Nolo's award-winning website has a page dedicated just to this book, where you can:

KEEP UP TO DATE – When there are important changes to the information in this book, we'll post updates

READ BLOGS – Get the latest info from Nolo authors' blogs

LISTEN TO PODCASTS – Listen to authors discuss timely issues on topics that interest you

WATCH VIDEOS – Get a quick introduction to a legal topic with our short videos

And that's not all. Nolo.com contains thousands of articles on everyday legal and business issues, plus a plain-English law dictionary, all written by Nolo experts and available for free. You'll also find more useful **books, software, online services,** and **downloadable forms.**

NOLO
LAW for ALL

Get updates and more at
www.nolo.com/back-of-book/NIRS.html

3rd Edition

Every Nonprofit's Tax Guide

How to Keep Your Tax-Exempt Status & Avoid IRS Problems

Stephen Fishman, J.D.

THIRD EDITION	JANUARY 2014
Editor	DIANA FITZPATRICK
Cover Design	SUSAN PUTNEY
Book Design	TERRI HEARSH
Proofreading	IRENE BARNARD
Index	SONGBIRD INDEXING SERVICES
Printing	BANG PRINTING

ISBN: 2330-8680 (print)

ISBN: 2330-8842 (online)

ISBN: 978-1-4133-1929-3 (pbk)

ISBN: 978-1-4133-1930-9 (epub ebook)

This book covers only United States law, unless it specifically states otherwise.

Please note

We believe accurate, plain-English legal information should help you solve many of your own legal problems. But this text is not a substitute for personalized advice from a knowledgeable lawyer. If you want the help of a trained professional—and we'll always point out situations in which we think that's a good idea—consult an attorney licensed to practice in your state.

Acknowledgments

Many thanks to:

Diana Fitzpatrick for her outstanding editing

Terri Hearsh for book design

About the Author

Stephen Fishman is a San Francisco-based attorney and tax expert who has been writing about the law for over 20 years. He is the author of many do-it-yourself law books, including *Deduct It! Lower Your Small Business Taxes, Every Landlord's Tax Deduction Guide,* and *Working for Yourself: Law & Taxes for Independent Contractors, Freelancers & Consultants.* All of his books are published by Nolo.

He is often quoted on tax-related issues by newspapers across the country, including the *Chicago Tribune, San Francisco Chronicle*, and *Cleveland Plain Dealer.*

His website and blog are at Fishmanlawandtaxfiles.com.

Table of Contents

Appendix

Your Legal Companion for Nonprofit Tax Compliance

This book is for you if you have a nonprofit that is up and running, whether it's been one day or one decade. You have dealt with the IRS already because you have your tax-exempt status. Now you're wondering what else the IRS has in store for you and your nonprofit? The answer is: "a lot."

Your nonprofit's relationship with the IRS doesn't end when you receive your tax-exempt status. Indeed, that's only the beginning. The IRS will continue to oversee its compliance with the myriad of complex tax laws and regulations governing nonprofits. Dealing with the IRS and its rules is the price all nonprofits pay in return for the substantial tax benefits they receive.

Failure to comply with these laws can lead to dire consequences—revocation of your tax-exempt status, or the imposition of taxes and penalties on your nonprofit, or even on your officers, directors, or employees personally. In the past, the IRS was relatively lax about monitoring and enforcing nonprofit compliance with tax rules. However, in response to widespread publicity about abuses by nonprofits and Congressional calls for better enforcement, the IRS has begun to more closely monitor nonprofits. These include more audits, requiring all nonprofits to file annual notices with the IRS, and substantially beefing up the annual information return filed by larger nonprofits—the IRS Form 990. Nonprofits need to take ongoing compliance with IRS rules and regulations more seriously than ever before.

In this era of fewer donations and grants and reductions in nonprofit staffing, the last thing a nonprofit wants to do is pay an accountant or lawyer to deal with IRS compliance issues. Fortunately, you can handle all or most compliance tasks yourself or with minimal help. This book can help. It contains step-by-step guidance on:

- how to file annual information returns with the IRS
- what types of records your nonprofit is required to keep

- classifying workers as employees or independent contractors and dealing with employment taxes
- how to comply with the tax laws governing the use of volunteers
- the deductibility of charitable contributions
- when you must provide written substantiation for contributions
- avoiding IRS taxes or penalties due to conflicts of interest, payment of excessive compensation, insider transactions, and other prohibited behavior
- how to avoid having to pay taxes on side businesses your nonprofit conducts to earn extra income
- what types of lobbying are and are not allowed, and
- how to steer clear of the prohibition on political activity.

Running a nonprofit is difficult enough these days without having to worry about the IRS looking over your shoulder. Turn to this book whenever you have a question about IRS rules or nonprofit compliance issues.

TIP

What this book is not. This book is not about how to form a nonprofit corporation or apply for IRS recognition of your nonprofit's tax-exempt status. For guidance on these tasks, refer to *How to Form a Nonprofit Corporation*, by Anthony Mancuso (Nolo). Also, this book has been written primarily for Section 501(c)(3) organizations that qualify as public charities and it does not cover the special tax rules applicable to private foundations. Moreover, while much of the material here is applicable to nonprofits other than Section 501(c)(3) organizations, this book has not been written with such organizations in mind.

Get Updates and More Online

When there are important changes to the information in this book, we'll post updates online, on a page dedicated to this book:

www.nolo.com/back-of-book/NIRS.html

You'll find other useful information there, too, including author blogs, podcasts, and videos.

Nonprofits and the IRS

This chapter provides an overview of what it means to be a non-profit and the role the IRS plays in regulating these organizations. Nonprofits and the IRS are inextricably intertwined: You create or run a nonprofit and you will have to deal with the IRS. How much will depend on what type of nonprofit you have and its size and activities. But nonprofits of any size need to be aware of the basic rules that govern their existence and operations. This chapter gives a brief overview of those rules and the IRS's role in the life of a nonprofit—from formation, to annual disclosures, to ongoing compliance, to audits, to winding up.

What Do We Mean When We Say "Nonprofit"?

What do the following organizations have in common: the United Way, Metropolitan Museum of Art, Harvard University, The Internet Archive, American Acupuncture and Herbs Research Institute, Talmudic Research Institute, Mothers Club of Grosse Point South High School, National Football League, Alcoholics Anonymous, National Rifle Association, Bill & Melinda Gates Foundation, MAYO Clinic, and YMCA? You guessed it, they are all nonprofit organizations. There are many terms that are used—sometimes interchangeably—to describe these organizations: "nonprofit," "charity," "charitable organization," "public charity," "private foundation," "501(c)(3) organization," and "tax-exempt." What they all share is that they exist for a purpose other than earning money for their owners.

Any organization or business that exists to earn a profit for its owners is a "for-profit" organization. Microsoft, Inc., of which Bill Gates is a principal shareholder, is a perfect example of a for-profit entity. It exists to enrich its owners—the shareholders. In contrast, a nonprofit has no owners and its purpose is not to enrich the people who run it. For example, the purpose of the Bill & Melinda Gates Foundation is not to earn money for Bill Gates. Rather, it is to use its money to "increase opportunity and equity for those most in need." Nonprofit organizations can and do earn money; however, they must use it for their stated nonprofit purposes, not for the private gain of any individual. Indeed, they are legally barred from distributing any profits they earn to the people that control them such as directors, officers, or members.

Not all nonprofits are tax exempt. Perhaps the best known nonprofit that is not tax exempt is the National Football League. Until recently, the New York Stock Exchange was also a nonexempt nonprofit. This is a small subset of nonprofits and not one that we deal with in this book. For the most part, the IRS and tax issues covered in this book would not be relevant to this group of nonprofits.

Tax-Exempt Nonprofits

At last count, there were an estimated 2.3 million nonprofits in the United States. Of these, approximately 1.6 million are registered with the IRS. Nonprofits have $2.71 trillion in total assets and over $1.5 trillion in annual revenue. They employ 13.7 million people, about 9% of the total United States workforce.

The most common and well-known tax-exempt nonprofits are Section 501(c)(3) organizations. These are nonprofits formed for charitable, educational, scientific, or religious purposes. When people use the term "nonprofit," they are usually referring to 501(c)(3) nonprofits. However, there are 27 other types of tax-exempt nonprofits. The most common of these are social welfare organizations. These are organizations operated exclusively to promote social welfare, such as volunteer fire companies, homeowners' associations, and advocacy organizations like the League of Women Voters. Other types of non-501(c)(3) nonprofits are membership organizations (social and recreational clubs), business leagues (chambers of commerce), fraternal organizations (college fraternities), cooperative organizations, and credit unions. A complete list of all 28 categories of tax-exempt nonprofits can be found at the end of IRS Publication 557, *Tax-Exempt Status for Your Organization*. This can be downloaded from the IRS website at www.irs.gov.

What all these nonprofits have in common is that they don't pay federal income tax on income they earn that is related to their nonprofit purposes. Tax-exempt nonprofits are also exempt from federal unemployment taxes and, depending on their state law, from most state and local taxes, such as state corporate income tax, sales tax, and property taxes. In some cases, the exemption from state and local taxes may equal or exceed the financial benefit derived from the federal exemption. Other than this tax exemption they all share, the 28 different types of nonprofits are subject to different tax rules and benefits depending on what type of nonprofit they are.

Section 501(c)(3) Charitable Organizations

By far the most common tax-exempt organization, and the type this book deals with, is the Section 501(c)(3) charitable organization. These organizations are not limited to what we normally think of as charities, such as homeless shelters or hospitals. Rather, they include any nonprofit organized and operated exclusively for one or more of the following tax-exempt purposes:

- charitable
- educational
- religious
- scientific
- literary
- testing for public safety
- fostering national or international amateur sports competition, and
- preventing cruelty to children or animals.

These nonprofits are referred to as Section 501(c)(3) organizations because they are governed by Section 501(c)(3) of the tax code. In addition to tax-exempt status, donations to Section 501(c)(3) organizations are tax deductible for the donor. This provides an enormous incentive for donors that almost no other type of nonprofit is afforded by the tax law. In return for this special tax treatment, Section 501(c)(3) organizations are subject to more tax rules and regulations than other nonprofits.

Charitable, Educational, and Religious Nonprofits

"Charitable," "educational," or "religious" nonprofits can be created for many different purposes. These terms are meant to be broadly construed and they encompass a broad range of activities.

Charitable. Charitable organizations conduct activities that promote:

- relief of the poor, the distressed, or the underprivileged
- advancement of religion
- advancement of education or science
- construction or maintenance of public buildings, monuments, or works
- lessening the burdens of government
- lessening neighborhood tensions
- eliminating prejudice and discrimination
- defending human and civil rights secured by law, and
- combating community deterioration and juvenile delinquency.

Educational. Educational nonprofits are involved in the "instruction or training of the individual for the purpose of improving or developing his capabilities" and "the instruction of the public on subjects useful to the individual and beneficial to the community." Such organizations include, but are not limited to:

- schools such as a primary or secondary school, college, university, professional, or trade school
- organizations that conduct public discussion groups, forums, panels, lectures, or similar programs
- museums, zoos, planetariums, symphony orchestras, theater groups, or similar organizations
- nonprofit day care centers, and
- youth sports organizations.

Religious. Religious nonprofits include all types of churches. "Churches" include synagogues, temples, mosques, and similar organizations. Other religious nonprofits include those that do not carry out the functions of a church, such as mission organizations, speakers' organizations, nondenominational ministries, ecumenical organizations, or faith-based social agencies.

Private Foundations and Public Charities

Every Section 501(c)(3) organization is classified by the IRS as either a private foundation or a public charity. This classification is important because private foundations are subject to strict operating rules and regulations that don't apply to public charities. For example, deductibility of contributions to a private foundation is more limited than for a public charity, and private foundations are subject to excise taxes that are not imposed on public charities. The bottom line is that private foundations get much worse tax treatment than public charities. Thus, you don't want your nonprofit to be a private foundation if you can avoid it.

The main difference between private foundations and public charities is where they get their financial support. A private foundation is typically controlled by an individual, family, or corporation, and obtains most of its income from a few donors and investments—a good example is the Bill & Melinda Gates Foundation. Because they are controlled by such a small group, private foundations can easily be misused and abused. This is why the tax law is so tough on them. Most foundations just give money to other nonprofits. However, some—called "operating foundations"—operate their own programs. As a practical matter, you need at least $1 million to start a private foundation; otherwise, it's not worth the trouble and expense. It's not surprising, then, that a private foundation has been described as a large body of money surrounded by people who want some of it.

Most Section 501(c)(3) organizations are public charities. They have a much broader base of financial support than private foundations and have more interaction with the public. Certain organizations, such as churches, schools, hospitals, and medical research organizations, automatically qualify as public charities. Others must prove that they are publicly supported, which generally means they must be able to show they receive at least one-third of their support from contributions, membership fees, or gross receipts from activities related to their exempt functions.

This book is primarily concerned with public charities, not private foundations. From here on, whenever we refer to "nonprofit," we are referring to public charities.

> ### Most Nonprofits Are Section 501(c)(3) Charitable Organizations
>
> According to the IRS Data Book, in 2012 there were 1,616,053 organizations exempt from tax. Of these, 1,081,891 were Section 501(c)(3) charitable organizations. The next largest groups were: social welfare organizations, 93,142; business leagues, 69,198; social clubs, 56,880; fraternal beneficiary societies, 50,763; labor, agricultural, and horticultural organizations, 50,046; and veterans organizations, 37,737.

The Life Cycle of a Nonprofit

The existence of a nonprofit for tax purposes can be divided into stages:

Stage 1: Creating Your Legal Entity

Stage 2: Applying to the IRS for Tax-Exempt Status

Stage 3: Ongoing Compliance, and

Stage 4: Ending Your Nonprofit.

This book is concerned primarily with the third stage—ongoing compliance with the tax law and IRS rules and regulations after your nonprofit has begun and obtained its tax exemption. However, we'll briefly review the other stages here.

Creating Your Legal Entity

You won't have much interaction with the IRS when you first start up your nonprofit. Indeed, all you need from the IRS is a federal employer identification number (FEIN), which can be obtained through the IRS website (www.irs.gov). Most of the initial work in creating a nonprofit involves state law issues. You must choose what entity you want for your nonprofit, and then comply with your state's legal requirements for creating it. Most people choose to organize their nonprofits as nonprofit corporations under the laws of the state where their nonprofit is located. However, some people create limited liability companies or trusts, while others choose to simply operate as unincorporated associations.

Forming a nonprofit corporation is very similar to forming a regular corporation. You must file articles of incorporation with the corporations division (usually part of the secretary of state's office) of your state government. But unlike regular corporations, you must also complete federal and state applications for tax exemptions. After filing this initial paperwork, you create corporate bylaws which lay out the operating rules for your nonprofit. Finally, you elect the initial directors of your nonprofit and hold an organizational meeting of the board.

You may also be required to register your nonprofit in all the states in which you solicit contributions.

RESOURCE

For detailed guidance on how to form a nonprofit corporation in all 50 states, refer to *How to Form a Nonprofit Corporation*, by Anthony Mancuso (Nolo). For complete information on how to register nonprofits with state charity offices, refer to *Nonprofit Fundraising Registration: The 50-State Guide*, by Stephen Fishman and Ronald J. Barrett (Nolo).

Obtaining Tax-Exempt Status

The first real interaction most nonprofits have with the IRS is applying for their tax exemption. You can do this as soon as your nonprofit is legally formed. You must complete a lengthy written application (IRS Form 1023, *Application for Recognition of Exemption Under Section 501(c)(3) of the Internal Revenue Code*) and provide other forms and documents, such as articles of incorporation. The IRS reviews the application and documentation to see if the nonprofit meets the two requirements for Section 501(c)(3) status. The nonprofit must be:

- organized as a corporation (including a limited liability company), trust, or unincorporated association whose organizing documents limit it to carrying out exempt purposes, and
- operated primarily to further one or more of these exempt purposes.

Welcome to the IRS Exempt Organizations Division

As you doubtless know, the IRS is a vast agency. Fortunately, it has created a single division to handle nonprofit matters. This is the IRS Exempt Organizations Division (EO), which in turn is part of the Tax Exempt and Government Entities Division (TE/GE Division for short). Exempt Organizations has about 900 employees divided among three offices: Examinations, Rulings and Agreements, and Customer Education and Outreach.

EO Examinations is responsible for enforcement activities, including both compliance checks and audits of exempt organizations.

EO Rulings and Agreements (R&A) is responsible for reviewing applications for exemption, issuing private letter rulings, and providing technical advice. It comprises Determinations and Quality Assurance, EO Technical, and EO Technical Guidance Quality Assurance.

Customer Education and Outreach (CE&O) spearheads EO's efforts to help exempt organizations understand their tax responsibilities through nationwide education and outreach programs. CE&O core staff is made up of ten full-time employees.

In response to the application, the IRS issues a determination letter either recognizing the nonprofit as tax-exempt or not. A favorable determination by the IRS is retroactive to the date that the nonprofit was created, if it files a completed Form 1023 within 27 months from the end of the month it was formed. Most nonprofits do, in fact, receive a favorable determination from the IRS. (In 2012, for example, only 1,148 of 52,608 completed exemption applications were rejected by the IRS.)

Certain nonprofits are not required to apply for IRS recognition of tax-exempt status to qualify as tax-exempt under Section 501(c)(3). These include:

- churches, including synagogues, temples, and mosques
- integrated auxiliaries of churches and conventions or associations of churches
- very small nonprofits—those with annual gross receipts that are normally not more than $5,000, and

- subordinate nonprofits that are covered by a group exemption letter from the IRS.

However, these nonprofits may voluntarily apply for IRS recognition of their exempt status, and many do so. A favorable determination letter from the IRS assures prospective contributors that their contributions will be tax deductible. Moreover, many institutional funders will only fund nonprofits with an IRS determination letter.

How Nonprofits Get Public Charity Status

Schools, churches, hospitals, medical research organizations, and nonprofits that support them are automatically classified as public charities by the IRS. Other nonprofits are not so lucky. The IRS initially presumes that they are private foundations. However, a new 501(c)(3) organization will be classified as a public charity, and not a private foundation, when it applies for tax-exempt status if it can show that it reasonably can be expected to be publicly supported. This is done by providing financial and other information on the exemption application. If the IRS classifies the nonprofit as a public charity, it keeps this status for its first five years, regardless of the public support it actually receives during this time. Beginning with the nonprofit's sixth tax year, it must show that it meets the public support test, which is based on the support it receives during the current year and previous four years. The nonprofit must file Schedule A along with its annual information return, containing detailed information about its sources of financial support. If a nonprofit passes the test, the IRS will continue to monitor its public charity status after the first five years by requiring that a completed Schedule A be filed each year.

RESOURCE

For detailed guidance on how to apply for IRS recognition of your nonprofit's tax-exempt status, refer to *How to Form a Nonprofit Corporation,* by Anthony Mancuso (Nolo).

Ongoing Compliance

After your nonprofit has obtained its exemption letter, it is the IRS's job to make sure you comply with the rules and regulations governing tax-exempt organizations. In return for tax-exempt status, all nonprofits must submit to IRS supervision. If the IRS determines that a nonprofit has not complied with the rules, it can impose monetary sanctions, and, in extreme cases, revoke the nonprofit's tax exemption. Revocation of tax exemption is usually tantamount to a death sentence for a nonprofit because it will make it difficult or impossible to obtain funding. This gives the IRS enormous power over nonprofits—a power it is threatening to exercise more than ever.

The Close Watch of the IRS

Since 2005, the enforcement climate for nonprofits has become much harsher. In 2006, Congress enacted a tax law called the Pension Protection Act of 2006 that contained several provisions making life harder for non-profits. Among other things, the law required even the smallest nonprofits to file an annual notice with the IRS, doubled the penalties for certain prohibited transactions, and tightened the rules for the tax deductibility of certain types of charitable contributions, such as motor vehicle donations. But things didn't stop there. Effective in 2008, the IRS adopted a significantly revised and beefed up Form 990—the annual information return filed by larger nonprofits. The agency also has called on nonprofits to practice good governance. Finally, the IRS has promised to audit nonprofits more often and has added staff to its Exempt Organizations Division.

The reason for these and other changes was widespread publicity about abuses by nonprofits, especially unreasonably large salaries and perks for nonprofit executives. These stories led to Congressional hearings, which led to legislation and IRS action. Although few nonprofits engaged in such abuses, all nonprofits will have to suffer the consequences.

Limitations on Your Nonprofit's Activities

In return for your nonprofit's tax-exempt status as a Section 501(c)(3) public charity, there are certain things you must do and certain things you cannot do. First, your nonprofit must be operated primarily to further its exempt purposes. For example, if your nonprofit's exempt purpose is to help the homeless, it must spend most of its time and money on homeless issues. Then, there are four things your nonprofit cannot do. You cannot:

- give or pay money or other benefits to insiders or other private individuals without receiving a fair return
- engage in substantial lobbying
- engage in any political activity, or
- earn excessive income from an unrelated business.

Doing any of these things can result in imposition of monetary sanctions and excise taxes by the IRS, and, in some cases, revocation of your nonprofit's tax-exempt status.

Here's a quick overview of each of these prohibited activities. They are all covered in later chapters.

Private benefit and inurement. A public charity is prohibited from siphoning money or other benefits to insiders such as officers, directors, or employees (private inurement) or to people who aren't insiders (private benefit). Private inurement and private benefit may occur in many different forms, including, for example, payment of excessive compensation or excessive rent, receipt of less than fair market value in sales or exchanges of property, inadequately secured loans or other questionable loans, or joint ventures with private individuals or companies. The prohibition against inurement is absolute. Any amount can jeopardize your nonprofit's 501(c)(3) status, or more likely, result in the imposition of IRS monetary sanctions on those involved in the transaction. See Chapter 7 for a detailed discussion of private benefit and private inurement.

Lobbying. A public charity is not permitted to engage in a substantial amount of lobbying. Lobbying is attempting to influence legislation— for example, by contacting legislators or publicly advocating approval or rejection of legislation under consideration by Congress, state legislatures, city councils, or other governing bodies. Your nonprofit may engage in a small amount of lobbying, but if it becomes substantial, you risk losing your tax-exempt status and you could be liable for excise taxes. See Chapter 9 for a detailed discussion of IRS restrictions on lobbying by public charities.

Political campaign activity. Political campaign activity is directly or indirectly participating in any political campaign on behalf of (or in opposition to) a candidate for any public office—for example, giving money to a political campaign or making public statements in favor of or opposed to a candidate. Unlike with lobbying, public campaign activity by public charities is absolutely prohibited. Any violation may result in the loss of your nonprofit's tax-exempt status and the imposition of excise taxes. See Chapter 9 for a detailed discussion of political campaign activity by public charities.

Excessive unrelated business activity. As stated above, your nonprofit must be operated primarily to further its exempt purposes. Obviously, you can't accomplish this if your nonprofit spends most of its time and effort running a business that is not related to its exempt purposes. If the IRS concludes that your nonprofit is operated for the primary purpose of conducting a trade or business that is not related to its exempt purpose, it may revoke its tax exemption. Some experts say that a nonprofit's tax exemption may be at risk if more than 50% of its total revenue comes from an unrelated business. See Chapter 8 for a detailed discussion of unrelated business income.

Documenting and Disclosing Contributions

Contributions to public charities are tax deductible by donors who itemize their deductions. However, your nonprofit must give written documentation to donors who make contributions over $250, or contribute more than $75 and receive a premium such as tickets in return. Failure to do so may prevent the donor from deducting his or her contribution. Additional documentation and disclosures to the IRS are required for certain types of property donations. See Chapter 5 for a detailed discussion of cash donations. See Chapter 6 for guidance on donations of property.

Annual Tax Filings

Once a nonprofit is up and running, it becomes subject to annual tax filing requirements. Which form you have to file will depend on the size of your nonprofit and the nature of its activities. Failure to file required returns can result in the imposition by the IRS of monetary sanctions and taxes on your nonprofit and, in some cases, on its managers and directors personally. Repeated failure to file can result in automatic termination of your nonprofit's tax-exempt status.

Information returns. Most nonprofits are required to file an annual information return with the IRS containing financial and other information, including the compensation paid to directors, officers, and top employees. Depending on your nonprofit's size, you file IRS Form 990 or Form 990-EZ (private foundations file Form 990-PF). Churches and very small nonprofits don't have to file an annual information return. See Chapter 2 for a detailed discussion of these filing requirements.

Electronic notice. Very small nonprofits (those with less than $50,000 in annual receipts) must submit an annual electronic notice to the IRS each year using Form 990-N, *Electronic Notice (e-Postcard) for Tax-Exempt Organizations not Required To File Form 990 or 990-EZ*, also known as the e-Postcard. The e-Postcard can only be filed electronically; there is no paper version. See Chapter 2 for guidance on filing the electronic notice.

Unrelated business income tax return. In addition to filing Form 990 or 990-EZ, if your nonprofit earns $1,000 or more in gross receipts from an unrelated trade or business during the year, it must file IRS Form 990-T, *Exempt Organization Business Income Tax Return*. You use this form to report income from a business that is:

1. regularly carried on, and
2. does not further your nonprofit's exempt purposes (other than by providing income).

You must also make quarterly payments of estimated tax on unrelated business income if you expect your tax for the year to be

$500 or more. See Chapter 8 for more information about the unrelated business income tax (UBIT).

Employment tax returns. If your nonprofit has employees, it will have to withhold employment taxes (Social Security and Medicare taxes) and income taxes from their salaries. You will also have to pay the employer's share of employment taxes. Failure to withhold and pay these taxes to the IRS can get you and your nonprofit into some of the worst tax trouble there is. Every year, your nonprofit must file IRS Form W-2, *Wage and Tax Statement*, for each of its workers. Additionally, quarterly employment tax returns must be filed with the IRS showing how much each employee was paid and how much tax was withheld and deposited. However, employment tax returns need only be filed once a year if your payroll is quite small. See Chapter 4 for a detailed discussion of employment taxes.

Reporting independent contractor payments. If your nonprofit hires an independent contractor—a nonemployee—and pays him or her $600 or more during the calendar year, it will have to file copies of IRS Form 1099-MISC with the IRS and your state taxing authority reporting how much the contractor was paid. See Chapter 4 for a detailed discussion of the tax ramifications of hiring independent contractors.

Public disclosure of returns. In addition to filing annual returns (Form 990 or 990-EZ), and, where applicable, 990-T, your nonprofit must make them available for public inspection and copying. See Chapter 2.

Record Keeping

In addition to filing returns with the IRS, nonprofits must keep adequate records. These include records of your nonprofit's income and expenses, documentation such as receipts and deposit slips, and payroll tax records if your nonprofit has employees. See Chapter 3 for a detailed discussion of record keeping and accounting for nonprofits. Proper and complete minutes and other records of all board meetings and actions must also be kept. For detailed guidance, see *Nonprofit Meetings, Minutes & Records*, by Anthony Mancuso (Nolo).

Ending Your Nonprofit

Nonprofits are not actually owned by anyone and therefore cannot be sold. If the directors of a nonprofit corporation decide to dissolve it, they must pay off all debts and obligations of the nonprofit and distribute all of its assets to another tax-exempt nonprofit corporation.

You must notify the IRS if your nonprofit is dissolved or terminated, or its assets are sold, or it is merged with another nonprofit. Usually this is done by filing a final Form 990, 990-EZ, or e-Postcard (990-N). Which of these to file depends largely on your nonprofit's gross receipts and assets. See Chapter 2 for a detailed discussion.

IRS Audits

By far the least welcome interaction your nonprofit can have with the IRS is an audit. Until recently, IRS audits of nonprofits were relatively rare, usually only involving extremely large nonprofits such as hospitals and colleges. However, this is changing. In the past few years, the IRS has placed a new emphasis on enforcement in all areas, including tax compliance by nonprofits. As a result it has increased audits and other contacts with all types of nonprofits. Here is an overview of this complex process.

What Is an Audit?

An IRS audit (also called an examination) is a review by an IRS examiner of your nonprofit's tax returns and books and records; it may also involve interviews and visits to your office. Most audits of nonprofits are conducted by the Examinations office of the IRS Exempt Organizations Division (EO). This is part of the Tax Exempt and Government Entities Division (TE/GE Division for short) which is in charge of all nonprofit matters. The Examinations office—EO Examinations for short—is made up of field exam groups: the Exempt Organizations Compliance Unit (EOCU), which conducts compliance checks; Review of Operations (ROO), which does follow-up reviews of nonprofits; and Compliance Strategies Critical Initiative (CSCI), which coordinates EO's strategic planning, monitors progress of critical initiatives, and analyzes the results of these projects. EO Examinations has over 450 employees.

The IRS says that audits of public charities are intended to accomplish the following objectives:

- ensure that nonprofits are operated for public purposes rather than private interests
- determine whether nonprofits are engaged in any substantial nonexempt activity, such as running unrelated businesses
- ensure that nonprofits protect and preserve their assets exclusively for exempt purposes
- evaluate procedures for accounting for money paid to individuals or noncharitable organizations
- determine if nonprofits pay any excessive compensation, fees, or benefits
- determine if nonprofits engage in lobbying, or participate in political campaigns, and
- determine whether nonprofits should be classified as public charities or foundations.

If the IRS determines that you have failed to comply with applicable tax laws and regulations it can, depending on the facts involved, impose monetary penalties, excise taxes, and, in extreme cases, revoke your nonprofit's tax exemption (see below). Excise taxes may also be imposed on directors, officers, employees, and others who participated in improper transactions with your nonprofit (see Chapter 7).

Who Gets Audited

When you're first contacted by the IRS about an audit, your first response is likely to be "Why me?" The IRS has many ways of selecting returns for audits.

The IRS uses a computerized system called RICS to select many nonprofit returns for audit. No one outside the IRS knows exactly how this works. The IRS simply says that "RICS applies the criteria selected by the Planning and Program Group to identify returns and line items for potential examination." For example, RICS could be used to identify returns in which nonprofits are allocating expenses to reflect unrelated business income and/or wages, but not filing an employment tax return (Form 941), and not filing Form 990-T.

Audits can also result from referrals from outside the examination group. These may come from other divisions of the IRS, Congress, other government agencies, watchdog groups, and the general public. The IRS has even created a special form members of the public can fill out to report inappropriate activities by nonprofits—Form 13909, *Tax-Exempt Organization Complaint (Referral)*.

The IRS also pays attention to media reports regarding questionable behavior by nonprofits. Thus, bad publicity can result not only in public embarrassment, but in an audit as well (so much for the old saying that "there is no such thing as bad publicity").

In addition, every year the IRS targets certain types of nonprofits for special scrutiny. In the past, these have included:

- nonprofits that conduct gambling fundraisers
- nonprofits engaged in joint ventures with for-profit companies
- nonprofits that sponsor travel tours
- credit counseling agencies
- donor advised funds
- hospitals
- colleges and universities
- community foundations
- nonprofits engaging in political activities
- student loan organizations, and
- nonprofits that fail to file required IRS returns.

The odds of any nonprofit being audited by the IRS in any given year are low. In 2012, for example, it examined only 10,743 of the 798,903 returns filed by tax-exempt organizations in 2011. Thus, only about 1.3% of all nonprofits filing returns were audited. In 2011, the odds of being audited were about the same: 11,699 of 858,865 returns filed in 2010 were audited, for an audit percentage of 1.3%.

Types of Audits

Not all audits are created equal. There are three different types:

- correspondence audits
- office audits, and
- field audits.

There are also special rules for audits of churches.

Correspondence audits. If you receive a letter from the IRS asking you to deliver documents to an IRS office by mail, the IRS is conducting a correspondence audit. Correspondence audits are part of the EO Examinations Office/Correspondence Examination Program (OCEP). They are by far the most common type of IRS audit. If your nonprofit earns less than $100,000 per year in gross receipts, this is likely the only type of audit you'll ever face. You might think of a correspondence audit as a mini-audit: it is ordinarily limited to one to three items the IRS has questions about on a return your nonprofit has filed or some other issue. These audits are handled by the least experienced examiners and are conducted via letters, fax, email, or phone calls. You'll often be able to clear up the matter in one or two phone calls or letters or by providing additional documentation of a questioned item. However, if the issues become complex, or if you don't respond to a letter or call, the examiner may require your officers or representatives to bring records to an IRS office. The examiner may also convert a correspondence examination into a field audit if he or she finds more serious violations.

Examples of problems with your information returns (Form 990 or 990-EZ) that can lead to a correspondence audit include:

- **Strange dollar amounts.** These are amounts that are unusual or disproportionate to the income or expenses shown on the return. It might be a large or unusual expense for your type of nonprofit—for example, if your return shows total disbursements of $30,000, $6,000 paid in legal fees might be questioned.

- **Inadequate descriptions on return.** The IRS may contact you if it's not possible to determine the validity of an item based on the way it is described on your return—for example, your return shows $30,000 of disbursements classified as "miscellaneous."
- **Presence on return.** Some items shown on a return invite close IRS scrutiny simply because they are there—for example, a balance sheet for liabilities lists $50,000 under "Loans from Officers."
- **Absence from return.** An item may be unusual because it does not appear on the return—for example, a nonprofit's balance sheet lists $75,000 in cash but shows no interest or dividend income.
- **Missing items.** Failure to file all the required schedules with your return will result in IRS scrutiny—for example, IRS Schedule A must be filed with Form 990 or 990-EZ each year to show whether your nonprofit should be classified as a public charity or private foundation.
- **Obvious errors.** Bad arithmetic or failure to properly sign a return will result in IRS questions.
- **Failure to file.** The IRS will question you if it appears your nonprofit has failed to file all required returns—for example, if your nonprofit has filed a Form 990 or 990-EZ that indicates you have income from an unrelated business, but you have not filed an unrelated business tax return (Form 990-T).

A correspondence audit begins when the IRS sends your nonprofit an initial contact letter. This letter will explain the tax years, forms, and issues involved in the audit and usually request that you provide additional documentation. This may include any or all of the following items for the year under examination:

- minutes of meetings of the board of directors and standing committees
- all books and records of assets, liabilities, receipts, and disbursements
- auditor's report, if any
- copies of other federal tax returns filed and any related workpapers (for example, Form 990-T for taxable income), and

- copies of employment tax returns and any related workpapers (Forms W-2, W-3, 941, 1096, 1099).

The auditor may also ask for:

- articles of incorporation and bylaws, including all amendments
- pamphlets, brochures, and other printed materials describing your nonprofit's activities, and
- copies of the Forms 990 for the years before and after the year under examination.

Review the letter and attachments for the necessary information that you need to gather. If you have questions after your review, you may do the following:

- write to the IRS at the address shown on the letter
- call the number on your letter, or
- obtain professional assistance (attorney, certified public accountant, enrolled agent).

Correspondence audits are often simple enough that they can be handled by your treasurer, president, or CEO. However, if you want a tax pro to represent your nonprofit, you'll need to sign and return an IRS power of attorney form—IRS Form 2848, *Power of Attorney and Declaration of Representative.*

CAUTION

Don't miss the IRS deadline for responding. Check the deadline in the IRS letter—normally 30 days—and be sure to reply by then. If you are unable to meet the deadline, call the number on the letter to discuss your situation with the examiner. If you fail to respond by the deadline, the examiner will send you a follow-up letter. If you don't respond to that, the examiner will attempt to contact a principal officer or authorized representative of your nonprofit by telephone to tell him or her that the organization's tax exemption could be revoked if you don't cooperate.

Attach photocopies of your original documents to the letter and send to the address provided. Do not send original documents. It's wise to mail your response by certified mail. Make sure you have copies of everything you send to the IRS. If you are unable to provide the necessary information by fax or mail due to a substantial volume of documentation, call the number listed on the letter for assistance.

Office audits. Like correspondence audits, office audits (also called interview examinations) are conducted when a nonprofit's annual gross receipts are less than $100,000. They are used when there is an issue or issues which cannot be dealt with by correspondence and the examiner requests the records be reviewed in an IRS office. Other than the fact that they are conducted face-to-face at an IRS office, office audits are much the same as correspondence audits, except they usually deal with more difficult issues. Office audits have become relatively rare because they take more time than correspondence audits.

Field audits. A field audit is a comprehensive heavy-duty audit conducted by one or more highly experienced IRS examiners, called field agents. As the name implies, these audits usually involve an IRS visit to your nonprofit's place of business. There are two types of field audits: the Team Examination Program (TEP) and the General Program. TEP examinations are field audits of large, complex nonprofits such as hospitals and universities that can require a team of specialized revenue agents. TEP audits are usually reserved for nonprofits with assets of at least $100 million or more. General Program audits are for smaller nonprofits and are typically performed by individual revenue agents.

These audits are multifaceted and can last one year, and often longer. They deal with the most serious audit issues and can result in the imposition of substantial taxes and penalties, and, in rare cases, revocation of your nonprofit's tax-exempt status. For this reason, you'll need to think seriously about getting help from a tax pro—an attorney, certified public accountant, or enrolled agent. The main violations the examiner looks for are:

- political activity
- substantial lobbying

- private inurement and private benefit—for example, payment of excessive compensation to employees, officers, or directors, or sweetheart deals with insiders
- failure to file information (Form 990) and income tax returns
- failure to report and/or pay tax on unrelated business income, or
- failure to file employment tax returns (Form 941), Form W-2, and Form 1099.

A field audit usually begins when the revenue agent notifies you that your nonprofit has been selected for examination. This first contact is by telephone or letter to schedule an initial appointment. In the appointment contact, the revenue agent will typically request a number of documents to begin the audit (see the list above). During the opening conference with your nonprofit's officers or representatives, the revenue agent explains the audit plan and the reason your nonprofit has been selected for an audit. The revenue agent usually conducts a comprehensive interview and tour of your offices or other facilities.

A field examination typically concludes with a closing conference. The revenue agent will discuss the audit with you, and if necessary, furnish a report explaining any proposed adjustments to your nonprofit's returns or exempt status. If you don't agree with the revenue agent's findings, you may request a meeting with the agent's manager to discuss the disagreement. If the manager cannot resolve the differences, you may pursue your case through the IRS appeals process. For additional information on the appeals process, see IRS Publication 892, *How to Appeal an IRS Decision on Tax-Exempt Status.*

Church audits. In general, churches are treated with kid gloves by the IRS. One reason is their political influence; another is legitimate concern about separation of church and state and the First Amendment right of all Americans to the free exercise of religion. A special provision of the tax law, called the Church Audit Procedures Act, imposes special restrictions on audits of churches. The Act permits the IRS to audit a church only if the Director, Exempt Organizations Examinations, reasonably believes, based on a written statement of the facts and circumstances, that the church:

- may not qualify for its tax exemption, or
- may not be paying tax on unrelated business or other taxable activity.

Thus, a church may be audited only after the matter has been reviewed by the highest levels of the IRS. Also, before beginning the audit, the IRS must provide the church with written notice and give it an opportunity for a conference with an IRS official if it so requests. If the church requests a conference, the IRS must schedule it within a reasonable time and cannot examine church records and activities until after the conference.

These restrictions on church inquiries and examinations apply only to churches (including organizations claiming to be churches if such status has not been recognized by the IRS) and conventions or associations of churches. They do not apply to related persons or organizations. Thus, for example, the rules do not apply to schools that, although operated by a church, are organized as separate legal entities. Moreover, the restrictions on church audits do not apply to the following situations:

- routine requests for information or inquiries on matters that do not primarily concern the churches' tax status or liability
- criminal investigations
- cases where tax assessments must be quickly imposed because delay may make them uncollectible
- any case involving the church's knowing failure to file a return or willful attempt to defeat or evade tax (including failure to withhold or pay Social Security or other employment or income tax required to be withheld from wages), or
- any inquiry or examination concerning the tax status or liability of people or organizations other than the church—for example, contributors.

IRS Soft Contacts

A "soft contact" is an interaction with the IRS that does not constitute an official audit. A soft contact will not, by itself, lead to imposition of taxes, penalties, or other punishments. Rather, it is intended to encourage tax compliance by nonprofits through a kinder, gentler approach. There are two main types of soft contacts—compliance checks and educational letters.

Compliance checks. The IRS has an active compliance check program that is run by the IRS's Exempt Organizations Compliance Unit (EOCU). In 2012, the IRS conducted 3,277 compliance checks. EO specialists conduct the checks by corresponding with or telephoning nonprofits. A specialist may ask about an item on a return, determine if specific reporting requirements have been met, or look at whether the nonprofit's activities are consistent with its stated tax-exempt purpose.

To begin, the specialist will inform you that the review is a compliance check and not an examination. The specialist will not ask to examine any books or records or ask about tax liabilities. The specialist may ask whether you understand or have questions about filing obligations and may also ask about your nonprofit's activities. If the specialist decides an audit is warranted, he or she will notify your nonprofit that EO is commencing an audit before asking questions related to tax liability.

Your nonprofit may refuse to participate in a compliance check without penalty. However, EO has the option of opening a formal examination, whether or not you agree to participate in a compliance check. For more information, see IRS Publication 4386, *Compliance Checks: Examination, Audit or Compliance Check*.

Compliance check questionnaires. The IRS also sends out compliance check questionnaires. These are a variation of compliance checks. The IRS mails compliance check questionnaires (or letters directing recipients how to complete the questionnaires online) to particular types of tax-exempt organizations to learn more about these types of organizations. When the IRS receives responses, it generally reviews them to determine whether and how those organizations are complying with applicable tax-exempt law and then decides what, if any, further action is appropriate to be taken. The IRS generally prepares reports on its findings based on review of the questionnaire responses, and publishes these reports on IRS.gov.

How Long Should You Worry About an Audit?

Ordinarily, the IRS only audits one or two years of returns at a time. However, the IRS can't wait forever to audit your nonprofit after you've filed a return. There is a statute of limitations on IRS audits. The IRS can't conduct an audit of a return after the limitations period expires.

The general rule is that the IRS may audit a return no later than three years from the due date of the return or the date it was filed, whichever was later. Nonprofits required to file an annual return must file the return by the 15th day of the fifth month after the close of their business year. For example, if your business year ends on December 31, you must file your information return for that year by May 15 of the following year. A return filed on May 15, 2013 can be audited no later than May 15, 2016.

However, the statute of limitations expiration date is extended from three years to six years if your nonprofit:

- fails to disclose on its return activities or expenses that could lead to the imposition of excise taxes—this includes excessive lobbying, political activities, and excess benefit transactions (see Chapters 7 and 9), or
- your nonprofit fails to report over 25% of its taxable income.

The IRS will usually commence an audit at least 12 months before the limitations period expires. It's common practice to ask your nonprofit to agree to waive the statute of limitations. Taxpayers undergoing audit usually agree to waive the statute—failure to do so could lead to IRS retaliation and make the audit much worse than it otherwise would be.

Audit Outcomes

At the conclusion of the audit, the IRS will send you a determination letter. An audit can result in any one or more of the following outcomes:

- no change to your nonprofit's exempt status or tax liability
- no change to your nonprofit's status or liability, with an advisory and later IRS follow-up to see if the advice has been followed

- imposition of tax (unrelated business income, employment, or excise) and/or penalties
- revocation of the IRS's determination that your nonprofit is tax exempt
- modification of the IRS's determination of your nonprofit's tax-exempt status—for example, reclassifying your nonprofit from public charity under Internal Revenue Code Section 501(c)(3) to a social welfare organization under Section 501(c)(4), or
- reclassification of your nonprofit's status as a public charity or foundation.

No-change audits. Obviously, the best result you can hope for is a no-change audit. However, today the IRS does a better job choosing nonprofits for audit: In 2008, only 20% of nonprofit audits resulted in no change.

No-change with written advisory. The next best result is no change with a written advisory. During the examination of Form 990 or 990-EZ, the examiner may encounter minor issues which, if they get worse, could jeopardize your nonprofit's exempt status. The examination is considered a no-change, but the examiner will issue a no-change with advisory letter. This letter will include the appropriate narrative addressing the issues revealed by the examination. The IRS says that no change with written advisory letters are appropriate for, but not limited to, the following situations:

- failure to timely file an annual information return—Form 990 or 990-EZ
- failure to timely file other required federal tax returns—for example, Form 990-T
- failure to follow the tax reporting rules for employees or independent contractors
- filing an incomplete or inaccurate Form 990 or 990-PF
- failure to identify special fundraising activities
- improperly combining income from different sources instead of reporting each source on appropriate lines of Form 990 or 990-EZ
- improper netting of income and expenses on Form 990

- failure to report required officer or trustee compensation and other data
- failure to notify the IRS of changes in purpose, character, or method of operation, or
- failure to maintain adequate books and records.

Imposition of taxes or penalties. The IRS can also impose taxes and/or penalties. These include income taxes on unrelated business income, employment taxes, and excise taxes imposed as a punishment for lobbying or political activities, or excess benefit transactions.

Loss of tax exemption. By far the most severe penalty the IRS can impose is revocation of your nonprofit's tax-exempt status. If this occurs, your ex-nonprofit is treated as a regular taxable corporation as of the date of revocation. This means all the income it receives will be taxable and donors will not be able to deduct their contributions. In addition, contributions received by the former nonprofit are treated as nontaxable gifts made during the years the organization was considered to be tax-exempt. However, gifts obtained under false pretenses—for example, donors who were lied to about how the money would be used—are taxable income to the ex-nonprofit. If that's not bad enough, the ex-nonprofit's officers and directors may have to pay excise taxes if they engaged in excess benefit transactions.

A nonprofit must engage in truly egregious conduct to lose its tax exemption: It must act in such a way that it fails to carry out its exempt functions—for example, a nonprofit spends all its time and effort running a for-profit business unrelated to its exempt purposes, or diverts contributions, grants, and other income to personal use.

Could Your Nonprofit Lose Its Tax-Exempt Status?

Virtually all IRS publications dealing with nonprofit issues make sure to mention that noncompliance with the tax law and IRS regulations can result in termination of a nonprofit's tax exemption. Is this just a scare tactic, or is the threat real? A look at IRS statistics shows that it's mostly a scare tactic. As the following IRS chart shows, nonprofits very rarely have their tax exemptions revoked by the IRS—for example, in 2001 a total of nine revocations were made—that's nine out of over one million nonprofits.

There's probably a better chance that your nonprofit's office will be hit by a meteor than lose its tax exemption. However, this doesn't mean that you can freely flout the tax laws. The IRS can, and often does, impose fines, penalties, and back taxes on nonprofits that break the rules.

Primary Reasons for Revocations by Fiscal Year, 1996-2001						
	Fiscal Year Ending					
	1996	**1997**	**1998**	**1999**	**2000**	**2001**
Delinquent filing of EO return	1	1	1	-	-	-
Discontinued operations	-	-	2	-	1	-
Inadequate records	1	-	2	-	2	-
Inurements	6	5	2	1	1	1
Nonexempt activities	2	-	1	1	11	1
Operating in a commercial manner	1	-	1	1	-	-
Met operational test	3	3	3	1	2	-
Private vs. public	2	1	2	-	-	-
Private use	-	-	-	-	3	-
Others*	-	2	9	4	7	7
Total	16	12	23	8	27	9

*Others include revocations for problems associated with grassroots lobbying and unrelated trade or business activities.

Appealing an IRS Audit

No audit result is set in stone. If you don't agree with the outcome of an audit, there are several ways you can appeal. Appeal procedures vary depending upon the outcome of the audit.

If your nonprofit's exempt status is revoked or changed, you may appeal to the IRS's Office of the Regional Director of Appeals. You may request a hearing before the regional office. If the regional office rules against you, you can appeal in federal court—that is, outside the IRS. A petition must be filed with the United States Tax Court, the United States Claims Court, or the United States District Court for the District of Columbia. Alternatively, you may forgo an appeal within the IRS.

Such appeals should be handled with the aid of an attorney experienced in representing nonprofits before the IRS.

If the IRS imposes additional taxes or penalties on your nonprofit, you have the right to appeal within the IRS, take the case to court, or both. What action you take should depend in large part on the amount of the taxes or penalties involved. There are special simplified procedures for small cases—those involving $25,000 or less.

For details on IRS appeals, refer to IRS Publication 892, *How to Appeal an IRS Decision on Tax-Exempt Status.*

CAUTION

Beware the 30-day deadline. If you wish to appeal, you must do so within 30 days of the date of the IRS determination letter. If your nonprofit takes no action, the IRS's decision becomes final after 30 days.

Annual IRS Filings—The Form 990

Nonprofits don't pay income taxes like other businesses, and they don't file tax returns like other businesses either. However, that doesn't mean they don't have IRS tax filings to deal with. All nonprofits are required to file a form each year with the IRS. For the smaller nonprofits (those with under $50,000 in gross receipts), this is simply an electronic postcard with minimal information. All others must file an information return—either the dreaded Form 990, or its less burdensome cousin, the Form 990-EZ.

An information return is just what it sounds like: a tax form that gives the IRS detailed financial and other information about your nonprofit. It is not used to calculate or pay taxes. Instead, it shows the IRS how your nonprofit spends its money, conducts its operations, and whether it is in compliance with the tax laws that govern tax-exempt organizations. These IRS filings are important for nonprofits because if they aren't done properly, you risk having to pay IRS sanctions and could even lose your tax-exempt status. In addition, all 990 filings are freely available for the public to read. Thus, they often serve as the single most important source of public information about your nonprofit.

The Nuts and Bolts of the Filing Process

Let's look at the basic why, who, what, when, where, and how of filing 990 information returns with the IRS.

Why an Information Return?

The 990 returns are a big deal for nonprofits ... bigger than ever with the recent changes to the forms. Unless you are a small nonprofit with gross receipts under $50,000, this annual filing is something you will need to pay attention to. Not only to avoid problems with the IRS, but also because for many nonprofits, it is their primary marketing document which can help enormously—or cause irreparable damage. A lot of information can be gleaned from this highly detailed, publicly available form, including how your nonprofit obtains and spends its money, how much it pays its staff and others, how it governs itself, and its program service accomplishments.

Moreover, almost all the information in the Form 990 and 990-EZ, including financial details about executive compensation and program expenditures, is available for public inspection. The nonprofit watchdog organization, GuideStar, posts electronic copies of all filed Form 990s and 990-EZs in an easy-to-use database (www.guidestar.org). As a result, in the words of the IRS, Form 990 is "the key transparency tool relied on by the public, state regulators, the media, researchers, and policymakers to obtain information about the tax-exempt sector and individual organizations."

Form 990 and 990-EZ are the IRS's primary tool to enforce compliance with nonprofit tax rules. The financial disclosures and answers to the questions about your nonprofit's activities will, among other things, help document whether your nonprofit is carrying out its tax-exempt purposes, engaging in excess benefit transactions, lobbying, or earning money from an unrelated business. The IRS uses this information to help it determine whether your nonprofit qualifies as a public charity or should be audited for any number of reasons. Wrong or misleading answers can lead to an audit of your nonprofit and the imposition of monetary sanctions against directors, officers, and other people who manage the organization.

In addition, some 40 states rely on 990 forms to perform charitable and other regulatory oversight, and to satisfy state income tax filing requirements for organizations claiming exemption from state income tax.

The first impression many people will get of your nonprofit will come from your Form 990 or Form 990-EZ. As we all know, negative first impressions are very hard to overcome.

Who Must File an Information Return

Most nonprofits that have been recognized as tax-exempt by the IRS must file an annual information return with the IRS. However, certain organizations are exempt from this annual filing requirement, including the following:

Religious organizations. The largest group of nonprofits that are exempt from any IRS informational filing requirement is churches and religious organizations. This exemption covers:

- any church (including synagogues, mosques, and temples); an interchurch organization of local units of a church; a convention or association of churches; or an integrated auxiliary of a church (such as a men's or women's organization, religious school, mission society, or youth group)
- schools below college level affiliated with a church or operated by a religious order
- any exclusively religious activity of any religious order, or
- religious missions in foreign countries.

Subsidiaries of other nonprofits. A nonprofit that is a subsidiary of another larger nonprofit is exempt from the IRS information filing requirement if the parent nonprofit files a consolidated return for its subordinate organizations, including the particular subsidiary nonprofit. For example, individual Boy Scout troops usually do not file their own information returns—they are covered by the Boy Scout parent organization's filing on behalf of all its subsidiary organizations.

A parent organization may file on a subsidiary's behalf only if the subsidiary nonprofit is covered by the parent's group exemption letter from the IRS. In addition, each subsidiary nonprofit covered by the exempt group must give the parent written authority each year for inclusion in the group return.

Parent nonprofits do not have to file a consolidated return for their subsidiaries—they can require them to file their own returns. Whether they do so or not, a parent nonprofit must file its own separate return. If you're not sure whether or not your parent organization will include you in a group return, contact the main office of the parent group and ask.

Nonprofits not registered with IRS. Any nonprofit that hasn't applied to the IRS for recognition of its exemption from federal income taxes. Nonprofit organizations that receive less than $5,000 in income each year don't have to file Form 1023 to obtain tax-exempt status and they don't have to file an information return. (See Chapter 1.)

Federal corporations and state institutions. This exemption applies to tax-exempt federal corporations such as federal credit unions, and to state and local agencies or other entities such as a state college or university or state hospital.

Foreign nonprofits. Foreign nonprofits, including those located in United States possessions, need not file an information return if their annual gross receipts from sources within the United States are normally less than $25,000.

Private foundations. These entities file IRS Form 990-PF each year, instead of one of the 990 forms discussed in this chapter.

> TIP
> **Look at your IRS determination letter.** If your nonprofit has received a determination letter from the IRS recognizing its tax-exempt status, the letter should state whether your nonprofit is exempt from filing an information return.

Which Form Should You File?

If you've heard about what a bear the IRS Form 990 is for nonprofits, don't panic. There's a good chance your nonprofit can file one of the simpler versions of the form. The IRS has created three different 990 forms, which differ greatly in size and complexity, from very simple to very complicated. Which form you have to file depends on your nonprofit's annual income and, in most cases, the value of its assets.

The three different 990 forms are:

- Form 990-N, *Electronic Notice (e-Postcard) for Tax-Exempt Organizations not Required To File Form 990 or 990-EZ*
- Form 990-EZ, *Short Form Return of Organization Exempt From Income Tax*, and
- Form 990, *Return of an Organization Exempt From Income Tax*.

Larger nonprofits are required to file the most complex form—Form 990—while small nonprofits can file the simplest—Form 990-N. Midsized nonprofits have the option of filing Form 990-EZ.

Should Your Nonprofit File a 990 Anyway?

Even if your nonprofit falls within one of the exempt categories, you may decide to file an information return anyway. If you do, you must file a complete and accurate return, including all required schedules. Why would a nonprofit that doesn't have to file an information return go to the trouble of filing one? There are several possible reasons:

- Information returns are an important way for nonprofits to gain recognition and provide information to the public about their organization. These forms are publicly available and many donors rely on this information when deciding which charities to donate to. Agencies that rate the effectiveness of nonprofits—such as Charity Navigator (www.charitynavigator.org)—also rely on Form 990s.

- In some cases, filing a Form 990 may be a condition of receiving a grant.

- Some states require nonprofits to file an annual return, even if they are exempt from the IRS filing requirements. Approximately 40 states will accept a Form 990 or 990-EZ in lieu of their own information return forms. Check your state law to see what the rules are.

- Filing Form 990 or 990-EZ starts the statute of limitations running on the IRS's authority to audit a nonprofit's tax compliance and impose monetary sanctions for "excess benefit transactions" against its managers, employees, directors, and others. Ordinarily, the IRS has three years to audit a return after its due date or filing date, whichever is later. The period is extended to six years if the return grossly understates the nonprofit's income or fails to adequately disclose improper activities. If a Form 990 return is not filed, there is no statute of limitations limiting the time the IRS has to audit your nonprofit regarding its activities for that tax year. (See Chapter 1.)

Form 990-N, the simplest e-Postcard form, was first introduced in tax year 2007. The following year, Form 990, the most complicated form, was radically redesigned, requiring more information and disclosures than ever before. To allow nonprofits time to adjust to the new forms, the IRS decided to phase these new forms in over a three-year transition period beginning in tax year 2008 and ending in tax year 2010. This phase-in period has been completed.

Filing Thresholds for Young Nonprofits

For nonprofits in their first few years of existence, the IRS has adopted special rules for determining their threshold levels for filing a 990 form. A nonprofit that is less than a year old can file a Form 990-N if it received, or donors have pledged to give, under $75,000 during its first tax year. For a nonprofit between one and three years old, it can file Form 990-N if it averaged $60,000 or less in gross receipts during each of its first two tax years.

As shown in the charts below, which 990 form a nonprofit can use will depend on its gross receipts and, in the case of larger nonprofits, the value of its assets. "Gross receipts" means the nonprofit's total income for the tax year from all sources without subtracting any costs or expenses.

Form 990 Filing Requirements

Annual Gross Receipts	Total Assets	Form to File
"normally" $50,000 or less	N/A	990-N
$50,001 to $199,999	Less than $500,000	990-EZ
$200,000 or more	$500,000 or more	990

> **TIP**
>
> **Consider filing a Form 990, even if you don't have to.** Even if it is not required, you should consider carefully whether your nonprofit should file a Form 990 rather than Form 990-EZ. See "Should Your Nonprofit File a 990 Anyway?" above.

When to File Your Return

No matter which form your nonprofit uses, the deadline for filing is the same: it is due by the 15th day of the fifth month after the end of your nonprofit's tax year—that is, four and one-half months after the end of the tax year. If your nonprofit uses the calendar year as its tax year, your tax year ends on December 31 and the return is due on May 15. If your nonprofit uses a fiscal year—that is, a year other than the calendar year as its tax year—the four-and-one-half-month rule still applies. For example, if a nonprofit's tax year ends on June 30, its information return would be due on November 15 of that year.

How to Determine Your Nonprofit's Tax Year

A tax year is usually 12 consecutive months. There are two kinds of tax years:

Calendar tax year. This is a period of 12 consecutive months beginning January 1 and ending December 31.

Fiscal tax year. This is a period of 12 consecutive months ending on the last day of any month except December—many fiscal years start on July 1 and end on June 30.

Your tax year (or accounting period) can usually be found in one or more of the following documents:

- your nonprofit's bylaws
- your application for federal tax-exempt status (Form 1023 or Form 1024) or the determination letter you received approving your tax-exempt status
- the application, Form SS-4, your nonprofit filed to get its employer identification number (EIN), or
- a copy of a prior year annual return (Form 990 or 990-EZ) that you filed with the IRS.

When to File Your Return	
Tax Year	Time to File Information Return
Calendar Year (ends on December 31)	May 15
Fiscal Year (ends any month other than December 31)	15th day of 5th month after year end

However, there is one exception to this general rule for filing deadlines. If your nonprofit is liquidated, dissolved, or terminated, its last return must be filed by the 15th day of the fifth month after the liquidation, dissolution, or termination, whether or not this coincides with the end of its tax year. See "Notifying the IRS If You Terminate, Merge, or Contract Your Nonprofit," below.

Beware of short deadlines for new nonprofits. When you start your nonprofit, your first tax year may be a "short year"—a tax year of less than 12 months. It all depends on when you file your articles of incorporation with your state government to establish your nonprofit's legal existence. For example, if your nonprofit uses the calendar year as its accounting period and your articles of incorporation were filed on December 1, your first tax year consists of one month—from December 1 through December 31.

Even though your first tax year is less than 12 months, you must still file a 990 form within four and one-half months after its end. In the case of the nonprofit with the one-month-long first tax year described above, the first 990 form must be filed by May 15 of the following year, only five and one-half months after its articles of incorporation were filed.

If your first tax year is a short year, there's a good chance that your federal tax exemption application will still be pending when your 990 form is due. That doesn't matter—you are still required to file the applicable 990 form.

There's also a good chance that you will be filing a Form 990-N in a short year, partly because it's likely your receipts will be low, but also because of special rules that apply. Namely, nonprofits that are less than one year old can file a Form 990-N if the nonprofit has received, or donors have pledged to give, less than $75,000 during its first tax year. Or, if a nonprofit is between one and three years old and averaged $60,000 or less in gross receipts during each of its first two tax years, it is also eligible to file a Form 990-N.

Obtaining an extension of time to file. All nonprofits are allowed one automatic three-month extension of time to file Form 990 or 990-EZ. Thus, you have as much as seven and one-half months to file either of these forms following the end your tax year. It is very common for nonprofits to obtain the automatic extension. To do so, you must file IRS Form 8868, *Application for Extension of Time to File an Exempt Organization Return*. The IRS will send you a notice that your request is granted. Do not attach Form 8868 to your return when you file it because it will delay IRS processing of your return.

You can get an additional three-month extension by filing a second Form 8868, but this extension is not automatic—it is granted only at the IRS's discretion. Your nonprofit must state a good reason for the additional extension in the Form 8868—for example, its financial records were lost or destroyed.

There is no extension of time for filing Form 990-N.

How to File Your Return

With the Form 990 and 990-EZ, you can choose between filing a hard copy by mail or private delivery service, or filing the form electronically. The one exception is for nonprofits with $10 million or more in total assets. These nonprofits must file their 990 form electronically if the total number of tax returns (of any type) that they file with the IRS in a calendar year—such as income, excise, employment tax, and information returns (including 1099 and W-2 Forms)—is 250 or more. For example, a nonprofit with 250 employees would have to file Form 990 electronically because it would have to file 250 W-2 forms each year plus all the other IRS forms—over 250 in all.

Electronic filings reduce normal processing time and allow the IRS to acknowledge more quickly that it has received your form. This can make it easier for you to comply with reporting and disclosure requirements. For example, with an electronic filing, you may find out more quickly from the IRS that you are missing a schedule or that there is some other defect in your filing.

If you file your Form 990 or 990-EZ electronically, you must do it through an IRS-approved provider for 990 electronic filings. For detailed guidance on electronic filings and a list of approved efile providers, see www.irs.gov/efile.

As indicated by its name, the Form 990-N (Electronic Notice (e-Postcard)) is always filed electronically. You file the Form 990-N online by going to http://epostcard.form990.org, a website operated by the Urban Institute. See "How to Complete and File Form 990-N," below, for more on how to file the Form 990-N online.

What If You Don't File?

Some bad things can happen if your nonprofit files an incomplete return or fails to file any return at all. As difficult as it may be to deal with this form every year, it's much worse to deal with the IRS and the consequences for failing to properly file your 990 return.

Revocation of IRS tax exemption. In the past, the only thing the IRS could do to a nonprofit that failed to file information returns, or filed incomplete returns, was to impose monetary penalties. However, this is no longer the case. Any nonprofit that fails to file a complete Form 990, 990-EZ, or 990-N for three consecutive tax years (starting with 2007), will automatically have its tax exemption revoked by the IRS. This occurs on the filing due date of the third year. For example, if your returns are due on May 15 each year, and you fail to file by May 15th of 2012, 2013, and 2014, your nonprofit will automatically lose its tax-exempt status on May 15, 2014.

If your nonprofit loses its tax-exempt status, you will have to apply all over again to get it back by filing IRS Form 1023. Moreover, donors may be reluctant to give you money until your tax-exempt status is restored—a process that can take many months. Reinstatement of tax-exempt status may be retroactive if you can show that you had a good reason for not filing.

IRS penalties. If you fail to file Form 990 or 990-EZ, or file an incomplete or false return, the IRS can impose monetary penalties against both your nonprofit and those responsible. There is no monetary penalty for failure to file Form 990-N.

You may be charged a penalty of $20 a day for a Form 990 or 990-EZ that is filed late, or is incomplete or inaccurate. However, this penalty can't exceed the lesser of $10,000 or 5% of your nonprofit's gross receipts for the year. Nonprofits with annual gross receipts exceeding $1 million are subject to a penalty of $100 for each day the failure continues, with a maximum penalty of $50,000 for any one return. The penalty begins on the due date for filing the Form 990 or 990-EZ. The IRS can excuse the penalty if you can show that your late filing was due to a reasonable cause—for example, you were unable to obtain the necessary records to complete the return despite reasonable efforts to do so.

If your nonprofit does not timely file a complete or accurate return, the IRS will send a letter that includes a date by which an accurate and complete return must be filed. After that date, the person failing to comply will be charged a penalty of $10 a day. If more than one person is responsible for the delay, then the penalties are shared. The maximum penalty on all persons for any one return may not exceed $5,000.

In especially egregious cases, those who willfully fail to file returns or file fraudulent returns can be criminally prosecuted and subjected to jail time and fines if convicted.

No Listing on IRS Website. Another possible adverse consequence of not filing is the risk of being dropped from the IRS's listing of tax-exempt organizations on its website. The IRS online *Exempt Organizations Select Check Tool* lists all nonprofits that it has recognized as tax-exempt. To ensure that their donations are tax deductible, donors will often check to see if a nonprofit is on this list before making a donation.

The 990-N Postcard Filing—
As Simple as It Gets

Until tax year 2007, nonprofits with annual gross receipts under $25,000 did not have to make any yearly filings with the IRS. That meant that many small nonprofits never filed anything with the IRS. However, the IRS introduced a new form in 2008—Form 990-N, *Electronic Notice (e-Postcard) for Tax-Exempt Organizations not Required To File Form 990 or 990-EZ*. Beginning in tax year 2007, all nonprofits with gross receipts "normally" under $25,000 were required to file the Form 990-N, a simple e-postcard that is filed electronically. In tax year 2010, the $25,000 threshold for filing went up to $50,000, so that more small nonprofits are eligible to file the e-Postcard.

What Does "Normally" Mean?

Nonprofits with annual gross receipts that are "normally" less than $50,000 can file Form 990-N. Your receipts will satisfy the "normally" requirement if they averaged $50,000 or less in the prior three consecutive tax years, including the year in which the return would be filed. This means that your nonprofit might have to file a Form 990 or 990-EZ one year and not the next. It all depends on your gross receipt average over the previous three tax years.

EXAMPLE: The Pauper's Institute, a nonprofit, earned gross receipts of $67,000 in 2012, $50,000 in 2013, and $25,000 in 2014. Its average gross receipts for the three years are $47,333, so it may file Form 990-N in 2013.

Congress imposed this new filing requirement because of concerns that small nonprofits were not keeping the IRS up-to-date on their address and other changes. Indeed, the IRS suspected that thousands of small nonprofits that ceased functioning failed to notify the agency of that fact. The 990-N form has enabled the IRS to create an up-to-date database with basic information on all active nonprofits: the IRS online *Exempt Organizations Select Check Tool*. This is important both for IRS administrative purposes and for donors who want to make sure they are contributing to recognized nonprofits.

If you are one of the many small nonprofits that must now file with the IRS, this form should not pose any problems for you. The 990-N form is so simple that, technically speaking, the IRS doesn't even consider it to be an information return. It should take you no more than ten or 15 minutes to complete. You don't even need to pay for a postage stamp to mail it to the IRS because it must be sent electronically—paper copies of the form will not be accepted. This is why the IRS calls the form an "e-Postcard."

How to Complete and File Form 990-N

Form 990-N is filed online through a website operated by the Urban Institute, a large nonprofit that has helped the nonprofit community with IRS compliance issues for many years. You do not need any special software to file the form, just access to the Internet and an email address for your nonprofit. Once you log on to the Urban Institute's website at http://epostcard.form990.org, you will be asked to create an account before you can access the system to complete and submit your Form 990-N. You will need your nonprofit's employer identification number (EIN) to do this. You will then be asked to fill out an online form requiring the following information:

Nonprofit's legal name. Your nonprofit's legal name is automatically provided by the online form. This is the name in the IRS's records. If your nonprofit has adopted a different name, the online form contains instructions on how to change the name in the IRS's records.

Any other names your nonprofit uses. If your nonprofit is known by, or uses, other names to refer to itself (and not to its programs and activities), these other names should be listed. These are commonly known as doing-business-as (DBA) names.

Nonprofit's mailing address. This should be the mailing address the IRS has on file for your nonprofit. Many small nonprofits change their mailing addresses frequently as the volunteers who run the organization come and go. If you've filed a change of address form with the post office with your latest address, the IRS should have it on file. If not, you should file Form 8822 to notify the IRS of your nonprofit's current mailing address.

Nonprofit's website address. This is only required if you have one. If you list a website here, make sure that its content is consistent with your nonprofit's mission.

Nonprofit's employer identification number (EIN). Every tax-exempt organization must have an EIN—called a taxpayer identification number (TIN)—even if it does not have employees. The EIN is a unique number that identifies the organization to the Internal Revenue Service. Your nonprofit would have acquired an EIN by filing a Form SS-4 prior to requesting tax exemption. The EIN is a nine-digit number—for example: 00-1234567. If you do not know your EIN, you may be able to find it on your nonprofit's bank statement, application for federal tax-exempt status (IRS Form 1023), or prior year return.

Name and address of a principal officer. This is usually the president, vice president, secretary, or treasurer.

Nonprofit's annual tax year. This is either the calendar year or a non-calendar fiscal year.

Answers to the following questions. Are your gross receipts normally $50,000 or less? See "What Does 'Normally' Mean?" above, for more information on how to answer this question. If you answer no to this question, you shouldn't be filing Form 990-N. You will also be asked if your organization has terminated or gone out of business. See "Notifying the IRS If You Terminate, Merge, or Contract Your Nonprofit," below.

After the form is completed, you need only click on the "Submit Filing to IRS" button to file it with the IRS. The IRS will notify you by email if your e-Postcard was accepted or rejected. If rejected, the email will contain instructions on whom to contact to resolve the problem.

If your form is accepted, you can view a copy by clicking the view button. Be sure to print out a copy for your files. Here's an example of a filed Form 990-N.

Form

990-N

Department of the
Treasury
Internal Revenue
Service

Electronic Notice (e-Postcard)
for Tax-Exempt Organizations not Required To File Form 990 or 990-EZ

OMB No.
1545-2085

20XX

Open to
Public
Inspection

A For the 20XX calendar year, or tax year beginning **1/1/20XX**, and ending **12/31/20XX**.

B Check if
applicable

☐ Terminated,
Out of Business

☑ Gross
receipts are
normally $50,000
or less

C Name of organization: **COMBAT VETERANS MOTORCYCLE
ASSOCIATION HAWAII INCORPORATION**
  d/b/a:

P O BOX 75417
Kapolei, HI, US, 96707-0417

F Name of Principal Officer: **Victor Ferrer**

91-1-038 Wahipana St
Kapolei, HI, US, 96707

D Employer
Identification
Number
20-4706623

E Website:
HIcombatvet.org

Privacy Act and Paperwork Reduction Act Notice. We ask for the information on this form to carry out the Internal Revenue laws of the United States. You are required to give us the information. We need it to ensure that you are complying with these laws.

The organization is not required to provide the information requested on a form that is subject to the Paperwork Reduction Act unless the form displays a valid OMB control number. Books or records relating to a form or its instructions must be retained as long as their contents may become material in the administration of any Internal Revenue law. The rules governing the confidentiality of the Form 990-N is covered in Code section 6104.

The time needed to complete and file this form and related schedules will vary depending on individual circumstances. The estimated average times is 15 minutes.

Note: This image is provided for your records only. Do NOT mail this page to the IRS. The IRS will not accept this filing via paper. You must file your Form 990-N (e-Postcard) electronically.

This Form 990-N (e-Postcard) was accepted by the IRS on 2/12/20XX.

Information Copy— Do Not Send to the IRS

Form 990-EZ: The E-Z Way Out

Nonprofits whose income is above the dollar threshold for filing Form 990-N and below the threshold for Form 990 can file Form 990-EZ, *Short Form Return of Organization Exempt From Income Tax.* As its title indicates, the Form 990-EZ is much simpler and shorter than the regular Form 990. It is only four pages long, while the regular Form 990 is 11 pages long (not counting the 16 additional schedules). And, unlike Form 990—which was radically redesigned in 2008 and made much more complicated and time-consuming to complete—the Form 990-EZ has not greatly changed. While not exactly simple, Form 990-EZ requires far less detailed financial information than Form 990.

A majority of nonprofits are able to file Form 990-EZ instead of Form 990. Is this so much better? Absolutely. Most nonprofits can prepare Form 990-EZ themselves if they have the proper records. Or, if you choose to hire someone to help, an accountant will usually charge less for a Form 990-EZ as opposed to a Form 990.

The following chart shows the thresholds for filing the Form 990-EZ:

Form 990-EZ Filing Thresholds		
May file 990-EZ for:	**If gross receipts are:**	**And if total assets are:**
2010 and later tax years (filed in 2011 and later)	Less than $200,000	Less than $500,000
2009 tax year (filed in 2010)	Less than $500,000	Less than $1.25 million
2008 tax year (filed in 2009)	Less than $1 million	Less than $2.5 million

CAUTION

You won't get a rating from Charity Navigator, the popular non-profit rating agency, if you file Form 990-EZ. If your nonprofit files Form 990-EZ, Charity Navigator, the nation's premier charity rating organization, will not list and rate your nonprofit. Moreover, if your nonprofit is currently listed and rated on its website, you will be removed for any year that you file a Form 990-EZ instead of Form 990. Charity Navigator says this is because Form 990-EZ does not provide enough financial information to rate a nonprofit's performance. If being listed and rated on Charity Navigator's website is important to you, you'll have to file Form 990, even if it is not required by the IRS. For more information about Charity Navigator, refer to their website at www.charitynavigator.org.

Form 990-EZ consists of a six-part four-page form and seven schedules. Which schedules you will have to complete will depend on your nonprofit's particular activities. The IRS has created a very thorough 39-page set of instructions on how to fill out the form. Read these carefully, particularly pages 9 through 21, which provide very helpful line-by-line instructions. Copies of the form are included in the appendix to this book.

An Even E-Zer Approach: 990-EZ Online

The National Center for Charitable Statistics at the Urban Institute has created a website where you can complete Form 990-EZ online and transmit it electronically to the IRS. The website has an online questionnaire that you will have to complete. The information you provide is automatically double-checked and used to create a completed Form 990-EZ. There is no charge to small nonprofits for these services and larger nonprofits pay only a small fee. You should look into this website's services if you're doing a Form 990-EZ. Refer to the Urban Institute's efile website at www.efile.form990.org.

We won't reiterate everything that you can find in the detailed line-by-line instructions to the form. Instead, we'll provide an overview of the form, the information required, and also give some helpful tips.

Form **990-EZ**	**Short Form** **Return of Organization Exempt From Income Tax**	OMB No. 1545-1150
	Under section 501(c), 527, or 4947(a)(1) of the Internal Revenue Code (except black lung benefit trust or private foundation)	**2012**

▶ Sponsoring organizations of donor advised funds, organizations that operate one or more hospital facilities, and certain controlling organizations as defined in section 512(b)(13) must file Form 990 (see instructions). All other organizations with gross receipts less than $200,000 and total assets less than $500,000 at the end of the year may use this form.

Department of the Treasury
Internal Revenue Service

▶ *The organization may have to use a copy of this return to satisfy state reporting requirements.*

Open to Public Inspection

A For the 2012 calendar year, or tax year beginning _____, 2012, and ending _____, 20____

B Check if applicable:	**C** Name of organization	**D** Employer identification number
☐ Address change		
☐ Name change	Number and street (or P.O. box, if mail is not delivered to street address)	Room/suite	**E** Telephone number
☐ Initial return		
☐ Terminated	City or town, state or country, and ZIP + 4	**F** Group Exemption
☐ Amended return		Number ▶
☐ Application pending		

G Accounting Method: ☐ Cash ☐ Accrual Other (specify) ▶ _____

I Website: ▶ _____

J Tax-exempt status (check only one) — ☐ 501(c)(3) ☐ 501(c) ( ) ◀ (insert no.) ☐ 4947(a)(1) or ☐ 527

H Check ▶ ☐ if the organization is **not** required to attach Schedule B (Form 990, 990-EZ, or 990-PF).

K Check ▶ ☐ if the organization is not a section 509(a)(3) supporting organization or a section 527 organization **and** its gross receipts are normally **not** more than $50,000. A Form 990-EZ or Form 990 return is not required though Form 990-N (e-postcard) may be required (see instructions). But if the organization chooses to file a return, be sure to file a complete return.

L Add lines 5b, 6c, and 7b, to line 9 to determine gross receipts. If gross receipts are $200,000 or more, or if total assets (Part II, line 25, column (B) below) are $500,000 or more, file Form 990 instead of Form 990-EZ . . . . ▶ $ _____

Part I Revenue, Expenses, and Changes in Net Assets or Fund Balances (see the instructions for Part I)

Check if the organization used Schedule O to respond to any question in this Part I . . . . ☐

Revenue	1	Contributions, gifts, grants, and similar amounts received	1	
	2	Program service revenue including government fees and contracts	2	
	3	Membership dues and assessments	3	
	4	Investment income	4	
	5a	Gross amount from sale of assets other than inventory	5a	
	b	Less: cost or other basis and sales expenses	5b	
	c	Gain or (loss) from sale of assets other than inventory (Subtract line 5b from line 5a)	5c	
	6	Gaming and fundraising events	
	a	Gross income from gaming (attach Schedule G if greater than $15,000)	6a	
	b	Gross income from fundraising events (not including $ _____ of contributions from fundraising events reported on line 1) (attach Schedule G if the sum of such gross income and contributions exceeds $15,000) . .	6b	
	c	Less: direct expenses from gaming and fundraising events . . .	6c	
	d	Net income or (loss) from gaming and fundraising events (add lines 6a and 6b and subtract line 6c)	6d	
	7a	Gross sales of inventory, less returns and allowances	7a	
	b	Less: cost of goods sold	7b	
	c	Gross profit or (loss) from sales of inventory (Subtract line 7b from line 7a)	7c	
	8	Other revenue (describe in Schedule O)	8	
	9	**Total revenue.** Add lines 1, 2, 3, 4, 5c, 6d, 7c, and 8 . . . . ▶	9	
Expenses	10	Grants and similar amounts paid (list in Schedule O)	10	
	11	Benefits paid to or for members	11	
	12	Salaries, other compensation, and employee benefits	12	
	13	Professional fees and other payments to independent contractors	13	
	14	Occupancy, rent, utilities, and maintenance	14	
	15	Printing, publications, postage, and shipping	15	
	16	Other expenses (describe in Schedule O)	16	
	17	**Total expenses.** Add lines 10 through 16 . . . . ▶	17	
Net Assets	18	Excess or (deficit) for the year (Subtract line 17 from line 9)	18	
	19	Net assets or fund balances at beginning of year (from line 27, column (A)) (must agree with end-of-year figure reported on prior year's return)	19	
	20	Other changes in net assets or fund balances (explain in Schedule O)	20	
	21	Net assets or fund balances at end of year. Combine lines 18 through 20 . . . . . . ▶	21	

For Paperwork Reduction Act Notice, see the separate instructions.   Cat. No. 10642I   Form **990-EZ** (2012)

Form 990-EZ (2012)   Page **2**

Part II	**Balance Sheets** (see the instructions for Part II)		

Check if the organization used Schedule O to respond to any question in this Part II . . . . □

		(A) Beginning of year		**(B)** End of year
22	Cash, savings, and investments		22	
23	Land and buildings		23	
24	Other assets (describe in Schedule O)		24	
25	**Total assets**		25	
26	**Total liabilities** (describe in Schedule O)		26	
27	**Net assets or fund balances** (line 27 of column (B) **must** agree with line 21) . .		27	

Part III	**Statement of Program Service Accomplishments** (see the instructions for Part III)	**Expenses**

Check if the organization used Schedule O to respond to any question in this Part III . . □

What is the organization's primary exempt purpose? _____

Describe the organization's program service accomplishments for each of its three largest program services, as measured by expenses. In a clear and concise manner, describe the services provided, the number of persons benefited, and other relevant information for each program title.

(Required for section 501(c)(3) and 501(c)(4) organizations and section 4947(a)(1) trusts; optional for others.)

28 _____

_____

_____

(Grants $_____) If this amount includes foreign grants, check here . . . . ▶ □ | 28a |

29 _____

_____

_____

(Grants $_____) If this amount includes foreign grants, check here . . . . ▶ □ | 29a |

30 _____

_____

_____

(Grants $_____) If this amount includes foreign grants, check here . . . . ▶ □ | 30a |

31 Other program services (describe in Schedule O) . . . .

(Grants $_____) If this amount includes foreign grants, check here . . . . ▶ □ | 31a |

32 **Total program service expenses** (add lines 28a through 31a) . . . . ▶ | 32 |

Part IV	**List of Officers, Directors, Trustees, and Key Employees** List each one even if not compensated (see the instructions for Part IV)

Check if the organization used Schedule O to respond to any question in this Part IV . . . . □

(a) Name and title	**(b)** Average hours per week devoted to position	**(c)** Reportable compensation (Forms W-2/1099-MISC) **(if not paid, enter -0-)**	**(d)** Health benefits, contributions to employee benefit plans, and deferred compensation	**(e)** Estimated amount of other compensation

Form **990-EZ** (2012)

Form 990-EZ (2012)   Page **3**

Part V	**Other Information** (Note the Schedule A and personal benefit contract statement requirements in the instructions for Part V) Check if the organization used Schedule O to respond to any question in this Part V . ☐		

			Yes	No
33	Did the organization engage in any significant activity not previously reported to the IRS? If "Yes," provide a detailed description of each activity in Schedule O	**33**		
34	Were any significant changes made to the organizing or governing documents? If "Yes," attach a conformed copy of the amended documents if they reflect a change to the organization's name. Otherwise, explain the change on Schedule O (see instructions)	**34**		
35a	Did the organization have unrelated business gross income of $1,000 or more during the year from business activities (such as those reported on lines 2, 6a, and 7a, among others)?	**35a**		
b	If "Yes," to line 35a, has the organization filed a Form 990-T for the year? If "No," provide an explanation in Schedule O	**35b**		
c	Was the organization a section 501(c)(4), 501(c)(5), or 501(c)(6) organization subject to section 6033(e) notice, reporting, and proxy tax requirements during the year? If "Yes," complete Schedule C, Part III	**35c**		
36	Did the organization undergo a liquidation, dissolution, termination, or significant disposition of net assets during the year? If "Yes," complete applicable parts of Schedule N	**36**		
37a	Enter amount of political expenditures, direct or indirect, as described in the instructions ▶	**37a**			
b	Did the organization file **Form 1120-POL** for this year?	**37b**		
38a	Did the organization borrow from, or make any loans to, any officer, director, trustee, or key employee **or** were any such loans made in a prior year and still outstanding at the end of the tax year covered by this return? .	**38a**		
b	If "Yes," complete Schedule L, Part II and enter the total amount involved	**38b**		
39	Section 501(c)(7) organizations. Enter:			
a	Initiation fees and capital contributions included on line 9	**39a**		
b	Gross receipts, included on line 9, for public use of club facilities	**39b**		
40a	Section 501(c)(3) organizations. Enter amount of tax imposed on the organization during the year under: section 4911 ▶ _____ ; section 4912 ▶ _____ ; section 4955 ▶ _____			
b	Section 501(c)(3) and 501(c)(4) organizations. Did the organization engage in any section 4958 excess benefit transaction during the year, or did it engage in an excess benefit transaction in a prior year that has not been reported on any of its prior Forms 990 or 990-EZ? If "Yes," complete Schedule L, Part I	**40b**		
c	Section 501(c)(3) and 501(c)(4) organizations. Enter amount of tax imposed on organization managers or disqualified persons during the year under sections 4912, 4955, and 4958 . . . . ▶ _____			
d	Section 501(c)(3) and 501(c)(4) organizations. Enter amount of tax on line 40c reimbursed by the organization . . . . ▶ _____			
e	All organizations. At any time during the tax year, was the organization a party to a prohibited tax shelter transaction? If "Yes," complete Form 8886-T	**40e**		
41	List the states with which a copy of this return is filed ▶ _____			
42a	The organization's books are in care of ▶ _____ Telephone no. ▶ _____			
	Located at ▶ _____ ZIP + 4 ▶ _____			
b	At any time during the calendar year, did the organization have an interest in or a signature or other authority over a financial account in a foreign country (such as a bank account, securities account, or other financial account)?	**42b**	Yes	No
	If "Yes," enter the name of the foreign country: ▶ _____ See the instructions for exceptions and filing requirements for **Form TD F 90-22.1, Report of Foreign Bank and Financial Accounts.**			
c	At any time during the calendar year, did the organization maintain an office outside the U.S.?	**42c**		
	If "Yes," enter the name of the foreign country: ▶ _____			
43	Section 4947(a)(1) nonexempt charitable trusts filing Form 990-EZ in lieu of **Form 1041**—Check here . . . . . ▶ ☐ and enter the amount of tax-exempt interest received or accrued during the tax year . . . . . ▶	**43**		

			Yes	No
44a	Did the organization maintain any donor advised funds during the year? If "Yes," Form 990 must be completed instead of Form 990-EZ	**44a**		
b	Did the organization operate one or more hospital facilities during the year? If "Yes," Form 990 must be completed instead of Form 990-EZ	**44b**		
c	Did the organization receive any payments for indoor tanning services during the year?	**44c**		
d	If "Yes" to line 44c, has the organization filed a Form 720 to report these payments? If "No," provide an explanation in Schedule O	**44d**		
45a	Did the organization have a controlled entity within the meaning of section 512(b)(13)?	**45a**		
45b	Did the organization receive any payment from or engage in any transaction with a controlled entity within the meaning of section 512(b)(13)? If "Yes," Form 990 and Schedule R may need to be completed instead of Form 990-EZ (see instructions)	**45b**		

Form **990-EZ** (2012)

Form 990-EZ (2012)   Page **4**

		Yes	No
46	Did the organization engage, directly or indirectly, in political campaign activities on behalf of or in opposition to candidates for public office? If "Yes," complete Schedule C, Part I **46**		

Part VI **Section 501(c)(3) organizations only**

All section 501(c)(3) organizations must answer questions 47–49b and 52, and complete the tables for lines 50 and 51

Check if the organization used Schedule O to respond to any question in this Part VI . . . . ☐

		Yes	No
47	Did the organization engage in lobbying activities or have a section 501(h) election in effect during the tax year? If "Yes," complete Schedule C, Part II **47**		
48	Is the organization a school as described in section 170(b)(1)(A)(ii)? If "Yes," complete Schedule E **48**		
49a	Did the organization make any transfers to an exempt non-charitable related organization? **49a**		
b	If "Yes," was the related organization a section 527 organization? **49b**		
50	Complete this table for the organization's five highest compensated employees (other than officers, directors, trustees and key employees) who each received more than $100,000 of compensation from the organization. If there is none, enter "None."		

(a) Name and title of each employee paid more than $100,000	(b) Average hours per week devoted to position	(c) Reportable compensation (Forms W-2/1099-MISC)	(d) Health benefits, contributions to employee benefit plans, and deferred compensation	(e) Estimated amount of other compensation

f   Total number of other employees paid over $100,000 . . . . ▶ _____

51   Complete this table for the organization's five highest compensated independent contractors who each received more than $100,000 of compensation from the organization. If there is none, enter "None."

(a) Name and address of each independent contractor paid more than $100,000	(b) Type of service	(c) Compensation

d   Total number of other independent contractors each receiving over $100,000 . . ▶ _____

52   Did the organization complete Schedule A? **Note**: All section 501(c)(3) organizations and 4947(a)(1) nonexempt charitable trusts must attach a completed Schedule A . . . . ▶ ☐ Yes ☐ No

Under penalties of perjury, I declare that I have examined this return, including accompanying schedules and statements, and to the best of my knowledge and belief, it is true, correct, and complete. Declaration of preparer (other than officer) is based on all information of which preparer has any knowledge.

Sign Here	▶	Signature of officer		Date		
	▶	Type or print name and title				

Paid Preparer Use Only	Print/Type preparer's name	Preparer's signature	Date	Check ☐ if self-employed	PTIN
	Firm's name ▶			Firm's EIN ▶	
	Firm's address ▶			Phone no.	

May the IRS discuss this return with the preparer shown above? See instructions . . . . ▶ ☐ Yes ☐ No

Form **990-EZ** (2012)

General Background Information

The heading of the form consists of items A through L, which require the following general background information on your organization.

Item A. You need to complete this item only if your nonprofit uses a tax year other than a calendar year. For example, if your tax year begins on July 1 and ends on June 30, you must list these months in item A. If you use a calendar year, you can leave this blank.

Item B. Most nonprofits won't need to check any of these boxes. However, be sure to check the last box if you've filed Form 1023 with the IRS, but have yet to receive your determination letter (IRS recognition of your nonprofit's tax-exempt status). If your nonprofit has changed its name, you must attach a copy of the filed amendment to your articles of incorporation establishing the new name. If you are filing an amended return, you must attach a statement to the form listing which portions of your previously filed return are being amended and describing the amendments. If it's the first time you are filing an information return, check the initial return box.

Items C–E. These items ask for basic contact information and your nonprofit's employer identification number (EIN).

Item F. This asks you to list your four-digit "Group Exemption Number." Your nonprofit will have this number only if it is a subsidiary of a parent organization and is listed in the parent's IRS determination letter. If so, you should file Form 990-EZ only if your parent nonprofit did not include your nonprofit in the group return it filed. Contact your parent organization if you're not sure about this.

Item G. This item asks you to indicate whether your nonprofit's accounting method is cash or accrual. Either method can be used to complete the form. To understand what these terms mean, see Chapter 3.

Item H. Check this box only if you're not required to file Schedule B. (See the discussion of Schedule B below.)

Item I. Complete this item if your nonprofit has a website. If you do list a website here, however, make sure that everything on the website is in accord with your nonprofit's charitable or other exempt purposes, and nonprofit tax rules. For example, your website should not exhort the public to vote for a particular candidate for political office, since this is strictly forbidden for tax-exempt nonprofits.

Item J. If, like most nonprofits, your nonprofit is a charitable organization, check the first box and place a "3" in the parentheses. If you're not sure how to complete this item, see Chapter 1 for a detailed discussion of the various types of nonprofits for tax purposes.

Item K. Check this box if your nonprofit is not required to file Form 990-EZ or 990, but you're doing it anyway. For example, check this box if your nonprofit's gross receipts are $50,000 or less, but you want to file Form 990-EZ instead of Form 990-N.

Item L. The IRS wants you to complete this item to make sure that your nonprofit is eligible to file Form 990-EZ instead of Form 990. This is based on your nonprofit's gross receipts for the year, which you are required to list in Part I. If your gross receipts are higher than $200,000 or your total assets are worth $500,000 or more, you must file Form 990. Most nonprofits can simply fill in the "total revenue" number listed in line 9 of Part I. However, if your nonprofit earned money from the sale of assets, inventory, or special events, you must add to the total in line 9 the expenses and other amounts listed in lines 5b, 6b, and 7b. This is required because gross receipts consist of all the income your nonprofit received during the year—that is, all the money that came in not subtracting any expenses.

Parts I and II: Financial Information

Parts I and II require you to provide financial information about your nonprofit. Small nonprofits that use the simple cash method of accounting may well be able to complete this part of the form simply by using their bank statements and checkbook register. Larger nonprofits should use an income and expense statement and balance sheet. (See Chapter 3 for discussion of nonprofit accounting.) This portion of the form is divided into three main categories: revenues, expenses, and net assets, followed by a very simple balance sheet.

Revenues. Lines one through nine of the form require you to list your nonprofit's revenues for the year in up to eight categories. A person reading this portion of the form can get an idea about how your nonprofit obtains its income—for example, whether your nonprofit relies primarily on donations or revenue generated by its activities, and whether it receives income from a variety of sources or just a few.

It is important to understand what types of income belong in each category. This can get tricky. The instructions provide a more detailed explanation of the following categories.

Line 1. Contributions. This is money or property voluntarily given to your nonprofit as a gift—that is, the donor does not receive something of equivalent value in return from your nonprofit. For many nonprofits, contributions will be their only source of revenue. You include in line 1 the total value of all:

- cash (including currency, checks, money orders, credit card donations, wire transfers, and other transfers to a cash account of your nonprofit)
- the fair market value of noncash contributions, such as corporate stock or an automobile, and
- the deductible amount of all quid pro quo contributions.

Include in line 1 all contributions received directly from donors as well as contributions received indirectly through organizations such as the United Way or from a parent organization. Grants from foundations or businesses belong here as well. You should also include grants from government agencies where the agency giving the grant receives nothing in return from your nonprofit. However, even if called a "grant" by the government agency, don't include money received from an agency in return for services performed for it—for IRS purposes, this is program service revenue, not a grant. See the Form 990-EZ instructions for several examples of this confusing rule.

These items are all lumped together in line 1. For example, there is no need to differentiate between donations from private, public, and government grants.

The value of noncash contributions such as corporate stock or automobiles is their fair market value at the time of the donation. You don't have to hire an appraiser to determine this value. Instead, you may use any reasonable method as long as you act in good faith. (See Chapter 6.)

Form 1099-K: Payment Card and Third Party Network Transactions

If your nonprofit receives contributions by credit card or through third party payment processors such as PayPal, it may receive copies of IRS Form 1099-K filed by credit card companies or third party networks reporting the amount of the payments to the IRS. You should receive a Form 1099-K if you had more than 200 transactions totaling $20,000 or more processed by the credit card company or a third party. Your nonprofit is not required to report the Form 1099-K information on any specific line of its return. However, be sure to include these amounts on lines 1 through 8 of your nonprofit's annual information return where you report contributions and revenue. Your nonprofit should retain all Forms 1099-K with its other records.

Line 2. Program service revenue. This is money your nonprofit earns in the course of performing its exempt functions—for example, the fees a nonprofit day care center charges its clients or revenue a performing arts nonprofit receives by charging admission to a concert. It does not include income from selling inventory—for example, money a nonprofit day care center earns from selling T-shirts. Inventory income is listed in line 7. Nor does it include income from special events—events like an auction or raffle that are undertaken to raise money, not further your nonprofit's mission. These are listed in line 6.

Line 3. Membership dues. Obviously, you'll have a value here only if your nonprofit has members who pay dues in return for their member-ship. Few nonprofits completing Form 990-EZ have such income. These dues are listed in line 3 only to the extent that their value "compares reasonably" with the value of the benefits your nonprofit provides to its members. Examples of such benefits include subscriptions to newsletters and other publications, free or discounted admission to nonprofit events, and discounts on goods or services the nonprofit sells to the public. For example, if the value of the benefits a nonprofit provides its members is $50 per year, and the membership fee is $200, $50 of the fee should reported as membership dues and $150 included as contributions in line 1. If your members pay dues primarily to support your nonprofit's activities and not to obtain benefits of more than nominal monetary value, the entire amount of their dues is a contribution that should be included on line 1.

Line 4. Investment income. This includes interest from savings, money market accounts, checking accounts, and certificates of deposit; dividends from stocks; and rent received from investment property— for example, a house a nonprofit owns and rents to the public. This is usually not a large source of income for smaller nonprofits without large endowments.

Line 5. Sales of assets other than inventory. This includes money earned from the sale of corporate stock, real estate, equipment, or any other property your nonprofit does not ordinarily offer for sale to the public. Sales of donated corporate stock are by far the most common form of income from sales of assets for most nonprofits.

Pledges Are Simply Promises—Don't Count Them Until You Receive Them

If your nonprofit uses the accrual form of accounting, you must count pledges as contributions received at the time the pledge is made—not when the pledged money or property is received. However, the IRS does not require you to do this on Form 990-EZ. You only include money or the value of property actually received. If your nonprofit has a lot of uncollected pledges, this may help you remain within the dollar threshold for filing Form 990-EZ instead of Form 990.

Special rules apply to quid pro quo contributions. These occur where a donor gets something in return for a contribution—for example, a premium such as event tickets, a pen, or membership in the nonprofit. The basic rule is that any amount a donor pays that exceeds the fair market value of the goods or services received in return is a contribution that should be included in line 1. Low-value premiums like pens can be ignored entirely. See Chapter 5 for a detailed discussion of such quid pro quo contributions.

Volunteer Time Doesn't Count as Revenue

Many nonprofits, particularly small ones, rely on free help from volunteers. You cannot include the value of volunteers' time in your revenues on line 1. Nor can you include the value of the free use of property—for example, free office space provided by a donor. This rule is unfortunate because its effect is to diminish the apparent size and importance of nonprofits that rely on volunteers and effectively understates their public support. However, the value of volunteer services can be mentioned in Part III where you describe your service accomplishments. Independent Sector (www.independentsector.org), a website for nonprofits, provides guidance on how to estimate the value of volunteer time.

You must list the total amount received from the sale in line 5a, and then in line 5b subtract the asset's "cost or other basis and sales expense." If your nonprofit purchased the asset, you would subtract its cost (less any depreciation if it is depreciable property such as real estate). If the asset was donated, you subtract its fair market value at the time of the donation. You need to have asset records to substantiate what you list in line 5 (see Chapter 3). Most nonprofits filing Form 990-EZ will have little or nothing to report here.

Line 6. Special event income. A "special event" is an activity designed primarily to raise money, not to further your nonprofit's exempt purposes. This is accomplished by selling goods or services to the public—examples include dinners, dances, carnivals, raffles, auctions, bingo games, other gaming activities, and door-to-door sales of merchandise.

Because it must be "special," an event belongs in this category only if it is not regularly carried on by your nonprofit, except for gambling, which is always considered a special event. For example, income earned from monthly dances held by a nonprofit whose mission is to promote folk dancing would not be special event income—instead, it would be program service revenue that belongs in line 2. On the other hand, income a day care center earns from an annual fundraising dance would be special event income.

You are required to report the total amount earned from special events ("gross revenue") in line 6a. This is straightforward unless the people who buy goods or services at your special event are really making quid pro quo contributions—that is, in order to support your nonprofit, they intentionally pay more than retail value for the goods or services you provide. In this event, the overage is a contribution. The amount of the contribution is listed in the parentheses in line 6a and also included in line 1 as a contribution. It is not included as part of the gross revenue from special events in line 6a.

For example, if your nonprofit held a fundraising dinner for which it charged $200, and the value of the dinner was $50, each person who purchased a ticket was really purchasing a dinner for $50 and also making a contribution of $150. The $150 contribution would be reported on line 1 and again on line 6a (within the parentheses). The revenue received ($50 value of the dinner) would be reported in the right-hand column on line 6a. See Chapter 5 for a detailed discussion of quid pro quo contributions.

You subtract from your gross revenue any direct expenses incurred by your nonprofit to sell the product or service. This includes such things as the cost of an item (if it wasn't donated) and shipping, or the cost of a special event such as a dinner. You do not include fundraising expenses here—for example, advertising or fees to professional fundraisers. The total is listed in line 6c as net profit or loss.

Money earned from sales of items of "nominal value," such as mugs and T-shirts, should all be included as contributions in line 1, not listed as special event income. The instructions list the monetary threshold for an item to be of nominal value.

If you list more than $15,000 in line 6a (not counting the amount in parentheses), you must complete Part I of Schedule G. This requires detailed financial disclosures, including the amounts paid to fundraisers. Additional disclosure must be made if you earned more than $5,000 from any one activity, or earned $15,000 from gaming.

Line 7. Sales of inventory. Inventory is goods or merchandise your nonprofit regularly offers for sale to the public. Such sales may arise from an unrelated business or from activities that are part of your nonprofit's exempt functions. For example, such sales would include money a nonprofit eye clinic earns through the sale of glasses to patients (part of its exempt function), and from operating a thrift shop (an unrelated business). You subtract the cost of the goods sold from the total amount earned from their sale ("gross sales") to determine your gross profit or loss from the sale. The cost of goods sold includes the cost of labor, materials, and supplies, the cost of transporting goods from suppliers ("freight-in"), and an appropriate proportion of your overhead expenses. If your nonprofit earns substantial sums from the sale of inventory, you should probably obtain professional accounting help. For more tax information about inventories, refer to IRS Publication 334, *Tax Guide for Small Business*, and Publication 538, *Accounting Periods and Methods*.

If your nonprofit earns more than $1,000 from the sale of inventory from an unrelated business, it must file IRS Form 990-T along with the Form 990-EZ. See Chapter 8 for a detailed discussion of unrelated business income.

Line 8. Other revenue. Include any revenue not already included in the previous seven categories—for example, income earned from banner ads on your website, or interest earned from loans made to officers, directors, or employees. You are not required to itemize each source of such revenue or list each on a separate schedule, although you may do so if you wish.

Line 9. Total revenue. The sum of lines 1 though 8 is reported in line 9. This is your nonprofit's total income for the year. This gives a reader of the form a rough idea of your nonprofit's ability to generate income—that is, does your nonprofit bring in a lot of money or is it a shoestring operation?

Expenses. This section of the form shows in general terms how your nonprofit spent its money during the year. Far less detailed information is required here than on Form 990. Unlike with Form 990, it is not necessary to allocate expenses among your nonprofit's functions such as program services, management and general expenses, and fundraising expenses. Instead, except for grants over $5,000, expenses are listed by what they are spent on, with no indication of whether the money was spent on programs, management, or some other function of the nonprofit. This makes your bookkeeping much easier. It also makes it impossible for readers of the form to determine if expenditures, other than grants to individuals, were made to further your nonprofit's mission or for some other reason, such as paying fundraisers.

Line 10. Grants. An amount other than zero is listed here only if your nonprofit gives money to individuals or organizations. Common examples include scholarships, fellowships, and research grants. You are required to attach to Form 990-EZ a schedule you create yourself giving details for each person or organization to which you gave more than $5,000. Among other things, you must disclose in the schedule whether the person who received the grant is related to any person with an interest in your nonprofit, such as a director, officer, or key employee. Most smaller nonprofits that file Form 990-EZ make no such grants and place a zero here.

Line 11. Benefits. This line ordinarily does not apply to public charities (501(c)(3) organizations). Place "N/A" here.

Lines 12-15. Various expenses. These categories are all very straight-forward. A couple of tips: be sure to include as part of compensation in line 12, the total amount of payroll taxes you pay for an employee. Also include expenses for employee events such as a holiday party. Line 13 should include all fees you paid to professional fundraisers, as well as fees for legal, accounting, and other professional help.

Line 16. Other expenses. Other expenses are items not listed in lines 12 through 15, such as travel and transportation costs; expenses for conferences, conventions, and meetings; website hosting and main-tenance; insurance; and supplies.

Line 17. Total expenses. This line is the sum of all your expenses listed above. Your total expenses provide a good guide to the size of your operations and show how much money you need to bring in each year to support them.

Net Assets. "Net assets" is the difference between your nonprofit's assets and liabilities. Assets are everything of value that your nonprofit owns, including cash, savings, investments like corporate stock, land, buildings, inventories, furniture, and equipment. Liabilities are everything your nonprofit owes to others. Thus, net assets represent your nonprofit's financial net worth—that is, its total financial resources. Net assets should not be confused with cash—cash is just one element of net assets.

Fundraising Expenses Are Buried

Fundraising expenses are not separately broken out and reported on Form 990-EZ. Instead, they are included with all other expenses reported on lines 12 through 16. For example, if your nonprofit pays for a fundraising mailing, the printing and postage costs are reported in line 15 along with all other printing and postage costs incurred during the year. Similarly, a fee paid to a professional fundraiser would be included in line 13, along with all other professional fees and payments to independent contractors—for example, legal and accounting fees. This makes it impossible for the IRS or public to determine from your Form 990-EZ how much your nonprofit spends on fundraising. You may well view this as one of the principal advantages of filing Form 990-EZ instead of Form 990, which requires detailed reports of all fundraising expenses.

Nonprofits with a small net worth must rely primarily on the income that comes in each year to finance their operations. If their income declines, they will have little or nothing to fall back on. A nonprofit whose net assets are equal to less than three months of its annual operating expenses may be headed for financial trouble. Nonprofits with a large net worth can better weather hard times because they have a cash reserve that can be used to make up for shortfalls in annual revenues. However, extremely large net assets may show that a nonprofit is more interested in making and hoarding money than spending it to carry out its charitable mission. The Better Business Bureau's standards for nonprofits provide that a nonprofit's net assets should be no more than the larger of (1) three times the size of the past year's expenses, or (2) three times the size of its current year's budget.

Line 18. Excess or deficit. Subtract your total expenses in line 17 from your total revenue in line 9 and insert the result in line 18. This is a particularly important number because it shows if your nonprofit took in more than it spent (ran a surplus), broke even, or ended the year with a deficit. Running a deficit for a single year may not be significant, but running substantial deficits year after year may indicate to potential donors that your nonprofit is not long for this world. On the other hand, ending the year with a large surplus may lead readers to believe that your nonprofit is spending too much time and money on fundraising and not enough money on programs. A nonprofit is supposed to use the money it takes in to further its charitable mission, not squirrel it away in the bank.

Line 19. Net assets at start of year. This is your nonprofit's net worth at the beginning of your tax year—January 1 of the previous year if your nonprofit uses the calendar year as its tax year. This number should be the same as shown in line 21 of the Form 990-EZ you filed the previous year, if any.

Line 20. Changes in net assets. This is the place to report changes in net assets that are not accounted for in line 18—for example, losses or gains in the market value of securities a nonprofit owns and did not sell during the year. You must attach a schedule explaining these changes. Most small nonprofits have nothing to report here and place a zero in line 20.

Line 21. Net assets at end of year. Combine the amounts in lines 18 through 20. The result listed in line 21 is your nonprofit's year-end net assets. You can see that this number is the result of combining your nonprofit's surplus or deficit for the year with its net worth at the start of the year.

Simplified Balance Sheet. This simplified balance sheet shows your nonprofit's financial position on the first and last days of the year. The beginning year totals in column A should be the same as the end of the year totals you listed in the Form 990-EZ (or 990) you filed the previous year, if any. You then list in column B your assets at the end of this tax year.

Line 22. Cash. This includes cash, savings, and investments such as securities and investment real property. If your nonprofit is small, all you may have to list is some cash.

Line 23. Land and buildings. List here the book value of any land and buildings you own that are not held as investments—that is, are used for your nonprofit's operations. Book value is the cost of the asset (or, if donated, its market value at the time of the donation) less any accumulated depreciation (cash basis nonprofits ordinarily don't take such depreciation). Most nonprofits filing Form 990-EZ have no such assets and place a zero here.

Line 24. Other assets. This includes such things as inventories and equipment. If your nonprofit uses the accrual method of accounting, accounts receivable and prepaid expenses are also assets.

Line 25. Total assets. This is simply the total of lines 22 through 24. If your total assets listed on line 25(B) are $2.5 million or more, you need to file Form 990 instead of Form 990-EZ.

Line 26. Liabilities. Your nonprofit's liabilities are listed in line 26. If your nonprofit uses the accrual method of accounting, these would include accounts payable (money you owe to vendors), outstanding loans and mortgages, and vacation time owed employees. Nonprofits that use the cash method of accounting usually have no liabilities to list here, and should insert a zero in line 26. You subtract the value of your total liabilities in line 26(B) from your total assets in line 25(B) to arrive at your year-end net assets. The number in line 27(B) should be the same as in line 21.

By comparing the total in column A with column B, you can get an idea of your nonprofit's financial performance during the year. If your total assets at the end of the year (line 27(B)) are larger than at the beginning of the year (line 27(A)), it shows that your nonprofit's ability to generate revenue is growing; if smaller, it shows the opposite.

Part III: Program Accomplishments

This is the only place in the form where you get to describe your non-profit's mission and its accomplishments during the tax year. Remember that this form will not only be read by the IRS, it will be posted on the GuideStar website and be available for viewing by any member of the public. So you should view it as an annual report card that can show potential donors what great work your nonprofit is doing.

First, you must provide a short statement of your nonprofit's primary purpose. This is usually the same as stated in previous years' 990 forms.

If your primary purpose has changed, make sure its new purpose is consistent with the statement of purposes included in your articles of incorporation. If not, you'll need to file amended articles with your state government and include a copy with your Form 990-EZ. If this is your first Form 990-EZ, draft a succinct description of what you want your nonprofit to do.

In lines 28 through 30, you should list your three largest program services during the year in terms of the total amount spent on them. "Program services" are the activities that further your nonprofit's mission—for example, publishing journals or newsletters would be a program service for an educational nonprofit, and counseling troubled youth would be a program service for a social services nonprofit. If there are only one or two program services, just list those. Many smaller nonprofits that file Form 990-EZ have only one or two program services. You are then supposed to describe how you accomplished each program's objectives during the year. The IRS wants you to be specific here. You should describe your accomplishments with measurements such as clients served, days of care, number of sessions or events held, or publications issued. You can give reasonable estimates if you don't have exact figures for these measurements. You are supposed to indicate if you've made estimates. You should also discuss accomplishments that are not measurable.

You are required to list the total amount spent on each program service reported in lines 28 through 30, in line 28a, line 29a, line 30a, and line 31a. This should include both direct and indirect expenses. Grants reported in line 10 should be restated in the parentheses and also included in the expenses. You may, if you wish, include in the narrative description of program service accomplishments, the value of volunteer time, donated materials, equipment, or facilities used for that specific program service. You do not include that amount, however, in the expenses. One advantage of adding the value of volunteer time and donated items is that it will increase the amount of your total program expenses. For good guidance on how to calculate the value of volunteer time, refer to Independent Sector's website at www.independentsector.org.

Program Service Accomplishments

Here are some examples of statements of program service accomplishments from Form 990-EZs filed by several small nonprofits:

- Scholarship Programs: The Queer Foundation Effective Writing and Scholarships Program held the annual High School Seniors English Essay Contest and awarded two $1,000 scholarships to the top essayists to attend the U.S. college or university of their choice. (Two scholarship recipients)

- Provided $1,000 to Dr. Cathleen Fitzgerald so she could lead UN-Reno student trip to Kenya and Uganda to construct manual water well drilling rigs, drill two wells, and provide training to locals in drilling and completing drinking-water wells. About 300 community members benefited.

- Wrote and published four walking tour brochures detailing local GLBT history, distributed through local historical organizations and convention center to the general public. Added to historical periodicals collections for research base with purchase of *Blacklight* magazines, *Furies* newspapers, and began preservation of Friends Radio broadcast tapes, continued recording of oral histories.

- Youth sports: Ran 3 youth hockey teams over course of 12-week season, 15 10-year-olds, 18 11-year-olds, 20 12-year-olds rostered each team. Total ice-time in practices and games per team: 300 hours. Each team had coach and assistant coach present for all practices and games. In addition, open skate for teams sponsored with trainer present weekly throughout the season—3 hours per week.

- Rescued over 200 dogs and birds, provided them with medical attention, and then found them forever homes with families.

You can find many more examples among the hundreds of thousands of filed 990-EZs posted on the GuideStar website at www.guidestar.org.

If you have additional program services other than those already listed, you must list and briefly describe them (in a separate schedule if necessary). The amount spent on them must also be disclosed.

Add up all your program service expenses and insert the total in line 32. This is an important number. By comparing it with your nonprofit's total expenses in line 17, you can determine what percentage of your nonprofit's total expenses are for program services. The more you spend on program services, the better your nonprofit looks to donors, who generally don't like to see their money spent on fundraising or administrative expenses. Some donors will not give money to nonprofits that spend too little on program services. The Better Business Bureau Wise Giving Standards for Charity Accountability provides that at least 65% of a nonprofit's total spending should be for program services (see www.give.org).

Allocating Expenses Between Direct and Shared Costs

A direct expense is money spent entirely to help accomplish a specific program service, while shared or indirect expenses support all or many of your nonprofit's activities. For example, the cost of food purchased by a nonprofit that delivers food to the elderly would be a direct expense for this program service. On the other hand, the salary it pays its executive director would be a shared expense because the executive director works on many activities in addition to the food delivery program—fundraising and administration, for example.

Shared expenses must be allocated among your program services. You may use any reasonable method to do so as long as you do so consistently. For example, the executive director could keep track of the time he or she spends on the food delivery program—if it was 50% on program work, then 50% of his or her compensation could be allocated to that on Form 990-EZ. There is no single or best way to allocate shared expenses. See Chapter 3 for more guidance on this complex topic.

Part IV: ODTKE Disclosure and Compensation

ODTKE is an acronym for officers, directors, trustees, and key employees.

Officers are the people elected or appointed to manage your nonprofit's daily operations, such as a president, vice president, secretary, or treasurer (these positions should be listed in your bylaws). For purposes of Form 990 reporting, treat your top management official and top financial official (the person who has ultimate responsibility for managing your nonprofit's finances) as officers.

Directors are the members of your nonprofit's governing body.

Trustees are the same as directors.

Key **E**mployees are all employees (other than officers, directors, or trustees) who meet all three of the following tests:

- $150,000 test—they are paid over $150,000 during the tax year
- Responsibility test—they (1) have responsibilities, powers, or influence similar to those of officers, directors, or trustees, or (2) manage an activity accounting for 10% or more of the nonprofit's total activities, assets, income, or expenses, or (3) have or share authority to control 10% or more of the nonprofit's capital expenditures, operating budget, or employee compensation, and
- Top 20 test—they are one of the 20 employees (that satisfy the $150,000 test and Responsibility test) paid the most during the tax year.

These are all the people in charge of running your nonprofit. In Part IV you are required to identify and disclose the compensation of all the people who served as ODTKEs at any time during the tax year covered by the Form 990-EZ—this is true even if they are no longer serving at the time you file your Form 990-EZ.

This is the one part of the form that everybody reads because they want to know whether your nonprofit's ODTKE's are being paid, and, if so, how much. Remember that Form 990-EZ is a public document that must be disclosed to anyone who asks for it. Obviously, unreasonably large salaries or expense accounts don't look good; moreover, they can result in IRS sanctions. (See Chapter 7.)

You must provide the following information for any person who was an ODTKE of your nonprofit any time during the tax year, regardless of whether or not that person is still involved with your nonprofit at the time you file your Form 990-EZ:

Column (a) and (b): Basic information. List your ODTKEs' names and titles in column (a). In column (b), provide an estimate of the average hours worked per week on your nonprofit's affairs.

Don't Include Social Security Numbers or Home Addresses on Publicly Disclosed Forms

Because the IRS is required to disclose approved exemption applications and information returns, nonprofits shouldn't include personal information, such as ODTKEs' home addresses or Social Security numbers, on these forms. By law, with limited exceptions, the IRS has no authority to remove such information before making the forms publicly available.

TIP

Directors should spend more than zero hours per week on non-profit business. A surprisingly large number of nonprofits filing Form 990-EZ state that their directors spend zero hours per week on nonprofit business. Your board of directors is supposed to provide adequate oversight of your operations. Stating that directors spend no time at all on nonprofit matters indicates that they are not exercising proper oversight. You are not required to round off numbers in this portion of the form. Thus, if a director spends only one hour per month on nonprofit business, you should list .25 in column (b) to show that the director spends 15 minutes per week on nonprofit affairs, not zero minutes.

Columns (c) through (e)—Compensation. You are required to provide a very complete disclosure of each ODTKE's compensation. This includes not just money, but other items of value given to an ODTKE as well, such as free housing. Many nonprofits have increased the amount of such noncash compensation paid to ODTKEs in order to make their salaries look as small as possible on Forms 990 and 990-EZ.

You use the calendar year to report the amount of this compensation. If your nonprofit uses a year other than a calendar year as its tax year, use the calendar year ending with or within your nonprofit's tax year. For example, if your nonprofit's tax year is July 1, 2013 through June 30, 2014, use the calendar year ending on December 31, 2013 to report the compensation paid to ODTKEs.

Column (c): Enter the amount of each ODTKE's compensation as reported to the IRS on IRS Form W-2 or 1099-MISC. Officers and other employees get a W-2, nonemployees such as directors get a 1099-MISC. If your nonprofit did not file a 1099-MISC because the amounts paid to a director or other nonemployee were below the $600 threshold reporting requirement, then report the amount actually paid. (See Chapter 4 for a detailed discussion of W-2s and 1099s.)

Column (d): List your nonprofit's contributions to the ODTKE's retirement plan, and the value of health benefits that are not taxable and therefore not included in the person's W-2 or 1099—for example, medical reimbursement payments or payments of health benefit plan premiums.

Column (e): Enter the value of taxable and nontaxable fringe benefits given to the ODTKE, but not already reported in columns (c) or (d). This includes the value of the personal use of housing, automobiles, or other assets owned or leased by the nonprofit (or provided for the nonprofit's use without charge). It also includes reimbursements or allowances not properly accounted for or spent for personal purposes-- for example, report the value of travel reimbursements if the travel was not to serve the nonprofit. You need not include in column (e) any item whose total value is less than $10,000 for the calendar year. Nor need you include the value of:

- working condition fringe benefits
- expense reimbursements and allowances paid under an accountable plan, or
- de minimis fringe benefits.

See Chapter 4 for a detailed discussion of these items.

Many smaller nonprofits that file Form 990-EZ are run largely by volunteers and pay no compensation to their ODTKEs. You should still list such individuals, and enter "0" in columns (c) through (e). A line of zeros in this column is great evidence of your ODTKEs' commitment to accomplishing your nonprofit's mission.

Can Board Members Be Compensated?

To avoid conflicts of interest, board members usually are not compensated, except possibly to reimburse them their costs for attending board meetings. These reimbursements don't need to be reported on Form 990-EZ, provided they are properly documented. (See Chapter 4.)

Nevertheless, particularly in smaller nonprofits, board members sometimes perform staff or other functions that are normally paid positions. For example, someone on the board of directors might provide legal or accounting services for the nonprofit. As long as all the conflict of interest and other IRS rules about compensating insiders are strictly adhered to, these directors may reasonably be compensated for their nonboard activities. (See Chapter 7.) But it's something you should try to avoid whenever possible. The Better Business Bureau says that no more than one or 10% (whichever is greater) of board members with voting rights should be directly or indirectly compensated.

Parts V and VI: Additional Information

Part V and most of Part VI of Form 990-EZ consist of a series of questions, most of which must be answered "yes" or "no." Most of these questions are intended to help show whether your nonprofit is in compliance with the tax laws governing nonprofits. Most nonprofits answer "no" to all of these questions. Any "yes" answer may require you to file additional schedules or other tax forms. However, failure to truthfully answer any of these questions can result in IRS penalties and sanctions. Pay particular attention to the following items:

Line 33—Changes in activities. Has your nonprofit begun any significant activities over the past three years that it hasn't reported to the IRS on a previously filed Form 990-EZ or Form 990? Has it discontinued any significant activities over the same period? The IRS wants to know. If you answer "yes" to either question, attach a statement to the form describing the activities. If these activities further your nonprofit's mission, they should also be listed in Part III, Statement of Program Activities.

Line 34: Articles and bylaws. If your nonprofit amended its articles of incorporation or bylaws during the tax year, you should answer "yes" in line 35 and attach to Form 990-EZ either a copy of the changes, or a copy of the entire articles or bylaws. If you only include a copy of the changes, the document must be a "conformed copy"—signed by an officer.

Line 35: Business income. If your nonprofit had $1,000 or more in gross income (income without subtracting expenses), from a business unrelated to your charitable mission that you regularly carried on, you must answer "yes" in line 35a. In this event, you may be required to file IRS Form 990-T, *Exempt Organizations Business Income Tax Return.* This is the form nonprofits file to report and pay taxes on income from an unrelated business. This form is filed separately from Form 990-EZ. It is due at the same time as the Form 990-EZ, but you may obtain an automatic six-month extension of the time to file. If you must file the form, check the "yes" box in line 35b. However, even if your nonprofit earned $1,000 or more from a regular unrelated business, there is a good chance you are exempt from filing a 990-T return and can safely check the "no" box in line 35b indicating that no 990-T was, or will be, filed. In this event, you should attach a statement explaining the reason for not filing Form 990-T—for example, the form does not need to be filed if the business was run by volunteers. See Chapter 8 for a detailed discussion of UBIT.

Line 36: Termination, merger, or contraction. Answer "yes" here if your nonprofit has terminated, merged with another nonprofit, or experienced a "substantial contraction" during the year. A substantial contraction means your nonprofit sold or otherwise disposed of at least 25% of its assets during the year. If any of these things occurred, you must file Schedule N with your return. See "Notifying the IRS If You Terminate, Merge, or Contract Your Nonprofit," below.

Line 37: Political expenditures. Political expenditures are payments intended to influence an election or appointment to any political office. Public charities (501(c)(3) organizations) are not allowed to make political expenditures—those that do can lose their tax-exempt status. Thus, you should answer "no" here. See Chapter 9 for a detailed discussion of IRS rules concerning political campaign activities by nonprofits. This line is primarily for nonprofits other than public charities (501(c)(3) organizations).

Line 38: Loans to ODTKEs. Unpaid loans to officers, directors, trustees, and key employees are a hot button issue for the IRS. If you check the "yes" box in line 38a, you must complete Schedule L and attach it to your Form 990-EZ and enter the amount of the loan in box 38b. See Chapter 7 for more information about loans to ODTKEs and Schedule L.

Line 40: Excess benefit transactions. This section of the form requires you to provide information about any excess benefit transactions between your nonprofit and disqualified persons such as directors, officers, employees, and their close relatives. Most nonprofits have nothing to report here. See Chapter 7 for detailed guidance on excess benefit transactions.

Line 41: State Filings of Form 990-EZ. Line 41 requires nonprofits to list the states in which a copy of Form-EZ has been filed. At least 28 states require that the form be filed as part of their state fundraising registration process, or accept it as an annual fundraising report: Arkansas, California, Connecticut, Florida, Georgia, Hawaii, Illinois, Kansas, Kentucky, Maine, Maryland, Massachusetts, Michigan, Minnesota, Mississippi, New Hampshire, New Jersey, New York, North Carolina, North Dakota, Ohio, Oregon, South Carolina, Tennessee, Virginia, Washington, West Virginia, and Wisconsin.

If you filed Form 990-EZ in any state for this purpose, list it here. If you have not filed your 990-EZ in a state where you should have filed, do not list it in Line 41. However, this could raise a red flag if your nonprofit is actively and visibly engaged in fundraising in any of these

28 states and has not registered. You should register in any such states as soon as possible.

For a detailed discussion of state fundraising registration requirements, refer to *Nonprofit Fundraising Registration: The 50-State Guide*, by Stephen Fishman and Ronald J. Barrett (Nolo).

Line 42: Foreign accounts. The IRS wants to know if nonprofits have foreign bank accounts or foreign offices. One reason is to help law enforcement agencies prevent nonprofits from funneling money to terrorist organizations.

A nonprofit that has money or assets in an account at a foreign financial institution may have to file an annual Foreign Bank Account Report (FBAR, Form TD F 90-22.1) with the IRS. A FBAR must be filed with the IRS whenever a taxpayer has an interest in, or signature authority over, a foreign financial account with a value over $10,000 at any time during the calendar year. Help with questions about FBAR filing requirements is available on the FBAR hotline at 800-800-2877. You can also submit written questions about the FBAR rules by email addressed to FBARQuestions@irs.gov.

Line 44: Donor advised funds. A "donor advised fund" is similar to a private foundation—an individual, family, or corporation contributes money to establish the fund with a charity and at any time thereafter can recommend grant distributions to qualified charities. (See Chapter 1.) If you answer "yes" here, you should file Form 990 instead of Form 990-EZ.

Line 45: Controlled entities. Some nonprofits—primarily large ones—create or buy into private businesses in an effort to obtain income away from the IRS's prying eyes. You must answer "yes" in line 45 only if your nonprofit owns such a business and it is a "controlled entity." A controlled entity is a business entity such as a corporation or partnership in which your nonprofit owns a majority interest. For example, a corporation in which your nonprofit owns more than 50% of the voting shares is a controlled entity. If your nonprofit has a controlled entity, you must file Form 990.

Line 46: Political campaign activities. Public charities (501(c)(3)) organizations) are barred from participating in political campaigns for any elective office. However, there are exceptions to this rule for certain activities, such as registering voters, hosting candidate appearances, and publishing voter guides. If your nonprofit engaged in any political campaign activities, it must file Schedule C with Form 990-EZ. See Chapter 9 for a detailed discussion of political activities by nonprofits.

Part VI: Payments to Key Employees or Contractors

In this section, the IRS wants you to disclose any substantial employee salaries not previously disclosed on the form, and any large payments to independent contractors.

Line 47: Lobbying. Before you answer "yes" or "no" here, make sure you understand what lobbying is. Many activities that you might think are lobbying are not considered to be so for tax purposes. See Chapter 9 for a detailed discussion of lobbying by nonprofits. If you answer "yes," you must file Schedule C along with your Form 990-EZ. This schedule requires detailed disclosures about your nonprofit's lobbying activities. See Chapter 9 for more information about Schedule C.

Line 50: Employees. You've already disclosed the compensation paid to your officers, directors, trustees, and key employees in Part IV. You are required to make the same disclosures in line 50 for the five highest-paid employees (other than those listed in Part IV) who were paid more than $100,000 during the tax year. If, like most nonprofits that file Form 990-EZ, your nonprofit has no employees who earn more than $100,000, you should state "None" in line 50(a).

Line 51: Independent contractors. Independent contractors are outside people or companies who provide services to your nonprofit—for example, accountants, lawyers, consultants, fundraisers, building contractors, and others. If your nonprofit paid more than $100,000 to one or more independent contractors during the year, you must complete the table in line 50 for the five highest-compensated contractors. The amount of compensation listed in line 50(c) should be the same as in any Form 1099-MISC you filed (or will file) with the IRS reporting the payments. (See Chapter 4.)

Few nonprofits filing Form 990-EZ make such large payments to contractors. If you're among those that don't, state "None" in line 50(a).

Signature Block

The Form 990-EZ must be signed by an officer—the president, vice president, treasurer, assistant treasurer, chief accounting officer, or other officer. An improperly signed form is considered to be incomplete by the IRS and is treated the same as not filing the form at all. Failure to properly sign the form is one of the most common mistakes filers make.

Schedules

There are up to seven separate schedules that may have to be filed along with Form 990-EZ. However, most nonprofits will only have to file one, Schedule A. These schedules are the same as those filed with Form 990, although Form 990 has more required schedules. They are intended to give the IRS and the public additional information on specific issues.

Schedule A, Public Charity Status and Public Support. All nonprofits that are public charities (501(c)(3) organizations) must file Schedule A with their Form 990-EZ. This schedule is used to establish that your nonprofit qualifies as a public charity instead of a private foundation. There are several ways your nonprofit can qualify as a public charity. Certain nonprofits automatically qualify, such as churches, schools, hospitals, medical research organizations, and government units. Most other nonprofits qualify by establishing that they receive a substantial amount of their financial support from the public or government, or from their program activities.

If your nonprofit applied for IRS recognition of its tax-exempt status by filing IRS Form 1023, you already had to deal with this complex issue and decide how your nonprofit qualifies as a public charity. If you've received a determination letter from the IRS, it will show whether, and how, your nonprofit qualified. You must file Schedule A every year to show the reason for your nonprofit's public charity status. If your public charity classification is based on public support, you must provide detailed financial information that is updated each year to support this classification. You've already listed most of this information on page one of Form 990-EZ. If you filed Form 990-EZ or Form 990 the past year, look at your Schedule A because it will contain financial information for previous years that must be updated on this year's form. The financial information in Schedule A must be based on the cash method of accounting, even if your nonprofit uses the accrual method for the other portions of the form.

Changes in IRS Rules

Under previous long-standing IRS rules, a nonprofit that wanted to be recognized by the IRS as a publicly supported charity instead of a private foundation had to go through an extended two-step process. First, the organization had to declare that it expected to be publicly supported on an ongoing basis. Then, after five years, it had to file Form 8734, *Support Schedule for Advance Ruling Period,* showing the IRS that it actually met the public support test. If it didn't meet the test, it was designated a private foundation instead of a public charity.

The IRS's new streamlined rules no longer require your nonprofit to file Form 8734 after completing its first five tax years. Moreover, your nonprofit retains its public charity status for its first five years, regardless of the level of public support actually received during that time. Instead, beginning with the sixth tax year, your nonprofit must establish that it meets the public support test by showing that it is publicly supported on its Schedule A. However, Schedule A must still be completed and filed every year.

For a detailed discussion of public charity status, refer to *How to Form a Nonprofit Corporation*, by Anthony Mancuso (Nolo).

Schedule B, Schedule of Contributors. This schedule must be completed only if you have donors who contributed (1) a total of $5,000 or more during the year, or (2) a contribution greater than 2% of your total contributions, gifts, and grants shown in line one of the form. If you don't file this schedule, be sure to check item H on the first page.

Schedule C, Political Campaign and Lobbying Activities. File this schedule only if you answered "yes" in lines 46 or 47. See Chapter 9 for a detailed discussion of this schedule.

Schedule E, Schools. This schedule is used to obtain information about private nonprofit schools' admissions and other policies to determine if there is racial discrimination. Only schools that answer "yes" on line 48 file this schedule.

Schedule G, Supplemental Information Regarding Fundraising or Gaming Activities. This form is filed only if your nonprofit earned $15,000 or more from special activities or from gaming.

Schedule L, Transactions With Interested Persons. See Chapter 7 for a detailed discussion of this schedule.

Schedule N, Liquidation, Termination, Dissolution or Significant Disposition of Assets. File this schedule only if you answered "yes" in line 36. See "Notifying the IRS If You Terminate, Merge, or Contract Your Nonprofit," below.

The New Form 990: Just Hold Your Nose and File It

Form 990 is the Big Daddy of the 990 form series. It is used by larger nonprofits and requires far more information than the other forms. This is one of the longest and most complex tax forms there is. The instructions alone total over 300 pages. We can't provide a line-by-line guide on how to fill out Form 990—that would take a whole book in itself (see the resources listed below). This discussion provides an overview of the form, shows how it has changed, how your nonprofit should go about completing it, and the things your nonprofit needs to do to prepare for Form 990 long before you actually file it.

Many donors, including foundations and government agencies, rely on the information contained in Form 990 to make their funding decisions. One study found that two out of three foundation donors asked for a Form 990. Organizations that grade nonprofits' effectiveness, such as Charity Navigator, rely primarily on this form to devise their ratings. Indeed, Charity Navigator will not grade any nonprofit that has not filed a Form 990. The media and nonprofit watchdog groups also check out 990 forms. Any embarrassing information in a 990 form, such as excessive executive salaries or perks, can easily find its way into a news story or blog.

Do You Really Have to File Form 990?

Form 990 was phased in over three years for smaller nonprofits. Thus, depending on your nonprofit's income, you may not have had to file Form 990 until as late as 2011. Moreover, many nonprofits that used to be required to file Form 990—those with an income between $100,000 and $200,000—are permanently relieved from filing the form and will always be able to file Form 990-EZ instead.

However, even if it is not required, some nonprofits choose to file Form 990 instead of Form 990-EZ. There are different reasons nonprofits may choose to do so including:

- some state governments require a Form 990 and won't accept Form 990-EZ
- certain nonprofit grantors, such as foundations and government agencies, may want a completed Form 990 as a condition of their grant
- the organization, Charity Navigator, will not list your nonprofit on its website or grade it unless you have filed a Form 990, and
- filing Form 990 shows your nonprofit's commitment to public accountability and transparency.

Form 990 Filing Thresholds		
Must file 990 for:	If gross receipts are:	And if total assets are:
2010 and later tax years (filed in 2011 and later)	More than $200,000	More than $500,000
2009 tax year (filed in 2010)	More than $500,000	More than $1.25 million
2008 tax year (filed in 2009)	More than $1 million	More than $2.5 million

How Many Nonprofits Must File Form 990?

Only a small minority of nonprofits have to file a Form 990. As the chart below shows, almost 80% of all nonprofits earn less than $100,000 per year. The income trigger for filing the Form 990 is $200,000, which only approximately 15% of all nonprofits meet.

Annual Income	Number of Registered Nonprofits	Percentage of Total Registered Nonprofits
Less than $100,000	776,817	79.7%
$100,000-$249,999	64,118	6.6%
$250,000-$499,999	38,465	3.9%
$500,000-$999,999	30,087	3.1%
$1-$5 million	41,317	4.2%
$5-$10 million	9,502	1.0%
$10-$100 million	12,149	1.2%
More than $100 million	2,171	0.2%
Total	974,626	100.0%

Source: Internal Revenue Service, Exempt Organizations Business Master File (2009, March); The Urban Institute, National Center for Charitable Statistics.

Resources for Form 990

To its credit, the IRS has gone to great lengths to educate the nonprofit community about the new Form 990. It has created an extraordinarily detailed and helpful set of instructions for the form—more than 300 pages in all. These instructions not only provide line-by-line guidance on how the form should be completed, they also include detailed discussions of applicable nonprofit law, and a helpful glossary. Everyone involved in completing the form should read these instructions carefully.

The agency has also posted on its website several background documents on the reasons for, and extent of, the form's redesign. You can find the latest version of the new Form 990, instructions, and background materials on the IRS's website at www.irs.gov/Charities-&-Non-Profits.

The IRS has also created special Form 990 training materials. These include a detailed online "mini-course" that helps explain what Form 990 contains and how to complete it. Go to the IRS's special nonprofit training website at www.stayexempt.irs.gov. Training materials can be found in both the "Virtual Workshop" and "EO Web-Based Mini-Courses" sections.

Two useful books on Form 990 are *Revised Form 990: A Line-by-Line Preparation Guide*, by Jody Blazek and Amanda Adams (Wiley); and *The New Form 990: Law, Policy, and Preparation*, by Bruce R. Hopkins, et al. (Wiley).

Who Should Prepare Form 990?

Form 990 is too important to be left to accountants to prepare on their own. Moreover, the form isn't just about numbers. Instead, it requires you to provide a complete picture of your nonprofit—including its activities, finances, governance, compensation, and tax compliance. As a result, about three-quarters of the form now deals with matters other than financial disclosures. Many questions require narrative descriptions, rather than quantitative information, that an accountant may be ill-prepared to deal with.

Remember that use of a paid preparer does not relieve your nonprofit from its duty to file a complete and accurate Form 990. Preparing Form 990 will have to be a group effort. The number of people who will need to be involved depends on your nonprofit's size and complexity. Start with your accountant, finance staff, lawyer, and anyone else who was previously involved in preparing the form. Then, consider whether you need to involve others. For example, you'll need to provide narrative descriptions of your nonprofit's activities: This may require the help of a program director. You'll also need to provide details about how your nonprofit's officers, directors, trustees, and key employees are compensated and whether they are engaged in any insider transactions: This will require input from accounting and human resources staff for larger nonprofits, or whoever takes care of your administration if you're a smaller nonprofit.

You may also want to involve your development and fundraising staff to provide information about your fundraising activities, business operations, and the work your volunteers do. If you provide grants, you may want to involve grant selection personnel and others who can help you report on how the grants are used.

Finally, don't forget to talk with your board members to make sure they are aware of the changes that the form may require. For example, you may want to educate them on the new governance questions, compensation reporting, and clarify the role they play in completing or reviewing Form 990. Your annual meeting would be an ideal time to do this.

TIP

Put someone in charge. Someone at your nonprofit should be in charge of preparing your Form 990. You can form a committee or assign one person to do this. Whoever is in charge should carefully review the form and instructions before determining what steps need to be taken to get ready for the form and who should be involved in the process.

Complete Your Form 990 Online

The National Center for Charitable Statistics at the Urban Institute has created a website that you can use to complete Form 990 online and transmit it electronically to the IRS. The site contains an online questionnaire that you complete. The information is automatically double-checked and used to create a completed Form 990. The system is free for nonprofits with less than $100,000 in gross receipts. A fee from $35 to $175 is charged to larger nonprofits, depending on their size. If you're completing Form 990 in-house, you should definitely consider using this website. Refer to the Urban Institute's efile website at http://efile.form990.org.

An Overview of the Form 990

Form 990 consists of an 11-page "core form" and 16 separate schedules —80 pages in all. Fortunately, you probably won't have to complete all the schedules. The Form 990 core form, which must be completed by all nonprofits, consists of the following parts:

- **Part I, Summary.** The first page of the form is intended to serve as a snapshot of your nonprofit. It summarizes key information that is recorded elsewhere in the form, including your nonprofit's mission, activities, governance, and current and prior years' financial results. This portion of the form should usually be completed last.
- **Part II, Signature Block.** Requires the signature of a nonprofit officer and, if applicable, paid preparer.
- **Part III, Statement of Program Service Accomplishments.** This part requires narrative descriptions of your program accomplishments during the year, and related revenue and expenses. This is where you can tell the world about the great work your nonprofit does.
- **Part IV, Checklist of Required Schedules.** The answers to the questions here are used to determine which of the 16 schedules must be completed.

- **Part V, Statements Regarding Other IRS Filings and Tax Compliance.** Used to report compliance with various federal tax requirements such as substantiation of contributions, filing of information returns, payment of employment and unrelated business income taxes, and others.
- **Part VI, Governance, Management, and Disclosure.** Requires information regarding your nonprofit's governing body, management, policies, and disclosure practices.
- **Part VII, Compensation of Officers, Directors, Trustees, Key Employees, Highest Compensated Employees, and Independent Contractors.** Used to report compensation paid to these persons that is reported on Forms W-2 and 1099-MISC, and certain other compensation.
- **Part VIII, Statement of Revenue; Part IX, Statement of Functional Expenses; Part X, Balance Sheet; and Part XI, Reconciliation of Net Assets.** These are your nonprofit's financial statements for federal tax reporting purposes.
- **Part XII, Financial Statements and Reporting.** Used to report information regarding your nonprofit's accounting methods and its compiled, reviewed, or audited financial statements.

Form 990 also contains 16 separate schedules lettered A through R (P and Q are reserved for later use). Each schedule is intended to elicit specific types of information and has its own filing requirements. No nonprofit will have to file all the schedules. Complete Part IV, *Checklist of Required Schedules*, to determine which of these schedules you must file with your Form 990. Following is a list and brief description of the schedules:

- **Schedule A, Public Charity Status and Public Support.** All nonprofits that are public charities (501(c)(3) organizations) must file Schedule A with their Form 990. This schedule is used to establish that your nonprofit qualifies as a public charity instead of a private foundation.
- **Schedule B, Schedule of Contributors.** This schedule must be completed only if you have donors who contributed (1) a total of $5,000 or more during the year, or (2) a contribution greater than 2% of your total contributions, gifts, and grants shown in

Part VIII, line 1h, of the form. If you don't file this schedule, be sure to check item H on the first page.

- **Schedule C, Political Campaign and Lobbying Activities.** This schedule must be completed only if your nonprofit engages in lobbying or political campaign activities. See Chapter 9 for a detailed discussion of this schedule.

- **Schedule D, Supplemental Financial Statements.** Many nonprofits will have to complete at least part of this schedule. It is used to supplement balance sheet information regarding certain assets and liabilities, and to provide additional information about conservation easements, donor advised funds, endowments, museums and other nonprofits maintaining art and other collections, and credit counseling organizations and others holding funds in escrow or custodial accounts.

- **Schedule E, School.** This schedule is used to obtain information about private nonprofit schools' admissions and other policies to determine if there is racial discrimination. Only schools need to complete this.

- **Schedule F, Statement of Activities Outside the United States.** This schedule is completed only if your nonprofit has more than $10,000 in total revenues or expenses from grantmaking, fundraising, and/or programs in foreign countries.

- **Schedule G, Supplemental Information Regarding Fundraising or Gaming Activities.** This schedule must be completed if your nonprofit raised money through special fundraising events or gambling. It requires expanded disclosures regarding your nonprofit's relationships with outside fundraisers, and compliance with state charitable solicitation laws.

- **Schedule H, Hospitals.** This schedule is only completed by hospitals.

- **Schedule I, Grants and Other Assistance to Organizations, Governments and Individuals in the U.S.** Used to report grants and other assistance provided by your nonprofit to organizations or individuals within the United States. Nonprofits that make more than $5,000 in such grants must describe their procedures for monitoring the use of the grant funds.

- **Schedule J, Compensation Information.** This schedule provides more detailed compensation information for officers, directors, trustees, key employees, and highest-compensated employees listed in Part VII of the core form, and information on compensation practices. Most nonprofits won't need to complete this schedule.

- **Schedule K, Supplemental Information for Tax-Exempt Bonds.** Only completed by organizations with outstanding tax-exempt bond liabilities.

- **Schedule L, Transactions with Interested Persons.** Must be completed if your nonprofit entered into transactions with insiders. See Chapter 7 for a detailed discussion of this schedule.

- **Schedule M, Noncash Contributions.** This schedule must be completed if your nonprofit received (1) noncash contributions over $25,000, or (2) contributions of art, historical contributions, or similar items, or (3) conservation easements.

- **Schedule N, Liquidation, Termination, Dissolution or Significant Disposition of Assets.** Completed only if your nonprofit is liquidating, dissolving, or experiencing a significant reduction in size. See "Notifying the IRS If You Terminate, Merge, or Contract Your Nonprofit," below.

- **Schedule O, Supplemental Information to Form 990.** Almost all filers will need to use this schedule to provide supplemental information to describe or explain their responses to questions contained in the core form or schedules.

- **Schedule R, Related Organizations and Unrelated Partnerships.** Filed only if your nonprofit has business relationships with other exempt and taxable organizations.

Getting Ready for Form 990

You need to prepare for Form 990 long before the end of your tax year—the sooner the better. As explained below, there are numerous policies and procedures recommended by the IRS that you may want to adopt, if you haven't done so already.

Common Errors Found on the Form 990

A study of numerous filed Form 990s found that the most common errors made by filers were:

- failure to complete Schedule A
- not stating the nonprofit's primary purpose
- arithmetic errors
- not properly reporting compensation of officers, directors, and employees
- failure to have a nonprofit officer sign the form in the signature block, and
- not listing the correct tax year on the form.

(Source: *Chronicle of Philanthropy*.)

Make sure your financial record keeping is adequate. Good record keeping is the key to preparing Form 990. Make sure your accounting and bookkeeping procedures provide all the information you'll need to complete the form. Whoever does your financial record keeping should look carefully at the expense categories in Part IX of the form. You may need to add new categories to your chart of accounts (and audited financial statements, if any) to ensure you're keeping track of all reportable expenses. See Chapter 3 for guidance on nonprofit accounting and record keeping for Form 990.

Review, revise, or adopt governance policies. The most revolutionary change in Form 990 is Part VI dealing with corporate governance, management, and disclosures. This portion of the form asks whether your nonprofit has adopted the policies listed below. The IRS believes that these policies "are hallmarks of a well-governed organization," and a nonprofit that lacks them is "exposed to a greater risk of abuse ... and more vulnerable to those who might use it for their personal benefit or to engage in nonexempt activities."

However, while adoption of these policies is strongly encouraged by the IRS, it is not required. Indeed, the IRS lacks the authority to impose such a requirement since such governance matters are largely the province of state nonprofit corporation law, not the federal tax law administered by the IRS. Nevertheless, IRS officials have indicated that nonprofits that fail to adopt such policies have a greater chance of being audited than those who do—the rationale being that nonprofits with such policies are more likely to be in compliance with the tax law. Moreover, a series of "no" answers in this section of the form just doesn't look good to members of the public who read the return. That said, you don't necessarily have to adopt all the suggested polices. The Form 990 instructions provide: "Whether a particular policy, procedure, or practice should be adopted by an organization may depend on the organization's size, type, and culture. Accordingly, it is important that each organization consider the governance policies and practices that are most appropriate for that organization in assuring sound operations and compliance."

If you haven't done so already, hold a board meeting to review key policies already in place at your nonprofit and discuss whether you should adopt or revise any of the following policies. Even if you've held such a board meeting in the past, you may wish to do so again this year to see if there are any new policies you should adopt or if changes should be made to your current policies.

- **Conflict of interest policy.** A conflict of interest policy is used to help all those associated with your nonprofit to identify, disclose, and deal with situations where there is a financial or other conflict. This is one policy all nonprofits, no matter how small, should have. For a detailed discussion of conflicts of interest policies, refer to Chapter 7.

- **Expense reimbursement policy.** Reimbursement or payment of expenses for nonprofit ODTKEs is a hot-button item for the IRS and the public. Form 990 contains a separate Schedule J dealing largely with this issue. The schedule specifically asks whether your nonprofit reimburses or pays ODTKEs for first-class or charter travel, companion travel, tax gross-up payments (payment of any taxes due on taxable perks such as travel), discretionary spending, housing, health or social club dues, and personal services such as use of a chauffeur. If your nonprofit reimbursed or paid an ODTKE for any of these things, you must disclose whether you have a written policy in place for such reimbursement or payment. If not, you must explain why not. See Chapter 4 for a detailed discussion of reimbursing or paying expenses for ODTKEs.

- **Whistleblower protection policy.** A whistleblower policy encourages employees to report financial and other improprieties by establishing procedures to keep whistleblowers' identities confidential and to protect them from retaliation. A small nonprofit without employees probably doesn't need this.
- **Document retention and destruction policy.** This policy provides guidance on how long records must be kept by your nonprofit before they are destroyed. This is a good policy for all nonprofits to have. See Chapter 3 for a detailed discussion of such policies.
- **Joint venture policy.** This policy requires a nonprofit to identify, disclose, and properly manage joint ventures—that is, relationships with for-profit businesses. Smaller nonprofits ordinarily are not involved in such ventures.
- **Gift acceptance policy.** A gift acceptance policy establishes procedures for reviewing, accepting, and substantiating non-standard contributions. These are contributions of items that are difficult to sell and/or value—for example, vacation time-shares or stock in a privately owned company. If your nonprofit accepts such nonstandard contributions, you should adopt such a policy. See Chapter 6.
- **Chapter, branch, and affiliate policies.** You would need such a policy only if your nonprofit has local chapters, branches, or affiliates.

Where to Find Sample Policies

If you need to adopt one or more of the suggested governance policies, you'll need to draft a policy and have it approved by your board of directors. There is no single way to draft any of these policies. They can be quite simple or complex. The smaller your nonprofit, the simpler they can be.

There are many places where you can find sample policies—some free, some for a fee. An excellent place to start is the book *Nonprofit Policy Sampler*, by Barbara Lawrence and Outi Flynn (BoardSource), which gives several versions of each policy. The organization, BoardSource, also has numerous sample policies that can be downloaded from its website for a small fee. They can be accessed at www.boardsouce.org. Other websites that have downloadable sample policies include:

- www.smartgivers.org
- www.independentsector.org
- www.foundationcenter.org
- www.probonopartner.org
- www.501commons.org
- www.idealist.org.
- www.councilofnonprofits.org, and
- www.managementhelp.org.

Are Your Management Practices Up to Snuff?

Various portions of Form 990 contain questions on whether your non-profit engages in certain management practices or procedures. Adoption of these practices is strongly encouraged by the IRS. However, as with the governance policies discussed above, it is not mandatory. Not every nonprofit will have to have every procedure in place. For example, if your nonprofit does not award grants, it won't need to have a written grantmaking procedure.

- **Compensation procedures.** You must disclose whether your nonprofit follows the procedures necessary to create a rebuttable presumption that the compensation paid your nonprofit's employees and officers is reasonable. This requires review and approval by independent board members, comparability data, and documentation and record keeping of the discussions and decision. It's highly advisable for all nonprofits with employees or officers it pays to use these procedures. They are covered in detail in Chapter 7. Obviously, all-volunteer nonprofits won't have to worry about this issue.

- **Financial statement review.** Form 990 asks whether your nonprofit's financial statements were compiled, reviewed, or audited by an independent accountant, and if so, whether you have an audit committee that selects the accountant and oversees the audit or review. Such audits or reviews are not required by the IRS, and smaller nonprofits may not need to have them. See Chapter 1 for a discussion of audits of nonprofit financial statements.

- **Corporate minutes.** Keeping accurate and contemporaneous records or minutes of key board meetings and decisions is an important element of good governance. Thus, Form 990 specifically asks if you keep such records. A "no" answer will not look good. For detailed guidance on how to keep proper records of board meetings and decisions and maintaining other corporate documents, refer to *Nonprofit Meetings, Minutes & Records,* by Anthony Mancuso (Nolo).

- **Grantmaking practices.** If your nonprofit awards grants to organizations, governments, or individuals in the United States or foreign countries, you must disclose whether you have procedures in place to substantiate the amount of such grants, the grantees' eligibility for them, and the selection criteria used to award them.

- **Procedures for filing Form 990.** Your nonprofit must disclose whether a copy of the completed Form 990 was provided to the governing board members before it was filed. This is not required, but it is a practice the IRS encourages. You are also required to describe the process, if any, your nonprofit uses to review Form 990—for example, is it approved by the entire board, or a board committee, before it is filed?

- **Public disclosure practices.** You are required to indicate how you make Form 990 and certain other forms available for public inspection. You are also required to describe whether and how your nonprofit makes its governing documents, conflict of interest policy, and financial statements available to the public. See the discussion of the IRS's public disclosure requirements below.

CAUTION

Watch out for the time limits for adopting policies and procedures. The policies and procedures discussed above have to be adopted by the end of your tax year for you to answer "yes" to the questions about them on your Form 990 you file for that year.

Identify and Disclose Family and Business Relationships

Another new feature of Form 990 is that it requires your nonprofit to: (1) list how many voting members of your board of directors (or other governing body) are independent, and (2) identify any family or business relationships among your ODTKEs. These two requirements are inter-twined because family or business relationships with ODTKEs may destroy a director's independence.

An ODTKE's family includes his or her spouse, ancestors, brothers and sisters (whether whole or half blood), children (whether natural or adopted), grandchildren, great-grandchildren, and spouses of brothers, sisters, children, grandchildren, and great-grandchildren. Business relationships include employment relationships, transactions not in the ordinary course of business, and common ownership of a business.

Identifying all the family and business relationships your ODTKEs have with each other could be a nightmare. Fortunately, the IRS says all you have to do is make a "reasonable effort" to obtain the necessary information. The easiest and best way to establish such a reasonable effort is to prepare and send a questionnaire to your nonprofit's ODTKEs each year requiring them to identify any such relationships. The IRS says that your nonprofit is legally entitled to rely on the answers in the questionnaire—it need not conduct any further investigations. The questionnaire need not be filed with your Form 990. Keep it in your records in case the IRS asks you about this issue. An example of such a questionnaire, to which you should attach a list of all your nonprofit's ODTKEs, is shown below.

Are You In Compliance With State Registration Requirements?

If your nonprofit spends more than $15,000 for fundraising services or grosses more than $15,000 from fundraising events, you must file Schedule G with your Form 990. This schedule requires you to list all the states where your nonprofit is registered to solicit funds or has been notified it is exempt from such registration (Schedule G, Part I, Question 3). Thus you'll have to determine if your nonprofit has complied with the state registration rules. Some 39 states, plus the District of Columbia, require nonprofits that solicit funds in their state to register with a state agency—typically the state attorney general or secretary of state. In the past, the IRS had little interest in this requirement, and many nonprofits failed to register. Each state has its own laws governing registration. For comprehensive guidance on how to comply with state fundraising registration requirements, refer to *Nonprofit Fundraising Registration: The 50-State Guide*, by Stephen Fishman and Ronald J. Barrett (Nolo).

Letting the Public See Your Report Card: Disclosure of Form 990

The tax returns filed by virtually all individuals and organizations are kept confidential by the IRS, with one exception: the information returns filed by nonprofits. The latest three years' worth of Forms 990

Family and Business Relationship Questionnaire

Attached is a list of all [*name of nonprofit*] officers, directors, trustees, and key employees during [*year*]. IRS Form 990 requires that the organization report if any of these individuals are related to each other through family or business relationships. Please check the appropriate boxes, provide the necessary information, and sign and date the questionnaire.

1. Family Relationships

Family relationships include an individual's spouse, ancestors, children, grandchildren, great-grandchildren, siblings (whether by whole or half blood), and the spouses of children, grandchildren, great-grandchildren, and siblings.

☐ I have no family relationship with anyone on the attached list.

Signed: _____

Date: _____

☐ I have a family relationship with someone on the attached list.

Name of related person: _____

Nature of family relationship: _____
(Use reverse of this form if more than one related person.)

Signed: _____

Date: _____

2. Business Relationships

Business relationships between two people include any of the following occurring during the tax year:

- One person is employed by the other in a sole proprietorship, or by an organization in which the other person is a trustee, director, officer, key employee, or greater than 35% owner.
- One person (1) directly transacts business with the other in one or more transactions involving transfers of cash

or property with a total value over $10,000, and (2) such transactions are not in the ordinary course of either party's business and not on the same terms as are generally offered to the public.

- One person transacts business with the other in the same manner as described in the previous paragraph but does so indirectly through an organization with which the person is a trustee, director, officer, key employee, or greater than 35% owner.
- The two people are each a director, trustee, officer, or greater than 10% owner in the same business or investment entity.

☐ I have no business relationship with anyone on the attached list.

Signed: _____

Date: _____

☐ I have a business relationship with someone on the attached list.

Name of person: _____

Nature of business relationship: _____
(Use reverse of this form if more than one person.)

Signed: _____

Date: _____

or 990-EZ filed by all nonprofits must be made available for public inspection and copying. Each year's return must be made available by the date it is required to be filed (not counting extensions). This date is May 15 if your nonprofit uses the calendar year as its tax year—for example, the Form 990 or 990-EZ you file for 2014 must be available for public inspection and copying by May 15, 2015. Your application for IRS recognition of your tax-exempt status, IRS Form 1023, must also be made available under these rules.

The requirements differ depending on whether the forms are inspected or copied.

What About Form 990-N?

If your nonprofit filed Form 990-N, you need not worry about the disclosure rules for information returns discussed here. When you file your Form 990-N electronically (which is required for all Form 990-Ns), your information is automatically placed in the IRS's database. The IRS has created a List of Automatically Revoked Organizations and posted it on its website at http://apps.irs.gov/app/eos/. It is updated monthly.

CAUTION

Don't disclose the names or addresses of contributors to the public. If your nonprofit had contributors who gave a total of $5,000 or more during the year, you are required to disclose their names, addresses, and contribution amounts on the Schedule B that you file with the IRS along with your Form 990 or 990-EZ. However, you can (and should) delete these names and addresses from the Schedule B you post on the Internet or make available for public inspection or copying. Each year, after filing your Form 990 with the IRS, prepare a copy for public inspection and disclosure omitting the names and addresses of all contributors.

Public Inspection of Returns

You must make copies of your original and amended annual information returns for the previous three tax years available for public inspection without charge. "Public inspection" is just what it sounds like: an individual comes to your office and looks at the returns. Any member of the public may inspect your returns. You may not require that someone asking to see your returns give you his or her name or address, or explain the reason for inspecting the returns. You may have an employee present during an inspection, but must allow the individual to take notes freely.

If your nonprofit has a principal office with regular business hours, you must permit members of the public to come to your office to inspect your returns at regular working hours. In-person requests for inspections must be allowed on the same day the request is made. Inspections must also be allowed at any regional or district offices with at least three employees.

If your nonprofit doesn't have a permanent office, you have two options:

- you can make the returns available for inspection at a reasonable location of your choice within a reasonable time after receiving the request for inspection (normally not more than two weeks) and at a reasonable time of day, or
- mail, within two weeks of receiving the request, copies of the returns to the requester instead of allowing an inspection (you can charge for copying and postage only if the requester agrees).

If your nonprofit has an office, but has no regular business hours or very limited hours during certain times of the year, you must make your returns available during those periods when office hours are limited or not available as though you had no permanent office.

Furnishing Copies of Returns

In addition to making your returns available for public inspection, you must furnish copies to any person who asks for them. There are two ways to do this—the easy way, and the hard way.

The Easy Way—post your returns on your website. The copying requirement is automatically deemed satisfied if your returns are "made widely available" to the public. You can do this by posting your returns on your website. In other words, if your returns are freely available to the public on your website, you need not honor requests to provide photocopies of them. Instead, you can tell the requester to download digital copies of the returns from the website.

The IRS has detailed regulations regarding the format of such posted returns. The format must exactly reproduce the image of the original document and allow an Internet user to access, download, and print the posted document without paying a fee. One format that currently meets the criteria is Portable Document Format (.pdf). You must advise requesters how to access the forms—a note on your website should do.

> **CAUTION**
>
> **Public inspection rules still apply.** Posting your returns on your website satisfies the requirement to provide copies of them. However, this requirement is separate from the requirement to make the returns available for public inspection. There is no exception to the public inspection requirement.

The Hard Way—provide hard copies. If, for some reason, you don't want to post your information returns on the Internet, you don't have to. Instead, you can provide hard copies to any individual who requests them. Photocopies usually must be provided immediately for in-person requests, and within 30 days for written requests (a request that is emailed is considered a written request). You may charge a reasonable copying fee plus actual postage, if any. The IRS says a reasonable copying fee is 20 cents per page. You may require payment before providing the copies, but must advise requesters of the total cost of the copies requested if adequate payment is not included with the initial request. The rules allow you up to seven days to mail a notice of prepayment after you receive the initial request. Individuals must also be allowed to make copies themselves without charge at your office if they provide their own photocopying equipment.

What If Someone Harasses You?

It's possible that a person or group may attempt to harass your nonprofit by making a large volume of requests for copies in the hope that it will disrupt your operations. Signs of a harassment campaign include: a sudden increase in the number of requests, multiple requests from the same person, requests made through form letters, or requests containing hostile language.

If You're Concerned About Harassment

If you're really concerned that a political or ideological opponent may attempt to harass you by deluging you with information requests, you can take the following steps to document to the IRS that a campaign of harassment is being waged against you.

- **Record the name, address, and date of every requester.** This enables you to make sure that no one requests more than two copies in a 30-day period or four within a year.
- **Keep written requests on file.** This enables you to compare the requests against each other to see if a form letter is being used, and provides evidence you can show the IRS that a form letter is being used or that requests contain hostile language.
- **Record the number and frequency of requests.** This enables you to document any sudden increase in requests or any extraordinary requests.

You may disregard requests for copies in excess of two requests from any individual sent from the same address within 30 days, or four within a one-year period. In addition, you may apply to the IRS for a determination that your nonprofit is the subject of a harassment campaign. To do so, you must file a written application containing the details of the harassment. If the IRS makes such a determination, your nonprofit can be relieved of having to comply with the harassing requests. While waiting for such an IRS determination, you may stop complying with any disclosure requests you believe are part of the harassment campaign. For details, refer to IRS regulation 301.6104(d)-3.

Penalties for Failure to Comply

Failure to comply with the disclosure rules can result in monetary penalties being imposed by the IRS. The normal penalty for noncompliance is $20 for each day that inspection was not permitted, up to a maximum of $10,000 for each return. However, if the IRS determines that the noncompliance was willful, it may impose an additional penalty of $5,000.

GuideStar Transparency Recommendations

The IRS rules discussed above are the minimum public disclosure requirements your nonprofit must comply with. However, you can do much more to increase your nonprofit's transparency to the public. The organization GuideStar, which maintains the largest private database of nonprofit information returns, suggests that all nonprofits with websites take the following steps:

- regularly update their websites with current, detailed program and evaluation information
- in addition to their names and titles, post brief biographic information on board members and key staff
- post annual reports, if any
- post audited financial statements, if any, and
- post their IRS Letter of Determination, if any.

Notifying the IRS If You Terminate, Merge, or Contract Your Nonprofit

In this period of economic difficulty, many nonprofits are ending their existence. This can be done in several ways:

- you can formally dissolve or liquidate your nonprofit by filing the required documents with your secretary of state or other state official
- you can simply sell or otherwise dispose of all of your nonprofit's assets, if any, and stop doing business, or
- you can merge with another nonprofit in an attempt to form an economically stronger entity.

You need not obtain IRS approval to end your nonprofit, but you are required to notify the IRS if it stops operating as an independent entity. This is done by filing a final Form 990, 990-EZ, or e-Postcard (990-N). Moreover, nonprofits that file Form 990 or 990-EZ must describe in detail what was done with their assets, if any, by filing Schedule N, *Liquidation, Termination, Dissolution, or Significant Disposition of Assets*, with their final return.

The reason that the IRS is so interested in what your nonprofit does with its assets upon termination is that one of the basic conditions for receiving tax-exempt status from the IRS is that you dispose of your assets in a certain way when your nonprofit terminates. Specifically, any assets left after all a nonprofit's debts and other liabilities are paid must be given to another nonprofit or used for another exempt purpose. They may not be given to members of the nonprofit—directors, officers, or employees—or any other private individuals. This requirement is ordinarily set forth in a nonprofit's articles of incorporation or other governing instruments. The IRS wants to make sure that no individual personally benefits from a nonprofit's termination.

Review and Follow Your State Law

The nonprofit corporation laws of many states contain detailed require-ments as to how nonprofits may be merged or terminated. Be sure to review and follow these rules. Many states require you to notify the state attorney general or other state official of your nonprofit's intent to dissolve, liquidate, or terminate. A list of these state officials can be found on the IRS website. at www.irs.gov/Charities-&-Non-Profits/State-Nonprofit-Incorporation-Forms-and-Information.

Which Form to File

Which form to file depends on your nonprofit's gross receipts and assets.

Form 990 Filing Requirements Upon Termination or Merger	
Gross receipts and assets	**Form to file**
Gross receipts "normally" $50,000 or less	990-N
Gross receipts $50,001 to $199,999 Total assets less than $500,000	990-EZ
Gross receipts $200,000 or more Total assets $500,000 or more	990

When the Return Is Due

If you are terminating your nonprofit or effectively going out of business by merging with another nonprofit or selling all your assets, you will need to file a final information return four months and 15 days after the date of your nonprofit's termination. For example, if your nonprofit terminates on September 1, 2014, your final information return must be filed by January 15, 2015.

Information You Must Disclose

Form 990 filers should check the "Termination" box in the header area on page 1 of the return and answer "yes" to the question whether the organization liquidated, terminated, or dissolved (line 31 of Part IV) and, if applicable, to the question whether the organization engaged in a significant disposition of net assets (line 32 of Part IV).

Form 990-EZ filers should check the "Termination" box in the header area on page 1 of the return and answer "yes" to the question whether the organization liquidated, terminated, dissolved, or substantially contracted (line 36 of Part V).

If you file the e-Postcard (Form 990-N), answer "yes" to the question about whether your nonprofit has terminated or gone out of business. This form is completed online at http://epostcard.form.org.

Schedule N. After you've indicated on the 990 or 990-EZ that you are terminating your organization or transferring assets, you'll need to file Schedule N: *Liquidation, Termination, Dissolution, or Significant Disposition of Assets.*

The information required on Schedule N includes a description of the assets distributed upon termination, any transaction fees paid, the date of distribution, the fair market value of the assets, and information about the recipients of the assets, including their EINs.

Schedule N also asks a series of specific questions, including:

- **Question 2:** Whether an officer, director, trustee, or key employee of your nonprofit is, or is expected to be, involved in the organization your nonprofit has merged with or transferred its assets to. If you answer "yes," you must provide the name of the person involved and an explanation of the circumstances.

- **Question 3:** Whether your nonprofit has distributed its assets in accordance with its governing instruments. If your nonprofit is incorporated, your articles of incorporation should require all assets remaining after debts are paid to be distributed to another nonprofit or for some other nonprofit purpose. If you answer "no" here, you must explain in Part III. This is the most important question on the form.

- **Questions 5 and 6:** Whether your nonprofit complied with your state's laws requiring notification of dissolution and payment of creditors.

Attachments to your return. You will need to provide a certified copy of your articles of dissolution or merger, resolutions, and plans of liquidation or merger along with your Form 990 or 990-EZ. You may also need to provide any other relevant documentation.

Significant Contraction of Your Nonprofit

You must also notify the IRS by filing Schedule N if, while not ending your nonprofit, you sell or otherwise dispose of 25% or more of the fair market value of its net assets during the year. It makes no difference if this occurred in a single transaction or a series of transactions.

In this time of substantial declines in the value of nonprofits' investments and other assets, it is important to understand that this does not include any decrease in value of assets due to market fluctuations, or to sales of publicly held securities. Nor does it include asset sales in the ordinary course of business, such as inventory sales. Rather, examples of the types of transactions required to be reported on Schedule N include:

- taxable or tax-free sales or exchanges of assets for cash or other consideration
- sales, contributions, or other transfers of assets to establish or maintain a partnership, joint venture, or a corporation (for-profit or nonprofit)
- sales of assets by a partnership or joint venture in which your nonprofit has an ownership interest
- transfers of assets because of a merger or other reorganization after which your nonprofit continues in existence, and
- a grant or charitable contribution of assets by your nonprofit to another nonprofit.

If a significant contraction of your nonprofit occurred, you must file Schedule N along with your annual information return—whether Form 990 or 990-EZ. These forms are filed at the normal time—four months and 15 days after the end of your nonprofit's tax year.

You must complete Part II of the schedule, which requires you to describe the assets distributed, their fair market value and how it was determined, and provide information about the recipients of the assets, including their EINs. You must also indicate whether any officer, director, or key employee has any personal involvement with the organization that received the assets.

What to Do If the IRS Has Revoked Your Nonprofit's Tax-Exempt Status

Over 400,000 nonprofits have lost their tax-exempt status due to failure to file Form 990, 990-EZ, or 990-N for three consecutive years. The IRS has created a List of Automatically Revoked Organizations and posted it on its website at http://apps.irs.gov/app/eos/. It is updated monthly.

A public charity (501(c)(3) organization) that loses its tax-exempt status cannot receive tax deductible contributions and will not be identified in the IRS Master File as eligible to receive tax deductible contributions, or be included on the IRS's Exempt Organizations Select Check (Pub. 78 Data) or the Exempt Organizations Business Master File extract (EO BMF). Contributions a donor makes to such a nonprofit after the date its name was published on the IRS list of automatically revoked organizations are not tax deductible.

Moreover, revocation of your nonprofit's tax-exempt status could have serious implications under your state's nonprofit laws. In some states, nonprofits listed on the IRS Auto-Revocation List may not be entitled to exemptions from real property, sales, or other taxes or they may be required to provide state authorities or the public with information concerning their changed federal tax status.

To receive tax deductible contributions and avoid problems with your state, you'll need to get your organization's tax exempt status reinstated by the IRS.

Reinstating Tax-Exempt Status

The IRS has no authority to undo an automatic revocation and there is no appeal process. So, you'll have to apply to the IRS to have your nonprofit's status reinstated. You must apply even if your nonprofit was not originally required to apply with the IRS for recognition of tax exemption. For example, if your nonprofit was a subordinate organization whose tax-exempt status was included in a group exemption letter that was automatically revoked, it must submit an application for reinstatement of its tax-exempt status on its own behalf.

This application process is much the same as filing for your tax-exempt status originally. Your nonprofit must:

- file Form 1023 if it is applying under section 501(c)(3), or Form 1024 if it is applying under a different code section
- pay the appropriate user fee. (The organization's annual gross receipts generally determine the amount of the fee.)
- write "Automatically Revoked" on top of the application and the envelope so the application goes to the proper personnel.

The application should be sent to:

Internal Revenue Service
P.O. Box 12192
Covington, KY 41012-0192

Effective Date of Reinstatement

Ordinarily, when the IRS reinstates a nonprofit's tax-exempt status, it is effective as of the date the new application for reinstatement was filed. This means that any gifts your nonprofit received during the period after it lost its tax-exempt status and before the application was filed are not tax deductible. However, you can request that the reinstatement be made retroactive back to the date of automatic revocation. This way, all gifts your nonprofit received will be tax deductible.

For your nonprofit to qualify for retroactive reinstatement, you must convince the IRS that you had "reasonable cause" for failing to file the returns for three consecutive years. To do so, include the following with your application:

- a written statement setting forth all of the facts that support your claim for reasonable cause for failing to file a required return in each of the three consecutive years and over the entire consecutive three-year period, including a detailed description of all the facts and circumstances that led to each failure and the continuous failure, the discovery of the failures, and the steps taken to avoid or mitigate the failures

- a written statement describing the safeguards your nonprofit has put into place to ensure that the organization will not fail to file returns or notices in the future
- evidence to substantiate all material aspects of the written statements described above
- properly completed and executed paper annual information returns (Forms 990, Forms 990-EZ, or Forms 990-PF, whichever is applicable) for all taxable years during and after the consecutive three-year period that the organization was required, but failed, to file an annual information return
- properly completed and executed Forms 990-EZ for all taxable years during and after the consecutive three-year period that the organization was eligible to file a Form 990-N e-Postcard but failed to file either a Form 990-N e-Postcard or an annual information return, and
- an original declaration, dated and signed under penalty of perjury by an officer, director, trustee, or other official who is authorized to sign for the organization in the following form:

I, _____(Name)_____ , _____(Title)_____ declare, under penalty of perjury, that I am authorized to sign this request for retroactive reinstatement on behalf of [*Name of Organization*], and I further declare that I have examined this request for retroactive reinstatement, including the written explanation of all the facts and information pertaining to the claim for reasonable cause and the evidence to substantiate the claim for reasonable cause, and to the best of my knowledge and belief, this request is true, correct, and complete.

If your nonprofit is not a small nonprofit that qualifies for special relief, write "Automatically Revoked" on top of the application and the envelope so the application goes to the proper personnel.

Reinstatement May Take Time to Appear on IRS Records

There can be a delay of up to one month between the time your nonprofit is reinstated and the time it shows up on Select Check (Pub.78 Data) and EO BMF as a tax-exempt 501(c)(3) nonprofit organization. During this time, donors can rely on your nonprofit's determination letter from the IRS as proof of your exempt status. So, even if your nonprofit remains on the list of automatically revoked organizations, donors can rely on an IRS determination letter dated on or after the effective revocation date. Donors also can confirm a nonprofit's status by calling the IRS (toll-free) at 877-829-5500.

Record Keeping and Accounting

This may not be the chapter you are most looking forward to reading. Well, do it anyway. Record keeping and accounting are to a nonprofit what paints are to an artist or marble to a sculptor: Without them, you have nothing. With them, you can keep the IRS off your back and show the world what a great job your nonprofit is doing.

In this chapter, we'll go over the nuts and bolts of record keeping—what you need to know and do to comply with IRS rules, keep adequate records, and run a good operation. Don't shortchange yourself by thinking this is something you can figure out on your own or as things come up. There are some basics that it pays to understand and do right—right from the beginning.

Why Keep Financial Records?

You probably didn't enter the nonprofit sector because you love accounting and bookkeeping. However, keeping good financial records is extremely important for all nonprofits, no matter how small you are. You've probably heard this before … but, in today's harsh economic climate, it's truer now than it has ever been. Here are a few of the reasons your nonprofit needs good records:

Accounting and Bookkeeping—What's the Difference?

The terms accounting and bookkeeping are often used interchangeably, but they have different meanings. Bookkeeping is the process of recording day-to-day financial transactions. Accounting is the process of taking this mass of bookkeeping information and using it to create financial statements, tax returns, and budgets. You might think of bookkeepers as the frontline troops in the financial wars, while accountants are the generals. However, both activities are equally important—you can't get the essential end product without the necessary and correct raw data.

Preparing Annual IRS Information Returns

All but the smallest nonprofits are required to file an annual information return with the IRS (Form 990 or 990-EZ). Nonprofits with under $50,000 in gross receipts file an electronic postcard instead. (See Chapter 2.) In all cases, you'll need an accurate record of your annual income to know which form you need to file. If you file a Form 990 or 990-EZ, you'll have to provide detailed financial information about your nonprofit. You can't just make up or guess at these numbers. You'll need accurate records of your income, expenses, and credits to report on the return. If the IRS audits your return, you'll need the records to explain the items you covered. And you'll be subject to IRS penalties if you fail to file an accurate return.

Showing You're Fulfilling Your Nonprofit Mission

In return for receiving a tax exemption, nonprofits are supposed to use the income they receive through contributions, grants, investments, and other means exclusively to further their nonprofit purposes. Neither you, your contributors, or the IRS will be able to determine if you are doing this unless you keep proper financial records. In extreme cases, the IRS can revoke the tax exemption of a nonprofit that can't show how it spent its money.

Showing You Qualify as a Public Charity

If, like most nonprofits, your nonprofit qualifies as a public charity because you receive substantial public support—that is, contributions from the public—you need to be able to identify where your income comes from. If you don't keep records showing how much support you receive from specific contributors, your nonprofit may not be able to show that it qualifies as a public charity. In this event, your nonprofit would be classified as a private foundation rather than a public charity—something you don't want to have happen.

UBIT

If your nonprofit sells goods or services to the public and the activity is not exempt from the unrelated business income tax (UBIT), you'll need records to substantiate the amount, if any, of unrelated business taxable income you earn during the year. You'll also need to track the financial revenues and expenses subject to UBIT reporting to prepare your unrelated business income tax return, Form 990-T, *Exempt Organization Business Income Tax Return*. (See Chapter 8.)

Preparing Financial Statements

You may need to prepare annual financial statements for state regulators, funding organizations, contributors, banks, and creditors. Some states require charities to make audited financial statements publicly available. These statements cannot be prepared without accurate and complete financial records.

Monitoring Your Budget

Unless you have accurate records showing your income and expenses, it will be impossible to determine accurately whether your nonprofit has stayed within its annual budget. The ability to monitor income and expenses to ensure that you are operating within budget is crucial to successful stewardship of a public charity.

RESOURCE

Educate yourself about nonprofit accounting. This chapter cannot provide a complete bookkeeping or accounting course—it is far too vast a subject. Fortunately, there are many good guides to nonprofit bookkeeping and accounting. These include:

- *Nonprofit Bookkeeping & Accounting for Dummies,* by Sharon Farris (Wiley)

- *Financial and Accounting Guide for Not-for-Profit Organizations,* by Malvern J. Gross, Jr., John H. McCarthy, and Nancy E. Sherman (Wiley)
- *Bookkeeping for Nonprofits,* by Murray Dropkin and James Halpin (Jossey-Bass)
- *Running QuickBooks in Nonprofits,* by Kathy Ivens (CPA911)
- *Bookkeeping Basics: What Every Nonprofit Bookkeeper Needs to Know,* by Debra L. Ruegg and Lisa M. Venkatrathnam (Fieldstone Alliance), and
- *Minding the Money: A Practical Guide for Volunteer Treasurers,* by Alden Todd and Joseph M. Galloway (ASJA Press).

Courses in nonprofit accounting and bookkeeping are also offered all over the country by four-year colleges and community colleges.

Who's in Charge?

If your nonprofit is incorporated, there should be a corporate officer whose duty it is to oversee your nonprofit's accounting and bookkeeping functions. Ordinarily, this is the treasurer or chief financial officer (CFO). In small nonprofits the treasurer or CFO is typically a board member who works on a volunteer basis. Larger nonprofits may have a paid employee serve as CFO. At a very small nonprofit, the volunteer treasurer may handle all the accounting and bookkeeping work, while a somewhat larger organization might employ a part-time bookkeeper under the treasurer's direction. The larger the nonprofit, the more people will be required to perform bookkeeping and accounting work. Large nonprofits may have an entire accounting staff or employ the services of an outside accounting firm.

Regardless of who performs and oversees the day-to-day accounting functions, your board of directors is ultimately responsible for everything your nonprofit does, including how it manages its financial affairs. All board members should read your nonprofit's financial statements and be knowledgeable about its finances so that they can make good management decisions.

What Does the IRS Require?

You may be surprised to discover that the IRS gives you a great deal of leeway in deciding how to do your bookkeeping and accounting. However, whatever system you use must contain a few basic elements:

- a tax year
- an accounting method
- a record of your nonprofit's income and expenses
- supporting documents showing income and expenses
- fixed asset records, and
- employment tax records (if your nonprofit has employees).

A Tax Year

Nonprofits must keep their financial records based on an annual accounting period called a tax year. A tax year is usually 12 consecutive months. There are two kinds of tax years:

- a calendar tax year—this is a period of 12 consecutive months beginning January 1 and ending December 31, or
- a fiscal tax year—this is a period of 12 consecutive months ending on the last day of any month except December.

You can use either one, but you must decide when you begin operating your nonprofit. When you apply for tax-exempt status from the IRS, you state your tax year on your application.

Make sure you know what your nonprofit does, so that you report the right items at the right time. If your nonprofit must file an annual information return with the IRS (Form 990 or 990-EZ), the due date is four and one-half months after the end of your tax year. Thus, for example, if your tax year ends on December 31, the return is due May 15 of the following year (however, you can get an automatic three-month extension).

Many nonprofits, especially small ones, use a calendar year as their tax year. It's easy to understand and coincides with the employment tax reporting for employees, bank reporting of interest income, and other financial items handled on a calendar year basis. However, it can be more convenient to use a fiscal year if your nonprofit's operations are seasonal. For example, if your nonprofit earns most of its income in the spring and incurs most of its expenses in the fall, a tax year ending in July or August might be better than a calendar tax year ending in December. That way, the income and expenses for each tax year will be more closely related.

Changing Your Tax Year

Once you've chosen your tax year, you need IRS permission to change it. Usually this is granted automatically. If your nonprofit files an annual information return with the IRS (Form 990 or 990-EZ) or an exempt organization business income return (Form 990-T), you would file the form within four and one-half months after the close of your new accounting year, which will be shorter than your previous year and is therefore called a short year. Write "Change of Accounting Period" at the top of your return. If you previously changed your tax year during the prior ten years, you must attach IRS Form 1128, *Application to Adopt, Change, or Retain a Tax Year* to the return. If your nonprofit doesn't have to file a Form 990 or 990-EZ, you don't need to notify the IRS that you have changed your tax year.

An Accounting Method

Your method of accounting is the set of rules you use to determine when and how income and expenses are reported to the IRS and others. A public charity must choose an accounting method when it files its first annual return (IRS Form 990 or 990-EZ). Thus, if you've already filed a return you've already chosen your method. However, you may be able to change your accounting method—many smaller nonprofits do so as they grow and their accounting needs change.

The IRS says that you can choose any method that clearly reflects your nonprofit's income. Your options include:

Cash method. The cash method is based on this commonsense idea: You haven't earned income for tax and accounting purposes until you actually receive the money, and you haven't incurred an expense until you actually pay the money. Thus, for example, you don't record any income when a donor gives you a pledge, only when the money is actually paid. Similarly, you don't record an expense when you receive a bill, only when you pay it. Using the cash basis method, then, is like maintaining a checkbook. Your nonprofit reports income only when the money is received and expenses only when they are actually paid. Although it's called the "cash" method, payments by check, credit card, or electronic funds transfer are also counted as cash payments. The cash method is by far the simplest and easiest to use and, for this reason, is the one used by many small nonprofits.

Accrual method. Under the accrual method, your nonprofit generally records income when it is earned, even if payment is not received until later. Likewise, expenses are recorded when they are incurred, whether or not they are paid at that time. Thus, for example, an unconditional pledge from a contributor would be recorded as income when it is made, not when the money is later received. Similarly, an expense is recorded when you receive a bill, even if you don't pay it until later. The accrual method is more difficult to use than the cash method because of complicated rules you must follow for figuring out when income or expenses accrue. The accrual method is used by all large nonprofits and is the only method that complies with generally accepted accounting principles (GAAP). Moreover, many states require that nonprofits whose income exceeds a certain threshold use the accrual method for their accounting.

Hybrid method. It is possible to combine elements of the cash and accrual methods. Your nonprofit could use the simple cash method for some accounts and the accrual method for others. There is no single way to devise a hybrid method. Under one type of hybrid method, unpaid bills are recorded on the accrual basis, while income is recorded on the cash basis. This way you know everything that your nonprofit owes, but only count as income money you actually have. Another type of hybrid method uses the cash method for most accounts and accrual for a few, such as payroll taxes payable to the IRS and state taxing authority.

Which method is best? There is no single answer to this question. It all depends on the size of your nonprofit, the number of transactions it has each year, and the expertise of people who do your accounting. For a small nonprofit that has few assets other than cash and has no significant accounts payable, the cash method can work just fine. Indeed, you'd end up with much the same results regardless of which method you use. On the other hand, the cash method will not give you an accurate picture of your nonprofit's financial position if you have many accounts payable and/or receivable—your books will only show the cash you have in the bank, not the large bills coming due or the donations or grants that will be paid in the future. Moreover, the accrual method must be used if you want your accounting and financial statements to comply with generally accepted accounting principles (GAAP). As discussed below, compliance with GAAP is necessary if you need to have audited financial statements. If you want to retain the simplicity of the cash method, but also want to comply with GAAP, one option is to keep your books using the cash method during the year and then have an accountant convert them to the accrual method at the end of your tax year.

Changing Your Method

You do not need to obtain IRS approval to choose your nonprofit's initial accounting method. However, once you choose your accounting method, you are supposed to use it consistently from year to year. You can't change it without getting permission from the IRS. To do this, you must file IRS Form 3115, *Application for Change in Accounting Method*, 180 days before the end of the year in which you want to make the change. The IRS will always permit you to change your accounting method from cash to accrual, because it prefers the accrual method. However, changing from accrual to cash may be more problematic.

A Record of Income and Expenses

Some people maintain no systematic record of their income and expenses during the year. Instead, they just throw all their bills, receipts, pay stubs, and other financial documents in a shoebox or other container and then deal with them come tax time. This is not a good idea for an individual, and it is a disaster for a nonprofit. For all the reasons discussed above, your nonprofit needs an accounting system that enables you to keep accurate track of your income and expenses.

There are many different ways to keep a nonprofit's financial accounts, from the exceedingly simple to the exceedingly complex. No one would expect a Little League team to use the same accounting system as a large nonprofit bringing in millions per year. Small nonprofits can usually use a very simple system; but, the larger a nonprofit gets, the more complex its accounting becomes.

The IRS does not require that a nonprofit use any specific type of accounting system. It says that "a public charity can choose any system, suited to its activities, that clearly shows the organization's income and expenses." In other words, you may choose any system that makes sense for your nonprofit. What makes sense depends on many factors, including:

- the amount and sources of your nonprofit's annual revenue
- the number of financial transactions you have each month
- whether your funds require any special financial reporting
- whether you have employees now or will in the future, and whether payroll will be handled in-house or by an outside service
- the experience of the person doing your bookkeeping, and
- whether you want a computerized accounting system.

If your nonprofit is quite small, you may be content to use "check-book accounting"—that is, all your nonprofit's financial transactions go through a single checking account and are recorded on the check register—either manually or in a computerized register. See "Journals and Ledgers," below for details on how to use such a simple system.

Getting Help

If you need help setting up your accounting system or figuring out ways to improve it, the cheapest alternative is to contact another nonprofit that is approximately the same size, and in the same or a similar field, and ask about the system they use. Nonprofits usually are willing to help each other. Alternatively, you can consult with an accountant—one or two hours with an accountant familiar with nonprofit issues may be all that's needed to help put you on the right track.

Larger nonprofits—those that must file IRS Form 990 or 990-EZ each year—usually need a more sophisticated system involving accounting journals and ledgers. Such a record-keeping system might include a:

- checkbook—including a check register showing each check written in chronological order
- cash disbursement journal—a chronological record showing all the checks that are written, organized according to specific categories
- cash receipts journal—a chronological record of all deposits, also organized by categories, and
- general journal—a record of all transactions which do not pass through the checkbook, including noncash transactions and corrections to previous journal entries.

As your nonprofit grows and you engage in more and more financial transactions, you may need to add journals to help you keep better track of more frequent transactions. These may include a payroll journal that records all payroll-related transactions and an accounts payable and accounts receivable journal that tracks income and expense accruals. Your accounting system is never set in stone. As your needs change, you are free to change your accounting system.

Journals and Ledgers

A journal is a book where you record each financial transaction shown on your supporting documents, such as expense receipts and deposit slips. A ledger is a book that contains the totals from all of your journals, organized into different accounts. The words "journal" and "ledger" come from the old days when all accounting was done by hand in actual written account books. Today, most people use computerized accounting systems. Such systems continue to use journals and ledgers, but they are simply modules in the overall computerized system.

Your chart of accounts. To make sense of all the individual financial transactions you record in your checkbook and various journals, the income coming in and expenses going out are divided into various categories called accounts. An account is a separate record of the increases and decreases of related items—for example, cash is always a separate account. A chart of accounts is the master list of all the accounts your accounting system tracks. Both a name and a number are often assigned to each account. A chart of accounts should include five basic areas:

- assets—things you own
- liabilities—bills you need to pay
- net assets—equity, a summary of your nonprofit's financial position
- income—money received or promised, and
- expenses—money you spent.

It is entirely up to you to decide what accounts you need within each major category. However, if your nonprofit files IRS Form 990 or 990-EZ, you (or your accountant) will have a much easier time if your chart of accounts flows into the line items that must be completed in the applicable form. Here is a chart of accounts that includes all the financial line items on Form 990-EZ (Form 990 contains a much more extensive list of line items).

Assets
- cash, savings, and investments
- land and buildings
- other assets

Net assets
- current year surplus/deficit

Liabilities
- Ordinarily, only nonprofits that use the accrual method of accounting will have liabilities such as accounts payable and loans payable.

Income
- contributions, gifts, and grants
- program service revenue
- membership dues
- investments
- noninventory sales—Gross
- noninventory sales—Cost
- special events
- special events—Gift revenue
- special events—Nongift revenue
- special events—Expenses
- inventory sales—Gross
- inventory sales—Cost of goods sold

Expenses
- grants
- member benefits
- salaries and employee benefits
- professional fees and payments to independent contractors
- occupancy, rent, utilities, and maintenance
- printing, publications, postage, and shipping, and
- other expenses.

Your chart need not match every account included on the form, only those relevant to your nonprofit. For example, if you don't sell goods or have inventories, you don't have to include accounts for those items. On the other hand, for your own purposes, you may want to have a more detailed chart of accounts—for example, you may want to have separate accounts for contributions, gifts, and grants. When you complete Form 990-EZ, you would simply combine all three accounts. It is usually best to provide a separate account for each type of expense that requires frequent entries.

Unified Chart of Accounts

The National Center for Charitable Statistics, in conjunction with several other nonprofit groups, has developed a Unified Chart of Accounts (UCOA) for nonprofits. This is a standardized list of accounts that non-profits may use. UCOA is designed so that nonprofits can easily translate their financial reports into the categories required on IRS Form 990. The UCOA is an excellent resource and can be downloaded for free from: http://nccs.urban.org/projects/ucoa.cfm.

If your nonprofit is a small all-volunteer organization that uses the cash basis and is supported solely by contributions, you likely only need a few accounts to be able to complete Form 990-EZ—for example:

Assets
- cash in bank
- savings

Net assets
- current year surplus/deficit

Income
- contributions

Expenses
- member benefits
- professional fees and payments to independent contractors
- occupancy, rent, utilities, and maintenance
- printing, publications, postage, and shipping
- other expenses
- supplies
- telephone

- website
- bank charges, and
- travel.

Allocating expenses. If you file IRS Form 990, a portion of the form requires you to allocate your annual expenses among three basic functions: administration (also called management & general), fundraising, and program services. This is also required to comply with GAAP if your nonprofit is a voluntary health and welfare organization. This is not required for smaller nonprofits that file IRS Form 990-EZ and don't need to comply with GAAP.

It is generally not difficult to tell if an expense is for fundraising. However, it can be difficult to determine which expenses are administrative and which are for program services.

- Program expenses are those directly related to carrying out your nonprofit's mission, and that result in goods or services being provided—for example, expenses to teach a class, put on a performance, provide health care, or deliver food or clothing to the indigent.
- Administrative expenses are those for your nonprofit's overall operations and management—for example, costs of board of directors' meetings, general legal services, accounting, insurance, office management, auditing, human resources, and other centralized services.
- Fundraising expenses include costs for publicizing and conducting fundraising campaigns, maintaining donor mailing lists, conducting special fundraising events, and any other activities that involve soliciting contributions.

Remember that an expense takes its function from the activity it supports—for example, the cost of a telephone call may be either program, fundraising, or administrative depending on the purpose of the call.

Form 990-EZ filers need not allocate their expenses by function. However, even 990-EZ form filers must list their total expenses for program services. If there is more than one program, shared expenses will have to be allocated among them. Also, if your nonprofit is selling goods or services to earn extra income, you'll have to allocate shared expenses between that activity and your other activities. (Form 990 filers allocate their total program expenses among their three major program accomplishments.)

All your expenses can be divided into two categories: direct and indirect.

- Direct expenses are clearly and easily attributable to a specific program—for example, the cost of food is clearly related to a nonprofit's program to deliver hot meals to the elderly, as is the salary of a driver hired to do the deliveries.

- Indirect or shared expenses are costs that cannot be identified specifically with an activity or project; instead they benefit, and are shared among, all programs and functions—for example, office rent, utilities, telephone, and website costs. If your nonprofit has an executive director, his or her salary is also an indirect cost that benefits all your programs and functions.

The IRS does not require you to allocate expenses in any particular way. But you are supposed to use a method that is reasonable, clear, and consistent. There are several methods. For example, indirect expenses, such as rent and utilities, could be allocated according to the total percentage of office space each program or function takes up. Salaries for employees whose work benefits more than one program or function could be allocated based on the amount of time they spend doing work in each expense area. Another method is to allocate indirect expenses based on the amount of income each program brings in. For example, if a nonprofit has two programs, one of which brings in 70% of its income and the other 30%, indirect costs could be allocated based on a 70%–30% split.

If you receive grants from the government or foundation, they may have their own rules about how you should allocate expenses. Detailed cost allocation rules have been promulgated by the federal Office of Management and Budget (OMB). See OMB Circular A-122, *Cost Principles for Nonprofit Organizations*, available at www.whitehouse.gov/omb.

Financial statements. A financial statement is a document that organizes and summarizes in various ways the financial data you collect and record over a given time period. There are two basic types of financial statements: internal and external. Internal financial statements are those you create for your own use and are not shown to people outside your nonprofit. External financial statements are those prepared for outsiders such as funders and government agencies.

The IRS does not require that you create any particular types of financial statements for your own use. However, if your nonprofit files IRS Form 990 or 990-EZ, you will have to complete the financial statements included on the form. For example, if you file form 990-EZ, you must complete the following simple balance sheet:

Part II	Balance Sheets. (see the instructions for Part II.) Check if the organization used Schedule O to respond to any question in this Part II . . . . ☐		(A) Beginning of year	(B) End of year
22	Cash, savings, and investments			22
23	Land and buildings			23
24	Other assets (describe in Schedule O)			24
25	**Total assets**			25
26	**Total liabilities** (describe in Schedule O)			26
27	**Net assets or fund balances** (line 27 of column (B) **must** agree with line 21) . .			27

Far more elaborate financial statements must be completed on Form 990.

However, regardless of IRS requirements, financial statements are important because they enable you to monitor your nonprofit's financial health—they can show whether your nonprofit earned a surplus or ran a deficit, what you spent your money on, where you got the money, and how much money you have left. There are several different types of financial statements. What statements your nonprofit needs depends on its size, the complexity of its affairs, and the demands and needs of external users, such as private foundations and government agencies that provide you with funding.

If your nonprofit is small and you have no need to provide audited financial statements to external users, such as government agencies or foundations, you can get by with something very simple. For example, your treasurer can create a periodic Treasurer's Report showing your nonprofit's cash balance at the beginning of the period, the income received during the period, the expenses paid during the period organized by categories, and the cash balance at the end of the period. The period can be one month, a calendar quarter, or a whole year.

However, the Treasurer's Report described above does not comply with generally accepted accounting principles (GAAP) and therefore cannot serve as an audited financial statement you show to outsiders. To comply with GAAP, you (or, more likely, your accountant) must create a more elaborate series of three or four year-end financial statements (see "Minding the GAAP," below).

A Simple Accounting System in Action

We Do Good, Inc., is a small public charity that provides tutoring services to children and adults with reading problems. It has an all-volunteer staff and earns less than $20,000 per year in gross receipts, so it doesn't have to file an annual information return with the IRS (Form 990 or 990-EZ). It receives no government funding, relying instead on small grants, income from special events, and contributions from the public. It uses the cash method of accounting. With money so tight, its volunteer treasurer watches every penny. Luckily, it has few expenses other than rent, phone, and supplies. Its accounting system is quite simple. It consists of four elements: a checkbook, income journal, expense journal, and periodic treasurer's reports.

Checkbook. All income and expenses pass through We Do Good's checking account. The treasurer is sure to include in the check register the date, number, amount of each check, and the name of the person or company to which the check is written. If it's not clear from the name of the payee what a check is for, the business reason for the check is described—for example, the items or services that were purchased are listed.

Income journal. The income journal is a chronological list of all income received, assigned to the appropriate account. As money is received (whether cash or checks), you enter the total amount received in

A Simple Accounting System in Action (continued)

the first column under "Deposits" and then enter the amount again under the applicable account.

Income Journal—July

Date	Received From	Deposits	Total Receipts	Grants	Donations	Special Events	Other
7/1	Balance forward		5,000				
7/2	Joan Blondell	100	100		100		
7/8	Literacy Institute	1,000	1,000	1,000			
7/15	Sam Granger	50	50		50		
7/18	Cindy Stone	25	25		25		
7/20	Ralph Carver	50	50		50		
7/25	Book Sale	500	500			500	
7/30	Jane Jones	50	50		50		
Total		1,775	6,775	1,000	275	500	

Expense journal. The expense journal is a chronological list of all expenses paid, assigned to the appropriate account.

Expense Journal—July

Date	Paid To	Check No.	Total	Rent	Phone	Utilities	Supplies	Other Description
7/2	ABC Realty	406	500	500				
7/5	Phone Co.	407	50		50			
7/5	Electric Co.	408	40			50		
7/15	Copy shop	409					25	
7/20	U.S.P.S.	410	30				30	
7/26		411	500					300 book sale
7/29		412	200					200 website
Total			1,155	500	50	50	55	500

A Simple Accounting System in Action (continued)

Treasurer's Report: Every month, We Do Good's treasurer creates a Treasurer's Report. It contains the:

- nonprofit's name
- the period that the report covers
- cash balance at the beginning of the period
- income received during the period
- expenses paid during the period
- the cash balance at the end of the period, and
- the treasurer's signature.

As you can see from the sample Treasurer's Report below for July, the cash balance at the end of the period equals the cash balance at the beginning of the period, plus total income, minus total expenses.

We Do Good, Inc.
Treasurer's Report
Month Ended July 31, 20xx

Cash Balance 7/1/20xx		$ 5,000
Income		
Grants	$ 1,000	
Donations	275	
Special events	500	
Total Income		1,775
Expenses		
Rent	(500)	
Utilities	(50)	
Telephone	(50)	
Supplies		
Book sale	(300)	
Website	(200)	
Total Expenses		(1,155)
Cash Balance 7/31/20xx		$ 5,620

Signature _____

Date _____

A Paper Trail

Having a complete and accurate set of books is great, but it's not enough. You also need documentation to back your records up. The IRS knows very well that you can claim anything in your books because you create them yourself. For this reason, you must have documents to support the entries in your books and on your tax returns. You don't have to file any of these documents with your tax returns. Just keep them available to back up your returns if you're audited.

Such documents should include:

- a treasurer's file with important records
- documents showing the source and amount of your income, such as bank deposit slips, invoices, and bank statements
- documents that support your expenses, such as receipts, canceled checks, and credit card statements, and
- documents regarding your nonprofit's assets and liabilities.

Keep your supporting documents in a safe place. If you don't have a lot of receipts and other documents to save, you can simply keep them all in a single folder. If you have a lot of supporting documents to save or are the type of person who likes to be extremely well organized, separate your documents by category—for example, income, travel expenses, or equipment purchases. You can use a separate file folder for each category or get an accordion file with multiple pockets.

Treasurer's file. First of all, your nonprofit's treasurer or CFO should keep a file containing important records in a secure place. A complete treasurer's file should contain the following:

- auditors' reports
- budgets
- certificates of insurance
- copies of all information returns (IRS Forms 990 or 990-EZ) filed with the IRS
- copies of all correspondence received from the IRS or other tax authorities

- a copy of the completed IRS application form for your nonprofit's tax exemption (Form 1023)
- a copy of your IRS determination letter recognizing your tax exemption
- descriptions and summaries of your nonprofit's programs
- employee records
- federal employer identification number (EIN)
- financial statements
- minutes of meetings of the governing board and any standing committees, such as the executive or compensation committees, and
- organizing documents, such as your nonprofit's articles of incorporation and bylaws, with amendments.

Income records. You should have documents showing all the income your nonprofit receives, including contributions. This includes:

- donor correspondence
- pledge documents
- grant award letters of agreement
- bank deposit slips, and
- receipt books.

If your nonprofit sells products or services to the public, you should have documents showing the income you earn such as cash register tapes, invoices, credit card charge slips, and Forms 1099-MISC.

Expense records. Expenses are the costs you incur to carry on your programs. Every expense should be supported by documentation showing: what, how much, and who. That is, your supporting documents should show:

- what you purchased
- how much you paid, and
- whom (or what company) you bought from.

The supporting documents could include:

- canceled checks
- cash register tapes
- contracts

- account statements
- credit card sales slips
- invoices, and
- petty cash slips for small cash payments.

Proving Payments With Bank Statements

Sometimes, you'll need to use an account statement to prove an expense. Some banks no longer return canceled checks, or you may pay for something with an ATM card or another electronic funds transfer method. Moreover, you may not always have a credit card slip when you pay by credit card—for example, when you buy an item over the Internet. In these events, the IRS will accept an account statement as proof that you purchased the item. The chart below shows what type of information you need on an account statement.

If payment is by:	The statement must show:
Check	Check number
	Amount
	Payee's name
	Date the check amount was posted to the account by the bank
Electronic funds transfer	Amount transferred
	Payee's name
	Date the amount transferred was posted to the account by the bank
Credit card	Amount charged
	Payee's name
	Transaction date

> ## Reimbursing Driving, Entertainment, Meal, Travel, and Gift Expenses
>
> If your nonprofit reimburses directors, employees, or volunteers for expenses they incur while on nonprofit business, you must be sure to do so under what the IRS calls an "accountable plan." This way, the reimbursement will not be taxable income to the recipient. Among other things, an accountable plan requires full documentation of the expense. For example, if you reimburse your directors for expenses incurred for driving on nonprofit business, the directors must document the time, place, and business purposes of each trip. The IRS is particularly suspicious of travel, entertainment, and meal expenses. The most thorough documentation is required for these expenses. For a detailed discussion of these requirements, refer to Chapter 4.

Asset and Liability Records

Assets are the property, such as investments, buildings, and furniture, your nonprofit owns and uses in its activities. Liabilities reflect the pecuniary obligations of the organization. A nonprofit must keep records to verify certain information about its assets and liabilities. These records should show:

- when and how the asset was acquired
- whether any debt was used to acquire the asset
- documents that support mortgages, notes, loans, or other forms of debt
- the purchase price
- the cost of any improvements
- deductions taken for depreciation, if any
- deductions taken for casualty losses, if any, such as losses resulting from fires or storms
- how the asset was used
- when and how the asset was disposed of
- the selling price, and
- the expenses of sale.

Documents that may show the above information include: purchase and sales invoices, real estate closing statements, canceled checks, and financing documents.

Employment Tax Records

All employers, including nonprofits, are required to withhold and pay both federal and state taxes for their employees. These taxes are called payroll taxes or employment taxes. Every year, employers must file IRS Form W-2, *Wage and Tax Statement*, for each of their workers. Additionally, quarterly and/or annual employment tax returns must be filed with the IRS showing how much each employee was paid and how much tax was withheld and deposited. If you have employees, your employment tax records should include:

- amounts and dates of all wage, annuity, and pension payments
- the fair market value of in-kind wages paid
- names, addresses, Social Security numbers, and occupations of all employees
- any employee copies of Forms W-2 that were returned to you as undeliverable
- dates of employment for each employee
- periods for which employees and recipients were paid while absent due to sickness or injury and the amount and weekly rate of payments you or third-party payers made to them
- copies of employees' income tax withholding allowance certificates (Forms W-4, W-4P, W-4(SP), W-4S, and W-4V)
- copies of employees' earned income credit advance payment certificates (Forms W-5 and W-5(SP))
- dates and amounts of tax deposits that you made
- copies of employment tax returns filed, and
- records of fringe benefits and expense reimbursements provided to your employees, including substantiation.

A detailed guide to these requirements can be found in IRS Publication 15, *Circular E, Employer's Tax Guide*. You can download it from the IRS website at www.irs.gov.

How Long Should Records Be Kept?

Nonprofits must keep records for federal tax purposes for as long as they may be needed to document compliance with the tax law. Generally, this means you must keep records that support an item of income or expense on a return until the statute of limitations for that return runs—usually three years after the date the return is due or filed, whichever is later. However, you may be required to retain records longer for other legal purposes, including state or local tax purposes.

Record retention periods vary depending on the types of records and returns. Develop a records retention policy based on this list.

Permanent storage: Some records should be kept permanently. These include:

- your completed application for IRS recognition of tax-exempt status (Form 1023)
- the IRS determination letter recognizing your nonprofit's tax-exempt status
- organizing documents for your nonprofit, such as articles of incorporation and bylaws with amendments, as well as board minutes, and corporate resolutions
- audit reports
- corporation exemption documents and corporation reports filed with the secretary of state (if your nonprofit is incorporated)
- legal correspondence
- ledgers
- depreciation schedules
- employee personnel files
- state and federal tax forms, as filed, and
- correspondence with state or federal agencies.

Seven years:

- payment authorization and expense forms (receipts attached) for payments to vendors or reimbursement to officers
- chart of accounts
- cash receipt records
- grant award letters of agreement

- financial statements (year-end) and budgets
- checks (other than those listed for permanent retention)
- bank statements that contain photocopies of canceled checks
- expired contracts and leases
- invoices
- purchase orders
- sales records
- withholding tax statements, and
- employee timesheets.

Four years:
- conflict of interest forms, and
- employment tax records.

Three years:
- general correspondence
- employment applications, and
- asset records—keep for three years after the asset is disposed.

One year:
- bank reconciliations
- correspondence with vendors if noncontested
- duplicate deposit slips
- certificates of insurance, and
- inventories of products and materials, updated yearly.

Do You Need an Independent Audit?

An independent audit is not the same as an IRS audit. Rather, it is an examination of your accounting records and financial statements by an independent auditor—normally, a certified public accountant (CPA). The auditor is an independent professional hired and paid by your nonprofit. The auditor will do an independent investigation to test the accuracy of your accounting records and internal controls. At the conclusion of the audit, the auditor issues a report in the form of a letter stating whether, in the auditor's professional judgment, your accounting records and year-end financial statements fairly represent your nonprofit's financial position according to generally accepted accounting principles (GAAP) (see below). The auditor's letter is attached to the front of your financial statements. A clean bill of health from an auditor shows the world that you're keeping your books in a responsible manner.

Why get an audit. Audits are expensive—at least $4,000 to $10,000 (or more) for smaller nonprofits. Larger nonprofits that file IRS Form 990 each year are required to state on their return whether they have obtained an audit. However, such an audit is *not* required by the IRS. So why would you get one? There are several reasons:

- **The federal government may require an audit.** Although the IRS does not require nonprofits to obtain audits, other federal government agencies do. For example, the federal Office of Management and Budget (OMB) requires any nonprofit that spends $500,000 or more in federal funds in a year (whether directly or by passing the money on to other nonprofits) to obtain what is termed a "single audit" to test for compliance with federal grants management standards. (This requirement is explained in OMB Circular No. A-133, which can be found on the Office of Management and Budget website at www.whitehouse.gov/omb/circulars_default/.)

- **Some states require audits.** About one-third of the states require nonprofits of a certain annual revenue size to be audited if they solicit funds from their state's residents. The revenue thresholds vary from state to state. For example, California requires annual audits for nonprofits registered with the state that have gross income of $2 million or more. Other states have lower income thresholds. Contact the secretary of state or office of the attorney general for regulations in those states where you raise money.

- **Some funders require audits.** Some funders, such as foundations, will not provide funding to a nonprofit unless they receive audited financial statements. The same holds true for many banks and other potential lenders.

- **Audits show your nonprofit can be trusted.** "Transparency" is the buzzword of the day in the nonprofit world, and having an independent auditor check your books is a great way to show that you have nothing to hide. Several nonprofit watchdog groups have established their own standards for when nonprofits should obtain audits. The income thresholds these organizations have adopted for audits vary widely: the Wise Giving Alliance on the Better Business Bureau's website (www.bbb.org/us) has a $250,000 annual income threshold for audits; the Standards for Excellence Institute's threshold is $300,000 (www.standards forexcellenceinstitute.org); and Independent Sector has an audit threshold of $1 million (www.independentsector.org). Remember, these organizations' recommendations are merely that—recommendations—they are not legal requirements.

RESOURCE

Need more information on audits? An excellent resource on non-profit audits is the *Not-for-Profit Entities Audit and Accounting Guide*, published by the American Institute of Certified Public Accountants (AICPA).

Alternatives to audits. Getting an audit sounds great in theory, but if it is not absolutely required by the government or an important funding source, it may not be worth the money, especially for nonprofits with smaller incomes. Think about it—if a nonprofit has an annual income of $100,000 or less, paying $5,000 to $10,000 for an audit would take up a substantial portion of its entire annual budget. Moreover, an audit is generally unnecessary for small nonprofits because they engage in a low number of financial transactions each year, and the veracity of their books can be checked in cheaper ways.

There are two cheaper alternatives to a full-blown independent audit. The first is called a review, which is like a mini-audit. A CPA examines your financial records, but much less thoroughly than in a full-blown audit. Unlike an audit, the CPA does not express an opinion as to whether your financial statements are in accordance with GAAP. Instead, the accountant merely states whether he or she is aware of any material modifications that should be made to the financial statements for them to be in conformity with GAAP. A review costs about half as much as an audit. Many funders will accept a review instead of an audit, but a review is not an audit and it may not be referred to as such.

The cheapest alternative to an audit is a compilation. This is where an accountant assembles your financial statements from the information you provide. The accountant does not subject your financial records to any audit or review and thus can express no opinion as to whether they comply with GAAP.

Minding the GAAP

GAAP is an acronym for "generally accepted accounting principles." These are the accepted standards (rules) used to prepare audited financial statements of both business and nonprofit organizations. GAAP is established by the nonprofit Financial Accounting Standards Board (FASB), which issues its rules in the form of numbered Statements of Financial Accounts Standards (SFAS). There is a special set of standards just for nonprofits. The most important of these are Standard (also called SFAS or FAS) 116 and 117. Standard 116 governs how nonprofits report contributions and pledges. Standard 117 dictates the form and content of the basic financial statements issued by nonprofits.

The IRS does not—repeat—does not require that your nonprofit comply with GAAP. For example, the IRS permits nonprofits to keep their books using the cash basis of accounting even though GAAP requires that the accrual method be used. Nor do you need to comply with GAAP when preparing financial statements for your own internal use. However, GAAP must be dealt with if you need to have audited financial statements for external users such as certain government agencies and institutional funders. To obtain a "clean" or "unqualified" opinion letter from the auditor, your financial statements must conform to GAAP requirements. To create the necessary financial statements, you must track your income and expenses in a very specific way. Failure to do so will make it very difficult for an accountant to create year-end financial statements for your nonprofit that comply with GAAP.

> **RESOURCE**
>
> **For an outstanding explanation of the nonprofit GAAP rules,** refer to *Not-for-Profit GAAP*, by Richard F. Larkin and Marie DiTommaso (Wiley). If you need to comply with GAAP, you should have this book.

Required Financial Statements

GAAP requires all nonprofits to have three or four financial statements:
- balance sheet
- statement of activities
- statement of cash flows, and
- statement of functional expenses.

Balance sheet. The balance sheet (also referred to as the Statement of Financial Position or Statement of Financial Condition) is a snapshot of your nonprofit's financial condition on a given date. It shows the amount you own (assets), such as cash and equipment, compared to the amount you owe (liabilities), such as loans. Net assets are the difference between your assets and liabilities—they are for a nonprofit what profits or owner's equity are for a for-profit enterprise. However, to comply with GAAP, the balance sheet for a nonprofit must break down net assets into unrestricted, temporarily restricted, and permanently restricted assets.

Statement of activities. The statement of activities (also referred to as the income statement) summarizes by categories all your nonprofit's financial activities over a period of time—for example, one month, one quarter, or an entire year. It shows whether your nonprofit's assets, liabilities, and net assets have increased or decreased. If your revenues exceeded your expenses during the time period, you ran a surplus. But, if your expenses exceeded your revenues, you had a deficit.

Cash flow statement. The cash flow statement shows where your nonprofit got its cash and where it spent it during the same period as covered by the statement of activities. It shows what cash you have on hand to pay bills and other obligations as they come due.

Statement of functional expenses. A statement of functional expenses shows how your nonprofit spent its money by function. There are three functions that must be tracked: program costs, management and general expenses, and fundraising expenses. GAAP requires a statement of functional expenses only for voluntary health and welfare organizations. However, all public charities that file IRS Form 990 must complete the statement of functional expenses included on the form.

Accounting for Restricted Funds

One important way nonprofits differ from for-profit organizations is that there may be restrictions imposed on the income they receive from the government, foundations, or individuals. For example, a donor may give your nonprofit $1,000 for the specific purpose of buying a new computer. This means the money may only be used for that purpose. The nonprofit GAAP rules require that contributions be divided into one of three classes as determined by the absence or presence of donor-imposed restrictions on how the funds may be used.

- **Unrestricted.** Contributions that may be used for any purpose, including administration, management, and fundraising.
- **Temporarily restricted.** Contributions donated for a specific purpose (usually a particular program), a specific time, or both. However, the donor-imposed restrictions will eventually expire with the passage of time or be released by some action by the recipient. Temporarily restricted funds become unrestricted once the restrictions are met. For example, a donor may donate $10,000 in 2014 that must be used to implement a program in 2015. The $10,000 becomes unrestricted when the nonprofit uses the money for this purpose in 2015.
- **Permanently restricted.** The restrictions imposed by the donor will never expire—for example, the principal of an endowment that must remain intact forever.

Recording Pledges and Donations

GAAP also contains special rules about how pledges and donations are recorded as income in your books.

Pledges. A pledge is a promise by a contributor to give a certain amount of money to your nonprofit at some time in the future. There are two types of pledges: conditional and unconditional. A pledge is conditional if it is contingent on some other event, such as your nonprofit implementing a program or receiving a matching grant. A pledge is unconditional if it is not subject to a restriction. Conditional pledges are not recorded as income in your books until the conditions have been substantially met. However, you must record all unconditional pledges as income in your books when they are made, even though the money pledged has not yet been received.

Donated goods. You must record in your books the fair market value of most donations of goods ("in-kind contributions"). However, there are some exceptions—for example, galleries, museums, and other groups with collections of art and other artifacts are generally exempt from recording the value of donated works.

Donated services. Ordinarily, the value of volunteer services contributed to your nonprofit is not recorded as income. However, there are two exceptions:

- the volunteer services create or enhance a nonfinancial (physical) asset—for example, your volunteers build a shelter for the homeless, or
- the volunteer services involve specialized skills that would otherwise have to be paid for by your nonprofit if volunteers were not available—for example, volunteer services performed by lawyers, accountants, doctors, electricians, and other professionals.

Bookkeeping by Hand or Computer?

Today, most organizations use accounting software to do their book-keeping. A huge array of software is available. These range from relatively simple checkbook programs like *Quicken* to complex and sophisticated accounting programs like *QuickBooks Pro* and *Peachtree Accounting*. There are a number of applications designed especially for nonprofits, such as *QuickBooks Premier for Nonprofits*, *Sage Nonprofit Software*, and Blackbaud's *The Financial Edge*.

You can use these in place of the handwritten ledger sheets. However, you'll be better off using handwritten ledger sheets, which are easy to create and understand and simple to keep up-to-date, instead of a complicated computer program that you don't understand or use properly. So, if you're not prepared to invest the time to use a computer program correctly, don't use it!

You don't want to spend your nonprofit's hard-earned money on accounting software only to discover that you don't like it. Before you purchase software:

- talk to others in similar nonprofits to find out what they use—if they don't like a program, ask them why
- think carefully about how many features you need—the more complex the program, the harder it will be to learn and use it, and
- obtain a demo version you can try out for free to see if you like it—you can usually download one from the software company's website.

Volunteers, Employees, and Independent Contractors

n the eyes of the IRS, people who work for a nonprofit fall into one of two broad categories: they are either unpaid help or paid help. Unpaid help consists of the volunteer workers that so many nonprofits rely on to accomplish their goals. Paid help—that is, workers who are compensated for their services—fall into one of two other categories: they are either employees or independent contractors. These three types of workers—volunteers, employees, and independent contractors—are all treated very differently for tax purposes. As a nonprofit, it's important to be able to distinguish among them so you know how to handle—and possibly avoid—tax issues related to each.

In this chapter, we explain how to distinguish among these categories of workers and the tax rules for each. Worker misclassification is a hot-button issue for the IRS. If you are audited, you can be sure this is something the IRS will look at. If you understand and follow the rules, you can avoid the risk of having to pay back taxes and penalties for improperly classifying your workers.

Volunteers—The Backbone Workforce of Nonprofits

Small nonprofits—those with budgets below $200,000—typically rely almost exclusively on volunteer help. Even larger charities are manned mainly by volunteers. According to a recent report on Form 990 filings, 85% of all charities have no employees at all. Everything these organizations do is being done by volunteers. Among the smaller nonprofits with employees, the paid staff is often tiny—perhaps an executive director and part-time bookkeeper. These organizations rely mostly on volunteers to perform the bulk of their work. Even larger nonprofits with paid staffs often have substantial numbers of volunteers working for them. With the bad economy and decline in donations to nonprofits, it's likely that nonprofits—big and small—will rely more and more on volunteers to get their work done. And, with the rapid rise in unemployment, more people than ever are seeking volunteer positions with nonprofits to keep busy while they look for paid work.

People often think that because volunteers are not paid for their work, there are no tax issues to consider when they work at an organization. This is far from true. There are two areas in particular where you need to be careful with how you handle volunteers—reimbursing them for expenses they incur and providing them with noncash benefits. If you do both these things properly, there will be no tax consequences or reporting obligation to the IRS for you or the volunteer. However, you must know and follow the rules or these payments or benefits will not qualify for tax-free treatment.

How Many of Us Volunteer?

An incredible 26.8% of all Americans said they engaged in volunteer activities in 2011—that's over 64 million people. The average person spent 2.31 hours volunteering during the days they volunteered. About 7.9 billion hours were volunteered in 2011. The total value of volunteers' time in 2011 was estimated at $171 billion.

The largest single use of volunteers is for administration and support, including fundraising, office work, computer use, phone calls, writing, editing, and reading. The second largest use is for social services and care, including preparing food and cleaning up; delivering clothing and other goods; tutoring, teaching, or counseling; and providing direct care services.

Who volunteers the most? Women, people 35 to 44 years of age, college graduates, married people, and those with part-time jobs.

Source: "Volunteering and Civic Life in America 2012: Key findings on the volunteer participation and civic health of the nation," Corporation for National and Community Service (December, 2012).

What Is a Volunteer?

To figure out what type of tax issues you may have with the various people helping out at your organization, you'll first have to know which ones are volunteers and which ones are paid workers. It's basically as straightforward as it sounds. A volunteer is anyone who performs services without any expectation of getting paid for those services. Certain volunteers are what might be called "pure volunteers"—they receive nothing of value for their services and they don't get reimbursed for any expenses they incur working for the nonprofit. The only things they might receive are token items of appreciation, like a mug or tote bag. Pure volunteers pose absolutely no tax issues for the nonprofit. If nothing of value changes hands, there is nothing to be taxed. These volunteers may be able to recoup some of the costs they incur for volunteering—gas money, for example—by claiming these expenses as a charitable deduction (if they itemize their personal deductions). But there are no tax consequences for the nonprofit.

Other volunteers might get reimbursed for expenses they incur while working or the nonprofit might offer them certain benefits, like discounts on parking, event tickets, or small gift items. While nonprofits are under no legal obligation to provide anything to volunteers, they are always free to do so. However, if your nonprofit chooses to do this, it must handle any reimbursements or benefits properly in order to avoid possible tax consequences for the organization and volunteer.

Volunteer Work—From Director to Intern

Volunteers perform a variety of services at nonprofits—everything from answering the phones to overseeing the organization. Some nonprofits carefully interview potential volunteers and require them to sign written contracts before commencing work. Other arrangements are less formal or project-based. Oftentimes volunteers are asked to perform certain tasks or work certain hours, usually under the direction of the executive director or another staff person. For example, a nonprofit may have volunteers who show up at regular hours to perform specific office work like doing client intake or delivering meals to the elderly.

The specific roles volunteers may play at an organization include the following:

Director. Incorporated nonprofits are run by a board of directors, which is responsible for overseeing the management of the organization.

Directors of nonprofits are almost always volunteers who are not paid for their services, although they sometimes get reimbursed for their expenses.

Officer. An incorporated nonprofit usually has officers such as a president, vice president, secretary, treasurer, executive director, and chief executive officer. Often the head of the organization—the executive director, president, or chief executive officer—is paid. Generally, the other officer positions are not. Officers who are not paid for their services are volunteers—in smaller nonprofits they are usually board members who take on one of the officer roles.

Intern. An intern is someone who works at a nonprofit on a temporary basis to get experience or make contacts in a particular field. Students are often hired as interns during their summer breaks and usually don't get paid for their services. If they get paid, whether a full salary or small stipend, they are considered employees.

Trainee. Trainees are people who participate in a government-approved program that provides them with training or instruction for future employment. Trainees are not paid wages for their services, but may be given nontaxable stipends for their expenses such as transportation, books, tools, and meal costs during training.

Reimbursing Your Volunteers—Know the Rules

Some nonprofits reimburse their volunteers for expenses. This may be out of a sense of fairness or to encourage people to volunteer, particularly those who might not be able to afford to work for free otherwise. Out-of-pocket expenses a nonprofit might reimburse include:

- travel to and from the place of volunteering
- postage, telephone calls, copying, and similar costs
- equipment or protective clothing
- attendance at training events and courses, and
- long distance travel, meals, and lodging while on nonprofit business.

Can Employees Be Volunteers?

The IRS doesn't care if a nonprofit's employees also serve as volunteers for the organization. Either way, anything of value given to the worker will be taxable, other than reimbursements for expenses and certain tax-free benefits (see below).

However, the United States Department of Labor does care if an employee volunteers for his or her employer. It wants to ensure that these employees are not taken advantage of. Under its rules, it is acceptable for an employee to serve as a volunteer only if the services the employee performs for the employer are:

- not the same type of services the worker is paid to perform, and
- take place outside the employee's normal working hours.

For example, employees who work from 9 a.m. to 5 p.m. during the week could volunteer on the weekend or evenings, as long as they don't do the same type of work they are paid to perform during their regular paid weekday hours.

These rules only apply to nonprofits that engage in a business activity—for example, a nonprofit that sells used clothing to the public would be covered. They wouldn't apply to a nonprofit that only provides counseling services.

There are different ways a volunteer might pay or seek reimbursement for expenses. In most cases, the volunteer will pay the expenses at the time they are incurred and then seek a cash reimbursement from your nonprofit. However, in some cases, the volunteer might get an advance payment to cover anticipated expenses. This is fine as long as it is not paid more than 30 days before the expense is incurred. Alternatively, a volunteer could be given a company credit card to use. There may also be instances where a volunteer handles expenses through a direct billing to the nonprofit. Using a company credit card or direct billing doesn't involve an actual reimbursement of funds to the volunteer because the expense is paid directly by the nonprofit. Nevertheless, the same rules apply as for an actual reimbursement where the volunteer pays an expense out of his or her own pocket and is later repaid by the nonprofit.

As long as the reimbursements are done properly, there should be no tax consequences for reimbursements for the nonprofit or its volunteers. The key to keeping them tax free is to make sure you have an accountable plan that follows IRS rules and that all reimbursements are made in accordance with that plan. If they are, these payments don't even need to be reported to the IRS.

Accountable Plans—The Key to Success With the IRS

An accountable plan is a plan that follows IRS rules on reimbursing employees or volunteers for business-related expenses. The IRS has adopted rules about reimbursements because these types of payments can be so easily subject to abuse. For example, someone on a business trip to Seattle might try to include in their business expenses the cost for a sightseeing trip to an island. To avoid these kinds of problems, the IRS has adopted a strict set of rules that must be followed for reimbursements to be a nontaxable and nonreportable event.

To pass muster with the IRS, the accountable plan must require that:

- any expenses being reimbursed are incurred for a nonprofit business purpose
- the volunteer adequately accounts for the expenses within a reasonable period of time—no more than 60 days after the expense was incurred, and
- the volunteer returns any amounts received in excess of the actual expenses incurred within a reasonable period of time—no more than 120 days after receipt of the excess money.

If you have an accountable plan that complies with these rules, then any payments made under the plan are not taxable and need not be reported to the IRS.

An accountable plan doesn't have to be in writing, although this isn't a bad idea. All you need to do is set up procedures for your volunteers and employees to follow that meet the requirements. However, you could include your accountable plan procedures in a volunteer handbook or orientation packet. Let's take a closer look at some of the accountable plan requirements.

Business expenses only. This is a threshold requirement. The expenses being reimbursed must be directly related to the work or services provided by the volunteer. The IRS doesn't want people to get reimbursed for any personal, family, or other nonbusiness expenses along with their business expenses. For example, a volunteer traveling to Las Vegas on nonprofit business cannot be reimbursed for a trip to the Grand Canyon. That is a personal expense that the volunteer must pay for out of his or her own pocket. Or, a volunteer could decide to bring a family member along on a business trip. As long as there is no added expense, that is okay. Otherwise, any expenses paid for by the nonprofit that are not business-related or are incurred on behalf of a family member or someone other than the volunteer must be included as taxable income for the volunteer and reported to the IRS.

> EXAMPLE: Phil is executive director of the Carbon Reduction Project, located in Colorado Springs. He travels to Washington, DC, to testify before a Congressional committee on climate change. He decides to take his wife and two children along so they can see the nation's capitol. Had he traveled alone, his hotel room would have cost $200. Instead, he books a "mini-suite" at $500 per night. His total lodging expense for the four-day trip is $2,000. The nonprofit reimburses Phil for the entire $2,000, even though his hotel would have cost only $800 had he traveled alone. The extra $1,200 is taxable income that must be included on Phil's W-2.

Adequate accounting. It is crucial to have good records for expenses to be reimbursable under an accountable plan. At a minimum, every expense should be supported by documentation showing:

- what was purchased

- how much was paid for it, and
- whom (or what company) it was purchased from.

The documentation can consist of canceled checks, sales receipts, account statements, credit card sales slips, invoices, or petty cash slips for small cash payments.

> **EXAMPLE:** Art, a volunteer for a nonprofit that documents toxic waste dumps, purchased a digital camera for himself and other volunteers to use to photograph dumps. The nonprofit agrees to reimburse him for the purchase. He provides the receipt for the camera and writes "purchase of camera to be used to document toxic dumps" to show the business purpose. This is adequate documentation.

Many nonprofits require volunteers to complete a written expense report to get reimbursed (see the sample Expense Report below). For certain expenses, such as local transportation, travel, entertainment, meals, and gifts, the IRS imposes additional documentation requirements. (See "Local Transportation Costs" and "Travel and Entertainment Expenses," below.)

An alternative to getting reimbursed for actual expenses is to use a per diem rate. Record-keeping duties are always easier if you choose to be paid at the IRS-approved per diem rate—although you usually won't get as much money. Under the per diem method, the IRS will accept the amount you claim for lodging, meals, and incidental expenses up to the maximum specified IRS per diem rate. You don't need to provide any receipts or documentation to back up your claimed expenses. The only thing you need to substantiate (by receipts or your own notes) is the time, place, and business purpose of the expense. Per diem rates for lodging, meals, and incidental expenses are set by the IRS and vary according to the destination. You can find these rates at www.gsa.gov (look for the link to "Per Diem Rates" in the "Featured Topics" section) or in IRS Publication 1542 (available on the IRS website at www.irs.gov).

Expense Report

Attach all receipts to this Expense Report

Name _____

Address _____

City/Zip _____

Telephone _____ Email _____

Expenditure was for: _____

List Expenditures:

_____ $ _____

_____   _____

_____   _____

_____   _____

_____   _____

Total Expense $ _____

Total Amount Claimed From Above $ _____

Minus Advance Received   _____

Reimbursement Claimed $ _____

Signature _____

Date _____

Expense Reimbursement Policy

Here is an example of actual expense reimbursement procedures used by a nonprofit. These comply fully with IRS accountable plan rules.

All requests for reimbursement shall be made in writing (preferably on the Expense Report) and shall be signed and dated by the person seeking reimbursement.

Expense Reports should be submitted within 60 days of incurring the expense. It is critical to receive all reports from a fiscal year (October 1–September 30) within 30 days of the close of the fiscal year (October 31). Any requests for reimbursements by volunteers or staff received after the close of the fiscal year-end books may not be paid. Any reimbursements in excess of actual substantiated expenses must be returned within 120 days after the expense was paid or incurred.

The Executive Director is authorized to reject or modify payment to comply with these policies and guidelines. Appeal of the Executive Director's decision shall be made to the Treasurer who may present the appeal to the Board of Governors if appropriate.

Prompt return of excess payments. Obviously, a volunteer can't be paid more than he or she actually spends on expenses. Volunteers who receive an advance or some kind of allowance for expenses must keep track of what they spend and return any excess within 120 days after the expense was paid. If any excess is not paid back within the required 120 days, the difference is gross income that the volunteer must pay income tax on.

EXAMPLE: The Canary In the Mine Project is a nonprofit that compiles climate change information by photographing its effects around the world. Hugo, a freelance photographer, volunteers to help photograph melting glaciers. Over six months, he travels to glaciers on five continents. The Project does not pay Hugo a salary, but gives him a $2,000 per month allowance that he can use to pay for his travel, meals, and lodging. It turns out that Hugo is a very frugal traveler. Of the $12,000 allowance the Project paid him, he actually spent only $8,000. If he doesn't pay back the $4,000 excess within 120 days, he must report it as income and pay income tax on it.

If you don't follow the accountable plan rules, any reimbursement a volunteer receives is income and subject to tax. Once the volunteer receives income, he or she becomes a paid worker and must be classified as either an employee or independent contractor under federal tax law. Most volunteers will be classified as employees because they typically work under the direction and control of the nonprofit and meet other criteria for being classified as an employee. The one exception is directors; they are classified as independent contractors because of their more independent role in overseeing the management and direction of the nonprofit. We cover this distinction and the tax reporting requirements for each in more detail later in this chapter when we discuss employees and independent contractors. However, we'll briefly go over the distinction now to show the two different ways you may have to report reimbursement income.

With volunteers who are classified as employees (which most are), any reimbursements they receive that were not paid under an accountable plan must be reported to the IRS on Form W-2. This means that for each volunteer who gets paid under an unaccountable plan, the nonprofit must file a Form W-2 with the IRS that reports the reimbursement as compensation. In addition, that payment is subject to all applicable employee payroll taxes. The volunteer must include that amount on his or her annual Form 1040 that reports his or her total income for the year. If any regular employees (not volunteers) receive improperly documented reimbursement payments, the nonprofit must include those amounts as well as additional compensation paid to the employee.

EXAMPLE: Ralph is the executive director of Buffalo Rising. He works full time and receives a salary so he is clearly an employee. Ralph goes on an out-of-town business trip and incurs $1,200 in travel expenses, but fails to properly document them. If Buffalo Rising reimburses Ralph, it must include the $1,200 in the W-2 form it files with the IRS reporting Ralph's total yearly compensation and it must withhold income and payroll taxes from that amount as well.

The tax reporting and withholding requirements for independent contractors work differently. Payments made to an independent contractor are reported to the IRS on Form 1099-MISC. If a volunteer (usually a director) is classified as an independent contractor and receives reimbursement for expenses that were not properly documented, the nonprofit must report those payments to the IRS on Form 1099-MISC, if the total amount for the year exceeds $600. The volunteer has to pay income and self-employment taxes on those amounts and report the payment in his or her total income for the year. The nonprofit does not need to withhold or pay any employment taxes on that amount.

> EXAMPLE: Jill, a director at Buffalo Rising, accompanies Ralph (from the above example) on a business trip and also fails to keep any receipts or otherwise document her travel expenses. The nonprofit pays her $1,200 for her expenses anyway. Because this money was not paid under an accountable plan, it is taxable income for Jill. Jill is a director of Buffalo Rising, so she is automatically classified as an independent contractor. This means that the nonprofit does not need to withhold tax from the payment, but it must report the payment to the IRS on Form 1099-MISC.

Local Transportation Costs

Unlike paid employees who can't be reimbursed tax-free for the cost of commuting to work, volunteers can be reimbursed for their daily commute costs without having to pay tax on the reimbursement. In addition, you can reimburse volunteers for any other local travel expenses they incur while doing volunteer work, such as delivering meals to the elderly or transporting disabled adults to medical appointments. Board members or other volunteers who have to travel to attend a board meeting can be paid for their local (not long distance) travel costs as well. The expenses that can be covered include gas and oil (using either the standard mileage rate or direct expenses as explained below) and the full cost of tolls, parking, cab fares, bus fares, and similar transportation expenses.

There are two different ways volunteers can be reimbursed for their gas and oil costs:

Actual expense method. Volunteers can choose to be reimbursed for the actual gas and oil costs they incur while driving for volunteer purposes. Other automobile expenses, such as repairs, depreciation, and insurance, generally are not reimbursable. To use this method, the volunteer must keep accurate records showing the date and purpose for any business travel and the mileage driven. While the record-keeping requirements can be burdensome, this method usually results in a higher reimbursement amount.

The standard mileage rate. Volunteers can elect instead to be paid using the standard mileage rate. Under this method, the person deducts a specified number of cents for every work-related mile he or she drives. This eliminates the need to keep track of how much is spent on gas, but the person must still keep track of the miles driven for volunteer-related work. Unfortunately, the standard mileage rate for volunteers is very low—only 14 cents per mile. This is far lower than the standard mileage rate for paid employees. Nonprofits have been complaining bitterly about this discrepancy for years, but so far to no avail.

Regardless of which method the volunteer chooses—the actual expense method or standard mileage rate—the volunteer must document the date, place, and business purpose of each trip and the mileage driven. Anyone who chooses to use the actual expense method will also need to have receipts or credit card slips for gas and oil purchased. There are cheap mileage diaries that can be purchased for this purpose.

If the volunteer doesn't have complete and accurate information, then any mileage reimbursement the volunteer receives must be included in his or her individual income.

Travel and Entertainment Expenses

The IRS is particularly suspicious of travel, entertainment, and meal expenses. These kinds of expenses are easy to take advantage of so the IRS has stringent documentation requirements for them. Specifically, for any business-related entertainment, meal, gift, or travel expenses, in addition to meeting the accountable plan requirements, volunteers must have the following documentation to get reimbursed:

- **The date the expense was incurred,** which generally appears on the receipt or credit card slip.
- **How much was spent,** which appears on the receipt or credit card slip.
- **The nature and place of the entertainment or meal.** This will usually be shown by the receipt or it can be recorded in an appointment book or calendar.
- **The business purpose.** There must be something that shows the expense was incurred for work-related purposes, such as a brief description of the meeting's purpose or an agenda or other relevant documentation.
- **The business relationship.** If entertainment or meals are involved, you must establish the business relationship of people at the event—for example, list their names and occupations and any other information needed to show their business connection to the nonprofit.

If the cost is less than $75, the IRS doesn't require that any supporting documentation be kept, such as receipts or credit card slips, although you must keep some kind of journal or other record documenting the five facts listed above. The only exception is for lodging. Lodging or hotel costs always require supporting documentation even if they are under $75.

One way people can have fewer documentation requirements for travel expenses is if they choose to be reimbursed using a per diem rate instead of actual expenses. If the volunteer's costs are equal to or less than the per diem rate the federal government pays its workers who travel, then the IRS will assume that any reimbursements for lodging, meals, and incidental expenses are accurate. The volunteer need only substantiate the time, place, and business purpose of the expense with his or her own records or notes. You can find the federal per diem rates at www.gsa.gov (look for the link to "Per Diem Rates" in the "Featured Topics" section) or in IRS Publication 1542.

Finally, volunteers serving in certain federal volunteer service programs may receive reimbursement from federal funds for approved out-of-pocket travel expenses and for a modest level of clerical support or other support services. Such payments are not taxable income regardless of whether the substantiation and accountable plan rules discussed above are satisfied. These volunteer service programs include the Retired Senior Volunteer Program (RSVP), the Foster Grandparent program, the Service Corps of Retired Executives (SCORE), and the Active Corps of Executives (ACE) programs. (Rev. Rul. 74-322.)

Unreimbursed Volunteer Expenses

Given the budget constraints facing nonprofits today, many nonprofits have a policy to not reimburse their volunteers for expenses they incur while performing work or services for their organization. If you choose not to reimburse your volunteers for their expenses, you should let them know that they may be able to deduct the expense as a charitable contribution, which will allow them to recoup some of the money. Although volunteers may be able to deduct their unreimbursed volunteer expenses, the IRS does not consider these expenses to be charitable contributions for purposes of tax reporting by nonprofits. Thus, nonprofits do not need to include their value in the total contributions they report to the IRS each year on Form 990 or 990-EZ.

Requirements for Deducting Unreimbursed Expenses

To be deductible, volunteer expenses must be:
- unreimbursed by your nonprofit
- directly connected with the volunteer services
- incurred only because of the volunteer services, and
- not personal, living, or family expenses.

EXAMPLE: George Jones spent $500 on car expenses and parking while volunteering for Acme Charities during the year. Acme does not reimburse him for this expense. He may deduct $500 as a charitable contribution.

Expenses incurred by a volunteer deemed by the IRS to be personal and that are not deductible include: babysitting expenses—a payment to a volunteer's babysitter for the time the volunteer spends performing the services to the charity; and the cost of the volunteer's food or drink while a volunteer is working if that work does not require the volunteer to be away from home overnight.

The Value of Services Donated Is Not Deductible

In contrast to certain unreimbursed out-of-pocket expenses, unpaid volunteers may never deduct as a charitable contribution the value of their time or services, or the value of the income they lost while volunteering.

EXAMPLE: During the year, Dr. Smith, a radiologist, volunteered 100 hours of his time and medical expertise to a nonprofit hospital in his community. Ordinarily, he bills his time at $250 per hour. Thus, his services to the hospital had a fair market value of $25,000. Even so, Dr. Smith may not take a charitable deduction for $25,000, or any amount, for the value of his time and services.

Nor may volunteers deduct the value of property they make available for a nonprofit's use for free.

EXAMPLE: The Spicerack Restaurant allows a local nonprofit to use its banquet room free of charge to conduct monthly meetings. The restaurant ordinarily charges $500 for use of the banquet room. However, the rental value of the banquet room is not deductible. It may not take any deduction for the value of property it permits a charity to use for free.

This rule may not seem fair to volunteers, but it is something that could be easily abused by those claiming the deduction and difficult for the IRS to monitor.

Car expenses. A volunteer can deduct unreimbursed out-of-pocket expenses, such as the cost of gas and oil, directly related to the use of his or her car in giving services to a charitable organization. However, volunteers cannot deduct general repair and maintenance expenses, depreciation, registration fees, or the costs of tires or insurance.

There are two ways volunteers can keep track of their car expenses. First, they can keep track and document what they actually spend for gas while volunteering. If they don't want to bother keeping track of actual expenses, they can use a standard mileage rate of 14 cents for each mile driving while volunteering. Given the cost of gasoline today, the 14-cent-per-mile limit is absurdly low, so volunteers would be better off keeping track of actual driving expenses. (See "Local Transportation Costs," above.) Whichever method is used, volunteers also can deduct parking fees and tolls.

Travel expenses. Travel expenses are one of the most common deductions by volunteers. These include:

- air, rail, and bus transportation
- car expenses where travel is done by car
- taxi fares or other costs of transportation between the airport or station and hotel
- lodging costs, and
- the cost of meals.

If unreimbursed by the nonprofit, the volunteer can deduct these expenses if they were incurred while the volunteer was away from home performing services for the nonprofit. A volunteer cannot deduct personal expenses for sightseeing, fishing parties, theater tickets, or other entertainment events or outings. Travel, meals, lodging, and other expenses for a volunteer's spouse or children are likewise not deductible.

Moreover, the trip must have been mostly for business, not pleasure, or it can't be deducted. The IRS says that a volunteer can claim a charitable contribution deduction for travel expenses only if there is "no significant element of personal pleasure, recreation, or vacation in the travel." This does not mean that the volunteer can't enjoy the trip, but he or she must have been on duty in "a genuine and substantial sense" throughout the trip. A volunteer gets no deduction at all if he or she had only nominal duties, or had no duties for significant parts of the trip.

EXAMPLE: Felicia is a troop leader for a tax-exempt youth group and goes with the group on a camping trip. She is responsible for overseeing the setup of the camp and providing adult supervision for other activities during the trip. Felicia participated in the group's activities and helped transport the group home. She can deduct her travel expenses.

EXAMPLE: Carlos works for several hours each morning on an archeological dig sponsored by a nonprofit. The rest of the day he is free for recreation and sightseeing. He cannot take a charitable contribution deduction for his travel expenses, even though he worked hard during those few hours.

The moral: If your nonprofit makes things too cushy, the volunteer may lose valuable tax deductions.

Conventions. If you want to send a volunteer to represent your non-profit at a convention, the volunteer can deduct unreimbursed expenses incurred in attending the convention. These include transportation expenses and a reasonable amount for meals and lodging.

Uniforms. Do your volunteers have to buy uniforms? A volunteer can deduct the cost and upkeep of uniforms that are not suitable for everyday use and that must be worn while volunteering for a nonprofit. For example, people who volunteer as Red Cross nurses' aides at a hospital can deduct the cost of uniforms they must wear.

Underprivileged youth. If your nonprofit's purpose is to reduce juvenile delinquency, volunteers can deduct any amounts they pay to allow under-privileged youths to attend athletic events, movies, or dinners. The youths must be selected by your nonprofit, not the volunteer. Volunteers may not deduct their own expenses incurred in accompanying the young people.

Substantiation of Volunteer Expenses

The substantiation requirements for deducting unreimbursed volunteer expenses differ according to the amount of the expenses.

Expenses less than $250. If the volunteer claims a deduction of less than $250, that person does not need to obtain any substantiation from the nonprofit. But the volunteer should keep records of his or her expenses in case they are ever questioned by the IRS.

Expenses of $250 or more. If the claimed expenses are $250 or more, they are treated much the same as a property (noncash) contribution. The volunteer must get an acknowledgment from the nonprofit that contains:

- a description of the services provided
- a statement of whether or not the nonprofit provided any goods or services to reimburse the volunteer for the expenses incurred
- a description and good faith estimate of the value of any goods or services (other than intangible religious benefits) provided to the volunteer as a reimbursement, and
- if applicable, a statement that the only benefit the volunteer received was an intangible religious benefit; the acknowledgment does not need to describe or estimate the value of an intangible religious benefit.

If goods or services are provided to the volunteer to reimburse him or her for expenses incurred, the quid pro quo contribution rules apply. This means that the amount of the volunteer's deduction might have to be reduced by the value of the quid pro quo benefits. (See the discussion of quid pro quo contributions in Chapter 5.)

The volunteer must get the acknowledgment by the earlier of:

- the date his or her tax return is filed for the year the contribution was made, or
- the due date, including extensions, for filing the return—usually October 15 of the year after the contribution was made.

EXAMPLE: George Jones volunteers for the Wildlife International Relief Fund by answering the phones and helping with its donor database for ten hours every week. He incurs $500 in car expenses during the year driving to and from its headquarters. Since WIRF does not reimburse volunteer expenses, he gets the following acknowledgment:

January 15, 20xx

Dear George Jones:

This letter serves to acknowledge for your tax records that you performed the following unpaid volunteer services for Wildlife International Relief Fund during 20xx: answered phones at head-quarters office, helped maintain computerized database of donors.

No goods or services were provided to reimburse you for the expenses you incurred while providing your volunteer services.

Thank you very much for your fine work.

Very truly yours,

Yolanda Allende

Yolanda Allende

Executive Director, Wildlife International Relief Fund

Benefits and Freebies—How to Show Your Appreciation Tax Free

Everybody likes to be appreciated, and what better way for a nonprofit to show appreciation than to give a volunteer something of value—for example, a small stipend, gift card, free membership, or meal. Just as with reimbursements, these benefits won't be considered taxable income as long as certain requirements are met. With benefits, generally this means the benefit must qualify either as a working condition fringe benefit or a de minimus benefit. It pays to understand how this works so you can make sure any benefits you give to volunteers are tax free.

Working Condition Fringe Benefits

Working condition fringe benefits include anything that an employer gives to employees to help them perform their work. As long as those costs would be deductible as regular business expenses by a business owner, then they qualify as tax-free working condition fringe benefits for a volunteer. Generally, this means the costs must be ordinary and necessary, directly related to the business, and reasonable in amount. Any type of cost can qualify as a working condition fringe benefit—a cell phone, a subscription to a legal journal, or a bus pass—as long as it is business related and there is proper documentation supporting it. This means that even when the nonprofit pays a bill directly—for example, a cell phone bill—there must be records showing that the calls were business related.

Here are some examples of working condition fringe benefits that a nonprofit can provide to a volunteer:

- professional association dues
- professional liability insurance
- professional publications
- business equipment, such as computers and telephones, and
- a company car.

If the volunteer uses the benefit 100% in connection with his or her volunteer work, then the benefit will be 100% tax-free. However, if the volunteer uses the benefit partly for nonprofit work and partly for personal use, then the volunteer must keep careful track of the item's use—allocating the time and percentage of use between personal and business. The value of the personal use is taxable income to the volunteer that must be reported to the IRS.

> **EXAMPLE:** Lloyd volunteers for a small nonprofit that helps the elderly by driving them to doctor appointments. The nonprofit gives him a cell phone that he uses to keep in touch with the office and clients when he's out driving. If Lloyd uses the cell phone 100% for this purpose, it is tax free to him. But if he uses it only 50% of the time for work and 50% of the time for personal purposes, he would have to pay income tax on 50% of its value.

To determine the value of personal use, you figure out the fair market value of the benefit received and multiply that by the percentage of personal use.

EXAMPLE: It costs Lloyd's nonprofit $50 a month to pay for the cell phone used by Lloyd. If Lloyd uses the cell phone 50% of the time for his volunteer driving and 50% of the time for nondeductible personal uses, the nonprofit would have to report $25 per month as income paid to Lloyd and Lloyd would have to report and pay tax on that amount. If Lloyd is classified as an employee (most volunteers are), the payment would be reported on Form W-2. If Lloyd is an independent contractor (usually only directors are), it would be reported on Form 1099-MISC, provided he was paid $600 or more during the year.

One very important working condition tax-free fringe benefit is liability insurance for a nonprofit's directors. This insurance can be expensive and, if the directors had to pay for it, a considerable tax burden and possible deterrent for people considering being a director. However, as long as the directors who receive the insurance are bona fide volunteers, they don't have to pay tax on the value of it and there are no IRS reporting obligations. To be a bona fide volunteer, the total value of any remuneration or other benefits received (not including the insurance) must be substantially less than the value of the volunteer services provided. (IRS Reg. 1.132-5(r).)

De Minimis Benefits—Those Token Freebies

What about those little freebies you might want to give your volunteers to show your appreciation for all their hard work—things like a free T-shirt, a mug, or a Christmas turkey? As long as these items are "de minimis"—that is, they are so small in value that accounting for them would be impractical—then they will be tax free and need not be reported to the IRS. Unfortunately, there is no set amount below which is considered de minimis. It depends on the circumstances. In one case, the IRS stated that an achievement award worth $100 was not de minimis.

Examples of some de minimis fringe benefits that are commonly provided by nonprofits to their volunteers include:

How One Nonprofit Rewards Its Volunteers

The Academy of Natural Sciences in Philadelphia provides its volunteers with an array of small tokens of appreciation that fall within the de minimis range for IRS purposes. They are tax free and don't need to be reported to the IRS.

Benefit	Grounds for Tax-Free Treatment
An invitation to the annual Volunteer Recognition Dinner held in the Spring.	De Minimis
Volunteers receive a certificate of appreciation for three years of service; and a pin for the completion of five years and ten years of service. There are also awards for exceptional volunteer service in a number of areas, and you may be nominated for our very own version of the "Academy Awards."	De Minimis
Free admission any time you visit the Academy Museum outside of your regular volunteer hours.	No Additional Cost Service
Free entry to the Butterflies exhibit at any time.	No Additional Cost Service
Upon request, free museum passes to be used by your family or friends.	No Additional Cost Service
A 20% discount on Museum Shop purchases.	Tax Free Discount
A discount on food and drink purchased at our restaurant.	Tax Free Discount
Free or reduced-cost trips organized from time to time for volunteers to visit other museums, nature centers, zoos, etc.	De Minimis
Use of the Volunteer Room for breaks or lunch and to find the latest information about the Academy and its programs.	De Minimis
A free copy of *Natural History Magazine* (issued 10 times a year) which you can pick up in the Volunteer Room.	De Minimis

- low-cost gifts such as a mug, T-shirt, or tote bag with the nonprofit's name on it
- personal use of the nonprofit's photocopier, fax machine, or other electronic equipment
- office parties, group meals, picnics
- theater or sporting event tickets
- coffee, doughnuts, or soft drinks
- flowers, fruit, or other niceties for special circumstances
- local telephone calls
- traditional birthday or holiday gifts (not cash) with a low fair market value, and
- pins and other low-cost tokens of appreciation.

RESOURCE

Want to know more? A detailed discussion of tax-free fringe benefits can be found in IRS Publication 15-B, *Employer's Tax Guide to Fringe Benefits.*

Tax-Free Benefits for Volunteer-Employees

Unlike working condition fringe benefits and de minimis benefits, certain benefits are tax free only if the volunteer qualifies as an employee (and not an independent contractor) for tax purposes. Basically, this IRS classification hinges on whether the nonprofit has the right to control the person's work. If they do, the person is an employee; if not, they are an independent contractor. The rules for classifying volunteers are the same as the rules used for paid workers and are explained in more detail below in "How to Tell the Difference."

Most volunteers at nonprofits are employees because they almost always work under someone else's supervision or direction. As employees, they can receive the benefits discussed below tax free. However, to avoid any confusion, a nonprofit can clearly define the employee role of volunteers in its handbook or contract with the volunteer. Here's an example of language one large nonprofit includes in its handbook:

> Each volunteer who is accepted to a position with the agency must have a clearly identified supervisor who is responsible for direct management of that volunteer. This supervisor shall be responsible for day-to-day management and guidance of the work of the volunteer, and shall be available to the volunteer for consultation and assistance.

Directors are the one exception to the general rule that volunteers are usually employees. Unlike other volunteers, directors don't perform regular supervised tasks or work. Instead, they are responsible for overseeing the management and overall direction of the organization. Because of this, they are normally classified as independent contractors. In some cases, this may depend on the role the person plays. For example, if an officer or director performs any significant non–board-related work for the nonprofit and is paid for that work, that person should be classified as an employee. Otherwise, where the director or officer's primary role is that of a board member, they should be classified as an independent contractor.

Now let's take a look at some of the types of benefits that a nonprofit can provide to its volunteer-employees (but not independent contractors) tax free.

Discounts. Volunteer-employees can buy goods or receive services from the nonprofit at a lower price than the price offered to the general public. For services, the amount of the discount is not taxable if it is no more than 20% of the price charged to the general public for the service. For merchandise or goods, the discount is limited to the nonprofit's gross profit percentage on the merchandise sold times the price charged to the public for the merchandise. To figure out gross profit percentage, you calculate the total amount earned from the sale of merchandise during the year and then subtract its cost. For example, if a nonprofit sold $100,000 worth of merchandise to the public and paid $60,000 for the merchandise, its gross profit percentage would be 40% (its $40,000 gross profit is 40% of its $100,000 gross income). The nonprofit could give its volunteer-employees a tax-free discount on its merchandise of up to 40%.

Parking and other transportation benefits. Many nonprofits provide volunteers with free parking, or reimburse them or give them an allowance for parking expenses. There is a cap of $230 per month in parking expenses that may be provided tax free to volunteer-employees. A nonprofit may also reimburse volunteers for the cost of using mass transit or provide them with an allowance. With reimbursements or an allowance, up to $120 per month may be provided tax free to volunteer-employees. (These dollar amounts are for 2013, and are adjusted each year for inflation.)

Meals and lodging at nonprofit premises. As long as they are provided for the nonprofit's convenience, then the value of any meals or lodging provided on the nonprofit's business premises is not taxable for volunteer-employees. Meals provided for the nonprofit's convenience would include, for example, where eating facilities are not close by, the meal period must be kept short, or the volunteer-employees are on call. Meals provided to improve general morale or goodwill or to attract new volunteers would not qualify for tax-free treatment. For lodging, there is an additional requirement: It must be necessary for the volunteer-employee to live at the nonprofit's premises in order to perform the volunteer services. For example, volunteers who traveled to New Orleans to help a community nonprofit rebuild housing destroyed by Hurricane Katrina could be provided tax-free housing while they were there performing their volunteer work.

No additional cost services. A nonprofit that provides services to the public as part of its mission may offer the same services for free to volunteer-employees, as long as it doesn't impose any substantial cost on the nonprofit and the volunteer is involved in providing the service. For example, a volunteer-employee who works at a nonprofit that provides low-cost health care to the poor may obtain free health care from the clinic if it can be done without any substantial additional cost for the clinic.

Education benefits. Nonprofits can pay certain education expenses for their volunteer-employees and it can be a nontaxable fringe benefit in either of two ways. First, expenses for education are a tax-free working condition fringe benefit if the course (1) maintains or improves job skills, (2) is required by the nonprofit, or (3) is required by law. For example, a nonprofit may pay for an accounting course for its volunteer treasurer. A nonprofit may also provide up to $5,250 per year in tuition assistance for undergraduate college education that is not work related. Graduate education may also be funded if the volunteer performs teaching or research activities.

Insurance coverage. Volunteer-employees can be provided with tax-free health and accident insurance, and up to $50,000 in group life insurance coverage (although few nonprofits provide these types of benefits to volunteers).

Other than what is listed above, any cash, discount, service, or benefit that a volunteer receives must be treated as taxable income and reported to the IRS. Benefits other than cash are valued according to their fair market value and then treated the same as taxable cash income.

> EXAMPLE: To encourage volunteers during a fundraising drive, a nonprofit offers a Hawaiian vacation to the volunteer who raises the most money. The fair market value of the vacation is taxable income. The vacation cost $2,000, so this is the amount that the nonprofit must report to the IRS and the winning volunteer must add to his or her taxable income for the year.

If a volunteer is classified as an employee for tax purposes (which is usually the case except for directors), you need to pay attention to employee withholding requirements if he or she is paid over a minimum amount during a pay period. See IRS Publication 15, *Circular E, Employer's Tax Guide.*

Special Benefits for Volunteer Firefighters

Volunteer firefighters and emergency medical responders who are part of a qualified volunteer emergency response organization don't have to pay federal income tax on the following benefits provided by their state or local government:

- rebates or reductions of their state or local property or income taxes, or
- annual payments of up to $30 multiplied by the number of months the person volunteered during the year.

Paid Help: Employees and Independent Contractors

Nonprofits that hire paid help face more tax issues than nonprofits that only have volunteers. The first and most important issue you will have to address with a paid worker is whether that person is an employee or independent contractor for tax purposes. Often, this is perfectly obvious. For example, someone you hire to work full time as an office manager and pay a salary is clearly an employee. On the other hand, if you hire an accountant solely to compile your annual financial statements, and the person is paid by the hour, owns their own company with its own employees, and has lots of other clients, that person is an independent contractor. But oftentimes, it is not so clear—a worker can have some attributes of an employee and some of an independent contractor. In these cases, a difficult judgment call may have to be made.

Initially, it's up to the hiring entity to make the employee or independent contractor classification. However, if the IRS determines that you have misclassified an employee as an independent contractor, you may have to pay back payroll taxes, interest, and penalties ranging from 1.5% to 3% of wages paid. You also may be required to pay the full amount (both the employee's and employer's share) of any pension plan contributions owed. These costs can be enormous. In one highly publicized case, the IRS claimed that a nonprofit youth soccer league in Connecticut owed $334,441 in back taxes and penalties for classifying approximately 60 soccer coaches as independent contractors instead of league employees. The case was ultimately settled when the league agreed to classify half of the coaches—those not employed by professional coaching associations—as league employees and withhold taxes from their pay. In return, the league only had to pay $11,600 in back taxes.

As you can see, it is important for a nonprofit to make its worker classifications correctly.

What's the Big Deal?

Employers have a strong incentive to classify their workers as independent contractors instead of employees because it can save them a lot of money. First of all, you don't have to pay half of the worker's Social Security and Medicare taxes (as you have to with employees). Nor do you have to comply with the complex and burdensome bookkeeping requirements required for employees. And, independent contractors don't receive workers' compensation, unemployment insurance, or other benefits, such as health insurance, sick leave, vacation, and pensions. All these things can add up to 10% to 25% of payroll costs. There are other important benefits of hiring independent contractors as well. Unlike employees, independent contractors can be hired to accomplish a specific task and then let go, and they often are not provided with office space or equipment. In addition, there is no such thing as severance pay for an independent contractor, and they don't benefit from most of the laws designed to protect employees, such as wage and hour laws and anti-discrimination rules. As a result, although independent contractors are often paid at a higher hourly rate than employees, it can be less costly to hire an independent contractor.

With employees, on the other hand, you must withhold income and Social Security taxes and pay those taxes directly to the IRS. In addition, you are responsible for paying half of the employee's Social Security and Medicare taxes. And there are much more complicated bookkeeping and IRS filing requirements for employees. As you might expect, the IRS prefers the employee setup—it ensures the government gets paid its taxes and also makes it difficult for employees to cheat on their taxes by underreporting their income.

CAUTION
Watch out for IRS scrutiny of worker classifications and worker conversions. The IRS and state agencies, such as state unemployment and workers' compensation agencies, are extremely suspicious of firms that convert

employees to independent contractors. If your nonprofit is audited, it will have to pay substantial taxes and penalties if the IRS concludes it misclassified an employee as an independent contractor. So even if, like so many nonprofits, you are under financial pressure and tempted to convert some of your employees to independent contractors to save money, beware—this is a dangerous move. You can only do this if the worker actually qualifies as a contractor. Saying that the person is an independent contractor does not change anything in the eyes of the IRS or other government agencies. The only thing that matters is whether the worker is actually engaged in an independent business—offering his or her services to the general public, servicing multiple clients or customers, incurring business expenses, and not supervised or controlled on the job. He or she can't simply go on working for your nonprofit the same way as before with a new title.

Hiring Employees	
Pros	**Cons**
Employees may be closely supervised.	Employer must pay federal and state payroll taxes for employees.
You don't need to worry about IRS auditors claiming you misclassified employees.	An employer is liable for an employee's actions.
Employees can be given extensive training.	Employer must usually provide workers' compensation coverage.
Employer automatically owns any intellectual property they create on the job.	Employer must provide office space and equipment.
Employees can't sue for damages if they are injured on the job, provided they are covered by workers' compensation insurance.	Employer ordinarily provides employee benefits such as vacation and sick leave.
Employees can generally be fired at any time.	Employer can be sued for labor law violations.

Hiring Independent Contractors

Pros	Cons
No need to pay federal and state payroll taxes.	Exposure to audits by IRS and other government agencies.
No office space or equipment need be provided.	Independent contractors can't be trained or closely supervised.
Hiring firm generally not liable for independent contractor's actions.	Independent contractors can sue for damages if injured on the job.
Hiring firm need not provide workers' compensation to independent contractors.	Independent contractors usually can't be terminated unless they violate their contracts.
No employee benefits.	They can work for others.
Less exposure to lawsuits for labor law violations.	Possible loss of copyright ownership in work product if an assignment of rights not obtained.

Other Agencies Concerned With Worker Classification

The IRS is not the only government agency that is concerned with how workers are classified. Other agencies also audit nonprofits on this issue. On the federal level, this includes the Department of Labor, which enforces the federal minimum wage and hours laws; the National Labor Relations Board, which enforces employees' federal right to unionize; and the Occupational Safety and Health Administration (OSHA), which enforces workplace safety laws. Many state agencies also get into the act, including the state income tax department, unemployment insurance agency, and workers' compensation agency. Although many of these agencies use the same test as the IRS to determine worker status, some use different ones that can be even stricter than the IRS. For a detailed discussion, see *Working With Independent Contractors* (Nolo), by Stephen Fishman.

How to Tell the Difference

As important as the distinction between employee and independent contractor status is, the IRS test for making this determination is deceptively simple. The IRS says that a worker is an employee if the hiring firm has the right to direct and control the way the worker performs his or her job. Put another way, an employer has the right to tell an employee not only what needs to be done, but also how to do it (even if the employer doesn't always exercise its right of control). In contrast, a worker is an independent contractor if the hiring firm has the right to tell the worker what needs to be done, but not how to do it. In other words, independent contractors are just that—independent. They have a high degree of autonomy because they run their own businesses.

The difficulty in applying this "right to control test" is determining whether you have the right to control a worker you hire. IRS auditors can't look into your mind to see if you are controlling a worker. They rely instead on indirect or circumstantial evidence indicating control or lack of it—for example, whether you provide a worker with tools and equipment, where the work is performed, how the worker is paid, and whether you can fire the worker.

A nonprofit may have a small regular staff of a few salaried employees. This might include the executive director, a bookkeeper, and an office manager. These are the people who run the organization on an ongoing basis. But sometimes people are hired to perform services on a temporary or project basis and it may not be as clear what their status is. For example, is a person who works full time for three months directing a special fundraising project an employee or a contractor? This is where circumstantial evidence relating to that worker will become important in making the determination about his or her status.

The chart below shows the primary factors used by the IRS and most other government agencies to determine if you have the right to control a worker. As you can see, the IRS has developed three broad categories of evidence:

- behavioral control
- financial control, and
- the relationship between the parties.

The single most important factor listed in the chart is instructions. In the worker classification context, instructions means telling—or merely having the right to tell—a worker how to get the job done. Instructions include telling a worker:

- when to do the work
- where to do the work
- what tools or equipment to use
- what workers to hire to assist with the work
- where to purchase supplies or services
- what work must be performed by a specified person
- what routines or work patterns must be used, and
- what order or sequence to follow in doing the work.

The more detailed the instructions the worker is required to follow, the more control the hiring firm exercises over the worker, and the more the worker looks like an employee. Requiring a worker to obtain prior approval before taking an action also constitutes instructions. For example, if you hire someone to revamp your website and you require her to obtain your approval for an assistant she wants to hire, then it's more likely that person will be considered an employee.

In contrast with the instructions listed above that tell a worker how to do the job, instructions about the end results a worker must achieve are perfectly consistent with independent contractor status. Indeed, virtually every hiring firm instructs its independent contractors about what must done. For example, if you hire an independent contractor to cater a fundraising dinner, you will likely give detailed instructions on what type of end product you are looking for—for example, the number of dinners required, cost per person, and type of food.

Additionally, analysis of court decisions has found that workers who hire, supervise, and pay for assistants are almost always found to be independent contractors. Conversely, workers who can be terminated at any time are usually found to be employees.

IRS Test for Worker Status		
Behavioral Control	Workers will more likely be considered independent contractors if you: • do not give them instructions • do not provide them with training	Workers will more likely be considered employees if you: • give them instructions they must follow about how to do the work • give them detailed training
Financial Control	Workers will more likely be considered independent contractors if they: • have a significant investment in equipment and facilities • pay business or travel expenses themselves • make their services available to the public • are paid by the job • have opportunity for profit or loss	Workers will more likely be considered employees if: • you provide them with equipment and facilities free of charge • you reimburse their business or travel expenses • they make no effort to market their services to the public • you pay them by the hour or other unit of time • they have no opportunity for profit or loss—for example, because they're paid by the hour and have all expenses reimbursed
Relationship Between Hirer and Worker	Workers will more likely be considered independent contractors if they: • don't receive employee benefits such as health insurance • sign a client agreement with the hiring firm • can't quit or be fired at will • perform services that are not part of your regular activities	Workers will more likely be considered employees if they: • receive employee benefits • have no written client agreement • can quit at any time without incurring any liability to you • can be fired at any time • perform services that are part of your core operations

Independent Contractor or Employee Self-Test

The following fact situations are taken from actual cases in which the status of nonprofit workers was contested. Read through them and see if you think the worker involved was an independent contractor or employee. We'll tell you how the courts or IRS ruled below.

1. The Community for Creative Non-Violence (CCNV), a nonprofit organization dedicated to helping the homeless, hired a sculptor named Reid to create a statue dramatizing the plight of the homeless. CCNV gave Reid highly detailed specifications on how the statue was to look: It was to be a sculpture of a modern Nativity scene in which, in lieu of the traditional holy family, the two adult figures and the infant would appear as contemporary homeless people huddled on a streetside steam grate. Reid supplied his own tools and worked in his studio in Baltimore. He was retained for less than two months. During and after this time, CCNV had no right to assign additional projects to Reid. Apart from the deadline for completing the sculpture, Reid had absolute freedom to decide when and how long to work. CCNV paid Reid $15,000 upon completion of the work to CCNV's satisfaction. Reid had total discretion in hiring and paying assistants.

   ☐ independent contractor   ☐ employee

2. Arlene Harris was hired by the Massachusetts Department of Mental Health to work as an educational coordinator for a project concerning special-needs children. She interviewed hundreds of children with special needs to provide data to the Department. She performed her duties independently and was not supervised daily. The project was, however, screened by the Department and she had periodic meetings with their personnel and submitted period reports. Arlene worked out of her home. When she had to travel, she used her own car and paid her own travel expenses.

   ☐ independent contractor   ☐ employee

Independent Contractor or Employee Self-Test (continued)

3. A biologist received a grant from a research lab to perform basic research. The funds were used to pay for the biologist's compensation, supplies and equipment, assistants, if desired, and overhead for the lab.

   The extent of the research and the place and manner of performance were determined by the biologist free from direction or control by the lab.

   ☐ independent contractor   ☐ employee

4. A nonprofit community health service planning center hired a part-time grant proposal writer. She was not given explicit instructions on the way her work was to be done. However, the nonprofit had the right to supervise her if it chose to. She worked at office space provided by the nonprofit, using its equipment. She was paid an annual salary in monthly installments. She received no employee benefits such as a paid vacation or sick days, insurance coverage, or pension, and the nonprofit did not carry workers' compensation insurance on her. It was understood that she would perform the services personally, and she hired no helpers. She worked only for the center and made no attempt to advertise her services to the public. The nonprofit also had the right to discharge her at any time.

   ☐ independent contractor   ☐ employee

5. Richard Greene, an Assemblies of God minister, worked as a missionary in Bangladesh on behalf of his church. The church did not provide Greene with any training or assign him to go to Bangladesh. He chose to go there on his own and the church did not direct Greene to work on a particular project while he was there. Instead, Greene independently chose to become involved in student ministry. The Church advanced Greene financial support and required that he keep records and file quarterly reports as to how the funds were spent. Greene was not directly supervised or evaluated by anyone

Independent Contractor or Employee Self-Test (continued)

from the church, and determined his own work days and hours. He was required to attend only one meeting every five years and did not communicate regularly with the church. He was free to resign at any time. Greene was provided with a mission manual that contained detailed instructions on how to conduct a foreign ministry, but the manual's provisions were not actually enforced by the church.

☐ independent contractor   ☐ employee

Answers:

1. Independent contractor. The United States Supreme Court held the sculptor was an independent contractor, not an employee. It said that all the factors, except for the extent of CCNV's control over the design of the statue, weighed heavily in favor of independent contractor status. (*Community for Creative Non-Violence v. Reid*, 490 U.S. 730 (1992).)

2. Employee. The court held there was sufficient control over petitioner Arlene by the Department of Mental Health to classify her as an employee. It was irrelevant that no control was actually exercised. (*Harris v. Comm'r*, T.C. Memo. 1977-358.)

3. Independent contractor. The biologist's freedom from control by the lab meant she was an independent contractor. IRS Rev. Rul. 57-127.

4. Employee. All the factors, except the lack of employee benefits, pointed toward employee status. (PLR 9231101 (1992).)

5. Independent contractor. The court found that the church lacked the control and lacked the right to control the manner and means by which Greene performed his duties as a foreign missionary. (*Greene v. Comm'r*, T.C. Memo. 1996-53.)

TIP

Part-time workers and temps can be employees. Don't assume that a person you hire to work part time or for a short period automatically qualifies as an independent contractor. If you have the right to control the way they work, they are employees.

There is no set number of factors that must point to independent contractor status for a worker to be classified that way. These cases require a highly subjective judgment call that must be made by using common sense.

The Safe Harbor Rule for Independent Contractor Status

If your nonprofit is ever audited, it is almost certain that the IRS will review any independent contractor classifications you have made. For this reason, any nonprofit that hires independent contractors should know about Section 530—a safe harbor rule in the tax code that protects you from IRS challenges of independent contractor status. If you qualify for safe harbor protection, the IRS cannot impose any assessments or penalties related to federal employment taxes (Social Security and Medicare taxes)—the safe harbor does not apply to federal income taxes. Moreover, you may continue to treat the workers as independent contractors and the IRS cannot question or contest their status.

To qualify for safe harbor protection, three requirements must be met. You must have:

- filed all required 1099-MISC forms for the workers in question
- consistently treated the workers involved, and others doing substantially similar work, as independent contractors, and
- had a reasonable basis for treating the workers as independent contractors—for example, treating such workers as independent contractors is a common practice for similar nonprofits, an attorney or accountant told the nonprofit they qualified as independent contractors, or your nonprofit relied on an IRS ruling.

Thus, your nonprofit may be safe to classify a worker as an independent contractor for employment tax purposes if it has consistently classified similar workers as independent contractors in the past. For example, if your nonprofit has always treated the people it hires to maintain its website as independent contractors because your accountant advised you that they qualified as contractors, then it can safely rely on this safe harbor. However, because Section 530 applies only to federal employment taxes (Social Security and Medicare taxes) and not federal income taxes, you may have to withhold income tax from the pay of a worker you treat as an independent contractor under Section 530. For more details on the safe harbor rule, see *Working With Independent Contractors* (Nolo), by Stephen Fishman.

Funded Positions

Many nonprofits receive outside funding from governmental or other sources that they use to pay some of their workers. Typically, these workers are involved with a particular program or project. If the nonprofit pays these workers directly, they are treated the same as any other workers the nonprofit uses—they will either be employees or independent contractors, depending on their role. The fact that the ultimate source of their pay is an entity other than the nonprofit is immaterial. The only exception is where the workers are paid directly by the outside funder. In this event, the workers are employees or independent contractors of the outside funding source. The nonprofit that uses their services need not put them on its payroll. As far as the nonprofit is concerned, these workers are volunteers.

EXAMPLE: The U.S. Department of the Census hires a nonprofit called the City Institute to conduct a detailed survey of residents in government subsidized housing in California. The Department pays the Institute $500,000 which the Institute uses to hire ten employees to conduct the survey. The Institute pays the workers directly, so they are employees of the Institute, not employees of the Census Department.

Getting an IRS Advance Determination

You can ask the IRS for its opinion on how a worker or group of workers should be classified. Either the worker or nonprofit can do this by filing IRS Form SS-8 with the IRS. After receiving the request, the IRS will issue a private letter ruling stating its determination. Depending on its backlog and the length of its investigation, it can take from three months to a year or more for the IRS to make its ruling. The private letter ruling is the IRS's official opinion on the issue. However, it can't be relied upon by anyone other than the taxpayer who asked for it. This means that you can't rely on other IRS classification rulings in making your decision about how to classify your workers.

There is usually no reason for a nonprofit to file an SS-8. If a worker's classification as an independent contractor is clear under the "right to control" test, there's no reason to ask the IRS for a determination on the issue. If a worker's classification is not clear, then chances are the IRS will rule that he or she is an employee. (Over 90% of all IRS rulings in response to Form SS-8s result in a determination that the worker is an employee.) Most SS-8 forms are filed by workers who are classified as independent contractors but want employee status either to get the nonprofit to pay one-half of their Social Security tax or because they discover they are ineligible for unemployment compensation after they are terminated by the nonprofit.

If you file a Form SS-8 and the IRS decides that your nonprofit misclassified a worker as an independent contractor instead of an employee, you are not required to reclassify the worker as an employee. You can continue to treat the worker as an independent contractor but it's probably not a good idea. If you are audited by the IRS, you will almost certainly be found to have misclassified that worker or group of workers. In addition, the IRS may decide that your continued misclassification of the worker after receiving the ruling was intentional and it could impose the maximum assessments and penalties for intentional worker misclassification. These are much higher than the assessments and penalties that may be imposed for an unintentional misclassification.

Classifying Corporate Officers and Directors

Usually, directors of a nonprofit are not paid for their services as directors so they are considered volunteers. Because they don't receive any compensation, you don't have to be concerned with any payroll tax issues. However, if directors are paid to attend board meetings or perform other services related to their role as directors, they must be classified as independent contractors for IRS purposes. Why? Because as members of the governing board, directors are responsible for the overall direction and management of the organization and would not meet the right-to-control test for employee status.

A nonprofit's officers include its president, vice president, secretary, treasurer, executive director, and chief executive officer (CEO). Officers are usually classified as employees because they work under the board of directors' direction and control. However, there is one limited exception: An officer is classified as an independent contractor if he or she receives no compensation and performs no services, or only minor services, for the nonprofit.

> EXAMPLE: Xavier is an accountant who serves as a nonprofit corporation's treasurer on a volunteer basis, keeping the nonprofit's books in order. His work as treasurer is subject to the board of directors' control, so he should be classified as an employee for IRS purposes. As a practical matter, however, this doesn't mean much. Because Xavier is paid no money by the nonprofit, there are no taxes to withhold or pay.

A director who also serves as an officer would be classified as an employee in his or her officer capacity and an independent contractor in his or her director capacity. Money paid to such a person for work as an officer would be subject to employment tax and withholding, while any money paid for that person's services as director would be treated as independent contractor payments.

Hiring Independent Contractors

Your nonprofit likely won't be able to rely on volunteers to do all the work that needs to be done, especially tasks that require specialized knowledge such as accounting, legal services, fundraising services, website design, or even plumbing. If you have a specific task that needs to be performed and you can't find a qualified volunteer to do it for free, the next best option is to hire an independent contractor. You'll have to pay an independent contractor for his or her services, but your nonprofit won't have the extra expense and headaches involved in hiring an employee. However, be aware that the IRS and other government agencies scrutinize nonprofits that classify workers as independent contractors rather than employees. Be sure to properly document your decision to treat any worker as an independent contractor. That way, you'll be prepared if the issue is raised by an IRS auditor or other government agency.

Procedures for Hiring Contractors

Here are some procedures you can follow to better ensure your independent contractor classifications withstand scrutiny.

Obtain documentation backing your classification. Obtain as much documentation as possible showing that any worker you classify as an independent contractor is really an independent contractor and not an employee. In cases where the worker involved is clearly an independent contractor—for example, he or she is an outside attorney, accountant, or fundraiser—this may not be as important. But where a worker's status might not be clear, it is vital and the more documentation, the better.

The type of documentation you will want to keep includes:

- copies of the independent contractor's business license (if required) and any professional licenses the independent contractor has, such as a contractor's license
- certificates showing that the independent contractor has insurance, including general liability insurance and workers' compensation insurance (if the independent contractor has employees)

- the independent contractor's business cards and stationery
- copies of any advertising the independent contractor has done, such as a yellow pages listing
- a copy of the independent contractor's white pages business phone listing, if available
- a printout of the home page of the independent contractor's website, if any
- if the independent contractor is operating under an assumed name, a copy of the fictitious business name statement
- the independent contractor's invoice form to be used for billing purposes
- a copy of any office lease and a photograph of the independent contractor's office or workplace
- the independent contractor's unemployment insurance number issued by the state unemployment insurance agency (only independent contractors with employees will have these)
- the names and salaries of all assistants that the independent contractor will use on the job
- the names and salaries of all assistants the independent contractor used on previous jobs for the past two years and proof that the independent contractor paid them (with copies of canceled checks or copies of payroll tax forms, if possible)
- a list of all the equipment and materials the independent contractor will use in performing the services and the cost; proof that the independent contractor paid for the equipment (with copies of canceled checks for example)
- the names and addresses of other clients or customers for whom the independent contractor has performed services during the previous two years, and copies of 1099-MISCs the independent contractor has received from other firms (in some cases, the independent contractor may be required to keep names confidential), and
- if the independent contractor is a sole proprietor and agrees, copies of the independent contractor's tax returns for the previous two years showing that the independent contractor has filed a Schedule C, *Profit or Loss From Business (Sole Propietorship)*.

Use a written independent contractor agreement. A written independent contractor agreement will *never* by itself make a worker an independent contractor in the eyes of the IRS. Nevertheless, it is always helpful. A well-drafted agreement that outlines the responsibilities and role of the worker as an independent contractor will demonstrate that you intended to create an independent contractor relationship. And because written agreements with independent contractors have become a routine fact of business life, not having one is a red flag.

You don't need to hire a lawyer to draft an independent contractor agreement. However, you should put some time and effort into creating your agreement. Many hiring firms simply use standard form agreements they obtain from the Internet or other sources. These forms typically contain standard one-size-fits-all legalese and are not tailored for any particular occupation. IRS auditors are well aware that hiring firms often have workers sign such generic independent contractor agreements before they start work. The worker may not even bother to read the agreement and certainly makes no changes in it to reflect the real work situation. The more an independent contractor agreement is custom-tailored for each worker or group of workers performing similar tasks and reflects the true relationship between the hiring firm and workers, the more helpful it will be.

Many independent contractors have their own agreements they have used in the past. If so, it's often wise to use that agreement as the starting point for your agreement. This will show that the agreement is a real negotiated contract, not a standard form you forced the worker to sign. Pay particular attention to whether the independent contractor's agreement contains any provisions that should be deleted or amended, or whether it needs new provisions.

RESOURCE

For detailed guidance on how to draft an independent contractor agreement and sample forms, see *Working With Independent Contractors*, by Stephen Fishman (Nolo).

Dos and Don'ts With Independent Contractors

- Don't supervise the independent contractor or his or her assistants. The independent contractor should perform the services without your direction. Your control should be limited to accepting or rejecting the final results the independent contractor achieves.
- Don't let the independent contractor work at your offices unless the nature of the services absolutely requires it—for example, where a computer consultant must work on your computers or a carpet installer is hired to lay carpet.
- Don't give the independent contractor employee handbooks or policy manuals. If you need to provide independent contractors with orientation materials or suggestions, copies of governmental rules and regulations or similar items, put them all in a separate folder titled "Orientation Materials for Independent Contractors" or "Suggestions for Independent Contractors."
- Don't establish the independent contractor's working hours.
- Avoid giving independent contractors so much work or such short deadlines that they have to work full time for you. It's best for independent contractors to work for others at the same time they work for you.
- Don't provide ongoing instructions or training. If the independent contractor needs special training, he or she should not obtain it in-house and should pay for it him- or herself.
- Don't provide the independent contractor with equipment or materials unless absolutely necessary.
- Don't give an independent contractor business cards or stationery to use that has your nonprofit's name on them.
- Don't give an independent contractor a title within your nonprofit.
- Don't pay the independent contractor's travel or other business expenses. Pay the independent contractor enough to cover these expenses out of his or her own pocket.

Dos and Don'ts With Independent Contractors (continued)

- Don't give an independent contractor employee benefits such as health insurance. Pay independent contractors enough to provide their own benefits.
- Don't require formal written reports. An occasional phone call inquiring into the work's progress is acceptable. But requiring regular written status reports indicates the worker is an employee.
- Don't invite an independent contractor to employee meetings or functions.
- Don't refer to an independent contractor as an employee, or to your nonprofit as the independent contractor's employer, either verbally or in writing.
- Don't pay independent contractors on a weekly, biweekly, or monthly basis as you pay employees. Rather, require all independent contractors to submit invoices to be paid for their work. Pay the invoices at the same time you pay other outside vendors.
- Obey the terms of your independent contractor agreement. Among other things, this means that you can't fire the independent contractor. You can only terminate the independent contractor's contract according to its terms—for example, if the independent contractor's services fail to satisfy the contract specifications.
- Don't give the independent contractor new projects after the original project is completed without signing a new independent contractor agreement.

Obtain the independent contractor's taxpayer identification number.
Some people work in the underground economy—that is, they are paid
in cash and never pay any taxes or file tax returns. The IRS may not
even know they exist. In order to find these people (who often work
as independent contractors), the IRS requires anyone who hires an
independent contractor to provide the IRS with the person's taxpayer
identification number. If an independent contractor won't give you his
or her number or the IRS informs you that the number the independent
contractor gave you is incorrect, you will be required to withhold taxes
from any money you pay that person and remit the funds to the IRS.
This is called backup withholding and ensures that the IRS receives
its share of taxes for the compensation paid. If your nonprofit fails
to backup withhold, the IRS will impose an assessment against your
organization equal to 31% of what the independent contractor was paid.

Backup withholding can be a bookkeeping burden. Fortunately, it's
very easy to avoid. Have the independent contractor fill out and sign IRS
Form W-9, *Request for Taxpayer Identification Number and Certification*,
and retain it in your files. Copies of the form can be downloaded from
the IRS website at www.irs.gov. You don't have to file the W-9 with the
IRS. This simple form merely requires the independent contractor to
list his or her name and address and taxpayer ID number. Partnerships
and sole proprietors with employees must have a federal employer
identification number ("EIN"), which they obtain from the IRS. In the
case of sole proprietors without employees, the taxpayer ID number is
the independent contractor's Social Security number.

If the independent contractor doesn't already have an EIN, but
promises to obtain one, you don't have to backup withhold for 60 days
after he or she applies for one. Have the independent contractor fill out
and sign the W-9 form, stating "Applied For" in the space where the ID
number is supposed to be listed. If you don't receive the independent
contractor's ID number within 60 days, start backup withholding.

Your Tax Reporting Obligations

Even though one of the great benefits of hiring independent contractors is that the tax reporting requirements are less burdensome, it's still important to comply with all the requirements. Failure to do so can result in fines and penalties and will make life much more difficult in the event of an IRS audit. Some nonprofits have their payroll services or outside accountants or bookkeepers file the necessary forms. However, these filings are so simple, you can easily do them yourself.

The basic tax reporting rule for independent contractors is that if you pay an independent contractor $600 or more during the year, you must file IRS Form 1099-MISC. This form tells the IRS exactly how much your firm paid the worker that year. You file the form with the IRS and give copies to the worker and your state tax agency. You must do a Form 1099-MISC for all independent contractors who are sole proprietors or partners in partnerships. This covers the vast majority of independent contractors. You don't have to file a 1099-MISC for independent contractors who are incorporated (but you do for those who have formed other types of business entities: partnerships or limited liability companies). This is one of the main advantages of hiring incorporated independent contractors—there are no filing requirements for them. The one exception is for doctors and lawyers. If their business is incorporated, you must file a 1099-MISC if you pay them $600 or more.

> **EXAMPLE:** Literacy for All pays $5,000 to Yvonne, a CPA, to perform accounting services. Yvonne has formed her own one-person corporation called Yvonne's Accounting Services, Inc. Literacy pays the corporation, not Yvonne personally. Because Literacy is paying a corporation, it need not report the payment to the IRS.

In determining how much you paid an independent contractor, it doesn't matter whether the sum is one payment for a single job or many small payments for multiple jobs. You add up all payments made to the independent contractor for services performed during the year. You also must include any payments you make for parts or materials.

EXAMPLE: The Friends School hires Jack, a self-employed painter, to paint its classrooms. Jack charges the School $2,000 for his labor and $500 for materials—paint, brushes, and drop cloths. The School's total payment to Jack that must be reported on Form 1099-MISC is $2,500.

With expenses, it's better to pay independent contractors enough so that they can cover their own expenses and do not have to bill separately for them. This is because independent contractors who pay their own expenses are less likely to be viewed as employees by the IRS or other government agencies. This cost would then be included as part of the total compensation paid to the independent contractor on Form 1099-MISC. However, it's sometimes customary for the client to reimburse the independent contractor for expenses. For example, a lawyer who handles a lawsuit will usually seek reimbursement for expenses, such as photocopying, court reporters, and travel. If this is the case, your nonprofit may pay these reimbursements. However, make sure the independent contractor documents expenses with receipts and then save them in case the IRS questions the payments. If the expenses are properly documented, you should not include the amount of the reimbursement on the 1099-MISC form because expense reimbursement is not considered income.

If an independent contractor doesn't properly document expenses, your nonprofit may still reimburse the contractor for the expenses. However, your nonprofit must include the amount of the reimbursement as income paid to the independent contractor on the independent contractor's 1099-MISC form.

Filling Out Form 1099-MISC

You must report on Form 1099-MISC payments to all independent contractors to whom you paid $600 or more during the year. Each 1099-MISC form contains three parts and can be used for three different workers. Send in all your 1099-MISC forms together along with one copy of Form 1096, which is a transmittal form—the IRS equivalent of a cover letter. Obtain these forms by calling the IRS at 800-TAX-FORM or by contacting your local IRS office.

		☐ CORRECTED (if checked)	
PAYER'S name, street address, city or town, province or state, country, ZIP or foreign postal code, and telephone no.	**1 Rents** $	OMB No. 1545-0115 20**13** Form **1099-MISC**	**Miscellaneous Income**
	2 Royalties $		
	3 Other income $	**4 Federal income tax withheld** $	**Copy B** **For Recipient**
PAYER'S federal identification number	RECIPIENT'S identification number	**5 Fishing boat proceeds** $	**6 Medical and health care payments** $	
RECIPIENT'S name	**7 Nonemployee compensation** $	**8 Substitute payments in lieu of dividends or interest** $	This is important tax information and is being furnished to the Internal Revenue Service. If you are required to file a return, a negligence penalty or other sanction may be imposed on you if this income is taxable and the IRS determines that it has not been reported.
Street address (including apt. no.)		
City or town, province or state, country, and ZIP or foreign postal code	**9 Payer made direct sales of $5,000 or more of consumer products to a buyer (recipient) for resale ▶** ☐	**10 Crop insurance proceeds** $	
	11 Foreign tax paid $	**12 Foreign country or U.S. possession**	
Account number (see instructions)	**13 Excess golden parachute payments** $	**14 Gross proceeds paid to an attorney** $	
15a Section 409A deferrals $	**15b Section 409A income** $	**16 State tax withheld** $ $	**17 State/Payer's state no.**	**18 State income** $ $

Form **1099-MISC**   (keep for your records)   www.irs.gov/form1099misc   Department of the Treasury - Internal Revenue Service

Filling out Form 1099-MISC is easy. Follow this step-by-step approach.

- List your nonprofit's name and address in the first box titled "Payer's name." Enter your nonprofit's taxpayer identification number in the box entitled "Payer's federal identification number."

- The independent contractor your nonprofit has paid is called the "Recipient" on this form, meaning the person who received the money. You must provide the independent contractor's taxpayer identification number, name, and address in the boxes indicated. For sole proprietors, you must list the individual's name first. Then you may list a different business name, although this is not required. You may not enter only a business name for a sole proprietor.

- Enter the amount you paid the independent contractor in box 7, entitled "Nonemployee compensation." Be sure to fill in the right box or the Form 1099-MISC will be deemed invalid by the IRS.
- Finally, if you've done backup withholding for an independent contractor who has not provided you with a taxpayer ID number, enter the amount withheld in box 4.

The Form 1099-MISC contains five copies. These must be filed as follows:

- Copy A, the top copy, must be filed with the IRS no later than February 28 of the year after you paid the independent contractor. If you don't use the remaining two spaces for other independent contractors, leave those spaces blank—don't cut the page.
- Copy 1 must be filed with your state taxing authority if your state has a state income tax. The filing deadline is probably February 28, but check with your state tax department to make sure. Your state may also have a specific transmittal form or cover letter you must obtain.
- Copy B and Copy 2 must be given to the worker no later than January 31 of the year after he or she was paid.
- Copy C is for you to retain for your files.

You file all the IRS copies of each 1099-MISC with Form 1096, the transmittal form. You must add up all the payments reported on all the 1099-MISC forms and list the total in the box indicated on Form 1096. File the forms with the IRS Service Center listed on the reverse of Form 1096.

You have the option of filing Form 1099-MISCs with the IRS electronically instead of by postal mail. You must get permission from the IRS to do this by filing IRS Form 4419, *Application for Filing Information Returns Electronically*. If you file electronically, the deadline for filing is extended to March 31. For more information, visit the IRS website at www.irs.gov (click on "IRS e-file"), or call the IRS Information Reporting Program at 304-263-8700.

Form 1099-MISCs may also be sent to independent contractors electronically—that is, by email. However, you may do this only if the contractor agrees to it. If he or she doesn't agree, you must deliver a printed copy of the 1099-MISC by mail or in person.

Hiring Employees

All but the smallest nonprofits eventually reach the point where they need to hire someone to work at their organization. This person will be an employee who receives a salary for his or her work. In a small nonprofit, there may only be one employee—an executive director who is in charge of everything. Larger organizations may also have a bookkeeper and office manager on staff. They may be full or part time but if they receive a salary and work under the director's supervision, they are employees.

The Tax Collector Role

Whenever anyone, including a nonprofit, hires an employee, it becomes an unpaid tax collector for the government. All employers are required to withhold and pay both federal and state taxes for their employees. These taxes are called payroll taxes or employment taxes. Federal payroll taxes consist of:

- Social Security and Medicare taxes—also known as FICA
- unemployment taxes—also known as FUTA, and
- federal income taxes—also known as FITW.

FICA is an acronym for Federal Income Contributions Act, the law requiring employers and employees to pay Social Security and Medicare taxes. FICA consists of a 12.4% Social Security tax on income up to an annual ceiling. In 2013, the annual Social Security ceiling was $113,700. Medicare taxes are not subject to any income ceiling and are levied at a 2.9% rate. This combines to a total 15.3% tax on employee income up to the Social Security tax ceiling.

Employers must pay half of this—7.65%—out of their own pockets. They must withhold the other half from their employees' pay.

FUTA is an acronym for the Federal Unemployment Tax Act, the law that establishes federal unemployment taxes. Most employers must pay both state and federal unemployment taxes. However, nonprofits that qualify as public charities (501(c)(3) organizations) need not pay FUTA. If your nonprofit uses an outside payroll service, bookkeeper, or accountant to do its payroll, make sure they know this.

FITW is an acronym for federal income tax withholding. The employer must calculate and withhold federal income taxes from its employees' paychecks. Employees are solely responsible for paying federal income taxes. The employer's only responsibility is to withhold the funds and remit them to the government.

Employers in every state are required to pay and withhold state payroll taxes. These taxes include:

- state unemployment compensation taxes in all states
- state income tax withholding in most states, and
- state disability taxes in a few states.

Employers in every state are required to contribute to a state unemployment insurance fund. Employees make no contributions, except in Alaska, New Jersey, Pennsylvania, and Rhode Island, where employers must withhold small employee contributions from employees' paychecks.

Employers must periodically pay payroll taxes to the IRS, either electronically or by making federal tax deposits at specified banks which transmit the money to the IRS. Every year, employers must file IRS Form W-2, *Wage and Tax Statement*, for each of their workers. The form shows the IRS how much the worker was paid and how much tax was withheld. Additionally, quarterly employment tax returns must be filed with the IRS showing how much each employee was paid and how much tax was withheld and deposited. However, employment tax returns need only be filed once a year if the employer's payroll is quite small.

You can find a detailed guide to all these requirements in IRS Publication 15, *Circular E, Employer's Tax Guide*, which can be downloaded from the IRS website at www.irs.gov.

Opting Out of Unemployment Taxes

Nonprofits that qualify as Section 501(c)(3) organizations don't have to pay federal unemployment taxes, but—subject to one exception—they must pay state unemployment tax. These taxes can be a real burden. They are based on your nonprofit's payroll and claims history. Employers with many claims pay higher taxes than those with few claims. Unfortunately, these taxes are likely to get worse. With unemployment at near record levels, most states are currently paying out far more in unemployment benefits than they are receiving in revenue. Most will have to increase unemployment taxes to make up the shortfall.

A 501(c)(3) organization has the option of opting out of its state unemployment insurance program. Instead of paying a set amount of unemployment tax to the state every year, regardless of how many of its employees file claims, it reimburses the state only for unemployment claims the state actually pays out to its former employees. This can save big money because nonprofits typically pay more in unemployment taxes than the state pays out for their former employees' claims. In the past, many nonprofits have saved 30% to 40% over five to ten years.

But there are obvious risks to this approach. If your nonprofit is forced to lay off substantial staff, the unemployment costs it will have to reimburse the state for could far exceed the unemployment tax it would otherwise have had to pay. This risk is doubtless greater now than it has been in the past because of the current economic climate. To mitigate these risks, thousands of nonprofits have joined grantor trusts that pool money from many organizations to pay off future claims. It is also possible to purchase private insurance to cover claims.

The reimbursement option works best for larger nonprofits with stable employment. Nonprofits with fewer than ten employees or that may have layoffs, are usually not good candidates for opting out of state unemployment taxes.

Always Pay Payroll Taxes

Nonprofits that are strapped for cash sometimes fail to pay their payroll taxes, or pay too little. A study by the Government Accounting Office found that nearly 55,000 nonprofits had nearly $1 billion in unpaid federal payroll taxes as of 2006. No matter how bad your nonprofit's financial situation is, failing to pay payroll taxes is extremely unwise. As far as the IRS is concerned, an employer's most important duty is to withhold and pay over Social Security and income taxes. Employee FICA and FITW are also known as trust fund taxes because the employer is deemed to hold the withheld funds in trust for the U.S. government.

If your nonprofit fails to pay trust fund taxes, it can get into the worst tax trouble there is. The IRS can—and often does—seize an employer's assets and force it to close down if it owes back payroll taxes. At the very least, your nonprofit will have to pay all the taxes due plus interest. The IRS may also impose a penalty known as the trust fund recovery penalty if it determines that your nonprofit willfully failed to pay the taxes. The agency can claim the failure to pay was willful if you knew the taxes were due and didn't pay them. Good evidence that your nonprofit knew such taxes were due is that it paid them in the past, but stopped.

The trust fund recovery penalty is also known as the 100% penalty because the amount of the penalty is equal to 100% of the total amount of employee FICA, FUTA, and FITW taxes the employer failed to withhold and pay to the IRS. This can be a staggering sum.

Don't think that the IRS won't go after your organization because it is a nonprofit that does good work in the community. In one case, the IRS placed a lien on property held by a small nonprofit Michigan health clinic that failed to pay $85,000 in payroll taxes. The amount soon grew to $110,000 due to interest and penalties. The IRS then gave the clinic six months to pay the full amount or face foreclosure on its property and closure of the clinic.

Moreover, any "responsible person" can and will be held *personally liable* if payroll taxes are not timely paid. This means the person must pay the back taxes and penalties out of his own pocket. A responsible person may include not only a nonprofit's accountant or bookkeeper, but anyone

Always Pay Payroll Taxes (continued)

who exercises significant control over the nonprofit's finances. This can include not only a nonprofit's treasurer, president, executive director, CEO, and other officers, but its board members as well.

Such liability can be found even where the person was not directly involved in paying payroll taxes. In one case, the chairman of the board of directors of a nonprofit was held personally liable for nonpayment of payroll taxes, even though the organization's in-house director and accountant were the ones who were charged by the board with the duty of seeing that the taxes were paid.

The IRS doesn't have to wait and see if the employer will pay the overdue payroll taxes before going after responsible persons. Rather, it can obtain a judgment against each responsible person for the full amount due. If more than 100% of the tax is ultimately collected, a refund is issued for the excess. Collecting this refund can take years, however. Also, a judgment for trust fund taxes is one debt you can't legally get out of—you won't even be forgiven the debt if you file for bankruptcy.

However, there is a limited exception: The trust fund recovery won't be imposed on a volunteer director who:

- serves only in an honorary capacity
- does not participate in the day-to-day or financial operations of the nonprofit, and
- does not have actual knowledge of the failure to pay payroll taxes. This exception can apply only where a board member has absolutely no personal involvement with a nonprofit's operations. Moreover, it won't apply if it results in no person being liable for the trust fund recovery penalty. (IRC Sec. 6672(e).)

If complying with payroll tax requirements sounds like a lot of work, that's because it is. For this reason, smaller employers typically hire a bookkeeper or payroll tax service to do the work. There are both large national payroll tax services and small local ones. There are even some that specialize in nonprofit payrolls. A good way to find a payroll tax service is to obtain a referral from a nonprofit similar to yours. You can also find a list on the IRS website at www.irs.gov.

Reimbursing Your Employees

There may be times when an employee must pay for a work-related expense. Most commonly, this occurs when an employee is driving, traveling, or entertaining while on the job. These payments have important tax consequences, whether reimbursed by the employer or paid by the employee.

The best way to reimburse or otherwise pay your nonprofit's employees for any work-related expenses is to use an accountable plan. When your nonprofit pays employees for their expenses under an accountable plan, three great things happen:

- your nonprofit doesn't have to pay payroll taxes on the payments
- the payments need not be included on the employee's IRS Form W-2, *Wage and Tax Statement*, and
- the employee won't have to include the payments in his or her taxable income.

EXAMPLE: The Coover Institute, a nonprofit think tank, sends its publicist Michele to a convention of publicity professionals in Detroit, Michigan. Michele pays all her expenses herself. When she gets back, she fully documents her expenses as required by Coover's accountable plan. These amount to $2,000 for transportation and hotel and $1,000 in meal and entertainment expenses. Coover reimburses Michele $3,000. Michele need not count the $3,000 reimbursement as income (or pay taxes on it), and Coover need not include the amount on the W-2 form it files with the IRS reporting how much Michele was paid for the year. Moreover, Coover need not withhold income tax or pay any Social Security or Medicare taxes on the $3,000.

The rules for an accountable plan for employees are the same as those for volunteers described in "Accountable Plans—The Key to Success With the IRS," above. In brief, the expenses must be work-related, adequately documented within 60 days, and any excess payments must be returned within 120 days. These payments to employees can be made through advances, direct reimbursements, charges to a company credit card, or direct billings to the employer. An accountable plan need not be in writing (although it's not a bad idea). All you need to do is set up procedures for your employees to follow that meet the IRS requirements for accountable plans.

> **EXAMPLE:** The Universal Yoga Center gives an employee a $1,000 advance to cover her expenses for a short business trip. When she gets back, she turns in an expense report and documentation showing she only spent $900 on business-related expenses while on the trip. If she doesn't return the extra $100 within 120 days after the trip, it will be considered wages for tax purposes and the Yoga Center will have to pay payroll tax on the amount.

Any payments you make to employees for business-related expenses that do not comply with the accountable plan rules are deemed to be made under an unaccountable plan. These payments are considered to be employee wages, which means all of the following:

- the payments must be included on the employee's IRS Form W-2, *Wage and Tax Statement*
- the employee must report the payments as income on his or her tax return and pay tax on them
- the employee may deduct the expenses—but only as a miscellaneous itemized deduction
- the employer must withhold the employee's income taxes and share of Social Security and Medicare taxes from the payments, and
- the employer must pay the employer's 7.65% share of the employee's Social Security and Medicare taxes on the payments.

EXAMPLE: The Urban Forest Coalition, a small nonprofit, pays Matthew, its secretary, $200 per month allowance to reimburse monthly business expenses he incurs on behalf of the nonprofit. Typically, he buys computer paper and other supplies. He doesn't substantiate the expenses or return any excess. The entire $200 must be reported on Form W-2 as wages subject to Social Security and Medicare taxes, state unemployment taxes, and income tax withholding.

This is a tax disaster for the employee and not a good result for you either. You will have to pay Social Security and Medicare tax that could have been avoided if the payments had been made under an accountable plan.

Unless it has agreed to do so, your nonprofit has no legal obligation to reimburse or pay employees for job-related expenses they incur. Employees are entitled to deduct from their own income ordinary and necessary expenses arising from their employment that are not reimbursed by their employers. However, it's much better for the employees to be reimbursed by the employer under an accountable plan and let the employer take the deduction. Why? Because employees can deduct unreimbursed employee expenses only if the employee itemizes his or her deductions and only to the extent these deductions, along with the employee's other miscellaneous itemized deductions, exceed 2% of his or her adjusted gross income. Adjusted gross income (AGI) is the employee's total income, minus deductions for IRA and pension contributions and a few other deductions (shown on Form 1040, line 35). An employee's unreimbursed expenses must be listed on IRS Schedule A, Form 1040, as a miscellaneous itemized deduction. Employees must also file IRS Form 2106 reporting the amount of the expenses.

Charitable Giving—The Basics and Cash Donations

The words, "your contribution is tax deductible," are music to a donor's ears. While getting a tax deduction is not the sole motivation for most charitable donations, it is an important factor—indeed, about 85% of all charitable contributions are made by individuals who deduct their donations.

However, not all charitable contributions are tax deductible. Whether a donation is deductible depends on whom it is given to, when, what for, and on the donor's particular tax situation. An identical contribution may be deductible by one donor, but not another. In addition, the IRS has imposed new, even more restrictive rules on donations. These new rules require more documentation and tax filings by nonprofits and donors than ever before. In some cases, they limit the amount that can be deducted. All this has made the charitable fundraiser's (and donor's) life more difficult than it used to be.

This chapter covers the basic tax rules for charitable giving and cash contributions. Property contributions are covered in Chapter 6.

Contributions, Donations, and Gifts

The words "contribution," "donation," or "gift" are typically used to refer to money or property received from a donor. These words mean essentially the same thing and are often used interchangeably. In the nonprofit world, however, people tend to use the word "donation" for small gifts—say an item of clothing—and reserve the word "contribution" for larger gifts—real estate, for example.

Your Role as a Nonprofit

Charitable deductions are claimed by donors on their individual tax returns, IRS Form 1040. It is up to the donor and his or her tax adviser—not the nonprofit that receives a donation—to determine how much to deduct, and when and how to deduct it. The nonprofit's role in the charitable tax deduction process is fairly limited. Subject to some important exceptions, a nonprofit is not required to report donations to the IRS or make any tax filings when it receives a donation. The nonprofit's main responsibility is to make sure it complies with any substantiation and documentation requirements for the donations it receives.

Whether, and to what extent, a donation is tax deductible depends on a donor's particular tax situation. Donors, with the help of a tax adviser if necessary, must apply the general rules discussed in this chapter to their specific circumstances. Each donor's situation is unique and will affect how much that person can deduct or whether a donation is deductible at all. Thus, no matter what role you have at your nonprofit, you should *never give a donor specific legal or tax advice* on donations. You are not the donor's lawyer or tax adviser.

This is also why blanket statements in fundraising solicitations such as "your contribution is tax deductible"—while technically accurate and perfectly legal—are often misleading. Instead, you should always tell donors to consult with their tax advisers to determine if a contribution is deductible. Never promise or assure a donor that it is.

That said, it is never in a nonprofit's interest to have a donor lose a valuable charitable deduction because he or she didn't understand the rules. Likewise, it is not good for a donor to make a contribution thinking it will be deductible when it is not, or that it will save more in taxes than it really will. In either case, you'll end up with a disappointed or angry donor who may decide not to make any more contributions to your nonprofit.

Many donors are abysmally ignorant regarding the charitable deduction rules. Moreover, many of these rules have changed over the last few years—changes that have made it more difficult for donors to claim deductions. Your nonprofit can help make sure that your donors understand the current IRS requirements for donations. Some nonprofits post this basic information on their websites, often in the form of FAQs (frequently asked questions). You can also refer donors to the IRS publication on the subject, IRS Publication 526, *Charitable Contributions*. It is available at the IRS website at www.irs.gov.

While everyone at your nonprofit doesn't need to become an expert on charitable contribution tax rules, it is helpful if some key people on your staff—particularly those involved in fundraising efforts—understand the basic charitable deduction rules. This might include your:

- executive director
- development director
- board of directors
- paid development staff
- paid staff in nondevelopment roles
- volunteers who help fundraise, and
- outside consultants.

IRS rules make some types of donations easier or more advantageous tax-wise than others. This ends up encouraging people to make certain types of donations while discouraging other types. Your fundraising strategies should always take into consideration the tax effect of a donation. You can use fundraising letters, emails, and other communications to explain to potential donors the tax benefits of particular types of donations—for example, in your fundraising letter, you could advise donors of the potential tax benefits of donating publicly traded stock that has gone up in value since it was purchased. (See "Stock and Other Securities," in Chapter 6.)

RESOURCE

For a highly useful guide to nonprofit fundraising strategies and tactics, refer to *Effective Fundraising for Nonprofits: Real-World Strategies That Work*, by Ilona Bray (Nolo).

Threshold Requirements for Deducting Donations

As you probably know, tax deductions (sometimes called tax write-offs) are expenses or payments that taxpayers subtract from their total income to determine their taxable income—that is, the amount of their income that is subject to tax for the year. The more deductions a taxpayer has, the less income tax will be due. Deductions are allowed for many different types of expenses—some of the most common ones are mortgage interest, real estate taxes, medical expenses, and charitable contributions.

> **EXAMPLE:** Ben has an annual income of $100,000. However, he doesn't have to pay income tax on this entire amount. He qualifies for various tax deductions—mortgage interest, real estate taxes, medical expenses, a personal deduction, and charitable contributions. Altogether these deductions amount to $40,000. Ben subtracts this amount from his annual income to determine his taxable income—$60,000. Thus, because of his many deductions, Ben only pays income tax on $60,000 instead of $100,000. This saves him $10,533 in federal income taxes.

It's easy to see why most taxpayers want as many deductions as possible. The more deductions a person has, the less money he or she will owe to the IRS. The IRS allows deductions as an incentive to promote or reward certain behavior—in the case of charitable deductions, it's to promote charitable giving. But there are also strict rules attached to deductions that dictate who can take them and under what circumstances. With charitable donations, there are two threshold requirements that must be met for any donation to be deductible.

The Donee Side—It Must Be a Qualified Organization

Only contributions to what the IRS calls "qualified organizations" are deductible. These consist mainly of public charities—organizations that come under Section 501(c)(3) of the Internal Revenue Code. These are the myriad of nonprofits that engage in charitable, religious, scientific, literary, or educational work. (See Chapter 1 for more on 501(c)(3)s and other nonprofits.) If your nonprofit has obtained a determination letter from the IRS recognizing its status as a 501(c)(3) public charity, then it is a qualified organization and donations to your organization are deductible. Many nonprofits include copies of their IRS determination letter on their website and their taxpayer identification number on fundraising solicitations so donors know that donations to their organization are deductible. The only 501(c)(3) organizations that are automatically considered qualified organizations without a determination letter from the IRS are churches and other religious organizations.

While Your Application Is Pending With the IRS

To obtain IRS recognition as a 501(c)(3) organization, a nonprofit must file IRS Form 1023. If all is in order, the IRS will send the nonprofit a determination letter stating that the organization meets the requirements to be classified as a 501(c)(3) tax-exempt organization. This review process may take some time, often several months. While a nonprofit's Form 1023 is waiting for approval from the IRS, the organization may operate as a tax-exempt organization and accept donations.

Contributions made while an application is pending are deductible if the application is ultimately approved. However, donors have no assurance that their contributions are tax deductible until the nonprofit's application is approved. If the application is disallowed, the contributions would not be deductible. Moreover, the nonprofit would be liable for filing federal income tax returns, unless its income is otherwise excluded from federal taxation.

If your nonprofit is in this situation, be honest with potential donors and inform them in fundraising solicitations that you have applied for IRS recognition as a 501(c)(3) organization and that contributions will be fully deductible *if* the application is approved by the IRS. Some donors may wish to wait until the application is approved so they don't take any risk about the deductibility of their contribution.

There are a few other types of nonprofits that do not obtain their tax-exempt status under Section 501(c)(3) but are still considered qualified organizations for IRS charitable contribution purposes. These are war veterans groups, volunteer fire departments, fraternal lodges that use all their net earnings for charitable purposes, and certain cemetery companies. Gifts to these organizations are tax deductible. In addition, gifts made for charitable purposes to a federal, state, or local government are also tax deductible. The documentation and substantiation rules for charitable contributions discussed here and in Chapter 6 apply to these organizations as well.

Not All Tax-Exempt Organizations Are Qualified Organizations

Some organizations obtain their tax-exempt status from the IRS under a section of the Internal Revenue Code other than Section 501(c)(3). They are often organizations that do "good work" in the community but they are not considered qualified organizations, so contributions to them are not deductible. These non–501(c)(3) tax-exempt organizations include:

- social welfare organizations
- labor unions
- civic leagues and associations
- country clubs
- social and sports clubs
- lodges
- chambers of commerce
- political candidates and organizations
- for-profit schools and hospitals
- homeowners' associations, and
- most state bar associations.

As a general rule, fundraising solicitations on behalf of tax-exempt organizations that are not qualified organizations are supposed to include an express statement that contributions to the organization are not tax deductible.

For more information on these organizations, refer to IRS Notice 88-120 (available at the IRS website at www.irs.gov).

The IRS maintains a database of qualified organizations, which can be searched using the IRS online Exempt Organizations Select Tool at: www. irs.gov/Charities-&-Non-Profits/Exempt-Organizations-Select-Check. You can also call the IRS at 877-829-5500 to find out if an organization is qualified. Other organizations maintain even more extensive lists of nonprofits. For example, the website www.guidestar.org lists over 1.5 million nonprofits. These are all valuable resources potential donors can check to see whether an organization they are making a donation to is a qualified organization.

Not all qualified organizations, however, are listed in the IRS database. Section 501(c)(3) nonprofits whose annual gross receipts are normally under $5,000 and religious organizations such as churches and synagogues don't have to apply to the IRS for tax-exempt status and are often not listed. If you are a small nonprofit or religious organization that is not listed in the IRS database, you might consider applying for IRS tax-exempt status so you will be included in the IRS list of qualified organizations. Many small nonprofits do this to reassure potential donors that their organization is a recognized qualified organization and donations to them are tax deductible.

The Donor Side—Only Those Who Itemize Can Deduct

Whether a donation is deductible depends first on whether the donation is made to a qualified organization. However, there is another critical component—whether the individual (donor) making the donation itemizes his or her deductions. Only people who itemize their deductions can deduct their charitable contributions. This greatly limits the actual number of people who can take deductions.

Itemized deductions are deductions taxpayers are allowed to take each year for certain personal expenses, such as mortgage interest, property taxes, state income taxes, certain medical expenses, casualty and theft losses, and charitable contributions. Individual taxpayers have the option to either itemize their deductions or take the standard deduction that is set by the IRS each year. In 2013, the standard deduction was $5,950 for single taxpayers and $11,900 for married taxpayers filing jointly.

Only taxpayers whose total itemized deductions are more than the standard deduction will itemize their deductions. Taxpayers who don't itemize get no deduction for their charitable contributions (or any other itemized deductions). Thus, from a tax standpoint, charitable contributions are useless for people who don't itemize. Efforts to allow nonitemizers to deduct at least some of their charitable contributions have thus far failed in Congress.

Thus, while in theory all charitable contributions are deductible, as a practical matter, only one-third of taxpayers each year actually deduct their contributions because that is roughly the percentage of people who itemize their deductions on their tax returns. This is why a statement such as "your contribution is tax deductible" in a fundraising solicitation is misleading. It would be far more truthful to say "Your contribution may be deductible if you itemize your deductions on your tax return. Consult your tax adviser for details."

Charitable Contributions Don't Save Taxpayers Money

Never tell potential donors that a contribution will "save them money," or "pay for itself" because it is deductible. This is simply not true, although many people mistakenly believe it. In reality, the tax savings from a deductible contribution is only a fraction of the total amount donated. The exact tax savings depends on the individual's top tax bracket. For example, if someone's top bracket is 25%, that person will save 25 cents in federal income taxes for every dollar he or she donates to a nonprofit. The combined federal and state tax burden for most donors who itemize their deductions is about 30%. Thus, most donors save only 30 cents in income tax for each dollar donated.

The only time taxpayers save money by making charitable contributions is when they cheat by overvaluing gifts of property. The IRS is well aware of this temptation and imposes many special rules on valuing property donations to prevent such cheating.

If potential donors ask you how much a gift will save them in taxes, tell those donors to multiply the amount of the gift by their top tax rate (both federal and state if they have state income taxes).

As you might expect, people who itemize their deductions are higher-income taxpayers. Over 90% of all taxpayers with taxable income over $100,000 itemize, while the majority of those with incomes below $50,000 take the standard deduction. Most people who itemize are homeowners with substantial mortgage interest and property tax payments. Others may itemize in a given year because of large medical expenses or casualty losses.

For taxpayers who itemize, the charitable deduction can be extremely valuable. For everyone else, charitable contributions have no tax benefit at all.

> **EXAMPLE:** Rosa, a single taxpayer, gives $1,000 to a nonprofit during the year. She has numerous itemized deductions, including substantial home mortgage interest and property taxes. All her itemized deductions amount to $10,000. This is more than the standard deduction, so she claims $10,000 in itemized deductions on Schedule A of her Form 1040. Because she itemized her deductions, she was able to deduct her $1,000 charitable contribution. Her top tax rate is 28%, so she saves $280 in income tax for the year for her $1,000 contribution; the net cost of her $1,000 donation is only $720. Had Rosa taken the standard deduction, she would not have gotten any deduction for her donation.

Does the tax deductibility of donations encourage people who itemize to donate to nonprofits? You bet it does—at all income levels, itemizers donate 40% more to nonprofits than nonitemizers. In fact, itemizers account for about 80% of all individual contributions to nonprofits. Eighty-nine percent of all itemizers take charitable deductions on their tax returns, meaning they made gifts to nonprofits. In 2005, this amounted to over $183 billion, while nonitemizers gave just $30 billion. If donations were not tax deductible, it is likely that the amount of giving would fall substantially.

The lesson of these statistics is clear: Your main source of charitable contributions is higher-income people who itemize their deductions, which is only about one-third of all taxpayers.

You may wish to stress the tax advantages of charitable gifts for itemizers to encourage them to donate. For nonitemizers who get no tax benefits from charitable contributions, you should stress the other benefits of donating—for example, feeling good about doing good.

When the Donor Is a Business

Businesses can make charitable contributions. And just like individuals, businesses like to get tax deductions because they reduce their taxable income. However, different rules apply for how these donations are deducted depending on what type of business entity is making the donation.

For all business entities other than C corporations, charitable contributions "flow through" the business to the individual business owners proportionately based on their ownership interest in the corporation. The individual business owners then claim their proportionate share of the deduction on their individual tax returns. All the rules that apply to individual donors claiming charitable deductions apply to these deductions. Tax deductions for C corporations work differently. Corporations are separate taxpaying entities that file their own tax returns, so the corporation claims the charitable deductions, not the individual shareholders.

If you receive a donation from a business, you should always address your acknowledgment or receipt for the donation to the company, not the individual owner or owners of the company. This is true regardless of whether the deduction is claimed by the individual owner or owners on their personal tax returns or, in the case of a C corporation, the corporation. You can tell that a contribution is from a business because it will come from a business bank account.

Annual Limits on Charitable Deductions

Donors are not allowed to avoid paying taxes entirely by making charitable deductions. This could happen, for example, if a taxpayer with very little income one year made a very large deductible gift that same year. To prevent this, there are overall limits on how much taxpayers can deduct each year as charitable contributions. However, these limits are quite high and usually only affect donors who make very substantial donations.

The specific limits vary according to whether cash or property is donated. However, the overall limit is that a taxpayer's charitable contribution deductions cannot exceed 50% of his or her adjusted gross income for the year. Adjusted gross income ("AGI" for short) consists of a taxpayer's total income minus deductions for IRA and pension contributions and a few other things. All the charitable contributions the donor makes during the year are combined and the total is applied against the percentage limits.

> **EXAMPLE:** Jerry, a waiter, had $30,000 of AGI this year. He inherits money from an uncle and decides to give $50,000 to his favorite nonprofit. Jerry may only deduct $15,000 of his contribution this year, because this amount is equal to 50% of his AGI.

For C corporations, the limit is 10% of the corporation's taxable income (not counting charitable contributions and a few other items).

Contributions that exceed the annual limit are not lost—instead, they may be carried forward and deducted over the following five years, subject to the annual limits. The taxpayer must first deduct his or her contributions for the current year before deducting carried-forward amounts from prior years. A donor has a total of six years to deduct a donation. After that time the deduction expires.

> **EXAMPLE:** Jerry (from the above example) may carry forward the remaining $35,000 of his donation and deduct it over the next five years, subject to the annual percentage limits. If his AGI is $30,000 the following year, he'll be able to deduct another $15,000, and carry forward the remaining $20,000 to the next year, and so on.

> **CAUTION**
>
> **Carrying over unusable deductions to future years can be complicated.** This is particularly true when a taxpayer's tax status changes—for example, due to marriage, divorce, or death of a spouse. Or where a donor contributes property rather than cash, or where donations are made other than to public nonprofits. You should advise donors whose total annual donations exceed 20% of their AGI to seek professional tax help.

Pease Limitation on Itemized Deductions

The so-called "Pease provision" limits the total amount of all itemized deductions—including charitable contributions—that can be taken by certain upper-income taxpayers. It was reinstated in 2013. The Pease limitation reduces a taxpayer's itemized deductions by 3% of the amount his or her adjusted gross income (AGI) exceeds a threshold amount. The Pease thresholds for 2013 are $300,000 for married taxpayers filing jointly and $250,000 for single taxpayers.

Thus, a married couple with an AGI of $400,000 and $50,000 in itemized deductions (including $10,000 in charitable contributions), would be $100,000 over the threshold. Three percent (3%) of $100,000 = $3,000, so their itemized deductions would be reduced from $50,000 to $47,000. The couple ends up with $3,000 more in taxable income.

However, no matter how high a taxpayer's AGI, the Pease reduction cannot exceed 80% of the amount of itemized deductions otherwise allowable for the year. But this still means that a very high-income homeowner could lose up to 80% of his or her itemized deductions for charitable contributions and other itemized deductions.

What Can a Donor Contribute?

A donor can give just about anything of value to a nonprofit and, if the requirements are met, receive a tax deduction. The IRS divides the universe of charitable contributions into two categories: cash and noncash.

Cash gifts include currency, checks, credit card contributions, electronic funds transfers, online payment services, and gift cards redeemable for cash. Cash contributions are by far the simplest and easiest for a nonprofit to deal with. Noncash contributions include all tangible property gifts—for example, cars, real estate, and old clothing. They also include certain intangible property, such as stocks, bonds, and patents. Noncash contributions are a minority of all the contributions most nonprofits receive, but require a majority of the work because they are subject to special documentation and valuation requirements. Noncash contributions (also called property donations) are covered in Chapter 6.

Planned Giving

Planned giving (also called deferred giving or gift planning) involves charitable gifts other than outright gifts. With planned giving, the donor leaves money or assets to a nonprofit at his or her death or the donor gives money or property to a nonprofit but retains the right to use, or earn income from, the gift until death or the elapse of a certain number of years. Planned giving is complicated and involves tax issues not covered by this book.

It is generally only larger nonprofits that have planned giving programs. Most nonprofits seek professional help to set up a planned giving program and hire staff or get advice from people educated in planned giving methods.

For more information on planned giving for nonprofits, see:

- *Effective Fundraising for Nonprofits: Real-World Strategies That Work*, by Ilona Bray (Nolo)
- *Conducting a Successful Major Gifts and Planned Giving Program: A Comprehensive Guide and Resource*, by Kent E. Dove, Alan M. Spears, and Thomas W. Herbert (Jossey-Bass)
- The National Committee on Planned Giving, at www.ppnet.org
- Planned Giving Coach, at www.plannedgivingcoach.com, and
- The Planned Giving Design Center, at www.pgdc.com.

A person may never receive a charitable deduction for the value of his or her time or services or lost income while working as an unpaid volunteer for a qualified organization. However, if a nonprofit volunteer incurs expenses in connection with his or her work at a nonprofit, that person may be able to deduct those expenses as a charitable contribution. (See "Unreimbursed Volunteer Expenses," in Chapter 4.)

When Is a Contribution Made for Tax Purposes?

A charitable contribution is deductible only when it is completed—that is, when the money or property is delivered to the nonprofit. Thus, the mere act of making a pledge to donate cash or property in the future does not constitute a deductible contribution—the donor must actually deliver the money or property to the nonprofit. This is why the heaviest month of the year for charitable contributions is December—taxpayers must make their contributions by the end of the year to deduct them for that year. It is also why nonprofits ramp up their fundraising efforts late in the year. So, if you're thinking about what time of year your nonprofit should devote the most resources to fundraising, the last quarter of the year is usually best.

Many donors wait until the very last minute to make their year-end contributions. Most are unaware that exactly when their contributions are considered delivered to your nonprofit for tax purposes depends on the type of contribution. Thus, it may be necessary for your nonprofit to give them some guidance. Here are some of the rules on delivery that you should be familiar with in case donors have questions.

Checks. A check is considered delivered on the date it is mailed. However, a postdated check is delivered as of the date listed on the check, regardless of when it's mailed. For example, a check mailed on December 31, 2014, but postdated to January 2, 2015, is considered delivered on January 2.

Credit card payments. Contributions charged on a donor's bank credit card are delivered on the date the card is charged by the bank or credit card company. Credit cards are a great way to donate cash because the donation is deductible in full in the year it is made even if the amount donated is not paid back to the credit card company until a later year. Thus, the donor doesn't have to actually lay out any cash to get a deduction for the current year. This rule applies to any contribution made with borrowed funds.

> **EXAMPLE:** Pete wants to make a $1,000 donation to Greenpeace by December 31, 2014 so he can deduct it from his taxes for the year. Unfortunately, Pete only has $500 in cash in the bank. Luckily, he has a credit card. He uses his credit card to make a $1,000 donation to Greenpeace on December 30, 2014. He can deduct his contribution for 2014 even though he won't be billed for the amount by his credit card company, or pay any part of it, until 2015.

Stock and other securities. When transferred electronically, a gift of stock is complete when it arrives in the nonprofit's brokerage account. When stock certificates are mailed, the gift is complete when it is postmarked. When certificates are hand delivered, the gift is complete when they are physically received by the nonprofit.

Real property and tangible personal property. Delivery of tangible personal property such as clothing, appliances, art, or collectibles, usually requires an actual transfer of possession of the property to your nonprofit.

> **EXAMPLE:** A donor calls you on December 31, 2014 and asks if he can take a charitable donation for 2014 if he mails his grandfather's antique watch to your nonprofit that day. What should you answer? You should tell him to mail a check instead if he wants to get a donation for 2014.

Special Gifts—Earmarked, Restricted, and Conditional

Not all donors make a straightforward contribution where they relinquish control over their gift and the use of funds. Sometimes people want to place restrictions or conditions on how the money they give is used.

Depending on how this is done and what the limitations are, this could make a donation nondeductible. Before you accept a gift with limitations or constraints, make sure your donors understand that there are rules about these gifts that could affect whether a gift is deductible or not.

Earmarked Gifts

Oftentimes, people want to make a donation to a nonprofit and have their funds earmarked for a particular person or small group of people. For example:

- someone knows a family that can't afford to pay their child's tuition and wants to donate money to a nonprofit school to cover that child's tuition
- someone wants to donate money to a nonprofit that runs a homeless shelter to provide housing for a particular person or family, or
- someone wants to donate money to a member of the clergy that can be spent as he or she wishes, such as for personal expenses.

While the intention on the donor's part is still charitable in nature, these types of gifts are not tax deductible. A donor can never deduct a charitable contribution earmarked for a particular individual. This rule applies even to gifts to widows and orphans.

> EXAMPLE: The residents of the small town of Mayberry, North Carolina, establish an account in the name of the widow of a town firefighter who died in the line of duty. They solicit contributions from the public that are to be deposited in that account and used only for the widow's benefit. Contributions to the account, although charitable in nature, are not tax deductible.

To be deductible, gifts must be given to a "charitable class," not a single individual or small group of individuals. A charitable class must be either large enough or indefinite enough that providing aid to members of the class benefits the community as a whole, and not a pre-selected group of people. For example, a charitable class could consist of all individuals located in a city, county, or state.

EXAMPLE: A hurricane causes widespread damage to property and loss of life in several counties of a coastal state. Over 100,000 homes are damaged or destroyed by high winds and floods. The group of people affected by the disaster is large enough so that providing aid to this group of people or geographic region benefits the public as a whole.

If your organization receives a contribution that is earmarked for a particular person, then the person making the donation can't take a tax deduction for it. But that doesn't mean you can't accept the gift. Just make sure the donor understands that if it is earmarked for a particular person, it will not be deductible. To make sure your donors understand this, in your thank-you letter for the gift, you could send the donor a letter stating that you will use the funds as directed but the contribution is not deductible.

EXAMPLE: Bill wants to help Al, a homeless person who camps out near Bill's house. Which of the following would be tax deductible:
- a. gift of $100 from Bill to Al
- b. gift of $100 by Bill to a homeless shelter with directions that the money be used to help Al
- c. $100 gift from Bill to a homeless shelter with no directions on how the money must be spent.

Answer: c—and only c.

Restricted Gifts

In contrast to gifts for the benefit of a particular person, restricted gifts are tax deductible. A restricted gift is one that the donor limits for a specific purpose or time period, or both. For example, a donor could say that his or her donation should only be used to pay construction costs for a new building, or for Thanksgiving and Christmas dinners at a nonprofit senior center. A gift can be restricted in this way as long as the money furthers the nonprofit's overall mission.

Gifts to Foreign Charities

A donor who wants to help people in foreign countries, and also deduct his or her contribution, must donate to a United States nonprofit—a qualified organization as described earlier in this chapter. That nonprofit can either spend the funds abroad itself, or transfer funds to a charitable foreign organization—but the United States nonprofit must control how the funds are used.

Canadian, Mexican, and Israeli charities receive special treatment because the United States has signed tax treaties with them requiring it. Americans may deduct donations to charities in these countries only if, and to the extent that, the donor has income from that country.

Donors may deduct contributions only to Canadian or Mexican nonprofits that satisfy the requirements to be a qualified nonprofit under United States law. Usually, the foreign charity will know if it qualifies.

In addition, contributions to these foreign organizations are subject to the IRS percentage limits on charitable contributions, which are applied to the donor's income from Canada or Mexico. These rules limit the annual deduction to 50% of the donor's adjusted gross income from the foreign country. (The limits do not apply to contributions to a Canadian college or university at which the donor or a family member is or was enrolled.)

An American may deduct contributions to any nonprofit recognized under Israeli law. However, the total deduction allowed for contributions to Israeli nonprofits is limited to 25% of the donor's adjusted gross income from Israeli sources.

Conditional Gifts

Sometimes nonprofits or donors wish to make a gift subject to conditions—that is, the contribution is conditioned on the performance of an act by the nonprofit or the occurrence of an event. If the act or event doesn't occur in the time allotted, the contribution is returned or need not be made.

While this may sound like an interesting fundraising strategy, it has one significant drawback for donors: The contribution won't be deductible by the donor until the act or event occurs, unless the chances of it not happening are "so remote as to be negligible." This means the donor might have to wait years to deduct his or her contribution. If your organization receives or solicits a conditional gift, you should make sure your donors understand this rule before you accept the gift. One way to do that would be to include a statement in your fundraising materials making this clear. Although not required by law, it's a good practice to follow up when the condition has been met to let donors know they can deduct their contributions.

> **EXAMPLE:** The Friend's School, a nonprofit grammar school, commences a three-year fundraising drive to raise funds to renovate its classrooms. It plans to hold all the funds it raises until it receives enough money to pay for the renovations, at which time it would transfer the funds to the construction fund. The School tells donors that if the contributions are not enough to complete the renovations, they will be returned. The donors' contributions are not deductible until the nonprofit determines that enough money has been raised and the contributions need not be returned.

If Your Nonprofit Provides Goods or Services

Only gifts to qualified organizations are deductible. A gift occurs when someone gives money or property to a nonprofit without getting anything of value in return. Gifts do not include money received by a nonprofit in exchange for something of value provided by the nonprofit. Thus, if your nonprofit sells goods or provides services, any payments people make for those goods or services are not deductible charitable gifts. For example—if someone buys a T-shirt from your nonprofit for its fair market value, that person has not made a charitable contribution.

This also means that when qualified organizations perform some type of work or services (as is often the case), people can't deduct the cost of payments for any services received—even though the work performed is often charitable in nature. For example, payments to a hospital for a specific patient's care cannot be deducted, even if the hospital is operated by a qualified organization. Deducting those payments would violate two sets of rules on charitable deductions—the rules against deducting payments earmarked for a particular individual and the rules against deducting payments for services.

Other types of payments that cannot be deducted include:

- payments to a 501(c)(3) retirement home for room, board, maintenance, or admittance of a particular individual, and
- tuition or other fees paid to enroll a child in a 501(c)(3) private or parochial school.

However, if someone pays for goods or services and the payment is intended partly as a gift, then the payment is deductible to the extent it is worth more than the value of the goods or services provided. For example, if someone pays $150 for a benefit dinner where the value of the meal is $25, then that person can deduct $125 (see "Quid Pro Quo Contributions" below).

Nonprofits often raise money by selling raffle or lottery tickets or hosting bingo games. Any money a nonprofit receives in connection with any of these fundraising activities is not a deductible charitable contribution because someone who purchases lottery or raffle tickets from a nonprofit or plays in a bingo game is not making a gift to the organization. He or she is getting something in return for the money paid—the chance to win a prize.

EXAMPLE: St. Mary's Church of Peoria, Illinois, holds a bingo game in its basement every Friday night. Lorene plays every week, spending about $100 per month on bingo cards. She may not deduct any portion of this expense as a charitable contribution. However, she also places $20 in the church's collection plate every Sunday. These contributions are tax deductible because they are charitable gifts for which Lorene receives nothing of monetary value in return.

!

CAUTION

Special tax rules for bingo and other games. If your nonprofit earns income from conducting gaming activities such as bingo, lotteries, raffles, pull-tabs, punch boards, tip boards, pickle jars, 21, casino nights, and so forth, you may need to comply with special tax rules. Specifically, IRS rules require that you:

- report to the IRS any participant's winnings over a specified amount on Form W-2G
- withhold income tax from winnings over specified amounts for certain games and pay it to the IRS
- pay unrelated business income tax (UBIT) on the profits earned from the games (see Chapter 8), and
- pay a wagering excise tax to the IRS.

For details, refer to IRS Publication 3079, *Gaming Publication for Tax-Exempt Organizations.*

Cash Contributions

From a nonprofit's point of view, there is nothing better than a cash contribution. The public seems to agree, since cash donations account for over 75% of all charitable gifts made each year. Gifts of cash are by far the simplest way for your nonprofit to receive donations. Cash means not only hard cash (currency), but also includes checks, credit card contributions, electronic funds transfers, online payment services, and gift cards redeemable for cash. It does not include stocks or bonds—these are considered noncash property donations (see Chapter 6).

Under relatively new rules, donors must have a written record for *all* donations—no matter how small. Without written documentation to support a cash donation, a donor can't claim a tax deduction. For cash donations under $250, donors can use a bank statement or other documentation that substantiates that the payment was made. For all cash donations above $250, the donor must have a document or receipt from the nonprofit. What that document or receipt must contain depends on the size of the contribution.

Contributions of $250 and Less

The rules for contributions under $250 are relatively new and many donors still don't realize they need documentation to support these contributions. While it is primarily the responsibility of the donor to make sure they have the proper records for these smaller contributions, nonprofits can and should help them. Donors who lose tax deductions because of failure to follow IRS technicalities are unhappy donors and unhappy donors often become ex-donors.

For any donation under $250, donors must have a written record that shows:

- the name of the nonprofit
- the date of the contribution, and
- the amount of the contribution.

A bank record or a receipt or letter from the nonprofit verifying this information will suffice. A bank record includes a statement from a financial institution, an electronic funds transfer receipt, a canceled check, a scanned image of both sides of a canceled check obtained from a bank website, or a credit card statement. If a bank statement does not include the name of the nonprofit, the donor can use a monthly bank statement and a photocopy or image obtained from the bank on the front of the check showing the name of the nonprofit.

Often, the donor won't have a bank record—for example, if he or she gives actual cash. In this event, the donor would need to ask the nonprofit for a written record of the donation, which could be a receipt, letter, email, or any other document or writing as long as it has all the required information. In real life, however, donors usually don't ask for receipts for small cash donations—for example, when someone places a few dollars on a church collection plate. In theory, the IRS could disallow any deductions that were taken for these types of small undocumented contributions. In practice, this rarely happens: The IRS has bigger fish to fry.

Nevertheless, the best practice is to always give donors a thank-you letter or email for any donations. Here is an example of a simple thank-you that also serves as a written record for the donor:

Dear Donor:

Do Good Charities received your generous cash gift in the amount of
$_____ on _____[date]_____ .

Thank you for your support.

Very truly yours,

Yolanda Allende

Yolanda Allende
Executive Director
Do Good Charities

(Please keep this receipt for your tax records.)

Instead of a letter, you can also give the donor a simple receipt form, such as:

[Nonprofit Letterhead] or
[Name and Address of Nonprofit]

This acknowledges receipt of a cash gift in the amount of $ _____
received on _____ .

(Please keep this receipt for your tax records.)

Contributions of $250 and More

Unlike with donations under $250, for any donation over $250, the donor must have a written acknowledgment of the contribution from the nonprofit to claim a deduction. Without it, the donor loses out on any potential tax benefit for a donation. The written acknowledgement is required for any *single* contribution of $250 or more—you don't combine the donor's donations to determine if the $250 threshold is met. Thus, a donor could contribute $249 every day for a year and would not need a written acknowledgment from your nonprofit to claim a $90,885 ($249 x 365) charitable deduction. (Although it would probably be a good idea to still have a written acknowledgment.)

Obviously, it is extremely important for donors to get proper documentation for any donation of more than $250 so they don't lose out on the tax benefit of their donation. It is your responsibility to make sure they get the documentation they need. While there is no penalty for nonprofits who fail to provide their donors with a proper acknowledgment, you don't want to be one of them. You will end up with angry donors on your hands at tax time and probably fewer donors in future years.

The written acknowledgement or receipt from you to the donor must contain:

- the nonprofit's name
- the amount of the cash contribution
- the date of the contribution, and
- a statement that no goods or services were provided by the organization in return for the contribution, if that was the case.

If your nonprofit gives the donor goods or services in exchange for the contribution, it constitutes a quid pro quo contribution and there are other rules that apply. (See "Quid Pro Quo Contributions" below.)

It is not necessary to include either the donor's Social Security number or any other tax identification number on the acknowledgment (and for security reasons, it's best not to do so).

There are no IRS forms for this acknowledgment. You can use a letter, postcard, email, or any type of document as long as it contains all the above information. Here is an example of what a form letter from your organization might look like:

Dear Donor:

A Better World Charities gratefully acknowledges our receipt of your generous gift of cash in the amount of $_____ . We received your gift on _____[date]_____ .

No goods or services were provided to you in exchange for this donation.

Again, we thank you for your support.

Very truly yours,

Yolanda Allende

Yolanda Allende
Executive Director
A Better World Charities

(Please keep this receipt for your tax records; your canceled check alone is not sufficient.)

If a donor gives more than one donation of $250 or more during the year, you can give a separate acknowledgment for each donation, or you can do one acknowledgment—such as an annual summary—at the end of the tax year. In either case, make sure the amount and date of each contribution is clearly stated. If you do a single acknowledgment for multiple contributions from one donor, you must keep careful track of all the donations you receive from each donor during the year. There is fundraising software available that can help you do this. The website techsoup.org is an excellent resource for guidance on all kinds of nonprofit software.

Your donors will need the documentation for their donations by the time they are ready to file their taxes. Make sure you get it to them by then. Of course, you have no way of knowing when a donor will file his or her income tax return. However, the earliest a donor can file a tax return is February 1 of the year after the donation is made. Thus, you can be assured that your donors will receive the paperwork in time if you get it to them by January 31 of the year following their donation.

Payroll Deductions

Some donors make cash contributions through payroll deductions taken directly from their paychecks by their employers. Each payroll deduction of $250 or more is treated as a separate contribution for purposes of the $250 threshold requirement for written acknowledgments. Because payroll deductions are automatically withdrawn from earnings by the employer, there are different documentation requirements. The donor needs both of the following documents to serve as the written acknowledgment for each contribution:

- a pay stub, Form W-2, *Wage and Tax Statement*, or other document furnished by the employer listing the amount withheld by the employer and paid to the nonprofit, and
- a pledge card or letter from the nonprofit that includes a statement that the nonprofit does not provide goods or services in consideration for contributions by payroll deduction.

When you first receive a payroll deduction, send a pledge card or letter to the donor (not the employer) acknowledging receipt of the donation and stating that no goods or services were received in exchange for the donation. Then keep track of the donations—the date and amount of each—as they come in. At the end of the tax year, (or by February 1 of the following year—see "Contributions of $250 and More," above), give the donor a year-end statement that lists all the payroll deductions you received and includes the required statement that no goods or services were provided in exchange for the donations.

The best practice—particularly with gifts of more than $250—is to acknowledge them as soon as you receive them. That way, donors know you got their gift and don't have to follow up with you to make sure. You can also acknowledge and thank them for their support immediately. And, you aren't stuck with a year-end rush of preparing paperwork for all your donations at the same time.

> ### Even Nonprofit Presidents Need Written Acknowledgements of Donations
>
> The rules requiring a written acknowledgement of cash donations of $250 or more apply to everyone. Everyone means everyone, including a nonprofit's employees, officers, directors, and founders. Jolene Villareale, the co-founder and president of a ferret rescue organization, found this out the hard way. She made numerous cash donations to the nonprofit, but never asked for or received a written acknowledgment. The IRS denied her deductions for all of these undocumented contributions over $250. As a result, she lost over $10,000 in charitable deductions for the year. She was allowed to deduct her undocumented contributions under $250, but these amounted to only $2,393. (*Villareale v. Comm'r*, TC Memo. 2013-74).

Cash Gifts From IRAs

With the economy mired in recession, many donors don't have as much cash lying around to donate to their favorite charity as they used to. Indeed, many donors are experiencing difficulty in fulfilling pledges they have already made. You should know about an additional source of cash that some donors may have for donations—their individual retirement accounts (IRAs).

Many people have IRAs that they have been contributing to for years. Under normal tax rules, the owner of an IRA pays income tax on money he or she withdraws from a traditional IRA, even if it goes directly to a nonprofit. However, during the years 2008 through 2013 only, donors age 70½ or older can make cash contributions to nonprofits directly from their IRAs without paying any income tax on the amount withdrawn. This IRA charitable rollover provision has enabled many nonprofits to collect cash donations they might not otherwise have received, including pledges that donors made and then later satisfied with an IRA tax-free rollover. The charitable rollover rule applies only to IRAs and not other types of retirement plans. However, owners of ineligible plans, such as 401(k)s and Keoghs, can roll over money from these accounts into an IRA.

The IRA charitable rollover is particularly useful because—unlike tax deductions for charitable contributions—everyone who makes a charitable rollover can take advantage of the tax benefit. With charitable donations, you only get a tax benefit if you itemize your deductions (see "The Donor Side—Only Those Who Itemize Can Deduct," above). With the IRA charitable rollover, everyone gets the tax benefit—namely, not ever having to pay income tax on money that would normally be taxable income.

A donor who makes an IRA charitable rollover contribution doesn't get a tax deduction for the donation in addition to the tax-free withdrawal treatment. However, these contributions (up to a maximum of $100,000 per person per year) count toward the minimum annual withdrawals people 70½ and older must make each year from their IRAs.

To get tax-free treatment, the distribution from the IRA must be made directly to the nonprofit by the custodian of the IRA. If this rule is not followed, the transfer won't be tax free. The best procedure is for the IRA custodian to transfer the IRA rollover funds by check or electronic transfer directly to the nonprofit.

The donor must obtain a written acknowledgement for the contribution from the nonprofit. This is the same acknowledgement required for any cash donation of $250 or more as described above in "Contributions of $250 and More."

Unless the deduction is extended, IRA contributions made during 2014 or later will not be deductible. For other rules that apply to IRA charitable rollover contributions, see IRS Publication 590, *Individual Retirement Arrangements,* at the IRS website (www.irs.gov).

Interest-Free Loans

An interest-free loan to a nonprofit is treated as a gift of cash. IRS rules allow donors to lend up to $250,000 to any one nonprofit. However, if and when the nonprofit pays back the loan, the payments are taxable income to the donor-lender. Oftentimes, donors will lend money to a nonprofit and not require repayment for many years or will include a provision in their will forgiving the loan upon their death.

To make such a gift, the donor will often sign a promissory note—a document in which the donor-lender promises to pay money to the nonprofit under the terms set forth in the note. The donor can't start taking any deductions for the interest-free loan until he or she makes a payment to the nonprofit under the note. Then the donor can deduct only the amount that has been actually paid to the nonprofit. Simply signing and delivering a promissory note to a nonprofit does not result in a deductible contribution.

Quid Pro Quo Contributions

"Quid pro quo" is a famous Latin expression meaning "this for that." Charitable contributions often take the form of a quid pro quo—that is, a donor makes a donation to a nonprofit and receives goods or services from the nonprofit in exchange for the gift. For example, a nonprofit might offer tickets to the ballet in exchange for a donation of $1,000 or more. This is a quid pro quo exchange—cash for opera tickets—and the charitable contribution is the amount by which the donor's cash donation exceeds the fair market value of the opera tickets. If the ballet tickets are worth $100, then the donor can take a charitable deduction of $900.

Donors love quid pro quo contributions. Nonprofits are well aware of this and commonly offer quid pro quos to motivate donors to give. Typical items offered by nonprofits in exchange for donations to their organization include tickets to cultural, social, or sporting events; books and DVDs; travel deals; or items such as mugs, pens, tote bags, and T-shirts.

With a quid pro quo contribution, the donor can deduct the amount by which his or her contribution exceeds the fair market value of the goods or services received from the nonprofit. Donors must take the deduction in the year the donation is made, regardless of when they receive the goods or services from the nonprofit. And, it doesn't matter whether the donor actually uses the goods or services—donors can't deduct more if they don't use the baseball tickets they received or they don't attend the dinner banquet.

> **EXAMPLE:** On December 20, 2014, James pays the Washington Opera, a 501(c)(3) nonprofit, $400 for concert tickets with a fair market value of $100. The concert is scheduled for January 5, 2015. The gift is a quid pro quo contribution that James can deduct in 2014. Even though he ends up missing the performance, the amount he can deduct is $300—the amount his payment exceeded the fair value of the tickets.

To be a quid pro quo donation, the donor must intend to make a gift to the nonprofit; it can't be a simple purchase of goods or services. For example, if someone buys something at a charity thrift shop, it is not a quid pro quo contribution—even if the customer paid more than the item was worth. The transaction was intended as a purchase and sale and not a donation.

Disclosure Statements

Anytime your nonprofit gives a quid pro quo benefit to a donor in return for a donation of more than $75, your nonprofit must provide a written disclosure statement to the donor. Unlike with written acknowledge-ments for ordinary donations of $250 or more, the IRS can fine you if you don't give this statement to your donors. The penalty is $10 per contribution, up to a maximum of $5,000 per fundraising event or mail-ing. The only way to avoid the penalty is if you can show your failure to provide disclosure statements was due to reasonable cause.

The disclosure statement must:

- inform the donor that the deductible portion of his or her contribution is limited to the amount of any money (and the value of any property other than money) contributed by the donor over the fair market value of goods or services provided by the nonprofit, and
- provide the donor with a good faith estimate of the fair market value of the goods or services that the donor received.

You will need to determine the fair market value of any goods or services you give to donors in exchange for their donation. To make this determination, you have to decide what a willing buyer would pay a willing seller for the item. It is not your actual cost—a common mistake many nonprofits make. According to the IRS, nonprofits often mistakenly value items they receive for free at zero ($0). For example, if your nonprofit receives books for free and then turns around and gives them as a quid pro quo, a good faith estimate of the fair market value of the books is the market price for comparable books—not zero because you got the books for free.

You can use any reasonable method to estimate the fair market value of goods or services you provide to a donor, as long as you apply the method in good faith. If the same goods or services are commercially available, their cost in the marketplace would be a reasonable method of valuation. This can usually be ascertained fairly easily. If the item was donated by a business, ask the business to provide an invoice listing its cost.

> **EXAMPLE:** A local tennis pro offers to give a free one-hour lesson to the first person who contributes $500 to Acme Charities. The pro ordinarily charges $100 for one-hour lessons. A good faith estimate of the lesson's fair market value is $100.

Nonprofits sometimes provide donors with goods or services that are not commercially available. In this event, their value may be estimated by using the fair market value of similar or comparable goods or services.

EXAMPLE: For a payment of $10,000, a museum (the nonprofit donee) allows a donor to hold a private event at the museum. A good faith estimate of the fair market value of the right to hold the event in the museum can be made by using the cost of renting a hotel ballroom with a capacity, amenities, and atmosphere comparable to the museum room, even though the hotel ballroom lacks the unique art displayed in the museum room. If the hotel ballroom rents for $2,500, a good faith estimate of the fair market value of the right to hold the event in the museum is $2,500.

You can make the disclosure statement available to potential donors when you solicit gifts—for example, in a fundraising letter. Or, it can be given upon receipt of the quid pro quo contribution from the donor. If the former, you don't have to give another disclosure statement when you actually receive the contribution.

There is no IRS form for a disclosure statement. It can be in the form of a letter, receipt, postcard, email, statement on a printed ticket to an event, or just about any other written form. However, it must be made in a manner that is likely to come to the donor's attention—a disclosure in small print within a larger document might not meet this requirement.

EXAMPLE: The Poughkeepsie Food Bank sends a fundraising letter to potential donors promising two free tickets to the charity's annual dinner in return for contributions of $500 or more. The value of each ticket is $50. The fundraising letter provides: "In appreciation for a contribution of $500 or more, you will be given two free tickets to the Food Bank's annual dinner on March 1. The fair market value of each ticket is $50. You may be entitled to claim a tax deduction for the difference between the cash donated and the value of the tickets."

EXAMPLE: Sally donates $500 to the Orangutan Rescue Fund and receives two books worth $100 in return. The charity provides Sally with a disclosure statement in the form of a thank-you letter.

Dear Donor:

The Orangutan Rescue Fund gratefully acknowledges our receipt of your generous gift of cash in the amount of $500. In exchange for your contribution, we gave you two books with an estimated fair market value of $100.

You may be entitled to claim an income tax deduction for the difference between the cash donated and the value of the benefits you received.

Again, we thank you for your support.

Very truly yours,

Yolanda Allende

Yolanda Allende
Executive Director
Orangutan Rescue Fund

(Please keep this receipt for your tax records.)

Donations of less than $75. If your nonprofit gives a quid pro quo benefit to a donor in return for a donation of less than $75, you are not required to give the donor a disclosure statement. The donor's deduction is still limited to the amount the donor gave minus the fair market value of the benefit received in return (unless it falls within one of the exceptions discussed below). Although not required by law, your nonprofit should provide the donor with a thank-you letter, email, receipt, or other writing stating the value of the benefit.

EXAMPLE: Chandra donates $60 to the Puppetry Art Society and receives in return a pen that cost the charity $15. Chandra can deduct $45; the rest is a quid pro quo contribution. Although not required, the Puppetry Art Society sends her a thank-you note listing the cost of the pen. Chandra would have to follow the other documentation rules for donations under $250 discussed above in "Contributions of $250 and Less."

Exceptions to the Quid Pro Quo Rules

There are lots of things your nonprofit can give a donor without having to worry about the quid pro quo rules. The items discussed below are disregarded for IRS purposes—the donor can take them in return for a deductible contribution and doesn't need to report them or calculate their value for deduction purposes, and the donee nonprofit has no obligation to give any kind of acknowledgment or receipt to the donor.

Whenever you get a quid pro quo gift that doesn't need to be reported to the IRS, you should include a statement in your fundraising materials, such as:

"Under Internal Revenue Service guidelines, the estimated value of [*description of the benefits received*] is not substantial; therefore, the full amount of your payment is a deductible contribution."

No disclosure statement is required when a donor gives goods or services that fall within an exception to the quid pro quo rules. Instead, the contribution is treated as if the donee received no quid pro quo benefit. However, the donor must still follow the regular rules for contributions—it's just the quid pro quo benefit received from the nonprofit that is ignored. This means that if $250 or more is contributed, the donor must obtain a written acknowledgement from the nonprofit with the name of the nonprofit and amount of the donation. The acknowledgement doesn't need to mention that any benefits were provided to the donor or describe what they were. Instead, it should say that "no goods or services were provided in return for the contribution."

> **EXAMPLE:** Sid donates $350 to the Utah Grand Opera. In return, the charity gives him a yearlong subscription to its quarterly newsletter, which is not of commercial quality and therefore not a quid pro quo benefit. The Utah Grand Opera sends Sid the following thank-you letter:

Dear Donor:

The Utah Grand Opera gratefully acknowledges our receipt of your generous gift of cash in the amount of $350.

No goods or services were provided to you in exchange for this donation.

Again, we thank you for your support.

Very truly yours,

Yolanda Allende

Yolanda Allende
Executive Director
Utah Grand Opera

(Please keep this receipt for your tax records.)

Now let's look at what types of items are excepted from the quid pro quo rules. These are all circumstances where the IRS disregards the items or services given to a donee in connection with a contribution.

Token Items

Bookmarks, calendars, key chains, mugs, T-shirts, and similar items that bear your nonprofit's name or logo can be disregarded if they are given to donors as part of a fundraising campaign and:

- the item cost the nonprofit $10.20 or less, and
- the contribution received is $51 or more.

EXAMPLE: Save Our Kids, an inner city health clinic, sends its supporters a small calendar bearing its logo in return for a $250 contribution. The cost to produce and distribute the calendar is $1.50 per supporter. Because the cost of the calendar is below $9.70 and it was given in exchange for contributions over $51, it can be disregarded by both the donor and the donee.

These dollar figures are for 2013 and are adjusted for inflation each year. You can contact IRS Exempt Organizations Customer Account Services at 877-829-5500 for the latest figures.

If your nonprofit gives out numerous token items during the course of the year, then you must keep track of the total cost of the items you give each donor and make sure this total stays below $10.20. If you give items worth more than that amount to a single donor through multiple gifts in a year, then the quid pro quo rules apply and the donor will have to reduce the amount of his or her tax deduction by the value of the items received. Because of this rule, your nonprofit has to track all the gifts and token items it gives each contributor during the year. You can use fundraising software to help you with this task.

Low-Cost Items

As part of a fundraising campaign, nonprofits often send potential donors low-cost items that they didn't ask for in the hopes that it will encourage them to donate. These items can be disregarded if they cost the nonprofit $10.20 or less (adjusted for inflation each year).

> EXAMPLE: As part of a fundraising campaign, the Center for International Rights mails each potential contributor a packet of 20 return address labels containing the person's name, along with a solicitation letter requesting a donation. The packet has not been distributed at the potential contributors' request or with their consent. The solicitation states that the potential contributor may keep the packet whether or not a contribution is made. The cost of producing each packet is 75¢, well below the $10.20 limitation, so there is no reporting or acknowledgment obligation attached to it.

Other goods or services that you give donors in return for contributions can be disregarded if the item you give has a fair market value (not cost to you) of the lesser of:

- $102, or
- 2% of the amount of the contribution.

The 2% limit will exceed $102 only for contributions of $5,100 or more, so the percentage limit usually applies.

EXAMPLE: In return for contributions of $1,000, a nonprofit private high school gives its contributors a framed print of the school campus. The print has a fair market value of $10. The value of the print may be disregarded if it cost the school the lesser of $102 or $20 (2% of $1,000). It cost $10, so it can be disregarded.

Intangible Religious Benefits

If a donor receives intangible religious benefits in exchange for a charitable donation, these benefits are not considered quid pro quo contributions. Usually these are things that are not sold commercially, such as:

- admission to a religious ceremony
- wine, wafers, or other food or items provided as part of a religious ceremony
- pew rents, and
- a religious wedding or funeral service.

EXAMPLE: Temple Sinai charges its members and the general public $100 for a ticket to attend services at the synagogue on Yom Kippur. The payment is not a quid pro quo contribution; it is simply a fully deductible charitable contribution.

The documentation rules are different with intangible religious benefits. When a donor contributes $250 or more and receives intangible religious benefits, the nonprofit must state in its written acknowledgment to the donor that intangible religious benefits with no tax value were provided.

EXAMPLE: Sid pays Temple Sinai $300 for a ticket to attend services at the synagogue on Yom Kippur. The temple mails him a ticket with the following statement printed in large type:

> Thank you for your contribution of $300. The Sinai Temple furnished intangible religious benefits that need not be valued for tax purposes. You may claim the full value of your gift as a donation.

If the contribution is for less than $250, no acknowledgement is required from the nonprofit. But the donor must have a bank record or receipt or other written document from the nonprofit recording the name of the nonprofit, the date, and the amount of the donation. (See "Contributions of $250 and Less," above.)

Membership Benefits

Some nonprofits such as museums, libraries, and arts organizations use membership packages to build a following and base of support. Payments for membership packages are not quid pro quo contributions if they cost $75 or less each year and the benefits provided under the package are used frequently by members. Instead, the entire donation is considered a charitable contribution. Membership packages might include:

- free or discounted admission to the nonprofit's facilities or events
- free or discounted parking
- preferred access to goods or services
- discounts on the purchase of goods and services, and
- admission to members-only events if the nonprofit reasonably projects that the cost per person (excluding any allocated overhead) is not more than $10.20 (as adjusted for inflation each year).

EXAMPLE: The Milwaukee Performing Arts Center offers a basic annual membership package for $75. Benefits include the right to purchase tickets one week before they go on sale to the general public, free parking in the arts center garage during evening and weekend performances, and a 10% discount at its gift shop. There are approximately 50 productions at the performing arts center during the 12-month period. The center's gift shop is open for several hours during the week and during performances. The $75 fee for the membership package is not a quid pro quo contribution—the donor can treat the payment as a $75 cash donation and follow the applicable rules.

However, these rules apply only to frequently available benefits, not those that are available to members only once or a few times a year.

EXAMPLE: The Dayton Thespians, a community theater group in Dayton, Ohio, performs four different plays each summer and each play is performed twice. In return for a membership fee of $75, the theater offers a membership package that consists of free admission to any of its performances. Nonmembers may purchase tickets for $15 each on a performance-by-performance basis. Because the benefit provided admission to a limited number of performances, it is not a benefit that can be frequently exercised and, therefore, cannot be disregarded. Thus, the value of the benefit received must be subtracted from the $75 membership fee to determine the amount of a member's charitable contribution. The four tickets have a fair market value of $60, so a member who purchases a $75 membership may only deduct $15 as a charitable contribution.

Nonprofit Newsletters and Other Publications

Does your nonprofit provide a newsletter or other publication to donors? If so, you probably don't have to worry about the quid pro quo rules. This is because newsletters and other publications a nonprofit publishes and distributes to inform contributors about its activities are considered to have no value if they: (1) are not of commercial quality, and (2) are not available to the public through subscriptions or newsstands.

When is a newsletter or other publication of commercial quality? When the publication has articles that were paid for and accepts advertising. Professional journals are considered commercial quality publications.

EXAMPLE 1: The Southwest Folk Art Museum, a nonprofit museum in Tucson, sends a newsletter to all its patrons who made contributions of $250 or more. The primary purpose of the newsletter is to inform patrons about forthcoming art exhibits and lectures. It contains no commercial advertisements or articles, and is only available to people who made those contributions. The newsletter is treated as having no fair market value for tax purposes.

EXAMPLE 2: Assume that the museum upgrades the newsletter and includes high-quality photographs of artworks and articles and reviews written by experts, critics, historians, and art collectors. Announcements of art openings held in commercial art galleries are also included for a fee. The newsletter is printed on quality paper in a magazine format, and is sold to the general public in the museum's gift shop for $60 per year. The cost of producing the newsletter is $20. This newsletter is now a commercial quality publication with a fair market value of $60 per year. Thus, a person who makes a $100 donation and receives a one-year subscription may only deduct $40 as a charitable contribution to the museum.

Charity Auctions

Another common way for nonprofits to receive cash donations is through charity auctions. The nonprofit auctions off donated goods or services to the public and raises cash. For example, a nonprofit may hold an annual auction to sell artwork, appliances, electronics, and other items donated by local businesses or the public. Often, the items sold at the auctions go for prices at near, or below, their fair market value. Purchasers who pay more than an item is worth can claim a charitable deduction for the excess, as long as they can show that they knew the value of the item was less than the amount they paid for it.

Your nonprofit can encourage auction participants to pay more than the value of the auctioned items by making it easy for them to claim a charitable deduction. One way to do this is to give each person who attends the auction a catalog listing your good faith estimate of the fair market value of the items that will be available for bidding. Labels listing the estimated values could also be placed on the items. Assuming the donor has no reason to doubt the accuracy of the estimates, if he or she pays more than the estimated value, the difference between the amount paid and the estimated value is a charitable deduction.

Your nonprofit should provide every purchaser with a disclosure statement that states the estimated fair market value of the item sold to that person.

> **EXAMPLE:** Isaac pays $500 for an Apple iPod at a nonprofit auction held by Save the Bay Charities. Prior to the auction, Save the Bay gave Isaac and the other auction goers a catalog listing its estimate of the fair market value of the items available for bidding. The fair market value of the iPod was listed at $100, the amount it sold for at the Apple website. Isaac is entitled to a $400 charitable deduction. Save the Bay gives him the following receipt, which serves as a disclosure statement:

Isaac Allgood

Thank you for your purchase of auction item number 17, Apple iPod, for $500 in cash on September 23, 20xx. We estimate that the fair market value of this item is $100.

You may be entitled to claim an income tax deduction for the difference between the cash you paid and the value of the item.

Save the Bay Charities

Most nonprofits spend the bulk of their fundraising efforts seeking contributions of cash. This is understandable since it's both the easiest way to give and receive a donation. However, the vast majority of the world's wealth consists of property, not cash. Noncash property includes tangible things like cars, real estate, household goods, business inventory and equipment, clothing, jewelry and artwork, and intangible items like stocks and bonds. It shouldn't be surprising, then, that charitable contributions of property (called "noncash donations" by the IRS) are very popular. They are likely to become even more popular during tough economic times when people have less cash to give away.

Property donations can represent a great fundraising opportunity for your nonprofit. However, they can also present challenges that don't exist with donations of hard cash. For one thing, it can be hard to fairly value property donations for tax purposes. For another, it's easy (and tempting) for taxpayers to try to overvalue their property donations to get higher tax deductions. In fact, concern about these kinds of abuses has led the IRS to adopt tough new valuation rules for property donations. These rules make property donations much more complicated than cash contributions. Just how complicated depends on the type and value of the property being donated.

CAUTION

Your nonprofit doesn't have to accept property donations. Property donations can be more trouble than they are worth—for example, where an item has little or no value or is hard to resell. You also need to consider the costs involved in accepting, processing, and selling property donations. Your nonprofit never has to accept an offer of a property donation. Indeed, many nonprofits refuse to accept property donations, except for publicly traded stock. If you don't want to get involved with property donations, you can always ask donors to sell the property themselves and give you the cash. This is easy to do these days through websites such as eBay and Craigslist.

Establishing a Gift Acceptance Policy

The IRS advises nonprofits to adopt a formal written gift acceptance policy—a document explaining which types of gifts will and will not be accepted by your nonprofit, and describing any special acceptance procedures for certain types of gifts such as real estate. This may seem like overkill for a very small nonprofit, but is an excellent idea for most others. You can find several examples of gift acceptance policies on the Foundation Center website at www.foundationcenter.org. Take a look at several policies. They aren't all the same. What yours should include depends on your nonprofit's particular circumstances—for example, whether you have the expertise and desire to deal with hard-to-sell items like nonpublicly traded stock, or unusual or specialized items such as vacation time-shares.

Annual Deduction Limit for Property Donations

There are overall limits on how much donors can deduct each year for charitable contributions (see "Annual Limits on Charitable Deductions," in Chapter 5). These limits are generous and only donors who make extremely large donations relative to their incomes would be affected by them. The overall annual limit for all of a donor's charitable contributions combined—cash and all forms of property—is 50% of the donor's adjusted gross income ("AGI") for the year. However, a different 30% limit applies to contributions of long-term capital gain property.

Long-Term Capital Gain Property

Many property gifts to charitable organizations are gifts of long-term capital gain property (also referred to simply as capital gain property). Long-term capital gain property is capital gain property (see "Capital

Gain Property," below) owned for one year or longer before it is donated, sold, or otherwise disposed of.

Capital Gain Property

The term "capital gain property" can be confusing. First of all, it refers only to property, not cash. Capital gain property is any capital asset that has increased in value since it was created or acquired. So what's a capital asset? Capital assets include all the property a person or business owns except for: business inventory (property held for sale to customers), business equipment and other property used in business that is owned for over one year, and a few other items. So, most everything an individual owns is a capital asset—for example, vehicles, household furnishings, a home occupied by the individual, coin or stamp collections, jewelry, gold, and silver.

There are special rules for artistic works like paintings, books, and inventions. Such works are not capital assets while owned by their creators; but they are capital assets when they are acquired by someone else.

Donors can deduct the full fair market value of gifts of long-term capital gain property in a single year only if the total value of the gifts is less than 30% of the donor's AGI for the year. If the property is worth more than this, the excess can be deducted over the following five years.

> EXAMPLE: Jean purchased stock for $10,000 in 1990 that has a fair market value of $40,000 in 2014. She decides to donate the stock to the United Way. Her AGI that year is $50,000. The stock is long-term capital gain property and is thus subject to the 30% of AGI annual deduction limit. As a result, Jean can deduct $15,000 of the stock's value in 2014 (30% × $50,000 AGI = $15,000) and deduct the remaining $25,000 over the next five years.

Many donors are unaware of the 30% limit for long-term capital gain property donations. Thus, someone considering making a substantial property donation may be counting on a much larger deduction than he or she will actually get in the current year. To avoid having disappointed donors on your hands, you should always let them know of these limits whenever you are about to receive a large property donation.

There is one exception to the 30% AGI limit for long-term capital gain property donations: It does not apply if a donor elects to deduct only the cost of the property instead of its full fair market value. In this event, the property is treated the same as gifts of short-term capital gain property.

Ordinary Income and Short-Term Capital Gain Property

The 30% of AGI limitation for gifts of long-term capital gain property does not apply to gifts of short-term capital gain property (capital gain property owned less than one year) or ordinary income property (inventory, works of art, or manuscripts created by the donor). Instead, these donations are subject to the 50% of AGI overall annual limit for donations.

Why is the tax law more generous for these contributions? Because the charitable deduction for this type of property is limited to the cost of the property (its "basis" in tax parlance), not its fair market value. Thus, the donor gets no deduction for any appreciation the property enjoyed. With most other property donations, donors can deduct the fair market value. (See "Basic Valuation Rule: Fair Market Value," below.) Thus, these gifts are usually worth less to the donor.

> **EXAMPLE:** Patty donates stock she owned for five months to her church. She paid $800 for the stock but its fair market value on the day she donated it is $1,000. The stock is short-term capital gain property, so she can only deduct what she paid for it—$800.

Valuing Property Donations— An Art, Not a Science

The value of most property donations is the item's fair market value on the day of the donation, not its original cost. Thus, the challenge with property donations is determining the item's fair market value. In the past, many taxpayers overvalued their donations and took charitable deductions far in excess of what their donated property was actually worth. This cost the government billions of dollars in income taxes. To prevent these kinds of abuses, the IRS cracked down on many types of property contributions and adopted a series of rules for valuing different kinds of property, such as vehicles, stock, and clothing. These rules are intended to fit the different circumstances and risks for valuation abuses by donors associated with each.

Even though as a nonprofit you aren't responsible for valuing donated property, it's important that you understand these rules if you accept property donations.

Your Nonprofit's Role in Determining Value

It is the donor's responsibility to determine the value of donated property—not the nonprofit's. A nonprofit should not get involved in giving estimates or values for donated property. It's a no-win situation. If the donor thinks your estimate is too low, he or she may decide it's not worth making the donation. If it's high, the IRS could question it later and you could end up with an unhappy donor who is in trouble with the IRS.

Any problem that develops with donated property valuations will always be between the donor and the IRS. It would most likely come up during an audit of the donor. If the IRS found that a property valuation was too high (and the corresponding charitable deduction amount was too much), the IRS could require the donor to pay back taxes, interest, and penalties. You don't want your donors getting into trouble with the IRS over donations to your organization. It pays to know the rules and help your donors understand how the valuation process works. You can also help by referring them to resources for property valuations (discussed below).

Basic Valuation Rule: Fair Market Value

With cash donations, valuation isn't an issue. Donors always get to deduct the amount of cash they contribute. With property donations, it's different because there isn't always an easily ascertainable value for the property being donated. How much is an old computer worth, or an antique clock, or a conservation easement? The IRS has developed rules to address both how to value different types of property donations and how much a donor can deduct.

The basic rule is that a donor may deduct no more than the property's "fair market value" at the time of the donation. But fair market value can be a tricky thing. For IRS purposes, it means the amount that a "willing buyer would pay and a willing seller would accept for the property, when neither party is compelled to buy or sell, and both parties have reasonable knowledge of the relevant facts." In other words, it's a fair price—not too high and not too low.

For property donations of under $5,000, the donor can determine the fair market value him- or herself and no appraisal is required. The IRS recommends that the donor consider all relevant factors, including:

- the item's cost or selling price
- sales of comparable items
- the item's replacement cost, and
- an expert opinion.

> **EXAMPLE:** Joe donates a one-year-old Macintosh portable computer to his church. He paid $1,500 for it new, but he knows it's worth much less than that because of its age. He looks at sales of comparable computers on eBay and finds that the average price similar computers are going for is $500. He decides this is its fair market value for tax purposes.

IRS Publication 561, *Determining the Value of Donated Property,* gives a good explanation how these factors should be used to determine an item's fair market value. You can refer donors to this publication, which can be downloaded from the IRS website at www.irs.gov.

For any property donations worth $5,000 or more, the donor must obtain a formal appraisal from a qualified appraiser. The only exception is for marketable securities, because they have a clear market value. (See "Property Valued at $5,000 or More," below.)

The IRS has created special rules for valuing certain types of property, including clothing, vehicles, easements, and short-term capital gain property. In some cases, this was because the regular fair market value rules are difficult to apply. In others, it was because taxpayers engaged in widespread overvaluation for that type of property. We discuss the rules for these and some of the other more commonly donated items below.

Different Types of Property Donations

Any nonprofit that accepts property donations should have a basic understanding of the IRS valuation, documentation, and reporting rules—particularly for the more commonly donated property items like clothing, furniture, and vehicles. We cover those basics—and more. However, we don't cover the rules for every possible property donation item you might receive. If you need more information on IRS rules on property donations, see IRS Publication 561, *Determining the Value of Donated Property.*

Clothing and Household Items

The most commonly donated property items are clothing and house-hold items. Household items include furniture, furnishings, electronics, appliances, linens, and other similar items. Things that are not considered household items include food, artwork and other art objects, antiques, jewelry, gems, and collectibles. Valuation abuses by taxpayers have been particularly widespread for donations of clothing and household items. In many cases, people donated used items that were worthless or nearly worthless and valued them for tax purposes as if they were new. To prevent this, the IRS tightened the rules on valuing household donations in 2005.

The first new restriction for any donated clothing or household items is that the items must be in "good used condition or better." If they are not, the donor cannot take a tax deduction for the donation. The IRS provides no guidelines for determining what constitutes "good used condition or better." However, some nonprofits have guidelines that describe what they will and will not accept and these can be helpful for providing guidance on what the IRS might consider acceptable. For example, the Salvation Army says it does not want torn, dirty, or broken items; Goodwill Industries advises "If you would give it to a relative or friend, then the item is most likely in good condition and is appropriate to donate." Your nonprofit should follow these examples and not accept items that are in poor condition.

The tax law contains an exception to the good used condition requirement for any *single* item of clothing or *single* household item that is worth $500 or more. If a donor gives such an item, it can be in less than good used condition. However, the donor must have a qualified appraisal of the item's value and must file IRS Form 8283, *Noncash Charitable Contributions,* with his or her tax return.

> **EXAMPLE:** Caroline donates a vintage French designer ball gown that belonged to her mother to her local symphony orchestra. The gown is over 30 years old and is in poor condition. Caroline hires an appraiser who determines that the rare item is worth $2,000, despite its poor condition. Caroline may deduct this amount, provided that she files Form 8283 with her tax return.

In addition to the requirement that clothing or household items be in good used condition, a donor must also obtain a receipt from the nonprofit that includes a written description of the donated property (not the value). (See "Documenting Property Donations," below.) It's a good idea for donors to photograph any items they donate as additional proof of their condition in case any questions come up later with the IRS.

Although you don't want to be the one actually doing the valuation of property, you can recommend that donors use one or more of the following resources to help them determine their property's fair market value:

Online valuation guides. Several well-known nonprofits have created value guides for clothing and household goods. It's hard to imagine that the IRS would complain if a donor used one of these guides. They can be found at the following websites (the Salvation Army guide is the most detailed):

- Salvation Army Donation Value Guide: http://satruck.org/donation-value-guide, and
- Goodwill Industries Donation Valuation Guide: www.goodwill.org/wp-content/uploads/2010/12/Donation_Valuation_Guide.pdf.

Tax software. Tax-preparation software, including H&R Block's *TaxCut* and Intuit's *TurboTax*, can provide donors with estimated values for clothing and other household goods based on the condition of each item. There are also two specialized software programs taxpayers can use to determine the fair market value of used property: *ItsDeductible* from Intuit (www.itsdeductible.com), and *DeductionPro* from H&R Block (www.hrblock.com). The donor describes the item being donated and the program gives an estimate of its value based on surveys of thrift store sales and online auctions. A comparison of the results obtained using these programs and the price guides created by nonprofits found that the software usually gives higher valuations.

Websites. There is also a subscription website called www.nonprofit deductions.com that provides values for clothing and household items and allows donors to keep track of all their donations during the year and print out an annual summary.

Past sales of similar items. Prices obtained in the past for the sale of similar items are always a good indicator of value. Good evidence of value would be the price at which similar items are sold in thrift stores, such as Salvation Army Family Stores and Goodwill Industries. Online auction sites, such as eBay, can also provide guidance on what used items are worth. The donor may simply check to see what similar items have sold for and could use the average price of a few recent sales.

Vehicles—Used Cars, Boats, and Aircraft

Vehicles have their own set of rules—different from other property donations. Historically, they have been a very popular donation item, which was in large part because, under the old rules, a taxpayer could donate a used car to a nonprofit and deduct whatever he or she claimed was the vehicle's fair market value. Hundreds of thousands of taxpayers donated vehicles and then grossly inflated the value to get larger tax deductions. In one case, a taxpayer claimed a $2,915 deduction for a 1980 Mercury station wagon that was ultimately sold for $30 by the nonprofit it was donated to. The IRS figured it was losing hundreds of millions of dollars every year because of these kinds of abuses.

In 2005, the rules changed. Under the new IRS rules, if a person donates a used car to a nonprofit and claims a deduction greater than $500, his or her charitable deduction is limited to the amount the nonprofit receives when it sells the car. Thus, the owner of the Mercury station wagon mentioned above would get a $30 deduction today. The nonprofit must document the sales price by providing the donor with IRS Form 1098-C, *Contributions of Motor Vehicles, Boats, and Airplanes* (see "Documentation Rules for Cars, Boats, and Airplanes," below). These rules apply not only to cars, but also to SUVs, trucks, motorcycles, boats, airplanes, and any motor vehicle manufactured primarily for use on public roads.

Since these new rules have been in effect, vehicle donations to nonprofits have plummeted: In 2005, the number of people claiming charitable deductions for automobiles dropped to under 300,000, a two-thirds reduction from the prior year. Donations of higher-value cars (those worth over $500) have dropped the most. Overall, the total amount deducted for car donations dropped from $2.4 billion in 2004 to just $470 million in 2005, a decline of over 80%. Auto donations have declined even more in recent years because people are holding on to their old cars instead of buying new ones.

Typically, nonprofits do not sell donated vehicles themselves. Instead, they contract with a broker (also called a liquidator) to manage the sale. There are many for-profit businesses and nonprofit organizations that act as brokers in return for a percentage of the vehicle's sales price. The vehicle is either sold to the public at a wholesale auction or to a used car dealer for a flat rate—often as little as $75 per car. Either way, it usually sells for far less than its retail value—and donors are stuck with that amount as their charitable deduction.

Using Brokers to Manage Vehicle Donations

Using a broker to manage the sale of donated vehicles is convenient and easy, but comes at a price. The convenience: the broker will pick up the car (including nonoperational vehicles), arrange for the sale, and handle all the paperwork. The price: The broker takes a percentage of the sales proceeds. For example, if a car sells at auction for $1,000, the auction company receives 25%—$250—and the broker will receive 25% to 45% of the remaining $750. So, at most, the charity will get about $550.

If you do use a broker, make sure it is reputable—there are many horror stories about unscrupulous brokers who cheat charities. Ask for and check references. The broker's percentage of the sales price received for the donated vehicles should be reasonable—no more than 25% to 30%.

Also, it's important to understand that your nonprofit cannot simply grant a for-profit broker the right to use its name to solicit donations of used vehicles. A charity cannot license its right to receive tax-deductible contributions. For a vehicle donation to be deductible, the broker must act as your nonprofit's agent. This means that the broker is acting under your nonprofit's direction and control and your nonprofit is ultimately responsible for everything it does.

You should sign a contract with the broker giving your nonprofit the right to review all contracts; establish rules of conduct; choose or change auction companies, car dealers, and towing companies; approve of or change advertising; and examine the broker's books and records. You should actively monitor the process—for example, make sure the broker tells donors how much of the sales proceeds will go to your nonprofit.

Nonprofits that sell donated vehicles themselves usually get more money and the donor gets a better deduction. You should let donors know how you handle donated vehicles so they can make an informed choice about their vehicle donation. The Salvation Army, which conducts online auctions of donated vehicles every month, includes the following information on its website:

> If your vehicle is operable, it will be auctioned at the monthly Salvation Army online auction. It typically results in a much higher sale price for vehicles compared to sales at conventional car auctions. The price it sells for at auction will determine the amount of your tax deduction, according to new IRS rules.

Exceptions to the vehicle deduction rules. There are three exceptions to the deduction rules for vehicles. If one of these exceptions applies, the donor may deduct the vehicle's fair market value as shown in a used vehicle pricing guide, such as the *Kelley Blue Book*. (However, the value cannot exceed the private party sales price listed in the guide.) Except where the car is an old clunker worth $500 or less, this will usually give the donor a much larger deduction than using the actual selling price for the vehicle. Make sure potential donors know this.

If a donor is relying on any of these exceptions, your nonprofit will have to give a written acknowledgement within 30 days of receiving the vehicle that includes a statement about what you intend to do with the vehicle, such as improvements or actual use. (See "Documentation Rules for Cars, Boats, and Airplanes," below.)

Exception 1. Deductions of $500 or less. If a donor is claiming a deduction of $500 or less for a donated vehicle, then the vehicle's valuation does not need to be based on the sales price. Instead, the taxpayer may deduct the smaller of $500, or the vehicle's fair market value on the date of the donation.

EXAMPLE: Bill donates a Yugo he purchased 15 years ago to a local nonprofit. The car's fair market value according the *Kelley Blue Book* is $100. Bill may deduct this amount even if the nonprofit later sells the car for only $10.

Exception 2: Vehicle used or improved by nonprofit. A donor may deduct a vehicle's fair market value at the time of the donation (as opposed to its sales price) if the nonprofit makes a "significant intervening use of or material improvement to" the vehicle before selling it. "Significant intervening use" means that the nonprofit uses the car on a regular basis as part of its regular activities.

> **EXAMPLE:** Homeward Bound, a nonprofit that delivers meals to the needy, receives a donation of a used van with a fair market value of $1,000. Homeward Bound uses the van to deliver meals every day for one year and then sells it for $400. This use qualifies as a "significant intervening use" because it significantly and substantially furthers the nonprofit's regularly conducted activity of delivering meals to needy people. The donor can deduct the $1,000 fair market price instead of the sales price.

A "material improvement" is a major repair or improvement made by the nonprofit (and not paid for by the donor) that significantly increases the vehicle's value. Material improvements do not include cleaning, minor repairs, routine maintenance, painting, removal of dents or scratches, cleaning or repair of upholstery, or installation of theft deterrent devices.

> **EXAMPLE:** Save Our Streets receives a donation of a used Ferrari race car with a fair market value of $8,000. It pays to have a new, more powerful, engine installed and then sells the car at auction for $12,000. This qualifies as a material improvement because the Ferrari was worth substantially more with the new, improved engine. The donor can deduct $8,000—not the sales price Save Our Streets received after making the improvement.

Exception 3: Vehicle given or sold to needy person. A donor can deduct a vehicle's fair market value at the time of the donation if the nonprofit intends to give it to a needy person, or sells it directly to a needy person for a price well below fair market value. The vehicle can't be sold at an auction. For this exception to apply, one of the nonprofit's purposes must be to help the poor or underprivileged who need transportation.

EXAMPLE: Carla donates her 2001 Toyota Corolla to the nonprofit Let's Go, whose mission is to help the poor get to work by providing them with low-cost transportation. Let's Go sells the car for $1,000 to Gene, one of its poor clients in need of transportation. The car has a fair market value of $10,000. Carla may deduct $10,000 because the car was given to a needy client.

Deductible Amount for Charitable Contributions of Vehicles		
Claimed value of $500 or less	Claimed value of over $500	
	General rule	Exceptions
Lesser of fair market value or $500.	Proceeds from sale (unless an exception applies).	Fair market value at the time of donation if the nonprofit intends to: • make significant use of vehicle • make material improvement to vehicle, or • give or sell the vehicle to a needy individual in direct furtherance of the nonprofit's charitable purpose.

Stock and Other Securities

Gifts of stock and other securities are a popular way to give to nonprofits, although with the recent decline in the stock market, there may not be as many of these donations as there have been in the past. Gifts of securities include not only publicly traded stocks like Microsoft or Wal-Mart, but also gifts of mutual funds, Treasury bills and notes, corporate and municipal bonds, and stock in nonpublicly held companies.

One reason gifts of publicly traded stock are popular with both donors and nonprofits, is that they don't present difficult valuation issues as with clothing or vehicles. Instead the main issue is how much the donor can deduct. The relatively simple rules covering this have a huge impact on why and when stock donations are made.

Stocks owned for more than one year. There are very favorable tax rules for donors who want to donate long-term stock (stock they have owned for more than one year) that has appreciated in value. Basically, the donor never has to pay capital gains on the appreciated stock. This can be a tremendous tax benefit and great incentive for donors to give stock to nonprofits.

Here's how it works: If someone owns stock for more than one year that has gone up in value, that person can donate the stock to a nonprofit, get a deduction equal to the fair market value of the stock at the time of the transfer (its increased value), and never pay capital gains tax on the appreciated value of the stock. The nonprofit will never owe that capital gains tax either. It can take the stock and either sell it right away and not pay any tax, or it can hold on to it—but it will never owe capital gains tax on the appreciated value the donor realized.

EXAMPLE: Ari owns 1,000 shares of Evergreen stock, which is traded on the New York Stock Exchange. He paid $1,000 for the shares back in 1995 and they are worth $10,000 today. He gives the stock to his favorite nonprofit, the Red Cross, and deducts its $10,000 fair market value as a charitable contribution. Ari need not pay the 15% capital gains tax on the $9,000 gain in the value of his stock. The Red Cross sells the stock and pays no taxes on the $10,000 it receives. Had Ari sold the stock he would have had to pay a $1,350 long-term capital gains tax on his $9,000 profit (15% × $9,000 = $1,350). This would have left him only $8,650 from the stock sale to donate to the nonprofit.

Make Sure Donors Know About Tax Benefits of Stock Donations

Most donors are unaware of the tax benefits of donating appreciated securities, other than the deduction for a charitable gift. Over two-thirds of those responding to a recent survey by Fidelity Investments didn't know that giving long-term appreciated stock to a nonprofit could avoid the 15% capital gains tax on the sale of such securities.

Many nonprofits use their websites to educate potential donors about the benefits of stock donations. Here is an example of a notice regarding such gifts from one nonprofit's website:

> **Gifts of Appreciated Assets:** Did you know that a direct transfer of appreciated stock is a good way to make a gift to your favorite non-profit? The donor avoids paying capital gains taxes on the stock and may also take a charitable deduction for its present market value.... Speak with your own broker or call us for instructions on how to make a gift of appreciated stock.

It's extremely easy for donors to give stocks and other securities that are marketable—that is, are sold to the public on stock exchanges or over-the-counter markets. No matter how large the donation, there is no need to obtain an appraisal. The value is simply based on what the stock or other security sold for on the exchange on the day of the donation (the average price between the highest and lowest quoted selling prices on the donation day is used).

Stocks that have gone down in value. These rules don't work as well in the case of a donor who owns stock that has gone down in value. The tax benefit of never paying capital gains on the appreciated value of the stock doesn't apply because there is no capital gain. In this situation, it is better for the donor to sell the stock, give the sales proceeds to the nonprofit, and deduct the loss. The donor can use the loss to offset gains he or she had from the sale of other capital assets during the year. In addition, taxpayers can deduct up to $3,000 in capital losses each year from ordinary income (such as salary income, interest, and dividends).

Any remainder can be carried forward and deducted in future years. So donors can potentially benefit by realizing the loss instead of simply giving the stock to a nonprofit where there is no tax benefit.

> **EXAMPLE:** Assume that Ari's Evergreen stock is worth only $100. He has lost $900 on his investment. He sells the stock and gives the $100 proceeds to a nonprofit, Building Bridges for Justice. He then deducts his $900 loss as a capital loss for the year (he has no other capital gains or losses for the year). He's in the 28% tax bracket, so this saves him $252 in income tax. Had Ari given the stock to a nonprofit instead of selling it, he would have had no capital loss deduction. Instead, he would have been able to deduct only the $100 fair market value of the stock.

With today's declining stock market, many potential donors own stocks on which they have lost money. Now might be the time to aggressively inform potential donors of the tax benefits of dumping their losing stocks and using the tax savings to donate to your nonprofit. Some nonprofits include detailed statements on their websites explaining the benefits of tax loss harvesting. Here's an example of what one nonprofit posts on its website:

> **Giving Property That Has Depreciated or Dropped in Value**
>
> If you have stock or other property that has decreased in value, you will normally save more in taxes by selling it and giving the proceeds to a charity. You may then be able to claim a capital loss on your tax return. You can also deduct the cash proceeds you give as a charitable gift. This can result in tax deductions that amount to more than the current value of the asset. The tax deduction for gifts of depreciated property will be based on the current value, not what you originally paid for it.

Stocks owned for less than one year. The rules for donating short-term stock (stock owned for less than one year) are different than the rules for long-term stock. With short-term stock, donors must reduce the amount of their charitable contribution by the amount of their short-term capital gain. In effect, this means that the donor's charitable contribution is limited to the original cost of the property, instead of its fair market value at the time of the donation.

> **EXAMPLE:** Sally purchases 1,000 shares of Blue Horizon, Inc., on February 1 for $50,000. By December 1 of that year, the stock is worth $70,000. She decides to donate the shares to her favorite nonprofit animal rights group. Because she owned the shares for less than one year, she can only claim a $50,000 charitable contribution.

Mechanics of Transferring Stocks to a Nonprofit

Publicly traded stocks and securities are usually bought and sold through brokerage companies. Most transfers are done electronically by brokerage companies. To receive electronic transfers, your nonprofit will need to set up one (or more) brokerage accounts. Setting up such an account is easy.

Alternatively, a donor who possesses a physical stock certificate can transfer it by delivering it to you by mail or by hand. In this event, the best practice is for the donor to mail (or deliver) an unsigned stock certificate and provide the necessary endorsement by signing a blank "stock power"—that is, a power of attorney enabling someone other than the owner to transfer ownership of the stock. For security reasons, it's wise for the donor to use registered or certified mail to send the certificate and mail the stock power in a separate envelope.

Nonmarketable securities. Nonmarketable securities are securities that are not sold to the public on stock exchanges—for example, the stock in a corporation owned by a family that runs a small business. If the claimed value of this property is greater than $10,000, it must be appraised by a qualified appraiser. (See "Property Valued at $5,000 or More," below.) This kind of gift can be very problematic for your nonprofit because this stock can be very hard to sell.

United States Savings Bonds. A person may not directly donate United States Savings Bonds to a nonprofit, such as Series EE or Series I bonds, because they are not transferable. Instead, the bond owner must redeem the bonds (cash them in) and give the cash to the nonprofit or use the cash to have new bonds registered in the nonprofit's name. Either way, the donor will have to pay income tax on the accrued interest earned on the bonds. As a result, this is not an attractive type of charitable gift. A donor is better off giving appreciated stock or real estate since he or she can usually deduct the entire fair market value of the gift without paying tax on the long-term capital gain from the property's increase in value. However, significant tax benefits are possible where a donor makes a charitable bequest of savings bonds in his or her will. Donors should seek professional advice for this type of gift.

Real Estate

Gifts of real estate usually involve substantial amounts of money and can be complex. They can also be fraught with peril for nonprofits. Some nonprofits have lost money on gifts of real estate—for example, where the property was hard to resell and expensive to keep. For these reasons, your nonprofit will probably want to obtain professional advice before accepting a gift of real estate.

TIP

Donating a vacation home for a fundraiser doesn't entitle the donor to a deduction. A popular auction item is to have someone donate their vacation home and auction it off at a fundraiser. It can raise a lot of money for your nonprofit, but it doesn't result in a tax deduction for the donor. Unfortunately, the owner of real property gets no deduction at all if he or she donates the right to use the property rent-free.

EXAMPLE: Ernie owns a three-bedroom cabin in Lake Tahoe. He donates the free use of the cabin for one week to a local nonprofit that auctions it off to the public as part of a fundraising effort. Ernie gets no tax deduction for donating the use of his cabin.

Should You Accept Gifts of Underwater Homes?

With the collapse of the real estate market, millions of Americans own homes that are worth less than the amount of their mortgages. A homeowner who donates this property to charity gets no deduction, because there is no equity. But some homeowners may offer to donate homes simply as a way to get rid of them and avoid foreclosure.

Should your nonprofit accept such a gift? Probably not. If you sell it, you'll get nothing because the mortgage must be paid off before any money goes to your nonprofit. If you rent it, you'll earn a profit only if the rent you receive is more than the cost of the mortgage, taxes, and other costs of maintaining the property. Moreover, your nonprofit will probably have to pay taxes on at least some of the rental income. Of course, the property may go up in value in future years—but don't count on it.

Art, Antiques, Collectibles, and Unusual Gifts

Donating property like art, antiques, and jewelry, or collectibles like coins, stamps, and rare books can be advantageous tax-wise for the donor. However, because there is always a strong temptation for a donor to overvalue these gifts, special tax rules apply. Some of the rules adopted in recent years have had the effect of discouraging these kinds of donations. If you have a donor who wants to donate any such property, you should recommend that they check the rules or consult with a professional. IRS Publication 561, *Determining the Value of Donated Property*, contains a thorough discussion of these rules.

Appreciated Property—The Related Use Rule

Most tangible property that people donate to nonprofits, such as used clothing or cars, is ordinarily worth much less than what the donor originally paid for it. However, this is generally not the case for art, antiques, collectibles such as stamps and coins, and similar items.

Typically, these items have appreciated—that is, gone up in value—since the donor acquired them.

Donations of appreciated property can be particularly attractive for donors because they not only get a charitable deduction, they also avoid having to pay any tax on the amount the property rose in value while they owned it—the "capital gain." Ordinarily, capital gains on property such as art and antiques are taxed at a particularly high rate—28% under current law.

However, donations of appreciated personal property held more than one year (long-term capital gain property) are subject to a special valuation rule called the "related use" rule. Under this rule, the amount of the donor's deduction depends on how the nonprofit uses the property. If the property is used for the nonprofit's exempt purposes for at least three years, the donor may deduct the property's fair market value at the time it was donated—a highly advantageous result because it maximizes the donor's deduction.

> **EXAMPLE:** Sam purchased a rare first edition of Charles Darwin's book, *On the Origin of Species,* for $25,000. Thirty years later, when he donates it to Goniff College for their rare book collection, it is worth $100,000. Sam may deduct $100,000, the book's fair market value, and he doesn't have to pay capital gains tax on the $75,000 in value the book gained while he owned it.

However, if the nonprofit uses the property in a way that is not related to its tax-exempt purpose, the donor's deductible contribution is limited to the property's cost basis—that is, what the donor originally paid for it. One type of unrelated use is if the nonprofit sells the item within three years, even if it spends the cash it receives for its exempt purposes.

> **EXAMPLE:** Assume that Goniff College, from the above example, sells the book that was donated one year later and uses the money to help support its library programs. The use is considered unrelated to the college's exempt purposes because the book was sold for cash. Thus, Sam may deduct only what the book originally cost him—$25,000.

As you can see, all of the appreciated value of the donated item is lost as a charitable deduction if the related use rule is not satisfied. Thus, a donor who owns appreciated personal property benefits most if the donated item is used (and not sold) by a nonprofit for its exempt purposes for at least three years. The broader your nonprofit's charitable purposes, the more "related uses" you'll be able to find for gifts of personal property. For example, a museum, university, library, or historical society could probably put a painting to a related use since display of the painting would further their broad educational purposes. However, a nonprofit whose mission is to help the homeless would have trouble finding a related use for such property.

Make sure to discuss with donors how your nonprofit intends to make use of a contemplated donation of appreciated property. You should also provide the donor with a written acceptance stating that it is a qualified public nonprofit, and that its intended use of the donation satisfies the related use rule. If the property is claimed to be worth more than $5,000, the donor will have to file IRS Form 8283, *Noncash Charitable Contributions*, and you will have to sign the form and indicate whether you intend to use the property for a related use (see "IRS Form 8283, Section B," below.)

When the Donor Sells the Property

What happens if a donor deducts the fair market value of an item in the belief that it would be used for an exempt purpose by the nonprofit, but the nonprofit later sells the property or stops using it for an exempt purpose? This presents no problem if the deduction claimed by the donor was $5,000 or less. However, if:

- the deduction was for more than $5,000, and
- the nonprofit sells the property any time within three years after the date of the donation,

then the donor might have to pay tax on the difference between the deduction taken and the property's cost basis—a process called recapture.

EXAMPLE: Assume that Goniff College, from the examples above, displays Sam's gift of a copy of *On the Origin of Species* for one year and then sells it to a rare book collector. Sam might have to add $75,000 to his income for the year he took his charitable deduction and pay tax on it.

Fortunately for donors, such recapture can be—and usually is—avoided if the nonprofit certifies in writing that it used the property for an exempt purpose prior to its sale or other disposition, or it intended to use it for an exempt purpose at the time of the donation but it became impossible or infeasible to implement this intent. This certification is made by the nonprofit filing IRS Form 8282, *Donee Information Return*, and giving a copy to the donor. (See "When a Nonprofit Sells Donated Property—IRS Form 8282," below.)

EXAMPLE: Assume that Goniff College files Form 8282 with the IRS certifying that it used *On the Origin of Species* to further its educational purpose prior to its sale and gives a copy to Sam. Sam can keep his full $100,000 charitable deduction and the recapture rules do not apply.

Gifts of Property Owned Less Than One Year

The charitable deduction for tangible appreciated personal property owned by the donor for less than one year (short-term capital gain property) is always limited to the property's original cost.

EXAMPLE: Assume that Sam acquired another copy of *On the Origin of Species* in February of 2012 for $95,000 and donated it to Goniff College in December 2012 when its value had gone up to $100,000. His deduction is limited to what he paid for the book in February, even though it increased in value by $5,000 over this time period.

Property That Has Declined in Value

If a donor gives property that has declined in value since he or she purchased it, his or her deduction is limited to the property's fair market value on the date of the donation, not its original cost. Unlike with stocks and other investment property, donors of personal use property, such as art, jewelry, and antiques, do not get a potential tax benefit by selling the property at a loss and then donating the proceeds to charity. Why? Because losses for personal use property are not deductible.

Donor-Created Property

A donor who created the property being donated may only deduct the cost incurred in creating the property, not its fair market value. The value of the donor's time is not included in this calculation, only the cost of the materials and other direct costs. This would ordinarily amount to very little. As a result, artists have no tax incentive to donate their works to a nonprofit. It's a good idea to make sure an artist understands this before accepting a donation of valuable donor-created art.

> **EXAMPLE:** Marketa, a well-known painter, creates a new painting and donates it to an art museum. Ordinarily, this type of painting would be worth $100,000 on the art market. However, Marketa may only deduct the cost of the canvas, paints, and any other materials she used to create the painting—a mere $100. Would it be better for her, taxwise, to sell the painting for $100,000 and then donate the proceeds to charity? If she did, she could deduct her entire $100,000 donation, but she'd also have to pay income tax on the $100,000 she earned from the sale so she wouldn't be better off.

This rule applies not only to artists, but to writers as well. An author who donates a manuscript to a nonprofit may only deduct the cost of creating the manuscript (basically, the cost of the paper), not the value of his or her time.

Gifts of Fractional Interests

Owners of valuable artworks, antiques, or other appreciated tangible personal property are allowed to make fractional gifts, and—until recently—many museums and art collectors took advantage of this rule. It allowed the donor to take an immediate charitable deduction for the fair market value of the fractional interest in the item donated, while retaining part ownership. The donor would then make additional partial interest donations in future years and take additional deductions based on the fair market value of the part interest at the time of the new gift. Thus, if the value of the work appreciated over time, the donor's charitable deductions would increase as well.

However, new rules implemented in 2006 have essentially eliminated any tax incentive to give fractional gifts to a nonprofit. Under these new rules, the deduction for a gift that is given in fractional increments over time is limited to the lesser of the value at the time of the initial gift, or the fair market value when a subsequent gift is made. Thus, if the value of the property goes up, the donor's deduction will not increase.

Moreover, a nonprofit that receives a fractional interest in an item of tangible personal property must take complete ownership of the item within ten years or the death of the donor, whichever occurs first. In addition, the nonprofit must take actual physical possession of the item for a period of time corresponding to its percentage ownership interest in the item and use it for the organization's exempt purpose. Failure to comply with these requirements results in the recapture of all tax benefits plus interest and the imposition of a 10% penalty.

These harsh new rules have eliminated any tax incentive to give a fractional gift of a work of art to a museum. As a result, these donations have almost ceased. Museums and art collectors have complained bitterly to Congress, which is considering liberalizing the rules.

Conservation Easements

In recent years, conservation easements have been a popular form of charitable giving by wealthy landowners. Landowners have been willing—indeed, in some cases, anxious—to grant conservation easements to nonprofits because they are allowed to deduct as a charitable contribution the decline in the fair market value of their property due to the easement, which can be substantial.

However, a landowner may take a deduction for a conservation easement only if the easement goes to a nonprofit that has a commitment to protect the conservation purposes of the donation, and the resources to enforce the easement restrictions. These conservation purposes—such as preserving open space, protecting wildlife, or preserving historic structures—should be set forth in the nonprofit's articles of incorporation or bylaws. If your nonprofit does not have conservation purposes, it may not play in the conservation easement game.

Conservation easement agreements are complex transactions that require the help of a professional. For a detailed explanation of all the legal requirements, see Treasury Regulation Section 1.170A-14.

Food Inventory

Effective until the end of 2013, businesses such as grocery stores, farmers, ranchers, and restaurants that donate "apparently wholesome food" inventory to nonprofits for the care of the ill, needy, or infants are entitled to an enhanced deduction equal to the *lesser* of:

- the cost of the food plus one-half of the difference between fair market value and cost, or
- twice the cost of the contributed inventory.

This gives businesses a terrific tax incentive to donate unsold or unused food to charity. If your nonprofit solicits food donations, make sure that potential donors are aware of these tax benefits, which are scheduled to expire at the end of 2013.

"Apparently wholesome food" is food intended for human consumption that meets all applicable quality and labeling standards, even though the food may not be readily marketable due to appearance, age, freshness, grade, size, surplus, or other conditions. For businesses other than C corporations, the deduction is limited to 10% of the business's total net income (figured without regard to the deduction for charitable contributions).

Business Inventory

Contributions of business inventory can be quite valuable to a nonprofit. Inventory includes the goods a business owns to sell to customers in the ordinary course of business, which means almost anything a business offers for sale, except real estate. As a general rule, a business owner may only deduct the lesser of the cost of donated inventory or its fair market value.

> EXAMPLE: Jane owns a jewelry store. In December, she donates some unsold inventory to the Salvation Army. The jewelry has a fair market value of $2,000, but cost Jane $1,000. Jane may only deduct $1,000.

Clearly, this rule does not encourage business owners to donate inventory to nonprofits. However, there are exceptions to the general rule that permit businesses to take much larger deductions for some inventory donations. To be able to take advantage of these exceptions, your nonprofit must actually use the inventory to help care for the needy or ill, or further education or scientific research. Your nonprofit may not sell the inventory and pocket the money.

If your nonprofit engages in these activities, these rules can help provide a boost in inventory contributions. Make sure that prospective donors are aware that your nonprofit qualifies under this exception.

Corporate Inventory and Equipment

The general rule for business inventory and equipment donations is that donors can deduct the lesser of the cost of the donated inventory or its fair market value. C corporations, however, are entitled to more favorable deductions for inventory deductions in certain situations. These special deduction rules can be a great boon for corporations that have inventory they want to get rid of. There are several organizations that facilitate donations of unsold inventory by corporations, including the National Association for the Exchange of Industrial Resources (NAEIR), at www.naeir.org.

Inventory for the needy or ill. The most favorable inventory deduction rules for C corporations are for donations for the needy, ill, or infants. As long as:

- the donated inventory is used solely for the care of the ill, the needy, or infants, and in a manner related to the nonprofit's exempt purpose
- the donated inventory is not transferred by the nonprofit in exchange for money, other property, or services, and
- the nonprofit furnishes a written statement to the donor that the above requirements will be met,

Then the corporation can deduct the lesser of:

- the cost of the donated inventory plus one-half of the inventory's appreciation, or
- two times the cost of the donated inventory.

Scientific equipment. Corporate donors can deduct the fair market value of scientific equipment donated to nonprofits engaged in scientific research and to institutions of higher learning if the equipment:

- was created or assembled by the donor
- is no more than two years old, and
- is scientific equipment used for research, training, or experimentation in the physical or biological sciences.

Computers. There is also an exception for corporate donations of computer technology or equipment for educational purposes to elementary or secondary schools, churches, or public libraries. These donations may be valued at their fair market value if the property:

- is less than three years old
- was not used when acquired by the donor
- will fit productively within the nonprofit's education plan, and
- is not resold by the nonprofit.

Documenting Property Donations

Because of the potential for abuses, the IRS requires more documentation for property donations than for cash donations. The more the property is worth, the more documentation is required. Your nonprofit must provide the donor with the required documentation or the donor could lose its charitable deduction, and, in some cases, your nonprofit could be liable for IRS penalties. This may involve providing the donor with a written acknowledgement, filling out part of a form the donor must file with the IRS, or filing your own form.

Deadline for Providing Documentation

It's usually a good practice to thank donors right away for their gifts. As part of your thank-you, you can provide them with the documentation they need to claim their tax deduction. If you don't do this right away though, make sure you get it to them in time for their taxes. This means the donor must receive the documentation from you by the *earlier* of:

- the date on which the donor actually files his or her individual federal income tax return for the year of the contribution, or
- the due date (including extensions) for the donor's return (normally October 15 of the year following the donation).

The IRS won't accept a receipt or acknowledgment any later unless the donor has a good excuse for missing the deadline.

The earliest a donor can file his or her income tax return is February 1 of the year following the donation. Thus, you can be assured you won't be late with the documentation if you get it to them by January 31 of the year following their donations. But, why wait? It just creates a year-end rush for your organization and won't endear you to donors who may not want to wait until the last minute to get all their paperwork together for the IRS.

Property Worth Less Than $250

Donors of property worth less than $250 must obtain a receipt from the nonprofit containing:

- the name of the nonprofit
- the date and location of the contribution, and
- a reasonably detailed description of the property contributed.

You don't have to give an estimate of the value of the donated property. And, as discussed above, it is usually better not to. Instead, you should include a statement that the contribution may qualify as a charitable deduction for federal income tax purposes, and advise donors to check with their tax adviser for details.

There is no IRS form for such a receipt. It can be in the form of a standard receipt, a letter, email, postcard, or any other written communication.

EXAMPLE: Sylvia donates a used oak baby crib and matching dresser to New Beginnings, a nonprofit for new mothers in need. The nonprofit sends Sylvia the following thank-you letter:

Dear Donor:

New Beginnings gratefully acknowledges our receipt of your generous gift of a used oak baby crib and matching dresser. New Beginnings received the gift on March 15, 20xx.

New Beginnings is a Section 501(c)(3) charitable organization, thus your gift may qualify as a charitable deduction for federal income tax purposes. Please consult your tax adviser or the IRS for details.

Again, we thank you for your support.

Very truly yours,

Yolanda Allende

Yolanda Allende
Executive Director, New Beginnings

(Please keep this receipt for your tax records.)

In some cases, it may be impractical for a donor of property to obtain a receipt from a nonprofit—for example, when a donor deposits property at a nonprofit's unattended drop site. In this event, the donor can support a deduction by keeping "reliable written records" containing the following information:

- the name and address of the nonprofit
- the date and location of the contribution
- a reasonably detailed description of the property contributed
- the fair market value of the property at the time of the contribution
- the method used to determine the fair market value, and
- the terms of any conditions attached to the gift of property—for example, whether the property has been earmarked by the donor for a particular use by the nonprofit.

Property Valued at $250 to $500

A donor who claims a charitable deduction of $250 to $500 for any single donation of noncash property must obtain a written acknowledgement from the nonprofit. This is required in every case, even if the donor drops off property at an unattended drop site.

The acknowledgement is largely the same as the acknowledgement required for cash donations of $250 or more. It must contain:

- the name of the nonprofit
- the date and location of the contribution
- a reasonably detailed description of the property contributed, and
- a statement that no goods or services were provided in exchange for the contribution (if that was the case).

It is not necessary to include either the donor's Social Security number or tax identification number on the acknowledgment.

There are no IRS forms for this acknowledgment. Letters, postcards, or computer-generated forms with the above information are all acceptable. A separate acknowledgment may be provided for each contribution of property worth $250 or more, or one acknowledgment, such as an annual summary, may be used to substantiate several single property contributions of $250 or more.

Your nonprofit can provide either a paper or electronic copy of the acknowledgment to the donor. An email addressed to the donor would be acceptable.

> **EXAMPLE:** John donates a used computer to Bright Start, a nonprofit preschool. He believes it has a fair market value of $1,000. He asks for and obtains the following written acknowledgment from the school:

Dear Donor:

Bright Start gratefully acknowledges our receipt of your generous gift of an Apple iMac computer. We received the gift on March 15, 20xx.

No goods or services were provided to you in exchange for your donation.

Bright Start is a Section 501(c)(3) charitable organization, thus your gift may qualify as a charitable deduction for federal income tax purposes. Please consult your tax adviser or the IRS for details.

Again, we thank you for your support.

Very truly yours,

Yolanda Allende

Yolanda Allende
Executive Director, Bright Start

(Please keep this receipt for your tax records.)

Property Valued at $500 to $5,000

The documentation requirements for noncash property contributions of $500 or more (and less than $5,000) are more burdensome. The donor must obtain documentation from the nonprofit, keep internal records, and file a report with the IRS.

Documentation Requirements

A donor who makes any single contribution of noncash property valued at $500 to $5,000 must obtain from the nonprofit the written acknowledgment described in "Property Valued at $250 to $5,000," above. In addition, the donor should keep the following information in his or her records:

- how the donor got the property, for example, by purchase, gift, bequest, inheritance, or exchange
- the approximate date the donor got the property (or, if created, produced, or manufactured by or for the donor, the approximate date the property was substantially completed), and
- the cost or other basis, and any adjustments to the basis, of property held less than 12 months and, if available, the cost or other basis of property held 12 months or more (this requirement does not apply to publicly traded securities).

It is up to the donor, not the nonprofit, to get and keep this information.

IRS Form 8283, Section A

For any claimed property deduction of $500 or more, the donor must also complete Section A of IRS Form 8283, *Noncash Charitable Contributions*, and attach it to his or her tax return. The donor must complete a separate Form 8283 for each item of contributed property that is not part of a group of similar items. Donors who fail to file this form lose their tax deduction.

Your nonprofit doesn't have to receive, review, or sign Form 8283, unless the donor claims that the donated property items (or groups of similar items) are worth more than $5,000. (See "Property Valued at $5,000 or More," below.)

Property Valued at $5,000 or More

As you might expect, the substantiation requirements are most onerous for large property donations—those valued at $5,000 and more. Not only does your nonprofit have to give the donor a written acknowledgment, you must file IRS Form 8283, *Noncash Charitable Contributions.* And, in most cases, the donor will have to get an appraisal for the property.

In determining whether the donor is claiming a property donation worth more than $5,000, the donor must combine all of his or her deductions for all similar items donated to all nonprofits during the year. "Similar items" means property of the same generic category or type (whether or not donated to the same nonprofit)—for example: clothing, jewelry, furniture, electronic equipment, household appliances, toys, everyday kitchenware, stamp and coin collections, lithographs, paintings, photographs, books, nonpublicly traded stock, land, buildings, china, crystal, or silver.

> **EXAMPLE:** Joe owns a sizable rare book collection. This year, he gave one book valued at $2,000 to Harvard University, one valued at $2,500 to Yale University, and a third valued at $900 to Columbia University. The books are similar items and his claimed deduction for all of them together is more than $5,000. Thus, Joe must get a qualified appraisal of the books, and for each donation he must attach a fully completed IRS Form 8283, Section B, to his tax return (see below).

Acknowledgment

The donor must obtain from each nonprofit that it contributed property to as part of a claimed deduction for $5,000 or more, the written acknowledgment that is required for property worth $250 to $5,000 (see "Property Valued at $500 to $5,000," above). In addition, the donor must keep the same records that are required for property donations of $500 to $5,000 (see "Property Valued at $500 to $5,000," above).

Appraisal

A donor who claims a charitable deduction of $5,000 or more for a single item or for multiple similar items of personal or real property must obtain a qualified appraisal of the item's or group of items' combined value. This can discourage large property donations because appraisals can be expensive. There are certain exceptions, however, including:

- personal property owned less than one year (this is because the donor's deduction is limited to the property's original cost, not its current fair market value)
- publicly traded stock, mutual fund shares, or other securities
- nonpublicly traded stock of $10,000 or less
- a vehicle (including a car, boat, or airplane) for which the donor's deduction is limited to the gross proceeds from its sale
- business inventory, or
- intellectual property, such as a patent.

The lack of an appraisal requirement is one reason gifts of publicly traded stock are the most popular noncash donations.

The appraisal must be arranged for and paid for by the donor—the nonprofit cannot help pay for it in any way. Moreover, the donor can't deduct appraisal fees as part of the charitable contribution. At best, a donor may claim them as a miscellaneous itemized deduction on Schedule A of IRS Form 1040. However, because not all taxpayers itemize their deductions, you should never promise a donor that his or her appraisal fees will be deductible as a miscellaneous itemized deduction. At most, you should say that the fee "may" be deductible depending on the donor's tax situation.

An appraisal must be "qualified" to satisfy the IRS. A qualified appraisal is one that:

- is made not earlier than 60 days before the property is donated
- is received by the donor before the due date (including extensions) of the return on which the deduction is claimed—usually not later than October 15 of the year after the donation was made
- includes certain specified information (see IRS Publication 561, *Determining the Value of Donated Property*)
- does not involve an appraisal fee based on a percentage of the appraised value of the property (with one narrow exception for certain fees to nonprofit appraiser associations) or the value of the property allowed as a charitable deduction

- is conducted in accordance with "generally accepted appraisal standards" and IRS rules, and
- is conducted, prepared, signed, and dated by a "qualified appraiser."

Donors often have old appraisals for expensive property items. Make sure they understand that the appraisal for the IRS must be new—made not more than 60 days before the contribution. And, insurance appraisals are not acceptable.

Not just anyone can conduct an IRS-approved appraisal. To satisfy the IRS, the appraisal must be done by a "qualified" appraiser. There are many professional appraiser organizations whose websites donors can use to help them find a qualified appraiser. These include:

- American Society of Appraisers: www.appraisers.org
- Appraisal Foundation: www.appraisalfoundation.org
- Appraisal Institute: www.appraisalinstitute.org
- Foundation of Real Estate Appraisers: www.frea.com
- Gemological Institute of America: www.gia.edu
- National Association of Independent Fee Appraisers: www.naifa.com
- International Society of Appraisers: www.isa-appraisers.org
- Appraisers Association of America: www.appraisersassoc.org.

It's perfectly legal and ethical for your nonprofit to recommend an appraiser. However, you cannot have a favorite appraiser who spends most of his or her time dealing with your donors. An appraiser who spends a majority of his or her time conducting appraisals for a single nonprofit cannot be a qualified appraiser under IRS rules.

For more information on appraisals, you can refer donors to IRS Publication 561, *Determining the Value of Donated Property*, and to IRS Revenue Procedure 96-15. Both can be obtained from the IRS website (www.irs.gov).

IRS Form 8283, Section B

Form 8283 must be filed with the donor's tax return for each item or group of similar items worth more than $5,000. If the donor claims that donated property items (or groups of similar items) are worth more than $5,000, he or she must complete Section B of IRS Form 8283, in addition to Section A. Section B requires the input of the donor, the appraiser, and your nonprofit. The donor and/or appraiser are required to complete Part I of Section B, which is a summary of the appraisal results, including the item's or items' appraised fair market value. The appraiser must sign Part III of Section B, declaring that he or she is a qualified appraiser.

The nonprofit must complete and sign Part IV of Section B, which is titled "Donee Acknowledgment." The "donee" is the recipient of the gift from the donor.

The donor is supposed to provide your nonprofit with the form to sign. The form does not have to be completed by the donor before it is signed by your nonprofit's representative, but the donor should have at least provided his or her name, tax identification number, and a description of the donated property (line 5, column (a)). If tangible property is donated, the donor should also describe its physical condition (line 5, column (b)) at the time of the gift.

By signing the Donee Acknowledgment, a nonprofit acknowledges that it is a qualified organization—that is, donations to it are tax deductible—and that it received the donated property described in the form. The nonprofit must provide the date the donation was received and its contact information. The person signing the form must be an official authorized to sign the nonprofit's tax returns—for example, the treasurer or a person specifically designated to sign Form 8283.

Signing the Donee Acknowledgement does not mean that your nonprofit agrees with the appraised value for the donated items stated on the form. It just means that it received the listed items on the date indicated.

The form also asks the nonprofit to answer whether it intends to use the donated property for an unrelated use. This is important information for the donor because it could affect the tax deduction allowed. (See "Appreciated Property—The Related Use Rule," above.) By checking "no," here, the donor will be allowed to deduct the full fair market value of the property at the time of the donation as long as it is not sold by your nonprofit within three years.

Form **8283**	**Noncash Charitable Contributions**	OMB No. 1545-0908
(Rev. December 2012) Department of the Treasury Internal Revenue Service	▶ **Attach to your tax return if you claimed a total deduction of over $500 for all contributed property.** ▶ **Information about Form 8283 and its separate instructions is at** *www.irs.gov/form8283.*	Attachment Sequence No. **155**
Name(s) shown on your income tax return		Identifying number

Note. Figure the amount of your contribution deduction before completing this form. See your tax return instructions.

Section A. Donated Property of $5,000 or Less and Certain Publicly Traded Securities—List in this section **only** items (or groups of similar items) for which you claimed a deduction of $5,000 or less. Also, list certain publicly traded securities even if the deduction is more than $5,000 (see instructions).

| Part I | Information on Donated Property—If you need more space, attach a statement. |

1	**(a)** Name and address of the donee organization	**(b)** If donated property is a vehicle (see instructions), check the box. Also enter the vehicle identification number (unless Form 1098-C is attached)	**(c)** Description of donated property (For a donated vehicle, enter the year, make, model, condition, and mileage, unless Form 1098-C is attached.)
A		☐	
B		☐	
C		☐	
D		☐	
E		☐	

Note. If the amount you claimed as a deduction for an item is $500 or less, you do not have to complete columns (e), (f), and (g).

	(d) Date of the contribution	**(e)** Date acquired by donor (mo., yr.)	**(f)** How acquired by donor	**(g)** Donor's cost or adjusted basis	**(h)** Fair market value (see instructions)	**(i)** Method used to determine the fair market value
A						
B						
C						
D						
E						

| Part II | Partial Interests and Restricted Use Property—Complete lines 2a through 2e if you gave less than an entire interest in a property listed in Part I; Complete lines 3a through 3c if conditions were placed on a contribution listed in Part I; also attach the required statement (see instructions). |

2a Enter the letter from Part I that identifies the property for which you gave less than an entire interest ▶ _____
If Part II applies to more than one property, attach a separate statement.

b Total amount claimed as a deduction for the property listed in Part I: **(1)** For this tax year ▶ _____
(2) For any prior tax years ▶ _____

c Name and address of each organization to which any such contribution was made in a prior year (complete only if different from the donee organization above):
Name of charitable organization (donee)

Address (number, street, and room or suite no.)

City or town, state, and ZIP code

d For tangible property, enter the place where the property is located or kept ▶ _____
e Name of any person, other than the donee organization, having actual possession of the property ▶ _____

		Yes	No
3a	Is there a restriction, either temporary or permanent, on the donee's right to use or dispose of the donated property?		
b	Did you give to anyone (other than the donee organization or another organization participating with the donee organization in cooperative fundraising) the right to the income from the donated property or to the possession of the property, including the right to vote donated securities, to acquire the property by purchase or otherwise, or to designate the person having such income, possession, or right to acquire?		
c	Is there a restriction limiting the donated property for a particular use?		

For Paperwork Reduction Act Notice, see separate instructions.   Cat. No. 62299J   Form **8283** (Rev. 12-2012)

Form 8283 (Rev. 12-2012)   Page **2**

Name(s) shown on your income tax return	Identifying number

Section B. Donated Property Over $5,000 (Except Certain Publicly Traded Securities)—List in this section only items (or groups of similar items) for which you claimed a deduction of more than $5,000 per item or group (except contributions of certain publicly traded securities reported in Section A). An appraisal is generally required for property listed in Section B (see instructions).

Part I **Information on Donated Property**—To be completed by the taxpayer and/or the appraiser.

4 Check the box that describes the type of property donated:

a ☐ Art* (contribution of $20,000 or more)	b ☐ Qualified Conservation Contribution	c ☐ Equipment
d ☐ Art* (contribution of less than $20,000)	e ☐ Other Real Estate	f ☐ Securities
g ☐ Collectibles**	h ☐ Intellectual Property	i ☐ Vehicles
j ☐ Other		

*Art includes paintings, sculptures, watercolors, prints, drawings, ceramics, antiques, decorative arts, textiles, carpets, silver, rare manuscripts, historical memorabilia, and other similar objects.

**Collectibles include coins, stamps, books, gems, jewelry, sports memorabilia, dolls, etc., but not art as defined above.

Note. In certain cases, you must attach a qualified appraisal of the property. See instructions.

5	(a) Description of donated property (if you need more space, attach a separate statement)	(b) If tangible property was donated, give a brief summary of the overall physical condition of the property at the time of the gift	(c) Appraised fair market value
A			
B			
C			
D			

	(d) Date acquired by donor (mo., yr.)	(e) How acquired by donor	(f) Donor's cost or adjusted basis	(g) For bargain sales, enter amount received	See instructions	
					(h) Amount claimed as a deduction	(i) Average trading price of securities
A						
B						
C						
D						

Part II **Taxpayer (Donor) Statement**—List each item included in Part I above that the appraisal identifies as having a value of $500 or less. See instructions.

I declare that the following item(s) included in Part I above has to the best of my knowledge and belief an appraised value of not more than $500 (per item). Enter identifying letter from Part I and describe the specific item. See instructions. ▶ _____

Signature of taxpayer (donor) ▶ _____   Date ▶ _____

Part III **Declaration of Appraiser**

I declare that I am not the donor, the donee, a party to the transaction in which the donor acquired the property, employed by, or related to any of the foregoing persons, or married to any person who is related to any of the foregoing persons. And, if regularly used by the donor, donee, or party to the transaction, I performed the majority of my appraisals during my tax year for other persons.

Also, I declare that I perform appraisals on a regular basis; and that because of my qualifications as described in the appraisal, I am qualified to make appraisals of the type of property being valued. I certify that the appraisal fees were not based on a percentage of the appraised property value. Furthermore, I understand that a false or fraudulent overstatement of the property value as described in the qualified appraisal or this Form 8283 may subject me to the penalty under section 6701(a) (aiding and abetting the understatement of tax liability). In addition, I understand that I may be subject to a penalty under section 6695A if I know, or reasonably should know, that my appraisal is to be used in connection with a return or claim for refund and a substantial or gross valuation misstatement results from my appraisal. I affirm that I have not been barred from presenting evidence or testimony by the Office of Professional Responsibility.

Sign Here

Signature ▶	Title ▶	Date ▶

Business address (including room or suite no.)	Identifying number
City or town, state, and ZIP code	

Part IV **Donee Acknowledgment**—To be completed by the charitable organization.

This charitable organization acknowledges that it is a qualified organization under section 170(c) and that it received the donated property as described in Section B, Part I, above on the following date ▶ _____

Furthermore, this organization affirms that in the event it sells, exchanges, or otherwise disposes of the property described in Section B, Part I (or any portion thereof) within 3 years after the date of receipt, it will file **Form 8282,** Donee Information Return, with the IRS and give the donor a copy of that form. This acknowledgment does not represent agreement with the claimed fair market value.

Does the organization intend to use the property for an unrelated use? . . . . ▶ ☐ Yes ☐ No

Name of charitable organization (donee)	Employer identification number
Address (number, street, and room or suite no.)	City or town, state, and ZIP code
Authorized signature	Title	Date

Form **8283** (Rev. 12-2012)

Your nonprofit should return the signed Form 8283 to the donor. It's the donor's responsibility to file it with his or her tax return. The donor should also provide your nonprofit with a copy of the completed form.

When a Nonprofit Sells Donated Property—IRS Form 8282

Anytime a nonprofit sells or disposes of property worth over $5,000 within three years of receiving it as a donation, the nonprofit must file Form 8282, *Donee Information Return*, with the IRS and send a copy to the donor. Because of this requirement, your nonprofit should have a system for tracking when noncash contributions over $5,000 are sold. There are fundraising software programs that can do this for you.

This requirement has to do with the related use rules for donated property (see "Appreciated Property—The Related Use Rule," above). When a donor contributes tangible personal property worth more than $5,000, he or she is allowed to deduct its fair market value only if:

- the nonprofit uses it for its exempt purposes for at least three years, or
- the nonprofit intended to do so but was prevented because it was impossible or infeasible.

How the nonprofit fills out Form 8282 can have important tax consequences for the donor. If the nonprofit tells the IRS on the form that it did not use, or intend to use, the property to further its exempt purpose, the donor will have to give back to the IRS any amount he or she deducted in excess of the item's cost. On the other hand, if the nonprofit indicates on the form that it used the property for its exempt purpose—or at least intended to, but was prevented from doing so because it was impossible—the donor will be allowed to deduct the property's fair market value on the date of the donation and won't have to give any money back.

Exceptions to filing requirement. You don't have to file Form 8282 if:

- an item is consumed or distributed, without payment, in fulfilling its tax-exempt purpose or function—for example, no reporting is required for medical supplies consumed or distributed by a tax-exempt relief organization in aiding disaster victims

- the property is publicly traded securities, or
- the donor stated on Form 8283 that the appraised value of the specific item was not more than $500.

Contents of form. To completely fill out this form, the nonprofit must have a copy of the donor's completed Form 8283. The IRS anticipates that many donors will fail to provide copies of the form to nonprofits. If this is the case, the nonprofit only has to complete Part III, columns 1, 2, 3, and 4; and Part IV.

Part III contains information on the donated property. The nonprofit must complete four columns.

- Column 1: Describe the property sold or otherwise transferred and explain how it was used.
- Column 2: Answer "yes" or "no" as to whether your entire interest in such property was transferred—ordinarily, the answer will be "yes."
- Column 3: Answer "yes" or "no" as to whether your nonprofit's use of the property was related to its exempt purpose or functions.
- Column 4: If the "yes" box was checked in column 3, describe how your use of the property furthered your organization's exempt purpose or function. If the "no" box was checked, and the property is tangible personal property, you must describe your organization's intended use for the property when it was donated.

Part IV contains a certification to be signed by an officer of the nonprofit. By signing, the nonprofit certifies that the property was either:

- used to further its exempt purpose or function, or
- intended to be used for its exempt purpose or function but the intended use became impossible or infeasible to implement. Of course, you should only sign the certification if one of the two statements is true. If either one is true, the donor is allowed to deduct the property's fair market value at the time of the contribution—a good result for the donor.

Form 8282

(Rev. April 2009)

Department of the Treasury
Internal Revenue Service

Donee Information Return

(Sale, Exchange, or Other Disposition of Donated Property)

▶ See instructions.

OMB No. 1545-0908

Give a Copy to Donor

Parts To Complete

- If the organization is an **original donee**, complete *Identifying Information,* Part I (lines 1a–1d and, if applicable, lines 2a–2d), and Part III.
- If the organization is a **successor donee,** complete *Identifying Information,* Part I, Part II, and Part III.

Identifying Information

Print or Type

Name of charitable organization (donee)	Employer identification number

Address (number, street, and room or suite no.) (or P.O. box no. if mail is not delivered to the street address)

City or town, state, and ZIP code

Part I — Information on ORIGINAL DONOR and SUCCESSOR DONEE Receiving the Property

1a Name of original donor of the property	1b Identifying number(s)

1c   Address (number, street, and room or suite no.) (P.O. box no. if mail is not delivered to the street address)

1d   City or town, state, and ZIP code

Note. Complete lines 2a–2d only if the organization gave this property to another charitable organization (successor donee).

2a Name of charitable organization	2b Employer identification number

2c   Address (number, street, and room or suite no.) (or P.O. box no. if mail is not delivered to the street address)

2d   City or town, state, and ZIP code

Part II — Information on PREVIOUS DONEES. Complete this part only if the organization was not the first donee to receive the property. See the instructions before completing lines 3a through 4d.

3a Name of original donee	3b Employer identification number

3c   Address (number, street, and room or suite no.) (or P.O. box no. if mail is not delivered to the street address)

3d   City or town, state, and ZIP code

4a Name of preceding donee	4b Employer identification number

4c   Address (number, street, and room or suite no.) (or P.O. box no. if mail is not delivered to the street address)

4d   City or town, state, and ZIP code

For Paperwork Reduction Act Notice, see page 4.   Cat. No. 62307Y   Form **8282** (Rev. 4-2009)

Form 8282 (Rev. 4-2009)   Page **2**

Part III Information on DONATED PROPERTY

1. Description of the donated property sold, exchanged, or otherwise disposed of and how the organization used the property. (If you need more space, attach a separate statement.)	2. Did the disposition involve the organization's entire interest in the property?		3. Was the use related to the organization's exempt purpose or function?		4. Information on use of property. • If you answered "Yes" to question 3 and the property was tangible personal property, describe how the organization's use of the property furthered its exempt purpose or function. Also complete Part IV below. • If you answered "No" to question 3 and the property was tangible personal property, describe the organization's intended use (if any) at the time of the contribution. Also complete Part IV below, if the intended use at the time of the contribution was related to the organization's exempt purpose or function and it became impossible or infeasible to implement.
	Yes	No	Yes	No	
A					
B					
C					
D					

		Donated Property			
		A	**B**	**C**	**D**
5	Date the organization received the donated property (MM/DD/YY)	/ /	/ /	/ /	/ /
6	Date the original donee received the property (MM/DD/YY)	/ /	/ /	/ /	/ /
7	Date the property was sold, exchanged, or otherwise disposed of (MM/DD/YY)	/ /	/ /	/ /	/ /
8	Amount received upon disposition	$	$	$	$

Part IV Certification

You must sign the certification below if any property described in Part III above is tangible personal property and:

• You answered "Yes" to question 3 above, or

• You answered "No" to question 3 above and the intended use of the property became impossible or infeasible to implement.

Under penalties of perjury and the penalty under section 6720B, I certify that either: (1) the use of the property that meets the above requirements, and is described above in Part III, was substantial and related to the donee organization's exempt purpose or function; or (2) the donee organization intended to use the property for its exempt purpose or function, but the intended use has become impossible or infeasible to implement.

▶ _____   _____   ▶ _____
Signature of officer   Title   Date

Sign Here	Under penalties of perjury, I declare that I have examined this return, including accompanying schedules and statements, and to the best of my knowledge and belief, it is true, correct, and complete. ▶ _____ _____ ▶ _____ Signature of officer Title Date Type or print name

Form **8282** (Rev. 4-2009)

The certification should not be signed if the nonprofit checked the "no" box in Column 3 and its intended use for the property did not become impossible or infeasible to implement. In this event, the donor can only deduct what the property cost, not its fair market value at the time of the donation. The donor might have to pay tax on the difference between the deduction taken and the property's cost. (See "Appreciated Property—The Related Use Rule," above.)

Deadline for filing. The form is supposed to be filed with the IRS within 125 days after the property is sold or otherwise disposed of. However, if the nonprofit does not file because it had no reason to believe the substantiation requirements applied to the donor, and the nonprofit later becomes aware that the substantiation requirements did apply, it must file Form 8282 within 60 days after the date it becomes aware of this. There is a $50 penalty for each failure to file the form by the applicable deadline.

Documentation Rules for Cars, Boats, and Airplanes

There are special reporting requirements for cars, boats, and airplanes. The information that must be provided to the donor depends upon what happens to the donated vehicle and its claimed value.

Nonprofits often hire private for-profit companies to sell donated vehicles. If this happens, the for-profit company usually takes care of the acknowledgment requirements. Nevertheless, the for-profit company is the nonprofit's agent, acting on its behalf, so the nonprofit will be liable for any penalties incurred because of a failure on the for-profit's part. So you should actively monitor a for-profit in this situation to make sure it complies with the IRS rules.

Vehicles Sold for More Than $500

Whenever a donated vehicle is sold for more than $500, the nonprofit must provide the donor and the IRS with a written acknowledgment within 30 days after the sale. Fortunately, the IRS has created a special form for this purpose, IRS Form 1098-C, *Contributions of Motor Vehicles, Boats, and Airplanes.* You don't have to use this form, but it does make your life easier. The form or your own acknowledgment must contain the following information:

- the donor's name and taxpayer identification number
- the vehicle identification number—Box 3
- the date of the contribution—Box 1
- a statement certifying that the vehicle was sold in an arm's length transaction between unrelated parties—Box 4a
- the date of the sale—Box 4b
- the gross proceeds received from the sale—Box 4c, and
- a statement that the donor's deduction may not exceed the gross proceeds from the sale.

You must indicate whether the donation was a quid pro quo donation —that is whether goods or services were given to the donor in exchange for the vehicle. (See "Quid Pro Quo Contributions" in Chapter 5 for a detailed discussion of the rules applicable to such donations.) The nonprofit must either:

- state that no goods or services were provided by the nonprofit in return for the donation—Box 6a
- provide a description and good faith estimate of the value of goods or services that the nonprofit provided in return for the donation—Box 6b, or
- state that the goods or services provided by the nonprofit consisted entirely of intangible religious benefits—Box 6c.

Form 1098-C is a multipage form consisting of three identical parts: Copy A, Copy B, and Copy C. Copy B and Copy C must be given to the donor no later than 30 days after the date the nonprofit (or its agent) sells the donated vehicle (if box 4a is checked), or 30 days after the date of the contribution (if box 5a or 5b is checked). If none of these boxes is checked, the donor must obtain the form by the due date (including extensions) of his or her tax return for the year of the contribution. The donor must attach a Copy B of Form 1098-C to his or her tax return to take a deduction for the vehicle donation. The donor retains Copy C for his or her records. Copy A of Form 1098-C is filed by the nonprofit with the IRS. The form is due by February 28 of the year after the

7878 ☐ VOID ☐ CORRECTED

DONEE'S name, street address, city or town, province or state, country, ZIP or foreign postal code, and telephone no.		OMB No. 1545-1959	**Contributions of Motor Vehicles, Boats, and Airplanes**
	1 Date of contribution	20**13** Form **1098-C**	

	2a Year	**2b** Make	**2c** Model

DONEE'S federal identification number	DONOR'S identification number	**3** Vehicle or other identification number

DONOR'S name	**4a** ☐ Donee certifies that vehicle was sold in arm's length transaction to unrelated party

Street address (including apt. no.)	**4b** Date of sale

City or town, province or state, country, and ZIP or foreign postal code	**4c** Gross proceeds from sale (see instructions) $

5a ☐ Donee certifies that vehicle will not be transferred for money, other property, or services before completion of material improvements or significant intervening use

5b ☐ Donee certifies that vehicle is to be transferred to a needy individual for significantly below fair market value in furtherance of donee's charitable purpose

5c Donee certifies the following detailed description of material improvements or significant intervening use and duration of use

6a Did you provide goods or services in exchange for the vehicle? . . . . ▶ Yes ☐ No ☐

6b Value of goods and services provided in exchange for the vehicle
$

6c Describe the goods and services, if any, that were provided. If this box is checked, donee certifies that the goods and services consisted solely of intangible religious benefits . . . . ▶ ☐

7 Under the law, the donor may not claim a deduction of more than $500 for this vehicle if this box is checked . . . . . ▶ ☐

Copy A

For Internal Revenue Service Center

File with Form 1096.

For Privacy Act and Paperwork Reduction Act Notice, see the **2013 General Instructions for Certain Information Returns.**

Form **1098-C**   Cat. No. 39732R   www.irs.gov/form1098c   Department of the Treasury - Internal Revenue Service acknowledgement was made to the donor (March 31 if the form is filed electronically).

Donated Vehicles That Are Not Sold

The donor can deduct the fair market value of the vehicle at the time of the donation if, instead of selling the vehicle, the nonprofit intends to:

- make significant use of the vehicle
- make material improvements to it before it is sold, or
- give or sell the vehicle to a needy person.

See "Vehicles—Used Cars, Boats, and Aircraft," above, for more information on when these different rules occur.

If any of these situations applies, your nonprofit must provide the donor with a written acknowledgment within 30 days after the contribution is made. The acknowledgment is the same as for vehicles sold for more than $500 discussed above, except that the nonprofit must state what it intends to do with the vehicle, and, where applicable, describe the intended use or improvements. Form 1098-C can be used. Boxes 5a, b, c are filled in, while Boxes 4a, b, c are left blank.

Deductions of $250 to $500

If a donor is claiming a deduction of at least $250 but not more than $500 for a vehicle, the acknowledgment must include:

- the name of the nonprofit
- a description (but not value) of the vehicle, and
- a statement as to whether goods or services were provided in return for the donation.

You can use Form 1098-C for this purpose, or you can give the donor any type of written acknowledgement with the required information. The acknowledgment can be paper copy or electronic, such as an email addressed to the donor.

If you use Form 1098-C, be sure to check Box 7, which states that the donor cannot claim a deduction of more than $500. Your nonprofit should only provide Copy C of the form to the donor. It should not file Copy A with the IRS.

Deductions of $250 or Less

Donors who claim vehicle deductions of less than $250 must get a receipt from the nonprofit containing:

- the name of the nonprofit
- the date and location of the contribution, and
- a reasonably detailed description of the vehicle contributed.

Penalties for Failure to Comply

Where a claimed deduction for a vehicle is for more than $500, the IRS will impose a monetary penalty on a nonprofit that knowingly furnishes the donor with a false or fraudulent acknowledgment, or knowingly fails to furnish an acknowledgment with the required information. If the vehicle was sold, the penalty is the greater of:

- the product of the highest tax rate (currently 35%) and the sales price stated on the acknowledgment, or
- the gross proceeds from the sale.

In the case of an acknowledgment that is not based on gross proceeds, the penalty is the greater of the product of the highest tax rate (currently 35%) and the claimed value of the vehicle, or $5,000.

> EXAMPLE: A nonprofit receives a donation of a used car and sells it for $1,000. However, the nonprofit provides the donor with a Form 1098-C that states that the gross proceeds from the sale were $3,000. The nonprofit is subject to a penalty for knowingly furnishing a false or fraudulent acknowledgment to the donor. The amount of the penalty is $1,050 (35% × $3,000 = $1,050).

Obtaining IRS Form 1098-C

Form 1098-C is different from most other IRS forms. It is a three-page pressure-sensitive form—that is, writing on the first page also writes on the next two pages. A copy of the form is available on the IRS website (www.irs.gov), but this online form may not be filed with the IRS because it cannot be read by IRS computers. A penalty of $50 per information return may be imposed by the IRS for filing forms that are not computer readable. However, copies B and C of the form on the IRS website may be used to provide a written acknowledgment to the donor. You can obtain a printed version of Form 1098-C from the IRS by mail or any IRS office. You can also order it through the IRS website, or by calling 800-TAX-FORM (800-829-3676).

Filing IRS Forms 8283 and 8282. If the vehicle is sold for over $5,000, or a deduction for over $5,000 is otherwise claimed, the donor must provide the nonprofit with a copy of IRS Form 8283 to sign certifying that it received the vehicle. (See "IRS Form 8283, Section A" above.)

If your nonprofit is required to sign Form 8283 for receipt of a vehicle, you must file Form 8282, *Donee Information Return,* if you sell or otherwise dispose of the vehicle within three years after you receive it. The form must be filed within 125 days after you sell the vehicle. This form requires you to identify the donor, your organization, and the amount you received upon disposition of the vehicle. You must give the donor a copy of the completed Form 8282. (See "When a Nonprofit Sells Donated Property—IRS Form 8282," above.)

Excessive Compensation, Sweetheart Deals, and Other Ways to Get in Trouble With the IRS

n this era of economic calamity, when most nonprofits are cutting back their staffs and reducing pay and benefits, the premise of this chapter may seem ludicrous: that the IRS needs to police nonprofits to prevent them from paying their key employees too much or otherwise enriching "insiders." Nevertheless, this has become a hot-button issue for the IRS, largely because of the seemingly endless stream of stories about nonprofit insiders who have unlawfully used nonprofit funds for their own personal purposes. To prevent these kinds of abuses, the IRS has exercised its broad powers and imposed substantial monetary penalties on those who engage in improper financial transactions with nonprofits. In extreme cases, the IRS can revoke the tax exemption of a nonprofit involved in improper financial activities.

Most commonly, the transactions that nonprofits need to watch out for are paying excessive compensation to key employees and giving money or property to insiders without receiving a fair return. Fortunately, the IRS has established procedures that you can follow to avoid running into these problems and the wrath of the IRS.

TIP
Do you need to worry about this stuff? You probably don't have to worry about the issues covered in this chapter if you're running a small all-volunteer nonprofit or have only a few employees who are paid at or below market rates. However, even a small nonprofit may run afoul of these rules if directors, officers, or other insiders engage in financial transactions with the nonprofit.

A Nonprofit Is Not a Personal Piggy Bank

It should go without saying that the money and other assets a nonprofit obtains are to be used only for the organization's nonprofit purposes, not for the private gain or enrichment of insiders. We use the term "insider" to refer to those who run the nonprofit, helped found it, work for it, contribute to it, or are related to it in any way. The tax law provides that an organization is entitled to tax-exempt status only if it is "organized and operated exclusively for religious, charitable, scientific," and a few other specified purposes. Obviously, this requirement is not satisfied where a nonprofit's money is used to benefit insiders instead of furthering its exempt purposes.

Lawyers have coined the confusing term "private inurement" to describe when a nonprofit's money or other assets are devoted to private uses by insiders instead of the charitable purposes they were intended for. Here are just a few examples:

- A nonprofit executive used the organization's money to pay his child's college tuition, lease a luxury car for his wife, have his kitchen remodeled, and rent a vacation house at the beach. The nonprofit also permitted him to charge almost $60,000 in personal expenses to the organization's American Express card.

- The CEO at a tax-exempt hospital used charitable assets to pay for personal items such as liquor, china, crystal, perfume, an airplane, and theater tickets. The hospital also picked up the tab for the CEO's country club charges and catered lunches to the tune of approximately $20,000.

- A nonprofit paid $200,000 for its executive director's wedding reception and tropical island honeymoon. The nonprofit also plunked down $90,000 for the down payment on the director's home and had enough left over to pay for his trip to a desert health spa.

Most of the highly publicized cases of private inurement involve larger nonprofits. However, the problem is certainly not limited to large nonprofits. In one case, for example, the founder of a small church, who also served as its president and director, allowed his children to live rent-free in a house owned by the church. He also used church credit cards to pay for personal expenses, such as department store purchases, car repairs, food, hotel, and clothing charges—and even had the church hire a private investigator to surveil his daughter-in-law.

When a nonprofit engages in any type of conduct that results in an improper benefit to an insider, one of three things can happen:

- nothing

- the IRS can impose monetary sanctions, or
- the IRS can revoke the nonprofit's tax exemption.

The most likely IRS response is the imposition of sanctions, so we'll discuss that first.

The IRS Intermediate Sanctions Minefield

The IRS is very serious about preventing excessive compensation, sweetheart deals with insiders, personal use of nonprofit assets, and other such abuses, To this end, Congress has given the IRS the power to impose monetary penalties against insiders it finds to have engaged in this type of prohibited conduct. The IRS calls these penalties "intermediate sanctions" because they are more than doing nothing, but fall short of revoking a nonprofit's tax-exempt status. These penalties can be substantial. Moreover, they are levied—not on the nonprofit—but on the individuals who participate in the prohibited transaction. This may include not only the people who benefited from a transaction, but those within the nonprofit who approved it as well. A nonprofit's managers (directors, officers, or others) who approve a transaction that they know is improper may be subject to a 10% excise tax. And they have to pay these IRS penalties out of their own pockets!

How big can these penalties be? Very big. Consider this simple example: A small rape crisis prevention center pays Sam, its executive director, $90,000 in total compensation, for 20 hours of work per week. The compensation package is approved by Denise, Dave, and Donald, three of the nonprofit's directors, even though they knew that similar nonprofits in the area paid $40,000 or less for similar work. The IRS receives a complaint from a former employee of the nonprofit stating that it is paying excessive compensation to Sam. The IRS audits the nonprofit and determines that reasonable compensation for Sam is only $40,000. Thus, Sam received an "excess benefit" of $50,000. Here's what happens:

- Sam must pay the IRS a penalty tax equal to 25% of the excess benefit—in this case, $12,500
- Sam must pay the $50,000 excess benefit back to the nonprofit; if he doesn't, he will have to pay an additional tax to the IRS equal to 200% of the excess benefit—or $100,000, and
- Denise, Dave, and Donald, the directors who knowingly approved Sam's compensation, must jointly pay an excise tax equal to 10% of the amount of the excess benefit, up to a maximum of $20,000—in this case, $5,000 total between the three of them.

Thus, at a minimum, the IRS will receive $17,500 in penalty taxes—$12,500 from Sam out of his own pocket and $5,000 from Denise, Dave, and Donald. The IRS would receive an additional $100,000 if Sam failed to pay the $50,000 back to the nonprofit.

Have we got your attention now? Good. Read on, because it is certainly worth it for you to know how to avoid these kinds of potential problems with the IRS. First, a few basics.

Disqualified Person + Excess Benefit = IRS Sanctions

IRS sanctions are imposed only when insiders, such as board members, officers, or key employees, siphon off a nonprofit's money or assets for their personal enrichment. In IRS parlance, these people are known as "disqualified persons" ("DPs" for short) and their improper financial dealings are "excess benefit transactions." The intermediate sanctions rules come into play only when both of these elements—DPs and excess benefits—are combined. For example, you don't have to worry about IRS sanctions when determining the compensation of a low-paid bookkeeper, but you do have to worry when deciding how much to pay your nonprofit's president or executive director. This is because under the IRS's rules, the president is a disqualified person, but the bookkeeper is not. Likewise, you need not worry about sanctions when your nonprofit pays its president or CEO a reasonable amount because that transaction does not result in an excess benefit. The key to avoiding sanctions, then, is never to pay or give an excess benefit to a DP.

Who is a disqualified person? A disqualified person is anyone who is in a position to exercise "substantial influence" over your nonprofit's affairs. This includes your nonprofit's officers and directors and possibly a few other influential people in the organization. See "Identify Your Nonprofit's Disqualified Persons," below.

What is an excess benefit transaction? The fact that a person is a disqualified person does not mean that he or she cannot transact business with your nonprofit and benefit from it financially. Far from it. For example, your nonprofit's CEO or executive director is entitled to be paid, even though he or she is an automatic DP. Likewise, a DP may sell or lease property to the nonprofit. Sanctions may be imposed by the IRS only when a DP enters into a transaction with the nonprofit and receives benefits greater than she or he provides in return—for example, a key employee is paid excessive compensation or a DP sells or rents property to the nonprofit for more than its fair market value. The IRS calls such an unequal exchange an "excess benefit transaction." The excess benefit is the difference between the value of what is received by the nonprofit and what the nonprofit gives to the DP.

Excess benefit transactions can take a variety of forms, but by far the most common is paying excessive compensation to DPs such as presidents, CEOs, CFOs, or other highly compensated employees (defined as employees earning $115,000 or more in 2013). Other common excess benefit transactions include:

- excessive expense accounts—for example, payments for excessive travel and food expenses or misuse of the nonprofit's credit card
- personal use of nonprofit property by a DP, such as a car or dwelling
- paying personal expenses for members of a DP's family
- leasing property from a DP in return for excessive rent
- purchase of goods or services from DPs at above fair market value
- sale of goods or services to DPs at below fair market value, and
- loans to DPs with below market interest rates (or no interest at all).

TIP

Get a professional opinion. If you think that a proposed transaction with someone might be an excess benefit transaction, consider getting a written professional opinion from an attorney, certified public accountant or accounting firm, or an independent qualified valuation expert. If the directors or other managers of your nonprofit obtain and follow an opinion, the IRS cannot impose sanctions on them if it later determines that the transaction was an excess benefit transaction. To be relied upon, the opinion must explain why the transaction is not an excess benefit transaction.

Automatic Excess Benefits

In some cases, the IRS imposes intermediate sanctions automatically, without even having to determine if a DP was paid too much or some other transaction was unreasonable. This occurs in two situations. First, any payment or other economic benefit to a DP that is not clearly identified by the nonprofit as compensation for the person's services is treated as an excess benefit, even if the amount is reasonable. For example, if a nonprofit pays for a benefit, such as life insurance coverage for a DP, and does not document in writing that the payment is compensation for the DP's services, the payment will automatically be treated as an excess benefit. (See "Document All Taxable Compensation Paid to DPs," below.)

An automatic excess benefit also occurs whenever a nonprofit reimburses a DP for work-related expenses without following the record-keeping rules for accountable reimbursement plans. For example, if a nonprofit reimburses its director for a $5,000 trip without requiring him to document his expenses, the entire amount will be treated as an excess benefit, and the director will have to return the money to the nonprofit and pay IRS sanctions as well. This result can easily be avoided by following the accountable plan rules discussed below. (See "Reimburse Employee DP Expenses Under an Accountable Plan," below.)

Loans With Insiders

It is generally not a good idea for a nonprofit to lend money to a DP. About 20 states ban loans from a nonprofit to its directors or officers, while another seven place limits on them. You should check your state's nonprofit laws before even thinking about making a loan to a DP. If your nonprofit does make a loan to a DP, its terms should be fully set forth in a written promissory note and formally approved by the board using the procedure described in "Follow IRS-Approved Procedures," below. The promissory note should list the original amount borrowed, balance due, maturity date, repayment terms, interest rate, security provided, and purpose of the loan. The loan should be treated as such on the nonprofit's books. Also, the existence and terms of the loan must be fully disclosed to the IRS and public on the Form 990 or Form 990-EZ most nonprofits file with the IRS each year.

The DP must actually repay the loan under the terms of the agreement, and the nonprofit must demand repayment if the DP does not do so. If the interest rate is below-market, or there is no interest, the value of the forgone interest must be added to the DP's total compensation. The interest rate is below market-rate if the amount loaned exceeds the present value of all the payments due under the loan. (Present value is the total amount that a series of future payments is worth now—several present-value calculators can be found on the Internet.)

It is not uncommon for DPs who receive money that they can't otherwise account for to claim that the payments were loans from the nonprofit, or repayments of loans the DP previously made to the nonprofit. These claims will not be accepted by the IRS unless the loan is fully documented and treated like a real loan.

The Poster Child for IRS Sanctions

A used car salesman established a nonprofit to help the homeless. All of its revenues were obtained by selling used cars donated by the public. The car salesman served as the nonprofit's president and executive director. The board of directors consisted of the salesman, his wife, father-in-law, and an unrelated CPA. An IRS examination found that the nonprofit sold $200,000 worth of donated cars each year, but donated only $5,000 a year to homeless shelters. Among other things, the nonprofit:

- paid the president a salary of $120,000 per year, without obtaining approval from the board
- leased a vehicle for the president's use, without requiring him to account for how he used the car
- hired a towing company owned by the president's son to which it paid much more than the going rate for such services
- made payments to the president for an alleged loan he made to the nonprofit, although there was no promissory note or other evidence that the loan was ever made, and
- permitted the president and his relatives to make personal use of the nonprofit's business premises.

The IRS found that the president and his relatives were DPs and that all of these transactions were excess benefit transactions, upon which it imposed sanctions. (IRS Technical Advice Memo 200243057 (2002).)

Transactions With Disqualified Persons— How to Avoid Problems With the IRS

Perhaps your nonprofit would like to rent office space owned by a major contributor, hire a director's law firm to do legal work for it, or sell real estate given to it by its president. Transactions such as these carry the risk of being treated as excess benefit transactions by the IRS that could result in the imposition of intermediate sanctions. Fortunately, IRS rules provide a path through the sanctions minefield. If your nonprofit follows the procedures outlined below, it's highly unlikely the IRS would seek to impose sanctions on your DPs or managers. Moreover, implementing these procedures will ensure that the transactions you enter into are fair and reasonable for your nonprofit.

> **TIP**
> **Make the IRS's wish your command.** The IRS does not require that a nonprofit use the procedures described here, but it strongly recommends it. In fact, IRS Form 990, the annual information return bigger-sized nonprofits file with the IRS, specifically asks whether these procedures have been implemented. A "no" answer won't necessarily result in any action by the IRS, but it doesn't look good either—to the IRS or any member of the public who reviews the Form 990.

Identify Your Nonprofit's Disqualified Persons

The first thing you should do is identify and create a written list of all the people involved with your nonprofit who are "disqualified persons" (DPs) under IRS rules. For a small nonprofit, there probably won't be a huge number of DPs—the nonprofit's officers and directors and possibly a few other influential people in the organization, and their immediate families, and, possibly, some of their business interests. Once you have created your list of DPs, you will only need to update it when a DP leaves, changes jobs (or his or her job description changes), or if a new DP joins the organization. Any person who stops being a DP for more than five years can be removed from the list.

Some people are automatically considered DPs; others have this status thrust upon them by circumstances. The basic rule is that a disqualified person is anyone who, at any time within the five-year period ending on the date of the transaction in question, was in a position to exercise "substantial influence" over your nonprofit's affairs. It is not necessary that the person actually exercise substantial influence, only that he or she is in a position to do so.

Automatic DPs. The following people are automatically considered to be disqualified persons due to their influential positions:

- all board members who are entitled to vote
- the nonprofit's president, chief executive officer, chief operating officer, and any other person who, regardless of title, has ultimate responsibility for implementing the decisions of the board and managing the nonprofit
- the nonprofit's treasurer, chief financial officer, and any other person who, regardless of title, has ultimate responsibility for managing the nonprofit's finances
- any member of a disqualified person's immediate family— including a spouse, brother, sister, grandparent, child, grandchild, great-grandchild, and their spouses, and
- any company or other entity in which one or more DPs own more than a 35% interest.

EXAMPLE: Eve is the headmaster of the Progressive School, a non-profit grade school. She reports to the school's board of trustees and has ultimate responsibility for supervising the school's day-to-day operations. Eve can hire faculty members and staff, make changes to the school's curriculum, and discipline students without board approval. Because Eve has ultimate responsibility for supervising the nonprofit's operation, she is in a position to exercise substantial influence over its affairs. Therefore, Eve is a disqualified person for the school.

EXAMPLE: Arthur is a member of the board of directors of The Slovak Archive, a nonprofit archive dedicated to preserving Slovakian history. He is also a building contractor who owns a 50% interest in the ABC Building Co. His son Eugene owns his own company called Cleanup, Inc., that provides custodial services to businesses. Not only is Arthur a disqualified person for the Archive, his company is as well and so is his son and his son's company.

Fact and circumstance DPs. People who are not automatic DPs can still be DPs if the facts and circumstances show that they have substantial influence over the nonprofit's affairs. For a small nonprofit, those most likely to be deemed DPs by the IRS under this test are the organization's founder and its substantial contributors. A substantial contributor is anyone who contributes over 2% of the donations received during the current year and the prior four years, provided that this amount is over $5,000.

> EXAMPLE: Jane makes a $20,000 contribution to your nonprofit. The total contributions your nonprofit has received during this year and the previous four years amount to $500,000. Thus, Jane's gift exceeds 2% of all the contributions you've received for those years. Jane is a substantial contributor.

In larger nonprofits, DPs may also include:
- a person who has substantial budgetary authority—that is, he or she controls at least 10% of the nonprofit's budget, compensation for employees, or major expenditures—for example, the head of the human resources department
- a person who has substantial management authority—that is, he or she manages an activity that accounts for at least 10% of the nonprofit's assets, income, or expenses
- a person whose compensation is based primarily on the nonprofit's revenues, and
- a person who is a majority owner of a company or other entity that is a DP.

EXAMPLE: Save Our Youth (SOY), a nonprofit that provides mentoring for troubled youth, decides to use bingo games to generate revenue. SOY enters into a contract with Best Bingo, Inc., a company that operates bingo games. Under the contract, Best Bingo manages the promotion and operation of the bingo games, provides all necessary staff, equipment, and services for the games, and pays SOY 50% of the revenue from the activity. Best Bingo retains the balance of the proceeds. The annual gross revenue earned from the bingo games represents more than half of SOY's total annual revenue. Best Bingo is a disqualified person for SOY on two grounds:

- it manages an activity that accounts for more than 10% of SOY's annual income, and
- its compensation is based on the revenue it brings in.

Beware the Five-Year Look-Back Rule

You should never assume that because a person ceases to be in an influential position within your nonprofit, that he or she is no longer a DP. Remember, once someone becomes a DP, that person remains one for five years. So, on the date of the transaction in question, anyone who was a DP at any time over the previous five years is still a DP, even if that person no longer works for your nonprofit. Thus, an executive director of a nonprofit would remain a DP of that nonprofit for five years after he or she leaves. Any financial transaction with that person would be subject to the sanctions rules during that time period.

Employees. Employees are usually not DPs, unless they are in top-level positions. This is because they are deemed not to have substantial influence over the nonprofit. You don't ever need to worry about IRS sanctions when dealing with these fortunate souls. Any employee who meets the following three requirements will not be deemed a DP for IRS purposes:

- He or she is not a "highly compensated employee"—this means that the person's total compensation is less than a threshold amount established by the IRS each year. In 2013, the amount is $115,000.
- The employee is not an automatic DP (such as a member of the board, CEO, or CFO) or a family member of an automatic DP.
- The employee is not a "substantial contributor" to the nonprofit—that is, his or her monetary contributions to the nonprofit for the

current year and the prior four years must be less than a total of $5,000 and 2% of the nonprofit's total contributions.

EXAMPLE: Nathan, an artist, works part time at a local art museum. The museum pays Nathan a salary of $30,000 and free admission to the museum, a benefit it provides to all of its employees and volunteers. The total compensation Nathan receives is less than the threshold amount to be considered a highly compensated employee ($115,000). The part-time job is Nathan's only relationship with the museum and he is not related to any other disqualified person for the museum. Nathan is not a disqualified person.

All or most of your nonprofit's support and administrative staff should fall within this group, as long as they are not related to an automatic DP. Even if they don't meet the three requirements listed above, employees are not considered DPs if they don't participate in important management decisions. As a general rule of thumb, any employee whose supervisor is not a DP is very likely not a DP either.

Professional advisers. A person such as an attorney, accountant, or investment adviser that your nonprofit hires to provide professional advice (and not make decisions for you) is not a DP, as long as he or she does not personally benefit from the transaction involved other than receiving fees or other normal payment for the services. An accountant you hire and pay by the hour to provide accounting services and tax advice for your nonprofit would not be a DP, unless the advice concerns a transaction the accountant would personally benefit from, directly or indirectly.

EXAMPLE: Donald provides accounting services and tax advice as an independent consultant to a small nonprofit. He gets paid an hourly fee for his services. Donald is not a DP when he prepares the nonprofit's annual tax return. However, Donald becomes a DP when the nonprofit asks him to advise it about the tax consequences of selling some property it owns to his brother-in-law.

Theater of the Absurd—Disqualified Persons

Theater of the Absurd is a small nonprofit repertory company founded in 2005. It is governed by a three-member board of directors. Day-to-day operations are managed by an employee-executive director and part-time treasurer. One member of the original board—Bart Farnsworth—left the organization in 2008 and was replaced by Delilah Solano. Farnsworth and his family will cease being DPs in 2013. The executive director of the Theater drafts the following list of DPs for the organization using answers to a conflicts of interest questionnaire that officers, directors, and key employees fill out each year (see "Have a Conflict of Interest Policy" below):

Name of DP	Reason for DP Status	Date DP Status Began	Date DP Status Ends
Alan James and immediate family: Spouse: Sue James Parents: Bart James, Mary James Siblings and their Spouses: Janice James Johnson, Dennis James Children and their Spouses: Karen James	Board Member or Relative	2/1/2005	
Sue Jenkins and immediate family: Spouse: Al Jenkins Siblings and their Spouses: Connie Ames, Roger Ames	Board Member or Relative	2/1/2005	
Bart Farnsworth and immediate family: Parents: Ann Farnsworth Siblings and their Spouses: Janice James Johnson, Bill Johnson, Art James, Diane Olsen James Grandchildren and their spouses: None	Board Member or Relative	2/1/2005	6/1/2013 (resigned from board on 6/1/2008)

Theater of the Absurd—Disqualified Persons (continued)			
Name of DP	Reason for DP Status	Date DP Status Began	Date DP Status Ends

Delilah Solano and immediate family:
   Parents: Edgar Solano, Ruth Solano
   Siblings and their Spouses: Ken Solano, Janice Solano
   Children and their Spouses: Ronald Solano, Mary Solano
	Board Member or Relative	6/1/2008	

Anne Rutledge and immediate family: Parents: Jean Farnsworth	Executive Director or Relative	2/1/2005	

George Jones and immediate family
   Spouse: Diana Jones
   Parents: Jane Jones
   Siblings and their Spouses: David Jones, Agnes Jones, Bill Jones, Frederick Jones
   Children and their Spouses: Alice Jones
	Chief Financial Officer or Relative	4/30/2005	

ABC, Inc.	50% interest in corporation owned by George Jones	2/1/2005	

Follow IRS-Approved Procedures

The IRS has established procedures for approving transactions with DPs that, if followed, create a "rebuttable presumption" that the transaction in question was reasonable and therefore not an excess benefit transaction. This means that the IRS must presume that the transaction passes muster if you follow the IRS-recommended procedures. In addition, sanctions cannot be imposed on your nonprofit's managers if these procedures are followed. The IRS can still challenge what your nonprofit did, but it must come up with its own evidence showing that your board acted improperly. As a practical matter, the IRS will rarely make such an effort. To be effective, you must implement these procedures *before* you enter into the transaction with the DP.

These procedures require some time and effort. Do they have to be used for every transaction involving a DP? No. It would likely be overkill to use them for transactions with DPs involving very small amounts of money or low-value property—for example, you probably wouldn't have to obtain prior board approval before purchasing a used computer from a director of your nonprofit for $100. Keep in mind that if you don't follow these procedures, it doesn't mean the transaction was an excess benefit transaction. It just means that you don't get the benefit of the IRS's presumption that the transaction is not an excess benefit transaction. But you should follow these procedures before entering into major transactions with DPs—for example, purchasing or renting real estate from a DP or setting a key employee's compensation (see "Excessive Compensation for Services: The Most Common Excess Benefit," below).

The IRS-recommended procedures for approving transactions with DPs consist of the following:

Prior approval by authorized body. The transaction must be approved in advance by an "authorized body." This can be the entire board of directors, a committee of the board, or other person or persons authorized by the board to act on its behalf. Thus, it is not necessary to have the full board approve the transaction. It can be approved by a committee appointed for the purpose by the board. Such a committee, often the executive committee, usually consists of at least two board members. However, a committee of only one member is acceptable to the IRS if it's permitted under your state's nonprofit corporation law. If allowed by your state's nonprofit corporation law, an independent committee consisting of non–board–members can also be authorized by the board to approve such transactions—for example, a committee consisting of the executive director and chief financial officer.

No conflicts of interest. Whoever reviews and approves the transaction —whether the full board or a committee—must not have any conflicts of interest. Any person with a conflict of interest should not participate in the deliberations or vote on the issue. (See "Have a Conflict of Interest Policy," below.) No person voting on the transaction should be:

- a member of the DP's family
- in a position to benefit financially if the transaction is approved or disapproved
- an employee of the nonprofit who works under the DP's direction
- an employee of the nonprofit whose compensation is subject to approval by the DP, or
- involved in any financial transaction with the nonprofit that has been, or will be, subject to the DP's approval.

The DP may be present to answer questions during disclosure of all the relevant facts, but should leave the room during the vote and not otherwise participate in the discussion or meeting.

Use of data to back up decisions. The board or other authorizing body should look at and rely on hard data in deciding whether or not to approve a transaction. The purpose of the data is to determine whether the transaction with the DP is fair and reasonable—that is, that fair market value is being paid by, or received by, the nonprofit. If you can show fair market value (or less) was paid, then there is no excess benefit. Fair market value is what a willing buyer would pay a willing seller, where neither is under any compulsion to buy or sell, and both have knowledge of all the relevant facts.

What type of data is appropriate will depend on the nature of the transaction. If the transaction involves the sale or purchase of property to or from a DP, the authorizing body should determine if there is a readily established market price for the property—for example: Can identical property be purchased elsewhere? Have other competitive offers been made for the property? If there is no readily established market price, you may need to obtain an independent appraisal. In the case of rentals to or from a DP, the authorizing body should look at the going rate for similar rentals in the area, taking into account the length of the rental period, the type of property being rented, and the purpose of the rental. See Chapter 6 for more guidance on how to determine the fair market value of property.

Adequate and timely documentation. The authorizing body's decision must be adequately and timely documented. If the authorizing body is the board of directors, this would normally consist of written board minutes. If an executive committee or independent committee served as the authorizing body, it should prepare its own minutes or report. The documentation must contain:

- the terms of the transaction and the date approved
- the names and titles of all those who were present during the debate on the transaction and those who voted on it
- the data that was relied on by the authorizing body and how it was obtained—this data can be attached or referenced in the minutes (or other documentation) but should be available for later review, and
- a detailed explanation of how any potential conflicts of interest on the authorizing body were handled.

If the board or other authorizing body determines that fair market value for a transaction is higher or lower than the amount paid by the DP, it must record the rationale for its decision to go forward with the transaction, particularly if it approves paying above fair market value for something.

The documentation must be prepared before the later of the next meeting of the authorizing body or 60 days after the body's final action on the matter. In addition, the body must approve the documentation within a reasonable time after it has been prepared. In most cases, this would be taken care of in the normal course of business by preparing minutes of the meeting that include all the required information and then approving those minutes at the next board or committee meeting.

RESOURCE

For a detailed guide on how to prepare board minutes for a nonprofit, refer to *Nonprofit Meetings, Minutes & Records*, by Anthony Mancuso (Nolo).

EXAMPLE: The Orphan Relief Fund has been offered the rental of office space in an office building owned by John for $2,000 per month. John is one of the Fund's directors, and is therefore a DP. The Fund's five-member board, not including John, meets to consider whether to approve the transaction. At the meeting, Sylvia, the Fund's executive director, explains that she contacted two commercial real estate brokers and was told that comparable office space in the area where John's building is located rents for $2 to $3 per square foot. The office space offered by John is 1,000 square feet and is being offered for $2 per square foot, at the low end of the rental scale. The board votes unanimously to approve the transaction. Minutes of the meeting are prepared by the organization's secretary the week after the meeting and are approved by the board at its next regularly scheduled meeting two months later. The minutes include the following information: the terms of the deal, a copy of the lease, the names of the people who attended the meeting, how everyone voted, a statement that John was not permitted to vote on the matter because of his conflict of interest, and the rental data.

Have a Conflict of Interest Policy

Although not required by law, the IRS strongly encourages all nonprofits to implement a formal written conflict of interest policy. These are a set of policies and procedures that help DPs identify whether they have a conflict of interest. They also require that the nonprofit's board be advised of the conflict and excuse conflicted DPs from voting on matters where they have a conflict. A "conflict of interest" arises when a person in a position of authority over a nonprofit, such as a director, officer, or manager, may benefit personally from a decision he or she could make. For example, a conflict of interest would occur where an officer, director, or board member votes on a contract between the nonprofit and a business that is owned by the person.

The IRS is so serious about the need for conflict of interest policies that it has created a sample policy and included it in the instructions for

IRS Form 1023, the form nonprofits use to apply for tax-exempt status. Moreover, Form 990, the annual information return larger nonprofits must file with the IRS each year, asks whether the nonprofit has adopted a conflicts policy and monitors compliance with it. A "no" answer to these questions makes it appear that a nonprofit is not doing a good job dealing with conflicts of interest.

Section B. Policies		Yes	No
12a Does the organization have a written conflict of interest policy? *If "No," go to line 13*	**12a**		
b Are officers, directors or trustees, and key employees required to disclose annually interests that could give rise to conflicts?	**12b**		
c Does the organization regularly and consistently monitor and enforce compliance with the policy? *If "Yes," describe in Schedule O how this is done*	**12c**		
13 Does the organization have a written whistleblower policy?	**13**		

If your nonprofit doesn't already have a written conflict of interest policy, your board of directors should adopt one. This can be a stand-alone document or incorporated in your nonprofit's bylaws.

There is no single way to write a conflict of interest policy. The IRS's sample policy was developed for large health care institutions and may not be appropriate for smaller nonprofits.

RESOURCE
A copy of the IRS sample conflict of interest policy is contained in the appendix to this book. A digital copy can be found in the Instructions to IRS Form 1023 at www.irs.gov. A conflict of interest policy is also included in the sample nonprofit corporation bylaws in the book *How to Form a Nonprofit Corporation*, by Anthony Mancuso (Nolo). Other sources include:
- the website www.boardsource.org, which has several sample policies that can be downloaded for a small fee
- the National Council of Nonprofits at www.councilofnonprofits.org has a sample policy available online, and
- the Minnesota Attorney General's Office website at www.ag.state.mn.us/ Charities has a sample policy available online.

A useful brief guide on the subject that also contains sample conflict policies is *Managing Conflicts of Interest: A Primer for Nonprofit Boards*, by Daniel L. Kurtz and Sarah E. Paul. It is also available at www.boardsource.com.

Excessive Compensation for Services: The Most Common Excess Benefit

By far the most common type of excess benefit transaction, and the one that garners the most IRS attention, is paying excessive compensation for services performed by disqualified persons, whether as employees of the nonprofit or independent contractors. These DPs include your non-profit's officers and its key employees who have significant management, financial, or budgetary authority. It also includes these individuals' immediate family who perform services for your nonprofit—for example, if the spouse of your nonprofit's president is hired to do work for your nonprofit. (See "Identify Your Nonprofit's Disqualified Persons," above.)

> **EXAMPLE:** The nonprofit Center for Democracy hires Mark, the son of one of its directors, as an independent contractor to perform public relations work. The work includes drafting press releases and writing a monthly newsletter for the organization. The Center pays Mark $10,000 per month for his services. Mark is a disqualified person because he is the son of a DP. Thus, if Mark's compensation was deemed to be unreasonable by the IRS, he, and anyone at the Center who approved the arrangement, would be subject to the imposition of intermediate sanctions.

The IRS says that a DP who performs services for a nonprofit can only be paid a reasonable amount. Any amount above the reasonable threshold is an excess benefit that can result in IRS sanctions. Determining how much to pay key employees, such as an executive director or CEO, can be an agonizing decision for a board. The fact that board members can be subject to IRS sanctions if they pay an employee or other DP too much doesn't make things any easier.

Preapproval of Compensation

The IRS has adopted procedures and guidelines for nonprofits to follow in determining how much to pay DPs. If your nonprofit follows them, the compensation it pays the DP must be presumed to be reasonable by the IRS. These procedures are the same as the procedures used when purchasing or renting property from DPs. (See "Follow IRS-Approved Procedures," above.) If you use them, it's unlikely you'll run into a problem with the IRS.

To obtain the benefit of the IRS's presumption that compensation paid to a DP is reasonable, the person's compensation must be pre-approved by the entire board of directors, or a smaller compensation committee authorized by the board. The board or committee must be independent—that is, those with conflicts of interest cannot participate in approving the transaction. Appropriate data must be used to determine if the compensation is reasonable. (See "What Is Reasonable Compensation," below.) And the decision must be thoroughly and timely documented. (See "Follow IRS-Approved Procedures," above, for more on all of these requirements.)

Compensation Data Is Publicly Available

Keep in mind that the compensation your nonprofit pays to officers, directors, and key employees will likely be publicly available via the IRS filings most nonprofits make each year. Larger nonprofits file IRS Form 990, which requires that the nonprofit disclose the compensation paid to all current directors and officers. You also must list the compensation for all key employees who earned more than $150,000 per year, and the five highest-compensated employees who earned more than $100,000 per year. Smaller nonprofits file IRS Form 990-EZ, which requires that the compensation of all officers, directors, and key employees be listed, regardless of the amount. Nonprofits must make these forms available for public inspection. Moreover, digital copies of most of them are freely available to the public at the website guidestar.org. Thus, a good rule of thumb for determining compensation is that your nonprofit shouldn't pay more than it would be comfortable to see reported in the local newspaper.

The "First Bite" Rule

There is an important exception to the IRS rules about compensation to DPs for their services. Under the so-called "first bite" rule, the IRS won't impose sanctions on fixed payments made pursuant to an employment contract with a person who was not a DP when the contract was negotiated. This is because when a nonprofit first hires a person who is not a DP, he or she will likely not be in a position to substantially influence the organization.

To apply, the employment contract must be in writing and the amount to be paid must be specified in the contract or determined by a fixed formula—for example, based on increases in the cost of living. Discretionary payments, such as a discretionary year-end bonus, do not come within the first bite rule. A nondiscretionary bonus however—for example, a bonus based on the nonprofit's future revenue, would be considered a fixed payment and come within the exception.

> EXAMPLE: Save the Iguanas, a small environmental nonprofit, negotiates with an outsider, Stan, to serve as its executive director. They enter into a contract calling for a fixed salary of $100,000 per year and $5,000 for health insurance. Future increases are to be based on the Consumer Price Index. All of these payments are fixed payments or set by a fixed formula, so Stan's contract falls within the first bite rule. If the IRS determines that Stan's compensation is excessive, it cannot impose sanctions on Stan or the board members who approved the contract.

After the initial contract terminates, the person will be a DP and the new contract will be subject to the sanctions rules. The initial contract is deemed over for these purposes as of the earliest date the nonprofit or employee is allowed to end it without incurring a substantial penalty. "Material changes" to the contract are also deemed to terminate it—such as substantial changes in the DP's compensation or an extension or renewal of the contract not already called for in the agreement.

Even if the first bite exception applies, it is still advisable to follow the IRS approval procedures for DP compensation.

What Is Reasonable Compensation?

The IRS says that a DP who works for a nonprofit can only be paid a reasonable amount. Any amount above the reasonable threshold is an excess benefit that can result in IRS sanctions. Nonprofits would love to have concrete guidelines about how much is reasonable. Unfortunately, there aren't any. The IRS simply says that compensation is reasonable if the amount paid would ordinarily be paid for:

- comparable services
- by comparable enterprises (whether nonprofit or for-profit), and
- under comparable circumstances.

In other words, you have to look at what other people doing similar jobs for similar organizations are paid. Your nonprofit and a comparable organization should be competing for the same pool of talent.

Comparable compensation data. The single most important element in determining whether a DP's compensation is reasonable is comparable compensation data—that is, data about how much compensation is paid by similar organizations for people working in comparable positions.

Comparable services. In determining whether one person's services are comparable to another's, you should consider such factors as the type of work and skills involved, whether the job is full time or part time, the size and scope of the organization, the number of employees managed, the budget or assets managed, and whether the person manages multiple functions or departments.

Comparable enterprises. In determining whether another nonprofit (or profit) organization is comparable to your own, you should consider whether it is similar in:

- size—by budget, revenues, number of employees, and persons served, and
- mission—for example, a small private school should not be compared to a hospital or performing arts group.

Comparable circumstances. Consider such circumstances as whether the organization is located in a similar geographic area—for example, whether it is urban or rural, and whether the cost of living is similar.

Other factors. Other factors can be considered as well. Depending on the circumstances, these may include:

- the nonprofit's geographic location
- economic conditions
- the DP's duties and past performance history
- the amount of time the DP spends on the job
- the person's compensation history
- the DP's background, skills, education, and experience
- whether the DP has actual written job offers from other organizations, and
- how much other employees at the nonprofit are paid, and the availability of similar services in the nonprofit's geographic area.

A 2008 study of nonprofit CEO compensation by Charity Navigator, a nonprofit that evaluates and rates charities, found that, other than comparable compensation data, the most important additional factors are the nonprofit's size, mission, and location. The study reported that:

- Nonprofits with total budgets greater than $13.5 million paid higher than average compensation, while those with under $3.5 million paid less than average.
- Nonprofits in the Northeast and Mid-Atlantic regions paid above average compensation, while those in the South, Southwest, Midwest, Mountain West, and Pacific West paid less than average.
- Nonprofits whose missions were in the areas of the arts, culture, humanities, public benefit, and health paid more than average compensation, while those involved with animals, the environment, human services, and international affairs paid less than average.

If this all sounds pretty subjective, that's because it is. The compensation nonprofits pay their DPs for doing similar jobs can vary widely.

How Much Are Nonprofit Leaders Paid?

Despite the many stories in the media about highly paid nonprofit CEOs and other employees, most people who work for nonprofits receive very modest salaries. The large salaries that garner the most publicity are mostly confined to extremely large nonprofits, such as nonprofit hospitals and universities. The boards of most small and midsized nonprofits worry about paying key employees enough, rather than paying too much.

One well-known survey of nonprofit salaries is the annual national salary survey published each year by *The Nonprofit Times*, a bimonthly magazine for the nonprofit world; it is available at www.thenonprofittimes. com. The 2013 survey found the following range of average salaries for small nonprofits:

Nonprofit Job	National Median Salary 2013
Executive Director	$59,939
Program Coordinator	$35,238
Director of Development	$49,798
Administrative Assistant	$33,418

What Is Included in Compensation?

Small nonprofits usually pay their executive director and other employee DPs a salary and often provide some type of health insurance. DPs in larger nonprofits receive additional types of compensation and fringe benefits. To determine whether a DP's compensation is reasonable, the total compensation paid the DP must be considered. Virtually everything of value given to a DP is included in compensation, with the exception of certain tax-free employee fringe benefits and reimbursements for expenses made under an accountable plan (see "Reimburse Employee DP Expenses Under an Accountable Plan," below).

The following chart shows which payments and benefits are considered part of an employee DP's compensation and which ones are not.

Calculating DP's Total Compensation

Included in Compensation	Not Included in Compensation

• salary
• bonuses
• deferred compensation
• retirement benefits
• medical and dental insurance benefits
• disability benefits
• life insurance
• directors' and officers' liability insurance (except for volunteer directors—see Chapter 4)
• severance pay
• interest-free or low-interest loans
• nonaccountable expense accounts
• rent-free or low-rent use of nonprofit property for personal purposes
• educational assistance, and
• spousal travel.
	• accountable plan reimbursements
	• tax-free employee fringe benefits:
	  ▪ working condition fringe benefits—any property or services the employee needs to do his or her job
	  ▪ commuting and parking benefits
	  ▪ employee discounts on the goods or services the nonprofit sells
	  ▪ de minimus (low-cost) fringe benefits, such as low-value birthday or holiday gifts, event tickets, traditional awards (such as a retirement gift), other special occasion gifts, and coffee and soft drinks
	  ▪ no-additional-cost services, and
	  ▪ moving expense reimbursements.

DPs who are independent contractors are usually paid an hourly fee or a set fee for a project, and they may get some or all of their expenses reimbursed. Expense reimbursements are not included as contractor compensation if they are properly documented with receipts, canceled checks, credit card statements, or other proof of payment.

Before determining whether a DP's compensation is reasonable, the board or committee charged with approving it must make sure it has complete and accurate information about the person's total compensation package. The nonprofit's staff should provide this information upon request.

Using Comparable Compensation Data

A large nonprofit might decide to hire a consultant to conduct a customized compensation survey to determine comparability data. However, this is not required. The key is to obtain comparable data—that is, find out what other organizations pay for similar work in similar organizations in similar communities. A lot of data is available for free or from anywhere from $50 to $1,000 or more.

If the nonprofit earns less than one million dollars per year (including donations), all that is required is compensation data for three similar positions in similar communities. This data may be obtained by any means, including documented phone calls. In determining whether the one million dollar threshold is met, a nonprofit may average its gross annual receipts over the prior three tax years. For larger organizations, there is no set number of comparables required—presumably there should be more than three.

You should obtain your comparables by finding nonprofits that are as like yours as possible in terms of mission, budget, number of employees, and geographic area, and then look at what they pay for a similar position. You don't have to rely solely on data from nonprofits. For some positions, data from for-profit enterprises may be useful and appropriate where the work involved is similar. For example, if you're hiring an accountant, data about pay for accountants at similarly sized for-profit businesses may be useful.

Often this data will reveal a broad range of pay for a certain type of position. The IRS shouldn't complain if your nonprofit pays a DP an amount that is average or below the average that is paid for similar work at comparable organizations. At the same time, a compensation package that is more than average will not necessarily be viewed as unreasonable by the IRS. It all depends on the circumstances. For example, a higher than average salary may be reasonable because the nonprofit is located in an area with a high cost of living or because the person involved has performed exceptionally well.

An IRS expert prepared the checklist shown below for determining a DP's compensation:

Finding Comparable Compensation Data

Sources of compensation data for nonprofits include the following:

GuideStar, a directory of nonprofits, posts copies of Forms 990 and 990-EZs filed each year for all nonprofits with annual revenues of $25,000 or more. These forms contain compensation data for each nonprofit's directors, officers, and key employees. You can check the 990 forms for similar nonprofits in your geographic area to see how much they are paying. Access to the forms is free and at GuideStar's website at www. guidestar.org.

Charity Navigator, an organization that evaluates charities, compiles compensation data for CEOs and executive directors of thousands of charities. This data may be found at www.charitynavigator.org.

The Chronicle of Philanthropy, a newspaper for nonprofits, compiles an annual survey of salary information for top officials at several hundred non-profits throughout the United States. Its website is http://philanthropy.com.

The Nonprofit Times, a magazine for the nonprofit community, publishes an annual survey of salaries at nonprofits throughout the United States. Its website is www.thenonprofittimes.com.

The Economic Research Institute maintains a massive commercial database of salary information and sells database software to access it. ERI and its affiliates have four different websites that offer various services at various prices: www.erieri.com; http://salariesreview.com; (redirects to ERI site); www.paq.com.

The Society for Human Resource Management publishes an annual compensation survey covering both for-profit and nonprofit organizations. Online compensation reports for specific positions are also available for a fee. Its website is www.shrm.org.

Local surveys for a particular city, state, or region may be available—for example, the National Capitol Human Resources Association publishes an annual survey of compensation in Washington, DC, including nonprofits. A list of regional associations that may have local survey information may be found at www.fundsnetservices.com.

Your local United Way or community foundation may also have salary information. And similar nonprofits in your area may have data that they are willing to share with you.

Rebuttable Presumption Checklist

1. Name of disqualified person: _____

2. Position under consideration: _____

3. Duration of contract (1 yr., 3 yr., etc.): _____

4. Proposed Compensation:

   Salary: _____

   Bonus: _____

   Deferred compensation: _____

   Fringe benefits: _____

   _____

   _____

   Liability insurance premiums: _____

   Forgone interest on loans: _____

   Other: _____

5. Description of types of comparability data relied upon (for example, association survey, phone inquiries, etc.):

   a. _____

   b. _____

   c. _____

   d. _____

6. Sources and amounts of comparability data:

   Salary: _____

   Bonus: _____

   Deferred compensation: _____

   Fringe benefits: _____

   _____

   _____

   Liability insurance premiums: _____

   Forgone interest on loans: _____

   Others: _____

7. Office or file where comparability data kept: _____

8. Total proposed compensation: _____

9. Maximum total compensation per comparability data: _____

10. Compensation package approved by authorized body:

   Salary: _____

   Bonus: _____

   Deferred compensation: _____

   Fringe benefits: _____

   _____

   _____

   Liability insurance premiums: _____

   Forgone interest on loans: _____

   Other: _____

Theater of the Absurd Pays Its Artistic Director

Theater of the Absurd is setting the annual compensation for Anne, its artistic director. The theater had annual gross receipts ranging from $600,000 to $900,000 over its past three tax years. Because its annual revenue was under $1 million, it only needs compensation comparables from three organizations. George, the theater's CFO, conducts a telephone survey of the compensation paid to the directors of three similar-sized theater groups in the San Francisco Bay Area. A member of the board drafts a brief written summary of the annual compensation information obtained from this informal survey. The entire board, except for Anne's sister-in-law, meets to discuss and approve Anne's compensation package. Anne tells the board that she would like a 5% increase over her current salary of $70,000 and discusses her accomplishments over the past year. She then leaves the meeting.

The total compensation paid by the three nonprofits that were surveyed for comparable data ranged from $50,000 to $100,000. One of the nonprofits provided no employee benefits to its director, while the other two provided health insurance. All provided liability insurance coverage. The board decides to keep Anne's salary and benefits at the same levels as the previous year, providing her with total compensation of $75,000. However, it also elects to grant her a year-end bonus of $5,000, payable if the theater's total income for the year exceeds $900,000. The board fully documents its decision in its minutes, referencing the survey information, the current financial status of the theater, and Anne's past performance. Anne agrees to the board's decision and signs a new employment contract with the theater that contains all the terms of her compensation package.

Because the board's decision utilized comparable salary data and was properly documented, the IRS must presume that Anne's salary is reasonable.

Document All Taxable Compensation Paid to DPs

The IRS does not want DPs being given hidden, unreported payments or other economic benefits. For this reason, all payments or taxable benefits given to a DP are automatically treated as excess benefits unless the nonprofit clearly indicates in writing its intent to treat them as part of the DP's compensation. Absent such documentation, the IRS will impose intermediate sanctions, whether or not it was reasonable for the DP to be given the payment or benefit.

> EXAMPLE: The Board of Directors of the Peoria Food Bank, a nonprofit that delivers food to the elderly in Central Illinois, agrees to pay its executive director a salary of $80,000 and provide other employee benefits worth $20,000. A written employment agreement is signed to this effect. During the year, the director uses one of the nonprofit's vehicles for his personal use. This benefit was not mentioned in the employment agreement or otherwise approved by the board. Nor is its value—$10,000—reported to the IRS on the director's W-2 or listed as income on his tax return. The nonprofit is subsequently audited by the IRS. When the IRS discovers that the director has made personal use of the vehicle, it automatically treats its value as an excess benefit and imposes sanctions. This is regardless of whether its value, in addition to the other amounts paid the director, was reasonable or not.

It's easy to avoid this type of automatic sanction. All you need to do is provide "written substantiation that is contemporaneous with the transfer of the particular benefit" that you intend to treat the benefit as DP compensation. There are several ways to do this and, as long as it is done, the value of the benefit will not be subject to automatic sanctions. Instead, it will be added to the DP's total compensation to determine whether it was reasonable.

Board approval. First, a payment or taxable benefit will be properly documented if, in accordance with established procedures, it is approved by the board of directors, another appropriate decision-making body (such as a compensation committee), or an officer authorized to approve compensation. "Established procedures" are the nonprofit's usual practices for approving compensation, and don't require a formal written procedure. The approval must occur *before* the benefit is given to the DP and must be documented in writing—for example, included in a written employment contract or other document approved by the board before the date the benefit is transferred to the DP. If your nonprofit follows the procedures outlined in "Follow IRS-Approved Procedures," above, all the benefits considered and authorized by the board at that time will be properly documented. If the DP receives additional benefits later, they should be separately approved and documented. A written employment contract or independent contractor agreement that includes the benefit is also sufficient if it is signed before the date the benefit is transferred to the DP. Make sure any approval is done by independent board members or any other authorized person who doesn't have a conflict of interest. (See "Follow IRS-Approved Procedures" for rules about getting independent board approvals.)

IRS reporting by nonprofit. Even if your nonprofit failed to properly document the benefit when it was first approved, you have a second bite of the apple: A nonprofit will satisfy the documentation requirement by reporting the additional payments or other economic benefits to the IRS. If the DP is an employee, the value of the benefit should be included in the wages reported to the IRS on Form W-2. If the DP is an independent contractor, the benefit must be reported on IRS Form 1099-MISC. Alternatively, the benefits can be reported on the information return most nonprofits file each year: IRS Form 990 or Form 990-EZ. It isn't even necessary for your nonprofit to file these forms when originally due. They can be filed any time before the start of an IRS examination of either your nonprofit or the DP for the year when the transaction occurred. Amended W-2s or 1099s can be filed if necessary. Thus, if you realize you have an undocumented benefit that was paid to a DP sometime in the past, be sure to file the required forms. As long as you do so before an IRS audit, you'll be okay.

IRS reporting by DP. The documentation requirement is also satisfied if the DP reports the benefit's value as income on his or her individual tax return (IRS Form 1040). This must be done before the earlier of:

(1) the start of an IRS examination of either the nonprofit or the DP for the year when the transaction occurred, or (2) the first written documentation by the IRS of a potential excess benefit transaction involving either the nonprofit or DP. If necessary, the DP can file an amended 1040 to report the income. Because you can never really be sure what a DP reports in his or her tax return, nonprofits shouldn't rely on the DP to do the necessary reporting.

Only taxable benefits need be documented. To make life a little easier for nonprofits, the IRS only requires that cash compensation and taxable employee benefits be documented as described above. Nontaxable employee benefits need not be documented. These include health insurance, contributions to a qualified pension plan, and several other types of benefits. (See the chart below.) Although these benefits are not included in the documentation requirements, most are considered when determining whether a DP's total compensation is reasonable.

RESOURCE

For a detailed discussion of the tax treatment of employee benefits, refer to IRS Publication 15-B, *Employer's Tax Guide to Fringe Benefits*. It can be found on the IRS website at www.irs.gov, or you can obtain a copy by calling 800-TAX-FORM.

Reimburse Employee DP Expenses Under an Accountable Plan

It's common for nonprofits to reimburse key employees for various work-related expenses such as car, travel, meals, and entertainment. These payments to employees can be made through advances, direct reimbursements, charges to a company credit card, or direct billings to the employer. As long as these payments are made under an "accountable plan," they are not considered in determining whether the DP's compensation is reasonable. They are not taxable income for the DP and don't need to be reported to the IRS.

Nontaxable Employee Fringe Benefits Exempt From IRS Documentation Requirements

- Health and dental insurance
- Contributions to qualified pension plans
- Group term life insurance up to $50,00 in coverage
- Disability insurance
- Health savings account contributions
- Educational assistance up to an annual cap
- No-additional-cost services from the nonprofit
- Employee discounts up to 20%
- Achievement awards
- Adoption assistance
- Child care assistance
- Retirement plan services
- Dependent care assistance up to an annual cap
- Moving expense reimbursements
- Athletic facilities
- Lodging on business premises for employer's convenience
- Low-value meals and meals provided on business premises
- Tuition reduction for undergraduate or graduate education
- Working condition fringe benefits—any property or services the employee needs to do his job
- De minimis (low-cost) fringe benefits such as low-value birthday or holiday gifts, event tickets, traditional awards (such as a retirement gift), other special occasion gifts, and coffee and soft drinks, and
- Parking and transportation benefits.

An accountable plan is an arrangement in which the nonprofit agrees to reimburse or advance employee expenses if the employee:

- pays or incurs expenses that are work-related
- adequately accounts for the expenses within a reasonable period of time—the DP must keep receipts for all expenses (except for some expenses below $75), and
- returns to the nonprofit any amounts received in excess of the actual expenses incurred within a reasonable time.

These strict rules are imposed to prevent employees from seeking reimbursement for personal expenses (or nonexistent phony expenses) under the guise that they were work expenses. An accountable plan doesn't need to be in writing (although it's not a bad idea). All your nonprofit has to do is set up procedures for your employees to follow that meet the requirements. See Chapter 3 for a detailed discussion of accountable plans.

Any payments to employees for work-related expenses that do not comply with the accountable plan rules are considered taxable compensation to the employee, and must be reported as such to the IRS. They will also be subject to employment taxes. Moreover, if the employee is a DP, the payments will be an automatic excess benefit for which sanctions will be imposed unless they were reported to the IRS or otherwise documented by the nonprofit. (See "Automatic Excess Benefits," above.)

> EXAMPLE 1: The Plagiarism Archive pays Sally, its president, a salary of $50,000 per year. Last year, Sally took a trip to a national archivists' convention and incurred travel expenses of $2,500. Sally complied with the accountable plan rules and was reimbursed for the expenses by the Archive. The IRS audited the Archive and determined that the reimbursement was not compensation for Sally and did not have to be reported as such. Thus, it did not consider the $2,500 in determining whether Sally's compensation was reasonable.

EXAMPLE 2: Assume that the Archive reimbursed Sally $2,500 in expenses but the reimbursement was not made under an accountable plan. Under these circumstances, the reimbursement would be taxable compensation that must be reported to the IRS. Neither Sally nor the Archive reported the payment, so it is an automatic excess benefit. The IRS imposes sanctions of $625 on Sally (25% of $2,500 = $625) and she must return the $2,500 to the Archive or face further sanctions of $5,000.

The moral is clear: *Don't ever reimburse a DP for expenses without complying with the accountable plan requirements.*

Correcting and Reporting Excess Benefit Transactions

If your nonprofit discovers an excess benefit transaction, it should make good faith efforts to correct it. To do this, you must have the disqualified person repay or return the excess benefit, plus interest, and then adopt measures to make sure the same situation doesn't occur again. The IRS will take into account these efforts in deciding what penalties to impose —and especially whether to revoke the nonprofit's tax exemption.

In addition, you are supposed to report any excess benefit transactions you are aware of on the annual information return your nonprofit files with the IRS each year—Form 990 or Form 990-EZ. Part V, line 40b of the Form 990-EZ, the form used by smaller nonprofits, asks the following question all nonprofits must answer:

> **Section 501(c)(3) organizations.** Did the organization engage in any section 4958 excess transaction during the year or did it engage in an excess benefit transaction in a prior year that has not been reported on any of its prior Forms 990 or 990-EZ? If "Yes," complete Schedule L, Part I.

Part IV of Form 990, filed by larger nonprofits, contains a longer list of questions.

25a **Section 501(c)(3) and 501(c)(4) organizations.** Did the organization engage in an excess transaction with a disqualified person during the year? *If "Yes," complete Schedule L, Part I.*

b Is the organization aware that it engaged in an excess benefit transaction with a disqualified person in a prior year, and that the transaction has not been reported on any of the organization's prior forms 990 or 990-EZ? *If "Yes," complete Schedule L, Part I.*

26 Was a loan to or by a current or former officer, director, trustee, key employee, highly compensated employee, or disqualified person outstanding as of the end of the organization's tax year? *If "Yes," complete Schedule L, Part II.*

27 Did the organization provide a grant or other assistance to an officer, director, trustee, key employee, substantial contributor or employee thereof, a grant selection committee member, or to a 35% controlled entity or family member of any of these persons? *If "Yes," complete Schedule L, Part III.*

28 Was the organization a party to a business transaction with one of the following parties (see Schedule L, Part IV instructions for applicable filing thresholds, conditions, and exceptions):

a A current or former officer, director, trustee, or key employee? *If "Yes," complete Schedule L, Part IV.*

b A family member of a current or former officer, director, trustee, or key employee? *If "Yes," complete Schedule L, Part IV.*

c An entity of which a current or former officer, director, trustee, or key employee (or a family member thereof) was an officer, director, trustee, or direct or indirect owner? *If "Yes," complete Schedule L, Part IV.*

As you can see, the forms require you to disclose and describe any excess benefit transaction that occurred in the current year, and any such transactions that occurred in prior years that it became aware of.

There is a schedule for both forms—Schedule L—that must be used to report any excess benefit transactions, and any loans to or from insiders. Nonprofits filing Form 990 must also indicate on Schedule L whether grants or other payments were given to insiders, and list and describe all business transactions the nonprofit had with insiders (called "interested persons" on the schedule).

SCHEDULE L
(Form 990 or 990-EZ)

Department of the Treasury
Internal Revenue Service

Transactions With Interested Persons

▶ Complete if the organization answered
"Yes" on Form 990, Part IV, line 25a, 25b, 26, 27, 28a, 28b, or 28c,
or Form 990-EZ, Part V, line 38a or 40b.
▶ Attach to Form 990 or Form 990-EZ. ▶ See separate instructions.

OMB No. 1545-0047

2012

**Open To Public
Inspection**

Name of the organization

Employer identification number

Part I   **Excess Benefit Transactions** (section 501(c)(3) and section 501(c)(4) organizations only).
Complete if the organization answered "Yes" on Form 990, Part IV, line 25a or 25b, or Form 990-EZ, Part V, line 40b.

1	(a) Name of disqualified person	(b) Relationship between disqualified person and organization	(c) Description of transaction	(d) Corrected?	
				Yes	No
(1)					
(2)					
(3)					
(4)					
(5)					
(6)					

2   Enter the amount of tax incurred by the organization managers or disqualified persons during the year under section 4958 . . . . ▶ $ _____

3   Enter the amount of tax, if any, on line 2, above, reimbursed by the organization . . . . ▶ $ _____

Part II   **Loans to and/or From Interested Persons.**
Complete if the organization answered "Yes" on Form 990-EZ, Part V, line 38a or Form 990, Part IV, line 26; or if the organization reported an amount on Form 990, Part X, line 5, 6, or 22.

(a) Name of interested person	(b) Relationship with organization	(c) Purpose of loan	(d) Loan to or from the organization?		(e) Original principal amount	(f) Balance due	(g) In default?		(h) Approved by board or committee?		(i) Written agreement?	
			To	From			Yes	No	Yes	No	Yes	No
(1)												
(2)												
(3)												
(4)												
(5)												
(6)												
(7)												
(8)												
(9)												
(10)												
Total . . . . ▶ $												

Part III   **Grants or Assistance Benefiting Interested Persons.**
Complete if the organization answered "Yes" on Form 990, Part IV, line 27.

(a) Name of interested person	(b) Relationship between interested person and the organization	(c) Amount of assistance	(d) Type of assistance	(e) Purpose of assistance
(1)				
(2)				
(3)				
(4)				
(5)				
(6)				
(7)				
(8)				
(9)				
(10)				

For Paperwork Reduction Act Notice, see the Instructions for Form 990 or 990-EZ.   Cat. No. 50056A   Schedule L (Form 990 or 990-EZ) 2012

Part IV	**Business Transactions Involving Interested Persons.**

Complete if the organization answered "Yes" on Form 990, Part IV, line 28a, 28b, or 28c.

(a) Name of interested person	(b) Relationship between interested person and the organization	(c) Amount of transaction	(d) Description of transaction	(e) Sharing of organization's revenues?	
				Yes	No
(1)					
(2)					
(3)					
(4)					
(5)					
(6)					
(7)					
(8)					
(9)					
(10)					

Part V	**Supplemental Information**

Complete this part to provide additional information for responses to questions on Schedule L (see instructions).

IRS intermediate sanctions can only be imposed against the individuals involved in an excess benefit transaction—disqualified persons and nonprofit managers. They cannot be imposed against your nonprofit itself. However, if your nonprofit fails to report an excess benefit transaction, it will be subject to an IRS penalty of $20 per day, up to the lesser of $10,000 or 5% of its gross receipts. For organizations with gross receipts in excess of $1,000,000, the penalty is $100 per day, up to a maximum of $50,000. Moreover, depending on the circumstances, deliberate noncompliance with the reporting requirements could subject your nonprofit to criminal sanctions for tax fraud or other offenses. In addition, officers, directors, attorneys, accountants, and others involved in preparing and filing the Form 990 or Form 990-EZ could be personally liable for their role in submitting a false tax return.

One benefit of reporting an excess benefit transaction on Form 990 or 990-EZ is that the statute of limitations for assessing intermediate sanctions begins to run. The limitations period is three years after the return was filed, or if the transaction was not adequately reported, up to six years.

The IRS's Sentence of Death: Revocation of Tax-Exempt Status

Having to pay substantial monetary penalties to the IRS is pretty bad, but things can get even worse for nonprofits that engage in particularly egregious conduct—they can have their tax exemption revoked by the IRS. This means, among other things, that donors would not be allowed to deduct their contributions from their income taxes. This is tantamount to a sentence of death. For this reason, it doesn't happen very often. But it does happen where a nonprofit ceases to be "charitable" in nature and instead is used for private gain.

Private Inurement

The IRS can revoke a nonprofit's tax exemption in cases of extreme private inurement—that is, where, instead of furthering an exempt purpose, a nonprofit is used to benefit insiders, such as directors, officers, employees, and major contributors. This happens when the nonprofit engages in excess benefit transactions. The IRS considers the following factors in determining whether to revoke a nonprofit's tax exemption when there has been an excess benefit transaction:

- the size and scope of the excess benefit transaction or transactions (collectively, if more than one) in relation to the size and scope of the nonprofit's regular charitable purpose activities
- whether the nonprofit has been involved in multiple excess benefit transactions before
- whether the nonprofit has implemented safeguards that are reasonably calculated to prevent excess benefit transactions, and
- whether the excess benefit transaction has been corrected or whether the nonprofit has made good faith efforts to seek correction from the disqualified persons who benefited from the transaction.

IRS regulations provide the following examples of cases where a nonprofit's tax exemption would be revoked:

EXAMPLE: A nonprofit museum was created to exhibit art to the general public. After three years, a new board of directors was elected, consisting entirely of local art dealers. At the new board's direction, the museum used a substantial portion of its revenues to purchase art solely from its directors at prices that exceeded their fair market value. The museum exhibited the art and offered it for sale. The board never tried to correct these multiple excess benefit transactions by requiring return of the excess payments for the art. Nor did it implement safeguards to prevent them from occurring in the future. This is a situation where the IRS would revoke the nonprofit's tax-exempt status.

EXAMPLE: An educational nonprofit employed Carl, its founder, as its CEO. For several years, Carl diverted significant portions of the nonprofit's funds to pay his personal expenses. The diversions significantly reduced the funds available to conduct the nonprofit's ongoing educational programs. The board of trustees never authorized Carl to have the nonprofit pay his personal expenses. However, certain members of the board were aware of the payments. The board did not terminate Carl's employment or take any action to seek repayment from Carl or to prevent him from continuing to divert the nonprofit's funds for his personal use. Carl claimed that the payments represented loans from the nonprofit to him. However, no contemporaneous loan documentation exists, and Carl never made any payments of principal or interest. The IRS would revoke the nonprofit's tax-exempt status.

The regulations and examples make clear that it is vitally important for a nonprofit to correct an excess benefit transaction after it is discovered and make sure a similar transaction doesn't happen again.

Private Benefit

Usually, cases involving improper benefits involve a nonprofit's insiders, such as an organization's founder, directors, officers, key employees, major contributors, their families, or businesses owned or controlled by them. More rarely, a nonprofit can be used to improperly benefit an outsider—a person or company without such a relationship with the nonprofit. The IRS cannot impose intermediate sanctions where outsiders are improperly benefited by a nonprofit. However, under the "private benefit doctrine," transactions involving a nonprofit that primarily benefit an outside person or organization in a substantial way can result in IRS revocation of the nonprofit's tax exemption.

In one case, for example, the IRS revoked a nonprofit's tax exemption where it found that it was operated primarily for the private benefit of an outside fundraising company that kept 90% of the total donations as its fee. In another, the tax court held that a nonprofit school operated to train its students for careers as political consultants did not qualify as a tax-exempt Section 501(c)(3) organization because almost all of its students ended up working for the Republican Party—thus, the school provided a substantial benefit to an outsider: the Republican Party.

However, revocation of a nonprofit's tax exemption because of private benefit occurs rarely—usually only in the most extreme cases. Providing "incidental" private benefits to outsiders is not sufficient to revoke a nonprofit's tax exemption. Rather, the benefits must be substantial—both qualitatively and quantitatively.

Nonprofits That Make Money and UBIT

Nonprofits are said to be "tax-exempt." While true, this is a bit misleading. Nonprofits never have to pay tax on their unearned income—namely, donations, gifts, and grants. However, a nonprofit may have to pay income tax on earned income— that is, money it earns from selling goods or services, or from certain investments. The tax imposed on nonprofits' earned income is called the unrelated business income tax or "UBIT."

Nonprofits Rely More on Earning Money

The poor economy has resulted in a decline in donations and grants to nonprofits. Many nonprofits are turning to selling goods and services as a way to make up for this shortfall. A 2009 survey of 848 charities found that 54% of them ran businesses (Community Wealth Ventures, Washington DC). Of the nonprofits that did not already run a business, 57% said they were thinking about starting one.

Here are just a few examples of successful nonprofit businesses:

- The Louisiana SPCA earns income from running a pet day care and boarding facility and is considering adding obedience classes.
- The Habitat for Humanity Portland Metro/East operates a store that sells donated building materials and recently opened a second outlet.
- New Door Ventures, a San Francisco nonprofit that provides job training to low-income youth, runs a screen printing business.
- Triangle Residential Options for Substance Abusers, a Durham, North Carolina, nonprofit, runs five businesses, including a moving company.

The middle of a recession might seem like a bad time to start a business, but this is not necessarily true. Rents, salaries, and other business expenses have gone down, while more people than ever are volunteering their time to charities. Moreover, some businesses run by nonprofits, such as thrift stores, have experienced increases in sales due to the recession.

If your nonprofit doesn't sell any goods or services or engage in any moneymaking activities, then you won't have to worry about UBIT. However, even something as simple as a car wash, bake sale, or auction could trigger UBIT issues. Fortunately, most of the income nonprofits earn from moneymaking activities is not taxable because there are many exemptions that apply. Nevertheless, once your nonprofit earns income, you will need to understand UBIT.

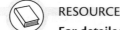

RESOURCE

For detailed guidance on the practical aspects of selling goods or services to raise money for your nonprofit, refer to *Effective Fundraising for Nonprofits: Real-World Strategies That Work,* by Ilona Bray (Nolo).

What Is UBIT?

UBIT is a tax imposed on income earned by nonprofits from businesses they conduct that are unrelated to their charitable mission. Before UBIT was imposed, a nonprofit could own and operate any type of business and not owe any taxes on the profits it earned. For example, New York University owned a macaroni company that was extremely successful. This success was partly because NYU—a tax-exempt nonprofit—didn't have to pay taxes on the profits it earned from the business. Other privately owned macaroni companies claimed this was unfair because they couldn't compete with a company that didn't have to pay taxes. To avoid this kind of unfair competition, the unrelated business income tax was created.

Today, a nonprofit that earns income from a business that is not related to its charitable mission may have to pay taxes on that income. Why "may"? Because not all unrelated income is subject to UBIT. There are three threshold questions to ask:

- whether the income is unrelated to the nonprofit's charitable mission

- whether the income-producing activity is a "business," and
- whether the income-producing activity is "regularly carried on."

Only income from activities that meet all three of these criteria will be subject to UBIT. However, even if income your nonprofit earns meets these threshold criteria, there are numerous exemptions that apply.

Do You Need to Worry About UBIT?

Most nonprofits—particularly smaller ones—don't have to worry about UBIT. Either they don't have income from any source other than donations or gifts or they fit into one of the many exemptions from UBIT.

Here is a checklist that covers some basic questions you can ask to see if your nonprofit is exempt from UBIT.

- Does your nonprofit earn income from an activity or business that is unrelated to its nonprofit mission? If your answer is "no," you will not be subject to UBIT.
- Does your nonprofit's activity come within one of the applicable exemptions? Income from the following sources is generally exempt from UBIT:
  - work done primarily by volunteers
  - thrift shops and donated merchandise
  - donor lists
  - business sponsorships
  - investment income, rental income, and capital gains
  - low-cost giveaways
  - bingo games, and
  - advertising income.
- Is your nonprofit's activity a "business"? If your answer is "no," you will not be subject to UBIT.
- Is your business "regularly carried on"? If your answer is "no," you will not be subject to UBIT.

All of the rules related to these exemptions are covered in more detail in the rest of this chapter. If you think you fit into one of these exempt categories, you can jump ahead and read more about the specific exemption that may apply to you.

Is the Activity Related to Your Mission?

No matter how much money a nonprofit makes from an activity, the income will not be subject to UBIT if the activity is substantially related to the nonprofit's exempt purpose or mission. It is only unrelated activities that are taxed—for example, the macaroni factory operated by New York University. There's nothing wrong with making macaroni, but it is not in any way related to a university's educational mission so it is subject to UBIT.

A business activity is unrelated if it does not contribute importantly to accomplishing your nonprofit's exempt purpose. It doesn't matter that the income earned from an unrelated activity is used to help fund your nonprofit's exempt purposes. For example, the fact that New York University used the profits from its macaroni factory to help fund its educational programs did not make the factory a related activity.

Your nonprofit's tax-exempt purpose determines what activities are related for UBIT purposes. This should be set forth in your nonprofit's articles of incorporation and may also be included or expanded on in your bylaws or a mission statement. If your nonprofit files IRS Form 990 or Form 990-EZ, your mission statement will be provided there. If you have more than one income-producing activity, you'll need to look at each one separately and ask whether it contributes significantly to achieving one or more of your nonprofit's purposes.

> **EXAMPLE:** Helping Out, Inc., is a California nonprofit whose articles of incorporation contain the following mission statement: "The purpose of Helping Out, Inc., is to provide counseling, case management, skills training, job placement, and follow-along services to adults with physical or mental disabilities who live in Los Angeles, California, to help them become more financially and vocationally independent."
>
> Helping Out owns a restaurant completely staffed by its disabled clients, which earns a healthy profit. The activity is not an unrelated business because it contributes importantly to the nonprofit's mission of helping disabled people become employable. Therefore, the profits the nonprofit earns from the restaurant business are not subject to UBIT.

In some cases, determining whether a business activity is substantially related to your nonprofit's exempt purpose can be difficult. The best way to get a feel for the problem is to look at real-life examples. Here are some activities the IRS found related enough to the nonprofit's charitable purpose to be exempt from UBIT.

Nonprofit's Exempt Purpose	Related Business Activity
Providing housing, counseling, and employment to recovering alcoholics	Halfway house furniture shop staffed by clients
Furthering education in the performing arts	Charging admission to performances by students of nonprofit performing arts school
Promoting the arts	Museum gift shop selling greeting cards containing art reproductions
Educating students about United States geography and culture	Nonprofit-led tours of national parks with formal educational component
Prevention of cruelty to animals	Operating a low-cost animal neutering service
Educating the public on the need for cleanliness in caring for the sick	Selling posters, buttons, stickers, and T-shirts urging children to wash their hands
Rehabilitating needy people and restoring them to useful life in the community	Operating a mushroom growing and processing facility to employ poor people and drug addicts
Art conservation training and education	Performing art conservation services for private collectors
Promoting health and welfare of senior citizens	A senior citizens' center operating a beauty shop and barber shop
Preserving a city's architectural heritage and unique city plan and educating the city's citizens and others about cultural history and restoration techniques	Renovating a Victorian era house and then leasing it to the public
Making new computer technology widely available	Selling computer software to the public

TIP

Check your Form 1023—activities listed there should be related activities. In Part VI of your Form 1023 federal tax-exempt application, you must state whether your nonprofit provides any goods or services to individuals that are in furtherance of your exempt purpose. If you list any activities there, the IRS will have a hard time claiming later that any of those activities are an unrelated business. Why? Because it approved them as related at the time you filed your application. However, any activity you began after you filed your 1023 application won't have been reviewed and approved by the IRS.

Here are some activities the IRS found were not related enough to the nonprofit's charitable purpose to be exempt from UBIT.

Nonprofit's Exempt Purpose	Unrelated Business Activity
Fostering public interest in the fine arts by sponsoring art exhibits and cultural events	Leasing studio apartments to artists and operating a dining hall primarily for them
Prevention of cruelty to animals	Providing pet boarding and grooming services to the public
Advancing public interest in classical music	Nonprofit classical music station selling advertising to for-profit businesses
Education	Selling membership mailing lists to businesses
Promoting education	A university alumni association conducting regular tours of foreign countries that contain no formal educational component
Promoting the welfare of young people	Operating a miniature golf course as a purely commercial business
Promoting the arts	An art museum selling scientific books in its gift shop
Advancing education	A school operating a for-profit tennis club open to the public
Advancing education	Selling items created in a vocational school's handicraft shop that were made by nonstudents
Religious	Church group selling members' labor to forest owners to plant seedlings on forest land
Promoting health and welfare of senior citizens	Selling of heavy-duty appliances to senior citizens by a senior citizens center

The IRS also considers the scale of the income-producing activity in deciding whether it's a related activity for UBIT purposes. If an activity is conducted on a scale that is greater than what is needed to accomplish the exempt purpose, it will be considered an unrelated business. The part of the activity that is more than is needed to accomplish the tax-exempt purpose will subject to UBIT. Or, in some cases, the nonprofit could lose its tax-exempt status and all its income would be taxed. Although this is rare, it has happened—for example, when a nonprofit is used primarily to run a significant commercial business.

Too Much Business Activity Can Jeopardize Your Nonprofit's Tax-Exempt Status

A nonprofit is supposed to exist primarily to perform its exempt functions —that's why it gets tax-exempt treatment. Unfortunately, the law in this area is far from clear. However, a nonprofit's tax-exempt status may be in danger if an unrelated business gets too big, earns too much money, takes up too much of the organization's time and effort, is run too much like a purely commercial enterprise, or competes with other for-profit businesses.

How big is too big? Some experts say that a nonprofit's tax exemption may be at risk if more than 50% of its total revenue comes from an unrelated business; others put the figure as low as 20%. This danger is especially great if most of the profits from the business are not used to further the nonprofit's exempt purposes. In one case, a nonprofit ran an extensive bingo operation, but spent less than 1% of its profits for exempt purposes. The IRS revoked its tax-exempt status.

To avoid possible problems with the IRS, some nonprofits legally separate themselves from their unrelated businesses by creating a separate corporation or limited liability company to operate the business. This is a complex area of the law; you should seek experienced legal counsel before embarking on such a venture.

Is the Activity a Business?

In order for income to be subject to UBIT, it must come from a business activity. For these purposes, business is broadly defined to mean "any activity that is carried on for the production of income from the sale of goods or the performance of services" (IRC Sec. 513(c)). Virtually any moneymaking activity your nonprofit conducts can qualify as a business under this definition. It could be a car wash, bake sale, or auction. It doesn't matter if the activity doesn't earn a profit for a period of time— many businesses incur losses.

The IRS looks at each moneymaking activity separately—a process called "fragmentation." Thus, a moneymaking activity carried on within a larger group of other moneymaking activities is looked at separately to determine whether its particular function is related to the nonprofit's exempt purposes. For example, income from selling commercial advertising in a nonprofit newsletter is considered an unrelated activity even though income from selling the newsletter might be exempt because it's related to the nonprofit's exempt purpose. (See "Periodical Advertising Income," below.)

When a nonprofit sells goods, each item is considered separately to determine whether income from its sale is subject to UBIT. In one case, a nonprofit school operated a shop where items made by students and local residents were sold. The IRS held that income from the sale of items made by the students was not taxable, but income from the sale of items made by local residents was subject to UBIT.

Is the Activity "Regularly Carried On"?

Only business activities that are "regularly carried on" are subject to UBIT. Although there is no precise definition for "regularly carried on," it is generally understood to mean that the activity is engaged in by the nonprofit as frequently and continuously as similar commercial activities by for-profit businesses. So, if a certain type of income-producing activity is ordinarily conducted year-round by for-profit businesses, a nonprofit that engages in a similar activity for only a few weeks a year would not be regularly carrying on a business.

For example, a nonprofit that operates a sandwich stand for two weeks at a state fair would not be engaged in a regular business activity. However, a nonprofit that had a business it conducted one day a week, year round, would be engaged in a regular business activity (such as operating a commercial parking lot on Saturdays). And engaging in a seasonal business would be considered regular if it is for a significant part of the season—for example, selling Christmas trees in November and December.

Business activities engaged in only periodically will not be considered regularly carried on if they are conducted "without the competitive and promotional efforts typical of commercial endeavors." For example, publishing advertising in programs for a sporting event or music or drama performance would not be considered regularly carrying on a business.

Certain fundraising activities occur so infrequently that the IRS does not regard them as a business regularly carried on, even though they take place every year. For example, income from an annual charity auction, concert, bake sale, car wash, charity ball, or street fair would not be considered income from a regularly carried on business.

Here is how the IRS viewed different activities for purposes of deciding if they were regularly carried on or not.

Activity Regularly Carried On	Activity Not Regularly Carried On
Operating a sandwich stand all year round	Operating a sandwich stand at a fair for two weeks per year
Selling ads for monthly newsletter	Selling ads for special program for annual charity concert
Continuous auction on eBay	Onetime auction on eBay
Running a bakery	Annual bake sale
Monthly dance	Annual charity ball

The Internet—A Gray Area

A nonprofit's use of the Internet for fundraising complicates the "regularly carried on" calculation. Fundraising activities nonprofits used to engage in for only a limited time each year in the nonvirtual world may now be conducted year-round online. For example, many nonprofits auction goods online instead of through a once-a-year live event. If a nonprofit has an online auction that it keeps posted all year or for some extended period, it probably would be considered a regularly carried on business by the IRS. On the other hand, an online auction limited to just a few days a year would not be considered regularly carried on.

Some nonprofits sell goods to the public through online virtual storefronts. These activities would likely be considered regularly carried on if the sales were made throughout the year.

Activities Exempt From UBIT

There are a host of profit-making activities that are exempt from UBIT. These exemptions cover many of the most common profit-making activities that nonprofits engage in, such as running a thrift shop or selling donor lists. If your nonprofit is small, there's a good chance your moneymaking activities fall within one of these exemptions.

When Your Volunteers Do the Work

Any profit-making activity where substantially all the work is performed by unpaid volunteers is exempt from UBIT. For example, the Girl Scouts organization doesn't pay any tax on its Girl Scout cookie income because substantially all the work related to earning that income is done by volunteer Girl Scouts. Any income-producing activities your nonprofit undertakes are likewise exempt from UBIT if they are conducted by volunteers. For many small nonprofits, this covers all of their for-profit activities.

EXAMPLE: The Sisters of Charity Orphanage operates a retail store that sells religious items such as crucifixes and religious statues. The store is run by ten unpaid volunteers—members of the community who donate their time to helping the Orphanage. The business is exempt from UBIT.

Don't Jeopardize Your Workers' Volunteer Status

Be careful not to inadvertently compensate a volunteer in a way that jeopardizes their volunteer status in the eyes of the IRS. Certain benefits, especially if substantial, could be considered compensation by the IRS and that worker would no longer be a volunteer for UBIT purposes.

In one case, a church group's members worked in an unrelated business that provided forestry, cleaning, and maintenance services. The members were not paid any money, but were given food, clothing, shelter, medical care, and other benefits. The IRS and courts held that the members were not volunteers because the substantial benefits they received from the church amounted to payment for their services. (*Shiloh Youth Revival Centers, Inc. v. Commissioner*, 88 T.C. 565 (1987).)

You won't risk jeopardizing your volunteer workers' status if you reimburse them for expenses directly related to their work, such as transportation or food. (Make sure they keep good records and return any excess payments.) You can also pay for volunteers' parking and provide them with meals if it is for the convenience of your nonprofit. And low-cost freebies, such as coffee, soft drinks, doughnuts, T-shirts, tickets to sporting or theater events, and office parties, are also okay. Just make sure you don't do anything that might amount to compensation or payment for services in the eyes of the IRS. See Chapter 4 for a detailed discussion of rewarding volunteers.

Volunteers don't have to do 100% of the work, but they must do "substantially" all of it. In this case, "substantially" means at least 80% to 85% measured by the total number of hours spent by everyone involved in the activity. Be sure to keep track of how much time each volunteer spends working on for-profit activities so you can rely on this exemption. The work done by volunteers can include anything related to the activity, such as phone calls, bookkeeping, working a cash register, purchasing merchandise, or supervising other volunteers. Paid staff can be involved as well, as long as their total hours stay below the 15% to 20% threshold.

TIP

Use volunteers to avoid UBIT. If your nonprofit conducts, or wants to conduct, a for-profit activity that would otherwise be subject to UBIT, get volunteers to run it and you'll be exempt from the tax.

Thrift Shops and Donated Merchandise

Have you ever noticed how every small town seems to have a thrift shop run by a nonprofit? Well, there's a good reason for that—nonprofits don't have to pay UBIT on any profits they earn from the sale of donated merchandise. This exempts all thrift shops operated by nonprofits that sell donated clothes, books, or other merchandise. All the proceeds from these sales can go to the nonprofit and are not subject to UBIT.

This exemption applies to the sale of any merchandise or products donated to a nonprofit. For example, if a nonprofit sells a used car that was donated to it, it does not have to pay UBIT on the proceeds it receives from selling the car.

EXAMPLE: The Seattle Foster Care Program conducts a highly publicized campaign to encourage donors to contribute their used cars. In one year, it received over 100 cars that it sold at its own used car auction for more than $50,000. Since this money was earned entirely from the sale of donated merchandise, it is not subject to UBIT.

Donor Lists

Any income a nonprofit receives from renting or exchanging its donor or membership list with another nonprofit is not subject to UBIT. This exemption applies only if you rent your list to another nonprofit that is eligible to receive tax deductible charitable contributions—primarily Section 501(c)(3) organizations. If you rent your donor list to a for-profit company, the income is exempt from UBIT only if you don't provide any services along with the list—for example, marketing services or database management. If you do, then the income you receive will be subject to UBIT.

Convenience Activities

Some nonprofits earn money from services or activities provided for the convenience of the nonprofit's employees, members, students, patients, or officers, rather than the general public. For example, a nonprofit may earn income from vending machines placed in its employee break room, or a college may operate a laundry for the purpose of cleaning dormitory linens and students' clothing. This income is not subject to UBIT.

Business Sponsorships

Sponsorship payments and donations from businesses are another important source of income for many small nonprofits. In order to build goodwill in the community, businesses often donate money to a nonprofit or provide their products or services for free. These payments or donations are not subject to UBIT if they are what the IRS calls a "qualified sponsorship payment." To qualify, the only benefit the sponsor should receive from the nonprofit is to have its name, logo, or product lines acknowledged or displayed by the nonprofit.

> EXAMPLE: Save Our Parks (SOP), a local charity, organizes a marathon and walkathon to help preserve local parks. During the event, it serves drinks and other refreshments provided free of charge by Goodwill Markets, a regional supermarket chain.

Goodwill also gives SOP prizes to be awarded to winners of the event. SOP recognizes Goodwill's help by listing its name in promotional fliers, newspaper advertisements for the event, and on T-shirts worn by participants. SOP even changes the name of the event to include Goodwill's name—it is now the "Goodwill Save Our Parks Marathon/Walkathon." SOP's activities constitute acknowledgment of Goodwill's sponsorship. Thus, the drinks, refreshments, and prizes provided by Goodwill are a qualified sponsorship payment, not subject to UBIT.

Your nonprofit can do all sorts of things for a sponsor without worrying about UBIT, including:

- enter into an exclusive sponsorship arrangement with the sponsor and acknowledge this relationship to the public
- display the sponsor's brand or trade names
- display logos and slogans that are an established part of the sponsor's identity
- list a sponsor's locations, telephone numbers, or Internet address on your nonprofit's publications, website, and displays
- include value-neutral descriptions or visual depictions of the sponsor's product line or services on your nonprofit's publications, website, and displays, and
- allow the sponsor to distribute—whether for free or for payment—its product at a sponsored activity.

Although it's fine for your nonprofit to acknowledge a sponsor's help, it can't cross the line from an acknowledgment to advertising. Income a nonprofit earns from advertising may be subject to UBIT—see "Periodical Advertising Income," below.

Audience response. If the amount a sponsor owes a nonprofit is based on audience exposure levels, then that income will be subject to UBIT. For example, if the number of people attending an event determines the amount the sponsor owes, then that income is taxable.

Exclusive provider agreements. Income from exclusive provider agreements is usually subject to UBIT. For example, if you hold a charity ball event and agree that only soft drinks made by a particular manufacturer will be sold at the event, that income is not a qualified sponsorship payment and is subject to UBIT.

Internet links. Simply including a link to a sponsor's website on your nonprofit's own website is not considered advertising, and thus will not subject your nonprofit to UBIT.

> EXAMPLE: The nonprofit Waukegan Symphony Orchestra maintains a website with its performance schedule and other information. The Music Shop, a local store, pays the Symphony $1,000 to help fund a concert series. The Symphony posts a list of its sponsors on its website, including the Music Shop's name and Internet address. It appears as a hyperlink from the Symphony's website to the Music Shop's site. The Symphony's website does not otherwise promote the Music Shop or advertise its merchandise. The Symphony's posting of the Music Shop's name and Internet address on its website constitutes acknowledgment of the shop's sponsorship. Thus, the entire payment is a qualified sponsorship payment, and is not subject to UBIT.

However, if a nonprofit provides a link to a sponsor's website where the nonprofit endorses the sponsor's product or services, the endorsement is advertising and is subject to UBIT.

Rental Income, Capital Gains, and Investment Income

Rental income, capital gains, and income from any passive investments is generally not subject to UBIT. The rules exempting this type of income are important to large nonprofits that may have substantial endowments or property or investment holdings, but tend to be less important to small nonprofits because they are less likely to have this type of income.

Rental income. If your nonprofit owns or leases office space or other real property that it rents out, the rental income it receives is tax free.

> EXAMPLE: The Boston Youth Literacy Center leases 3,000 square feet of office space in downtown Boston. Due to budget cutbacks, it no longer needs all this space. It subleases 1,000 square feet of

its space to an accounting firm for $4,000 per month. This rental income is exempt from UBIT.

There are certain situations, however, when rental income is taxable. Namely, you will have to pay UBIT on rental income if:

- the lease involves more personal property than real estate—for example, rental of computers or other equipment
- the rental income is based on the tenants' income or profits (other than an amount based on a fixed percentage of the gross receipts or sales), or
- the nonprofit operates a hotel, boarding house, parking lot, warehouse, or other enterprise in which significant services are provided to the tenants.

Capital gains. Gains from the sale of capital assets can be another important source of UBIT-free income for nonprofits. Capital assets include just about any property your nonprofit owns—tangible or intangible—other than inventory and any real estate or depreciable property used in a business. Examples of capital assets include stocks, buildings, equipment, land, and furniture, Any profit your nonprofit earns from the sale of these items is not subject to UBIT. For example, if your nonprofit owns stock or mutual fund shares that have gone up in value and you sell them, any profit you receive from that sale will not be subject to UBIT.

EXAMPLE: Due to the bad economy, the Midwest Folklife Center has experienced a significant reduction in donations. To help meet its budgetary needs this year, it sells corporate stock it received from a donor ten years ago. The stock was valued at $30,000 when it was donated and sells for $50,000. The entire amount received from the sale is not subject to UBIT.

Investment income. Income your nonprofit earns from passive investments is not subject to UBIT. For example, your nonprofit does not have to pay any UBIT on interest it earns on money in bank accounts, dividends from stocks, or payments from an annuity.

UBIT-free investment income also includes royalties—for example, payments for trademarks, trade names, copyrights, or for the use of a professional athlete's name, photograph, likeness, or facsimile signature. Payments from affinity cards may also be considered UBIT-free royalties if the nonprofit does not actively promote or market the card to its members or engage in other marketing efforts. (An affinity card is a credit or debit card issued by a bank and a nonprofit, whose logo appears on the card. The bank makes a donation to the nonprofit each time the card is used.)

Watch Out With Debt-Financed Property

There is an important exception to the rules exempting investment and rental property and capital gains from UBIT. If your nonprofit financed the purchase of any stocks, bonds, or other investment property, or any rental property, the portion of income from the property that is debt-financed may be subject to UBIT. For example, if your nonprofit purchased a rental property for $200,000 and has a $100,000 loan, 50% of the rent received from the property would be taxable. However, there is an exception to the exception: If at least 85% of the use of the debt-financed property is related to the nonprofit's exempt purposes, it is not treated as debt-financed property. This is a very complex area of UBIT. For more information, refer to IRS Publication 598, *Tax on Unrelated Business Income of Exempt Organizations.*

Low-Cost Giveaways

As part of their fundraising campaigns, nonprofits sometimes send potential donors unsolicited low-cost items in the hopes that it will encourage them to donate. For example, a nonprofit might give away free mailing labels, pens, or posters when it is soliciting donations. Selling these items to the public would result in income subject to

UBIT. However, money received by a nonprofit in connection with the distribution of such items for free is not subject to UBIT if:

- each item cost the nonprofit no more than $10.20 (adjusted for inflation each year)
- the recipient did not request the item or agree to receive it, and
- the item is accompanied by a written request for a charitable contribution and a statement that the recipient may keep the low cost item regardless of whether a contribution is made.

EXAMPLE: The Walton School, a small nonprofit private school, sends packages of greeting cards that cost $2.00 to prospective families along with a letter asking for donations. The school's solicitation letter makes clear that recipients of the greeting cards are under no obligation to make a contribution and are free to keep the cards at no cost. Because the greeting cards are low-cost articles incidental to the solicitation of a charitable donation, the activity is not a trade or business and the income is not subject to UBIT.

Research Income

Nonprofits engaged in science or education need not pay UBIT on income derived from their research activities if the research is:

- performed for the United States government, or a state or local government
- performed by a college, university, or hospital, or
- "fundamental" research (as opposed to applied research which is designed to create actual products) and the results are made freely available to the public.

This rule seems to be unnecessary because, even if it didn't exist, research income earned by nonprofits would usually be exempt from UBIT because it is usually related to their exempt purposes. It was apparently added to the law to make it abundantly clear that such income is UBIT-free, and thereby encourage nonprofits to engage in such useful research.

Bingo Games

Income from certain bingo games is UBIT-free. To qualify for this exclusion, the bingo game must be one in which wagers are placed, winners are determined, and prizes or other property are distributed in the presence of everyone who placed wagers in that game. In addition, it must be legal in the place where it is played, and it can't be in a state or locality where bingo games are regularly carried on by for-profit organizations. However, if you have a bingo game that is run by volunteers, then the income earned would be UBIT-free under the volunteer exemption discussed above.

RESOURCE
There are many legal rules—state, local, and federal—that apply to gambling activities. For more information on federal tax rules for income from bingo and other gambling activities, refer to IRS Publication 3079, *Gaming Publication for Tax-Exempt Organization.*

Periodical Advertising Income

If your nonprofit regularly publishes a newsletter, journal, magazine, or other printed material, any payment you receive in exchange for using a business's name, logo, or product lines in the publication may be subject to UBIT. Even though this income isn't exempt from UBIT, in practice few nonprofits end up paying UBIT on it because of the special rules that apply. Basically, you will be subject to UBIT only if the income you receive from the advertising is more than your direct advertising costs. In other words, you must end up with a net profit from the advertising. In addition, you can reduce your taxable advertising income by any amount that your readership costs exceed your circulation income. Readership costs include the cost of producing and distributing the periodical—for example, printing costs. Most nonprofits spend more money producing a publication than they receive from their circulation income, so they don't ever owe UBIT on it.

Strategies to Avoid UBIT

Here are some simple strategies any nonprofit can use to avoid UBIT:

Convert income to royalties. Convert income to royalties by contracting with a third party to carry on the activity and pay your nonprofit a portion of the earnings. For example, income from the publication and sale of a book on a topic unrelated to a nonprofit's exempt purpose is unrelated business income subject to UBIT. However, if you transfer the publication rights to a commercial publisher, you can receive royalty income that is not subject to UBIT. (Rev. Rul. 69–430.)

Have volunteers do the work. Any commercial activity can be "cleansed" of UBIT if it is conducted by volunteers. For example, income from raffles, casino nights, and similar gambling activities (other than bingo) is ordinarily subject to UBIT. However, if the raffle or other game of chance is conducted by volunteers, the income earned will be UBIT-free.

Restructure the activity. You may be able to turn an unrelated business into a related business by changing the structure or nature of the activity. For example, in one case, the IRS said that foreign travel tours sponsored by a nonprofit were an unrelated business because they had no formal educational component. Hiring teachers to accompany the tours and requiring tour members to complete a formal course of study could turn this into a related activity.

Expand your nonprofit's exempt purposes. In some cases, a nonprofit can make a profit-making activity a related business by expanding or amending its exempt purposes. This is usually done by amending the nonprofit's articles of incorporation. For example, an educational nonprofit that wants to engage in conservation work could add conservation as one of its exempt purposes.

EXAMPLE: Acme Charities, Inc. publishes a monthly newsletter. In one year, it earns $9,000 from selling advertising space and has $2,000 in direct advertising expenses. Thus, it has a net profit from advertising of $7,000. Meanwhile, Acme spent $12,000 in readership costs (printing, postage, and other costs) and had $2,000 in circulation income. Thus, Acme's readership costs exceeded its circulation income by $10,000. This amount is subtracted from the $7,000 net profit from advertising, leaving Acme with no taxable income from its advertising sales.

If your nonprofit has periodical income, you should work with a bookkeeper or accountant to determine if you will owe UBIT and to allocate and track the income and expenses from the periodical.

Website Advertising Income

Nonprofits sometimes earn income from their websites and other online publications, such as online newsletters. For example, if a nonprofit is paid to include a company's name, hyperlink, banner ad, or logo on its website or other online publication, the payment may be advertising income that can be subject to UBIT.

If a nonprofit's website qualifies as a "periodical," such advertising revenue can be treated the same as periodical advertising revenue from print publications. However, there is no clear test to determine when a website is a periodical. The IRS says to take advantage of the special rules available to compute unrelated business income from periodical advertising income, a nonprofit must show that the online materials are "prepared and distributed in substantially the same manner as a traditional periodical." This seems to mean that a nonprofit's website can constitute a periodical only if it is updated on a regularly scheduled basis. It may also mean that the website would need to have an editorial staff, marketing program, and budget independent of the organization's webmaster.

Unrelated business income earned from a website that is not a periodical is treated like any other income subject to UBIT: The gross advertising income is added to any other unrelated business income (other than advertising in periodicals).

Do You Owe UBIT?

If your nonprofit earns $1,000 or more in income from a regularly carried on unrelated business, you will have to file a UBIT tax return and you may have to pay UBIT to the IRS. UBIT is paid at corporate tax rates, which range from 15% to 35%. Fortunately, most nonprofits with unrelated business income end up paying little or no UBIT. Indeed, recent IRS statistics show that only about 4% of all nonprofits file UBIT returns, and of those filing a return, less than half pay any tax.

You only have to pay UBIT on net income from your unrelated businesses. To determine your net income, you are allowed to deduct your business expenses, just like any regular business. Basically, this means you can deduct any ordinary and necessary expenses directly connected to carrying on your unrelated business. For example, you can deduct salaries of employees who work full time to carry on the unrelated business and you can include depreciation for a building used entirely in the conduct of that business.

> **EXAMPLE:** The Contemporary Theater of Louisville owns and operates a dry-cleaning business as a means of earning extra income. The business took in $250,000 in gross receipts this year. However, the Theater doesn't have to pay UBIT on the total amount it earned. It first gets to subtract all applicable business deductions, including salaries, rent, cleaning supplies, depreciation, advertising, and insurance. These come to $200,000, leaving only $50,000 in net income. The Theater must pay UBIT only on its $50,000 in net business income.

Some of the most common business expense deductions for nonprofits include:
- compensation of officers and directors
- advertising costs
- attorneys' and accounting fees
- business start-up costs
- costs of renting or leasing vehicles, machinery, equipment, and other property used in the business

- depreciation of business assets
- insurance for the business—for example, liability, workers' compensation, and business property insurance
- interest on business loans and debts
- office supplies, utilities, postage, Internet costs
- repairs and maintenance for business equipment
- business related travel, meals, and entertainment
- charitable contributions, and
- wages and benefits provided to employees.

For more information on business tax deductions, refer to *Deduct It! Lower Your Small Business Taxes,* by Stephen Fishman (Nolo).

If your nonprofit sells goods, you can also deduct the cost of goods sold from your gross receipts to determine your net income from the sales. The cost of goods sold includes the cost of purchasing inventory to sell, and the cost of any labor and materials used to produce inventory.

> **EXAMPLE:** Associated Charities has an unrelated business selling T-shirts. This year, it earned $5,000 in total receipts from the sale of T-shirts. It paid $4,100 for the T-shirts so its gross income from the business is $900.

For more information on inventories, refer to IRS Publication 334, *Tax Guide for Small Business,* and IRS Publication 538, *Accounting Periods and Methods.*

Expenses related to your nonprofit's exempt purposes are not deductible because you can only deduct expenses incurred in connection with your unrelated business. Expenses incurred solely to accomplish your nonprofit's exempt purposes are not an "unrelated" business so you can't deduct them.

> **EXAMPLE:** Recall the Contemporary Theater of Louisville from the previous example, which operates a dry-cleaning business. It may deduct expenses incurred in running that business, but may not deduct expenses incurred solely to accomplish its exempt purpose of producing live theater. For example, it cannot deduct the cost of renting the theater, paying the actors, or advertising upcoming plays.

Expenses for dual use of facilities or personnel are deductible as long as they are properly allocated. It is very common, particularly in smaller nonprofits, for employees or facilities to be used both for an unrelated business and the nonprofit's exempt functions. If this happens, you will need to allocate the expenses between the two uses. Expenses allocated to the business are deductible, the others are not.

> **EXAMPLE:** The Rainforest Fund, a nonprofit that earns income from an unrelated business, pays its president $90,000 a year. The president devotes approximately 10% of his time to the business. In calculating unrelated business taxable income, the nonprofit can deduct $9,000 ($90,000 × 10%) of the president's salary from its unrelated business income as a business expense so it will have $9,000 less that it must pay tax on.

Determining how to do these allocations can be difficult when facilities are involved. The IRS gives little guidance other than to say that the allocation must be reasonable. Obviously, nonprofits with unrelated businesses have a strong incentive to allocate as many of their dual-use expenses as possible to the business side, rather than to their exempt activities. IRS officials have recently stated that many nonprofits have over-allocated dual-use facilities to the business side of the ledger to lower their income and pay less UBIT. If you are in this situation, you might want to get help from an accountant experienced with these issues.

Filing UBIT Tax Returns

If your nonprofit earns $1,000 or more in gross income from one or more unrelated businesses, you are supposed to file a special tax return with the IRS: Form 990-T, *Exempt Organization Business Income Tax Return.* If you have more than one unrelated business, you file a single Form 990-T for the year and report your gross income from all your unrelated businesses on that form. Your gross income is all the income you receive from your unrelated businesses before you subtract any deductions you are entitled to.

The fact that your nonprofit has to file a Form 990-T does not necessarily mean that you will have to pay tax. You only have to pay UBIT tax on the net income your nonprofit earns from an unrelated business—that is, the income left after subtracting all applicable deductions. Moreover, the first $1,000 of unrelated business income is tax-free. Thus, you will only owe UBIT if the net income from your unrelated business exceeds $1,000.

> **TIP**
>
> **Your Form 990-T is a public document.** As part of an ongoing effort by the IRS to make nonprofits' financial activities as transparent as possible, all nonprofits filing Form 990-T must make the completed form available for public inspection. (See Chapter 2.)

Deadline for Filing

You must file Form 990-T by the 15th day of the fifth month after the end of your nonprofit's tax year. If your nonprofit uses the calendar year as its tax year, this would be May 15 of the year after the income was earned. If the nonprofit uses a fiscal year that ends on June 30, Form 990-T would be due by November 15 of the same calendar year. However, you may obtain an automatic six-month extension of time to file the return by submitting IRS Form 8868, *Application for Extension of Time To File an Exempt Organization Return.*

Failure to File Form 990-T

If your nonprofit owes UBIT tax and fails to timely file Form 990-T, it will be subject to interest and penalties imposed by the IRS. The penalty is 5% of the unpaid tax for each month or part of a month the return is late, up to a maximum of 25% of the unpaid tax. The minimum penalty for a return that is more than 60 days late is the smaller of the tax due or $135. However, the penalty will not be imposed if you can show a reasonable cause for your failure to file on time.

Although you are supposed to file Form 990-T if you meet the $1,000 gross income threshold, there is no penalty for failing to file if you don't owe any UBIT tax. However, if your nonprofit files an IRS information return—Form 990 or 990-EZ—you are required to state whether your nonprofit earned $1,000 or more in gross income from an unrelated business. If you indicate that your nonprofit's earnings exceeded the threshold, you are then required to state whether you have filed Form 990-T. If you truthfully state "no," it's likely you'll be questioned by the IRS. If you lie and state, "yes," your nonprofit will be subject to penalties for filing an inaccurate return. A penalty of $20 a day, not to exceed the smaller of $10,000 or 5% of your nonprofit's gross receipts for the year, may be charged when a Form 990 or 990-EZ is incomplete or inaccurate. (See Chapter 2.)

Contents of Form

Form 990-T is very straightforward. You must list your gross income from the unrelated business and the deductible expenses you incurred running the business. You subtract your total expenses from your total gross income to determine your unrelated business taxable income. If you have multiple unrelated businesses, you can use losses from one unrelated business to offset profits from another.

The most important thing is to make sure you have accurate and complete records of the income and expenses for your unrelated businesses. You should have records to support all the numbers on your Form 990-T.

Paying UBIT

You must pay any UBIT due at the time you file your Form 990-T or by the filing deadline for the return (determined without extensions). The penalty for late payment of UBIT is usually half of 1% of the unpaid tax for each month or part of a month the tax is unpaid. The penalty cannot exceed 25% of the unpaid tax.

Moreover, you must make quarterly estimated tax payments of UBIT if you expect your UBIT for the year to be $500 or more. You must make your estimated tax payments by the 15th day of the fourth, sixth, ninth, and 12th months of your tax year. You will be subject to an underpayment penalty if you don't make estimated tax payments of at least the smaller of your actual tax liability for the year, or 100% of the prior year's tax. Use Form 990-W (Worksheet), *Estimated Tax on Unrelated Business Taxable Income for Tax-Exempt Organizations,* to figure this estimated tax.

Lobbying and Political Campaign Activities

Many people in the nonprofit community think that lobbying by nonprofits is completely prohibited. It is not. Some think it's okay for nonprofits to support political candidates. This is wrong too. The IRS rules on lobbying and political campaigning by nonprofits are some of the most misunderstood rules in the nonprofit world. In this chapter, we'll explain what nonprofits can and cannot do with respect to these two activities.

The context in which a nonprofit's role in lobbying and political campaigning comes up can be surprising. After reading this chapter, you'll have a better understanding of how to act in certain circumstances where there may be lobbying and political campaign issues, such as:

- Your city council is about to vote on cutting its grant to your nonprofit by 80%. Can you attend the council meeting and complain? Can you ask the public to email or call council members to complain?
- A proposition banning gay marriage is on your state's ballot. Can your church urge parishioners to vote for or against it?
- Joe Dokes is running for mayor of your town. Can your nonprofit host a fundraiser for him? Can it register people to vote? Can it hold a public forum in which all candidates for mayor are invited to speak?

Lobbying by Nonprofits—What's Allowed and What's Not

Let's assume that you are president of Peoria Clayworks, a small nonprofit arts organization in Peoria, Illinois, dedicated to teaching ceramic arts to the poor and elderly. Due to budget constraints, the Peoria City Council is considering reducing its grants to all local arts organizations by 80%. The new city budget containing these reductions comes up for a council vote in two weeks. If your grant is cut by 80%, your nonprofit will have to close its doors. You are a Section 501(c)(3) public charity and as such are subject to IRS restrictions on lobbying by nonprofits. Which of the following actions can you take without risking the IRS's wrath?

- call the mayor of Peoria to complain about the proposed cuts
- place a notice on your organization's website alerting the community to the cuts
- contact the Peoria city manager to discuss whether some of the cuts can be restored
- at the city council's invitation, testify before the city council about the effect the proposed budget cuts would have on your nonprofit
- send a letter to all the city council members protesting the proposed cuts
- ask the public to call and email their city council members to protest the cuts, or
- join a coalition of small arts groups that plans to hire a high-priced lobbyist in the state capital to persuade the state legislature to increase state funding for the arts.

The answer: *All of them.* That's right, despite what you may have heard about nonprofits not being allowed to lobby, nonprofits can and do engage in lobbying. The key is that they not engage in too much of it.

Many in the nonprofit community have the idea that lobbying by nonprofits is frowned upon by the IRS, or even prohibited. Some even fear that they will lose their tax exemption if they engage in lobbying. Perhaps as a result, only about 1% of the hundreds of thousands of nonprofits registered with the IRS report any lobbying expenditures. However, nothing could be further from the truth. Public charities (501(c)(3) organizations) are allowed to engage in lobbying as long as it does not constitute a substantial part of their overall activities. Moreover, many activities you might think of as lobbying are not considered such by the IRS.

Lobbying Congress, state legislatures, city councils, and other legislative bodies can be a nonprofit's most valuable public service, gaining attention for people and causes that would otherwise be overlooked. Lobbying by nonprofits has resulted in many important legislative achievements, including the passage of stricter drunk driving laws and improved funding for medical research and public health. There are over 17,000 registered professional lobbyists in Washington, DC, and thousands more in the 50 state capitals. The vast majority work to promote the interests of business and industry. If nonprofits don't fight for the interests of those who can't afford to hire lobbyists, who will?

Why the Limits?

Lobbying and political activity by nonprofits are subject to limitations that don't apply to other types of organizations. Why? Because nonprofits receive significant tax benefits that other organizations don't receive. Not only is their income tax free, but people who donate to a nonprofit can deduct their contributions. These tax benefits amount to a substantial financial subsidy by the government. In return, nonprofits are required to engage in charitable activities—this is what Congress wants to encourage. However, Congress also believes the federal government should be neutral in political affairs and not subsidize partisan political activity. Thus, it has imposed certain limitations on lobbying and political campaigning by tax-exempt nonprofits. These limitations have withstood court challenges that they deny nonprofits their First Amendment right of free speech or interfere with the free exercise of religion by churches.

CAUTION

Check for lobbying registration requirements. Nonprofits that engage in lobbying may have to register with the federal government in Washington, DC, and one or more state governments. The Lobbying Disclosure Act of 1995 requires nonprofits to register their in-house lobbyists with the House and Senate and file semiannual reports on their lobbying activities and expenses. The Act applies to any nonprofit that has at least one employee who devotes 20% or more of his or her time on lobbying and spends $20,000 or more on lobbying every six months. States have their own registration requirements. For more information, see www.citizen.org.

What Is Lobbying?

Basically, for IRS purposes, your nonprofit engages in lobbying anytime it attempts to persuade members of a legislative body to propose, support, oppose, amend, or repeal legislation. "Legislation" means anything a legislative body must vote to adopt or reject—whether a law, resolution, proposal, nomination, treaty, zoning rule, or anything else. It also includes things like referendums, initiatives, and constitutional amendments that must be placed on the ballot and voted on by the general public. Lobbying, then, means trying to persuade a member of Congress, a state legislature, city council, county board of supervisors, or even a foreign legislature or parliament, to vote in a certain way. It also means trying to help to enact or oppose a law or other item that would have to be voted on to take effect. For example, the nonprofit Peoria Clayworks (from the above example) would be engaged in lobbying if it attempted to persuade Peoria City Council members not to adopt a new budget containing drastic budget cuts for the arts.

However, there does not have to be a specific law pending in a legislative body for lobbying to occur. Lobbying includes support or opposition for proposed laws that are a long way from actually being voted on—for example, a church would be engaged in lobbying if it urged members of Congress to approve a constitutional amendment allowing school prayer, even if no such amendment was pending in Congress at the time.

There are many different ways a nonprofit can attempt to persuade a legislator; however, they can all be divided into two broad categories— direct lobbying and grassroots lobbying.

Direct lobbying. Direct lobbying occurs when your nonprofit or its members directly communicate with legislators or their employees. For example, Peoria Clayworks would be engaged in direct lobbying if its president, or any other person acting on its behalf, met with, called, wrote, or emailed any member of the Peoria City Council (or a member of a councilperson's staff) and asked him or her to vote "no" on proposed budget reductions for the arts. The nonprofit would also be engaged in direct lobbying if it urged its members to lobby the city council.

Grassroots lobbying. Grassroots lobbying occurs when you urge members of the general public—or any segment of the public—to contact their legislators to voice their opposition or approval of specific legislation or proposals. This can be a very effective form of lobbying, especially if lots of people become involved. Any method your nonprofit uses to get the public's attention and persuade them to contact their legislators constitutes grassroots lobbying—for example, mass mailings; public meetings and rallies; press conferences; websites; newspaper, radio and television advertisements; and any other efforts to reach the general public.

> EXAMPLE: The nonprofit, Peoria Clayworks, places an advertisement in its local newspaper urging all the citizens of Peoria to contact their city council members to protest proposed budget cuts that will hurt its operations. This is grassroots lobbying. On the other hand, if the nonprofit sent an email only to members of its organization, it would not be grassroots lobbying because it is not directed to the general public.

Not All Advocacy Is Lobbying

Lobbying is just one form of advocacy that your nonprofit can engage in to help accomplish its exempt purposes. And, although lobbying by nonprofits is allowed, it is subject to restrictions (see "How Much Lobbying is Too Much?" below). Advocacy, on the other hand, that doesn't fall within the IRS definition of lobbying is completely unrestricted. Such nonlobbying advocacy includes the following:

Actions by administrative bodies. Lobbying only involves something a legislative body can vote on, such as Congress, a state legislature, or city council or county board of supervisors. Lobbying does not include items voted on or otherwise approved by administrative bodies, such as school boards, housing authorities, sewer and water districts, zoning boards, and other federal, state, or local special purpose bodies (whether elected or appointed). Nonprofits can try to persuade members of administrative bodies and their staffs to take any action within their authority, including voting on laws, rules, proposals, budgets, or other items. For example, the president of the Peoria Clayworks would not be engaged in lobbying if he contacted the Peoria School Board and asked its members to provide more money for arts education in the schools.

However, it would be lobbying to ask an administrative body to propose, support, or oppose legislation that would have to be voted on by a legislative body. For example, if the president of Peoria Clayworks asked the Peoria School Board to support the Peoria City Council restoring funding for the city arts budget, it would constitute lobbying because the city's arts budget is a matter that must be voted on by a legislative body—the city council.

Actions by the executive. For the same reason that asking a school board or other administrative body to take (or refrain from taking) an administrative action is not lobbying, asking the executive branch to take or not take an executive action is also not lobbying. An executive action is anything an executive—such as the president, governor, mayor, or other elected executive—can do without obtaining approval from a legislative body. For example, it is not lobbying to ask the governor to commute the death sentence for a prisoner on death row because this does not require a vote of the state legislature. However, requesting an executive to support or propose legislation is lobbying because adopting the legislation would require a vote by the appropriate legislative body. For example, it would be lobbying to ask the governor to support a bill outlawing the death penalty.

Invited legislative testimony. Ordinarily, if a nonprofit testifies before a legislative committee regarding legislation, it will be considered lobbying. However, this is not the case when a nonprofit testifies (in person or in writing) in response to an official request from a governmental body or legislative committee for the nonprofit's technical advice. The request must be made in the name of the governmental body or committee rather than by an individual member. If requested to do so by the legislators, the nonprofit may even offer its opinions or recommendations regarding specific legislation.

Thus, for example, it would not be lobbying for the president of the Peoria Clayworks to testify about the impact of the proposed budget cuts for the arts if he was officially invited to do so by the Peoria City Council. However, if he asked to appear and testify before the city council to oppose the budget cuts and the council agreed to hear him, his testimony would constitute lobbying.

Lobbying by individuals. Only official acts are attributed to a nonprofit organization. Thus, lobbying by individual members of a nonprofit is not attributed to the organization if it is done without the organization's consent or approval. Similarly, lobbying by an employee, officer, or director of a nonprofit is not attributed to the organization where it is done in a purely private capacity, not as a representative of the nonprofit. So, when does a person act in an official, as opposed to private, capacity? This can be difficult to discern. The basic rule is that a person's actions on behalf of a nonprofit are "official" if the person acted within his or her authority, or the actions were later approved by the nonprofit.

For example, the president of Peoria Clayworks has the authority to represent and speak for the organization on all matters regarding government grants and fundraising. Thus, he is acting within his official capacity—and, therefore, lobbying—when he tells the Peoria City Council that he is the nonprofit's president and then attempts to persuade them to restore arts funding. On the other hand, Clayworks would not be engaged in lobbying if its president sent a personal letter to his state legislator urging him to support a bill allowing gay marriage and the letter did not mention his involvement with Clayworks.

Self-defense lobbying. "Self-defense" lobbying does not count as lobbying for IRS purposes. This type of lobbying occurs when a non-profit communicates with legislators about its own existence, powers, or tax-exempt status, or the deductibility of contributions to nonprofits. For example, a nonprofit might lobby Congress to reject a proposal by the president to limit the tax deduction for charitable contributions. Self-defense lobbying occurs relatively rarely.

Nonpartisan Education Is Not Lobbying

Educating the public or members of the government about public issues in a nonpartisan manner is not lobbying as long as you do not ask or advise a legislative body to take a particular action.

Discussion of broad social and economic problems. Discussing broad social and economic problems does not constitute lobbying if you do not address specific legislation or directly encourage people to take action on legislation. For example, a nonprofit may discuss problems such as environmental pollution or population growth that are being considered by Congress. The discussion must not directly address specific legislation being considered and the nonprofit cannot directly encourage people to contact Congress or others who participate in the legislative process to take specific action.

> EXAMPLE: A nonprofit group, Environmental Education Institute, sponsors a public forum in which several environmental scientists present the latest findings about global warming. Neither the institute nor the scientists recommend that Congress or other legislative bodies take any particular action on the issue, nor do they ask the public to do anything. They simply present the latest scientific facts. The forum does not constitute lobbying.

On the other hand, if your educational efforts also include a dose of advocacy, you would be engaged in lobbying.

> EXAMPLE: Assume that the Environment Education Institute sponsors a forum on global warming in which several scientists discuss the latest scientific research on the subject, and urge that the carbon cap and trade bill pending in Congress be enacted into law. This forum constitutes lobbying.

Nonpartisan education and analysis. Nonprofits often do studies of specific issues or problems and then publish their results. As long as they provide a nonpartisan analysis of the underlying issue, it won't be considered lobbying when they distribute or make their results available to the public. To be considered nonpartisan, it must be a full and fair explanation of the relevant facts so that people can form their own independent opinion on the issue. In addition, it must not encourage people to take any particular action, including contacting their legislators. If your reports are nonpartisan, then you can make them available by any means you want, including publishing, distributing copies of the reports, presenting information at conferences or meetings, or communicating through news media such as radio, television, or newspapers. In addition, the communications must be made available to anyone who wants them. Their circulation can't be limited to only those who are interested solely in one side of a particular issue.

> EXAMPLE: A nonprofit called Free the Bees establishes a research project to collect information on the dangers of using pesticides in agriculture. The information is distributed in a published report that analyzes the effects and costs of using various pesticides on humans, animals, and crops. The report discusses the advantages, disadvantages, and economic cost of allowing the continued use of pesticides, of controlling their use, and of developing alternatives to them. The report concludes that the disadvantages of using pesticides are greater than the advantages, and that regulation of their use is needed. Even though the report advocates a certain viewpoint, it is within the exception for nonpartisan analysis because it presents a full and fair explanation of both sides of the issue. Free the Bees is free to distribute and use the report to advocate its position and it would not be considered lobbying.

However, your nonprofit will be engaged in lobbying if it issues a report or study that recommends that specific legislation be adopted or opposed.

> EXAMPLE: Assume that Free the Bees' report on pesticide use recommends that legislation be enacted limiting the use of specific types of pesticides. The report is no longer nonpartisan and the nonprofit's efforts would constitute lobbying.

How Much Lobbying Is Too Much?

Remember, as a nonprofit, you are allowed to engage in some lobbying. The key is to make sure it remains at a level that is acceptable to the IRS. How do you do this? Unfortunately, this is where things can get confusing. There are two different tests for determining whether your lobbying activities are within IRS guidelines. A majority of nonprofits use the so-called "substantial part test." This is the default test that will be automatically applied to your nonprofit if you don't make an IRS election to use the other test, called the expenditures test. Although it is used less often, the expenditures test has certain advantages and may be a better choice depending on your circumstances.

Substantial Part Test

The substantial part test is used by the vast majority of nonprofits. Under this test, a nonprofit will qualify for tax-exempt status as long as no "substantial part" of its overall activities relates to influencing legislation or carrying on propaganda. Churches are required to use this test; it is also the default test applied to nonprofits that don't elect the expenditures test.

If your nonprofit engages in lobbying activities and, like most nonprofits, you use the substantial part test, you'll need to know at what point lobbying would be considered a "substantial part" of your nonprofit's overall activities. Unfortunately, this has never been clearly defined. The only IRS guidance on the issue is that it looks at "all the pertinent facts and circumstances in each case." Among the factors the IRS considers are the time devoted to lobbying by both your paid and volunteer workers and the amount of money your organization spends on lobbying. Other factors may be considered as well—for example, the amount of publicity your organization assigns to the activity, the continuous or intermittent nature of your attention to it, and the impact of the lobbying efforts.

Obviously, this is a highly subjective test—what might seem like substantial lobbying to one IRS auditor could appear like minor lobbying to another. In an attempt to find more clarity, experts have examined the few court decisions on this issue and tried to discern numerical guidelines. One court found that a nonprofit's lobbying was not substantial because it constituted less than 5% of the organization's total time and effort for the year. Another court found that lobbying was substantial where it exceeded 16% to 20% of a nonprofit's total expenditures. Many people use these figures as a rule of thumb— spending anything less than 5% of the nonprofit's total budget is minor lobbying, while spending anything over the 16% to 20% range is substantial lobbying. However, it's important to keep in mind that these figures have no official sanction from the IRS or courts. Indeed, some courts have explicitly stated that, while these percentages are relevant, they do not themselves determine whether lobbying is substantial.

According to one survey, 85% of nonprofits devote less than 2% of their budgets to lobbying—well under the 5% rule of thumb. However, the consequences are severe if you make a mistake and flunk the substantial part test. If the IRS determines that a substantial part of your overall activities relate to lobbying, it will revoke your tax-exempt status for that year. This is a death sentence for most nonprofits because it results in all of the nonprofit's income being subject to tax. In addition, donors to the organization cannot deduct their contributions, and you might have to pay a special excise tax equal to 5% of your lobbying expenditures. This tax can be imposed on your organization's managers personally if they agreed to the lobbying expenditures knowing that it would likely result in the loss of tax-exempt status. While it may be unlikely that you would find yourself in this position, it is something you want to be aware of because the consequences are so severe.

Expenditures Test

In order to provide more precise guidelines for determining how much lobbying is too much, Congress created the expenditures test. It's much easier for nonprofits to figure out whether the amount of lobbying they are doing is allowed under this test. You must elect to use the expenditures test for your nonprofit, and it can only be used by public charities or 501(c)(3) organizations—not churches or private foundations. If you don't elect to use this test, you will be governed by the substantial part test by default. Making the election is easy. You file IRS Form 5768, a simple one-page form. Regardless of when you file the form, you are considered to have made the election at the start of the tax year in which it was filed.

Although the expenditures test was created to make lobbying by nonprofits easier, few have chosen to take advantage of it. In fact, fewer than 5% of eligible nonprofits have made the election. This may be because people are unaware of it or because they believe it will increase their accounting burden or make their group an IRS audit target (which the IRS denies). Indeed, an IRS manual states that nonprofits that file the election are usually within the law and are poor audit targets.

The only thing that counts under the expenditures test is how much money a nonprofit spends on lobbying—for example, costs to print and distribute literature, maintain websites, travel to visit legislators, salaries of in-house lobbyists, and the cost of hiring outside lobbyists. The amount of time your nonprofit spends on lobbying is immaterial. Lobbying by unpaid volunteers doesn't count at all (unless they are reimbursed for their expenses). You also don't count any time spent lobbying legislators regarding regulations (as opposed to laws).

If you use this test, you must divide your lobbying expenses into the two categories discussed above: direct and grassroots (see "What is Lobbying?" above). The expenditures test establishes an annual ceiling on how much a nonprofit can spend each year on all lobbying (direct and grassroots), and on grassroots lobbying alone. As shown in the chart below, the ceiling varies according to the nonprofit's annual operating budget, which includes all the money a nonprofit spends in a year related to its exempt purpose (excluding capital expenditures and any separate fundraising unit).

These ceilings are fairly generous, especially for smaller nonprofits (those with annual budgets up to $500,000). These nonprofits are allowed to spend 20% of their total operating budget on lobbying. This is far more than the 5% to 10% rule of thumb under the substantial part test.

Total Annual Operating Budget	Annual Ceiling for All Lobbying Activities	Annual Ceiling for Grassroots Lobbying
Up to $500,000	20% of total budget	5% of total budget
$500,000 to $1,000,000	$100,000 + 15% of excess over $500,000	$25,000 + 3.75% of excess over $500,000
$1,000,000 to $1,500,000	$175,000 + 10% of excess over $1,000,000	$43,750 + 2.5% of excess over $1,000,000
$1,500,000 to $17,000,000	$225,000 + 5% of excess over $1,500,000	$56,250 + 1.25% of excess over $1,500,000
Over $17,000,000	$1,000,000	$250,000

EXAMPLE: Save Our Seniors, a nonprofit that provides free meals to the homebound elderly, has an annual operating budget of $250,000. It can spend a total of $50,000 (20% of its annual budget) on lobbying activities. Of this amount, it can spend $12,500 (5% of its annual budget) on grassroots lobbying.

If you are part of a group of affiliated nonprofits, then your lobbying expenditures will be counted together with the rest of the group's for purposes of the test. You will be considered affiliated with another nonprofit if one nonprofit has the right to control the lobbying activities of one or more other nonprofits through interlocking governing boards or governing instruments. This prevents a nonprofit from gaming the expenditures test by dividing itself into several separate nonprofits, each with its own annual limit.

The penalties for failing the expenditure test are less onerous than if you fail the substantial part test. If your expenditures on lobbying exceed the limit in any year, you will have to pay a 25% excise tax on the excess. Grassroots lobbying is considered separately. For example, if Save Our Seniors (the nonprofit in the example above) spent $25,000 on grassroots lobbying during the year, it would be $12,500 over its limit and it would have to pay an excise tax on that amount.

Your nonprofit will lose its tax exemption under the expenditures test only if its lobbying expenses are 150% over the limit over a four-year period. This means that if you elect to use this test, you can't have your tax exemption revoked until the end of four years.

The expenditures test may not be a good choice if your nonprofit engages in substantial grassroots lobbying, because the dollar limits for grassroots lobbying are relatively low. On the other hand, nonprofits that rely on volunteers to lobby benefit by electing the expenditures test because volunteer lobbying is not counted under the test. Any nonprofit that wants to have the absolute certainty that comes with the expenditure test should consider filing an election.

Reporting Your Lobbying Time and Expenses

If your nonprofit files IRS Form 990 or IRS Form 990-EZ, you must report your lobbying expenditures on Schedule C of that form. The only nonprofits that don't have to file either Form 990 or Form 990-EZ are those that earn less than $25,000 per year. Those nonprofits don't have to report their lobbying expenditures.

If you (like the vast majority of nonprofits) use the substantial part test, you must report on Schedule C what you spent during the tax year on lobbying-related activities. This includes the following: the amount you paid for staff or management engaged in lobbying; media advertisements; mailings, publications, or broadcasts; grants to other organizations for lobbying purposes; direct contacts with legislators or their staffs; and rallies, demonstrations, speeches, lectures, and other means of reaching the public. You must also provide a detailed description of any other lobbying activities you were involved in, including those carried out by unreimbursed volunteers. For this reason, you should always keep track of the time spent by volunteers on lobbying activities.

If you elect to use the expenditures test instead, you must separately report your expenditures for direct and grassroots lobbying. This requires a fairly sophisticated accounting system that allows you to allocate expenses between the direct and grassroots lobbying categories. You must also allocate a portion of your general overhead to lobbying. However, you don't need to report on volunteer lobbying activities (and, therefore, don't have to keep track of them for IRS purposes).

No matter which test you use, make sure your employees keep careful records of the time they spend on lobbying. That way you can correctly allocate their salaries, benefits, and expenses between lobbying and nonlobbying activities.

Lobbying via the Internet

The Internet has become one of the most powerful mediums for political activity in the world. Most nonprofits have websites which, among many other things, can be used for lobbying. For example, you might post documents on your website urging members of the public to lobby or send email to legislators regarding legislation that you support or oppose.

Lobbying via the Internet is subject to the same rules as any other form of lobbying. However, it does pose some unique issues that have yet to be clearly addressed by the IRS, such as:

- Does providing a hyperlink to an organization that engages in lobbying constitute lobbying by the nonprofit that provides the link? Answer: Probably not, unless the nonprofit is controlled by the linked-to site, or the nonprofit is lobbying on a particular issue and urges visitors to link to a website taking similar positions.

- To what extent are statements made by subscribers to a forum, such as a listserv or newsgroup, attributable to an exempt organization that maintains the forum? Answer: These statements cannot be attributed to the nonprofit unless they are made by the nonprofit itself.

- For the vast majority of nonprofits that use the substantial part test, how can you determine whether lobbying via the Internet is a substantial part of the nonprofit's activities? For example, is the location of the communication on the website (main page or subsidiary page) or number of hits it receives from Internet users relevant? Answer: Unclear, but the IRS has indicated that these factors are relevant.

Because lobbying on the Internet tends to be much less expensive than other forms of lobbying, nonprofits that engage in a lot of it may wish to elect to use the expenditures test. That way, only the money you spend on your Internet lobbying will be considered by the IRS, not its effectiveness or popularity.

If You Receive Federal Grants

Many nonprofits receive federal grants to fund various programs. Understandably, you cannot use federal money for lobbying. What constitutes lobbying for federal fund purposes is defined by the federal Office of Management and Budget instead of the IRS. While these rules on lobbying are similar to the IRS rules, there are also some differences. For example, under these rules, lobbying consists of attempting to influence through direct or grassroots lobbying federal legislation in Congress or state legislation in a state legislature. Attempting to influence local legislation—for example, city council laws or ordinances—is not lobbying. However, attempting to persuade the president or a state governor to sign or veto legislation is lobbying. Legislative liaison activities undertaken to support lobbying or prepare for a lobbying effort are also considered lobbying for these purposes. Such activities include attending legislative sessions or committee hearings, gathering information about legislation, and analyzing its effects. For more information, see Attachment B, Section 25, of OMB Circular A-122, *Cost Principles for Nonprofit Organizations,* available at www.whitehouse.gov/omb/circulars_default/.

This limitation does not mean that if your nonprofit receives federal grant money, you cannot lobby. You just have to make sure that you don't spend federal money on your lobbying efforts. This means you have to track how you spend your federal money to ensure that it doesn't go to support lobbying. A separate bank account for such funds is not required, although it can be used.

RESOURCE

Need more information? The nonprofit Center for Lobbying in the Public Interest has created an outstanding guide to all aspects of lobbying on its website at www.clpi.org.

Political Campaign Activities— An Absolute Ban

If a certain amount of lobbying is allowed by the IRS, electioneering or political campaigning is absolutely forbidden. Nonprofits are prohibited from intervening in political campaigns in any manner whatsoever, whether by endorsing or opposing candidates for public office, mobilizing supporters to help elect or defeat candidates, or giving money to political campaigns or political parties. This prohibition applies to *all* political campaigns for elective office, including those at the federal, state, and local level, and even includes elections in foreign countries. If you violate these rules, your nonprofit (or its managers) may have to pay excise taxes and you risk losing your tax-exempt status—not something any nonprofit wants to take a chance with.

Despite these harsh sounding rules, nonprofits can play a non-partisan role in an election. As described more below, nonprofits are allowed to educate voters about important issues, and can register voters and urge them to vote, as long as everything is done in a nonpartisan manner. Only then is it not considered a political campaign activity.

What Activities Are Prohibited

Quite simply, a nonprofit may not engage in *any* activity that favors or opposes a candidate for elective public office. This includes:

- endorsing a candidate for public office
- contributing money to political campaigns
- making verbal or written public statements supporting or criticizing candidates
- distributing statements prepared by others that favor or oppose any candidate
- allowing a candidate to use an organization's assets or facilities (unless other candidates are given the same opportunity)
- criticizing or supporting candidates on nonprofit websites or through links to other websites, and

- placing signs on nonprofit property supporting or opposing candidates.

If You Receive Federal Grants

As is the case with lobbying, nonprofits that receive federal grants can't use the money to help fund political campaigns. This includes attempting to influence the outcome of any federal, state, or local election through cash or in-kind contributions, endorsements, or publicity. Federal grant money may not be used to help pay the expenses of a political party, campaign, political action committee, or other organization established to influence the outcome of an election. For more information, see Attachment B, Section 25 of OMB Circular A-122, *Cost Principles for Nonprofit Organizations*, available at www.whitehouse.gov/omb/circulars_default/.

Voter Education, Voter Registration, and Get-Out-the-Vote Drives

Provided you do it in a nonpartisan, unbiased manner, your nonprofit may engage in voter education activities and voter registration and get-out-the-vote drives. For example, a nonprofit group can offer rides to the polls, canvass the neighborhood, and hand out voter information, or call voters about the election. However, you can't engage in any of these activities if you do them in a way that favors or opposes any candidate for office.

EXAMPLE 1: The Alinsky Brigade, a nonprofit that promotes community involvement, sets up a voter registration booth at a state fair. The signs and banners in and around the booth give only the name of the organization, the date of the upcoming election, and notice of the opportunity to register. No reference to any candidate or political party is made by the volunteers staffing the booth or in the materials available at the booth, other than the official voter registration forms that allow registrants to select a party affiliation. The nonprofit is not engaged in political campaigning because it is acting in a nonpartisan manner.

EXAMPLE 2: Green Thumb, Inc., a nonprofit involved with environmental issues, would like Candidate George to be elected governor of the state because he is proenvironment. Shortly before the election, it sets up a telephone bank to call registered voters. Voters who indicate that they support George are urged to vote and offered free transportation to the polls. If voters indicate they do not support George, the caller politely ends the call. The nonprofit is engaged in political campaign intervention because it treats voters differently depending on their affiliation.

Candidate Appearances

You may decide to invite political candidates to speak at events sponsored by your nonprofit, either in their capacity as a candidate or in their individual capacity. In either event, you'll need to make sure you do it properly or you will run into problems with political campaigning.

If you invite a candidate to speak at one of your events as a political candidate—that is, to solicit votes—you must ensure that:

- you provide an equal opportunity to other candidates seeking the same office
- your nonprofit does not voice any support for or opposition to the candidate (this should be stated explicitly when the candidate is introduced and in communications concerning the candidate's attendance), and
- no political fundraising occurs.

In determining whether candidates are given an equal opportunity to participate, you should consider the nature of the event, in addition to the manner of presentation. For example, a nonprofit that invites one candidate to speak at its well-attended annual banquet, but invites the opposing candidate to speak at a sparsely attended general meeting, will likely have violated the political campaign activity prohibition, even if the manner of presentation for both speakers is otherwise neutral.

Candidates may also appear or speak at nonprofit events in a non-candidate capacity. For example, you might invite a political candidate to one of your nonprofit events because he or she:

- currently holds, or formerly held, public office
- is considered an expert in a nonpolitical field, or
- is a celebrity or has led a distinguished military, legal, or public service career.

A candidate may also choose to attend an event that is open to the public, such as a lecture, concert, or worship service.

A candidate's presence at one of your nonprofit's sponsored events does not, by itself, mean you are engaged in political campaign intervention. However, if the candidate is publicly recognized at the event or invited to speak, you must ensure that:

- the candidate is chosen to speak solely for reasons other than candidacy for public office
- the candidate speaks only in a noncandidate capacity
- neither the individual's candidacy nor the election is mentioned
- no campaign activity occurs due to the candidate's attendance, and
- a nonpartisan atmosphere is maintained at the event.

In addition, you should clearly indicate the capacity in which the candidate is appearing and should not mention the individual's political candidacy or the upcoming election in any announcement of the event.

You can invite more than one candidate for the same office to speak at one of your events or some other public forum, as long as the event is conducted in an unbiased manner. The factors the IRS considers in determining if an event is unbiased include whether:

- questions for the candidates are prepared and presented by an independent nonpartisan panel
- the topics discussed by the candidates cover a broad range of issues that the candidates would address if elected to the office and are of interest to the public

- each candidate is given an equal opportunity to present his or her view on the issues discussed
- the candidates are asked to agree or disagree with positions, agendas, platforms, or statements of the nonprofit, and
- a moderator comments on the questions or otherwise implies approval or disapproval of the candidates.

EXAMPLE 1: The president of the Columbus Historical Society invites the three candidates in the upcoming congressional election to address the group's members, one each at a regular meeting held on three successive weeks. Each candidate is given an equal opportunity to answer questions on a wide variety of topics from the members. The nonprofit's publicity announcing the dates for each of the candidate's speeches and the president's introduction of each candidate include no comments on their qualifications or any indication of a preference for any candidate. The nonprofit's actions do not constitute political campaign intervention.

EXAMPLE 2: The Sunday before the November election, the minister of the Friends Church invites Senate Candidate Willie Slick to preach to her congregation during worship services. During his remarks, Candidate Slick states, "I am asking not only for your votes, but for your enthusiasm and dedication, for your willingness to go the extra mile to get a very large turnout on Tuesday." The minister invites no other candidate to address her congregation during the senatorial campaign. Because these activities take place during official church services, they are attributed to the church. By selectively providing church facilities to allow Candidate Slick to speak in support of his campaign, the church's actions constitute political campaign intervention.

Voter Guides

Voter guides are pamphlets or documents that are created to help voters compare candidates' positions on issues. Nonprofits are allowed to prepare, distribute, and otherwise help with voter guides, as long as the guide is neutral in form and content and covers a broad range of issues. If a voter guide focuses on a single or narrow range of issues, or if the questions or information reflect bias, then it would violate the prohibition against political campaign activity for the nonprofit to be involved in the preparation, distribution, or some other way with the voter guide.

The factors the IRS considers in determining if a voter guide is biased include whether:

- the questions and descriptions of the issues are clear and unbiased in both their structure and content
- the candidates are given enough space to explain their positions
- the candidates' answers are unedited and appear near to the questions they relate to
- all candidates for a particular office are included, and
- the questions cover most major issues of interest to the entire electorate.

CAUTION

A few words of caution on voter guides. If your organization's position on one or more issues is set out in the guide so that it can be compared to the candidates' positions, the guide will constitute political campaign intervention. In addition, a nonprofit that distributes a voter guide prepared by a third party is responsible for its own actions. Thus, if you distribute a guide that is biased, distributing that guide constitutes political campaign intervention even though you didn't write it.

Individual Activity by Directors, Officers, and Employees

Just because you work at or head a nonprofit, doesn't mean you can no longer express your political views or speak out freely on important issues of public policy. However, if you are a leader or possible representative of a nonprofit organization, you must refrain from making partisan comments at official functions or in any of your organization's official publications. Although they are not required to do so, to avoid potential problems, nonprofit leaders or employees who speak or write in their individual capacity should clearly indicate that their comments are personal and not intended to represent the views of their organization. Also, it is best that their names not appear on a candidate's campaign literature. Finally, staff members at a nonprofit may not engage in partisan political activity during normal working hours.

> EXAMPLE: Three weeks before the election, John Knox, a well-known minister of the Foursquare Baptist Church attends a press conference at Candidate Victor's campaign headquarters. Without stating that he is speaking on behalf of the church, Knox states that he hopes Candidate Victor is reelected. The next day, his endorsement is reported on the front page of the local newspaper and he is identified in the article as the minister of the Foursquare Baptist Church. Because Knox did not make the endorsement at an official church function, in an official church publication, or otherwise use the church's assets, and because he never said that he was speaking as a representative of his church, his actions do not constitute campaign activity by the church.

> EXAMPLE: Dave is the chairman of the board of directors of the Open Space Initiative, a nonprofit that educates the public on conservation issues. During a regular meeting shortly before a local election, Chairman Dave spoke on a number of issues, including the importance of voting in the upcoming election and concluded by stating, "It is important that you all do your duty in the election and vote for Candidate Wendy." Because Chairman Dave's remarks were made during an official organization meeting, they constitute political campaign activity by the nonprofit.

Issue Advocacy Versus Political Campaign Activity

Nonprofits may take positions on public policy issues, including those that divide the candidates in an election. For example, a nonprofit may advocate for the abolition of the death penalty by issuing publications, sponsoring public forums on the issue, or sending out mailings. However, nonprofits cannot engage in any issue advocacy that functions as political campaign activity. Even advocacy that does not expressly tell an audience to vote for or against a specific candidate can constitute impermissible campaign activity if it contains a message favoring or opposing a candidate.

Key factors the IRS considers in determining whether a communication constitutes political campaign activity include whether in the course of its issue advocacy the nonprofit:

- identifies one or more candidates for a given public office
- expresses approval or disapproval for one or more candidates' positions or actions
- engages in advocacy near in time to the election (increasing advocacy efforts during the election season is evidence of political campaign activity)
- refers to voting or an election (this is strong evidence of political campaign activity)
- addresses an issue that divides the candidates for a given office
- makes the statement as one of an ongoing series of statements on the same issue and it is independent of the timing of any election (a statement is far more likely to be seen as nonpartisan if the nonprofit has made similar statements in nonelection years), and
- times its advocacy in response to a nonelectoral event—for example, a scheduled vote on specific legislation by an office-holder who also happens to be running for reelection—this is the safest type of issue advocacy during an election season.

EXAMPLE: Three Rs, Inc., a nonprofit that educates the public about the need for improved public education, prepares and finances a radio advertisement urging an increase in state funding for public education in the state. The ad is run during the reelection campaign of Governor Ed, the governor of the state. The ad cites numerous statistics indicating that public education in the state is underfunded. While the ad does not say anything about Governor Ed's position on funding for public education, it ends with "Tell

Governor Ed what you think about our underfunded schools."
Governor Ed's veto of a state income tax increase to fund public
schools was made an issue in the campaign by Ed's opponent.
At the time the ad is broadcast, no legislative vote or other major
legislative activity is scheduled in the state legislature regarding state
funding of public education. The nonprofit has violated the political
campaign prohibition because the advertisement identifies Governor
Ed, appears shortly before an election in which Governor Ed is a
candidate, is not timed to coincide with a nonelection event such as
a legislative vote on the issue, and takes a position on an issue that
Governor Ed's opponent has used to distinguish himself from Ed.

Business Activity as Political Campaign Activity

Your nonprofit's business activities could be considered political
campaign activity if they are done in a biased or partisan manner. For
example, if you sell your mailing list to the local Republican Party but
then refuse to sell it to members of the Democratic Party, your conduct
could be considered illegal political campaign activity. Other types of
business activities that might be considered political campaigning if they
are done improperly include leasing space to third parties or accepting
paid political advertising. The key here is that your nonprofit must offer
the goods or services to a candidate solely as a business decision—that is,
to earn money—not as part of an effort to help a candidate get elected.

The IRS can't read your mind to determine whether you have a
partisan motive, so it looks at your behavior. Your decision to sell goods
or services to a candidate will look like a business decision if:

- you offer the same goods or services on an equal basis to any
  political candidate
- the goods, services, or facilities are available to the general public
- the fees charged to candidates are at your nonprofit's usual rates, and
- providing the goods or services is an ongoing activity.

On the other hand, your nonprofit will appear to have a partisan motive if:

- you offer goods or services to some candidates but not others
- the goods or services are only made available to political candidates, not the general public
- you charge a candidate less than (or more than) your usual fees, or
- you only provide the goods or services during a particular election.

EXAMPLE: The San Antonio Cowboy Museum, a nonprofit museum, owns an historic building that has a large hall suitable for hosting dinners and receptions. The campaign committee of Candidate Quilty, who supports increased funding for museums, asks to rent the hall for a fundraising event. Although it has never rented the hall for a political event, the museum agrees to do it for a fee that would be charged to any other group renting the hall. However, later that year, the group declines similar requests from other campaign committees of other candidates involved in other elections. The museum has intervened in a political campaign because:

- it did not offer its service—rental of its hall—on an equal basis to all political candidates
- it did offer the service to the general public, and
- it made the service available only during a particular election.

The museum would not have engaged in political activity if it had made the hall available for rent to anyone who agreed to pay its usual fee.

Websites

The IRS treats material posted on a nonprofit's website exactly the same way as any other material. Thus, if a nonprofit posts something on its website that favors or opposes a candidate for public office, it will be treated the same as if it distributed printed material, oral statements, or broadcasts that favored or opposed a candidate.

> **EXAMPLE:** A church maintains a website that includes information on its ministers, the hours the church is open for worship, details on its community outreach programs, and the activities of congregation members. Bill, a member of the congregation, is running for a seat on the town council. Shortly before the election, the church posts the following message on its website, "Lend your support to Bill, your fellow parishioner, in Tuesday's election for town council." The church has intervened in a political campaign on behalf of Bill.

The rules discussed above regarding voter education, voter guides, voter registration, and candidate appearances apply to websites just as they do to the physical world. Thus, for example, you may post a nonpartisan voter guide on your website, urge people to register to vote (but not vote for a particular candidate), inform voters where to vote, and use your website as a nonpartisan public forum for political candidates. For example, you could post articles or speeches by candidates, so long as you do so for all candidates. You may also use your website to pursue issue advocacy—for example, an environmental nonprofit could post on its websites articles and other information about global warming.

One unique feature of websites is the use of hyperlinks—links that automatically take users to other Web pages when they click on them. Your nonprofit has control over whether it establishes a link to another site. Thus, the IRS says that when your nonprofit links to another website, you are responsible for the consequences of establishing and maintaining that link, even if you do not have control over the content of the linked site. This means that linking to a website that contains partisan political material could constitute impermissible political campaign intervention. However, the IRS has recently stressed that this is not always the case. Rather, all facts and circumstances must be taken into account, including:

- the context for the link—for example, whether it was created for a partisan reason
- whether the linked site contains material about all the candidates as opposed to only a single candidate—the IRS says that links to

websites containing information about all the candidates for an office are permissible

- whether any tax-exempt purpose, such as educating voters, is served by the link, and
- how direct the link is between the nonprofit's website and the Web page favoring or opposing a candidate—for example, a link that goes directly to a Web page that prominently endorses a candidate is more problematic than a link to a Web page that does not contain any specifically partisan material.

EXAMPLE 1: The Homeless Coalition, a nonprofit that serves the homeless, posts an unbiased, nonpartisan voter guide on its website. It includes a link to the official campaign website of each candidate included in the guide. These links are presented on a consistent neutral basis, with text saying "For more information on Candidate X, you may consult [URL]." The nonprofit has not intervened in a political campaign because the links are provided for the exempt purpose of educating voters and are presented in a neutral, unbiased manner that includes all candidates running for that office.

EXAMPLE 2: The Church of Nature maintains a website that includes such information as directions to the church, and descriptions of its programs, including an extensive treatment program for homeless veterans. On one page of the website, the church describes a particular type of treatment program for homeless veterans. This section includes a link to an article on the website of the *New York Enquirer*, a major national newspaper, praising the church's own treatment program for homeless veterans. The page containing the article on the newspaper's website does not refer to any candidate or election and has no direct links to candidate or election information. Elsewhere on the newspaper's website, however, there is a page displaying editorials that the paper has published, several of which endorse candidates in an upcoming election. The church has not intervened in a political campaign by linking to the newspaper's website because the link was provided for the exempt purpose of educating the public about its programs. In addition, there was a nonpartisan context for the link, and the way the links went from the church's website to the endorsement on the newspaper's website did not indicate that the church was favoring or opposing any candidate.

The IRS says that your organization is responsible for checking the link during the time it is posted on your website to make sure that there are no updates or changes that would cause it to violate the political campaign activity rules. So if you do post links on your website, be sure to monitor the links and their content; otherwise, you could end up violating the ban on campaign activity without even knowing it.

RESOURCE

For more on this topic ... In 2007, the IRS released its most detailed-ever guidance on the political campaign intervention rules in IRS Revenue Ruling 2007-41. It's an excellent resource to turn to for more information on this topic. IRS Publication 1828, *Tax Guide for Churches and Religious Organizations*, also contains a good discussion of these issues from the point of view of churches. Both are available at www.irs.gov.

Consequences of Violating the Rules

If the IRS finds that your organization violated the prohibition on political campaign activity, you could be required to pay a special excise tax equal to 10% of each prohibited political expenditure. Your nonprofit's managers could also be personally liable for a tax equal to 2.5% of each expenditure (up to a ceiling of $5,000) if they agreed to the expenditure even though they knew it was prohibited. Your organization could also have its tax-exempt status revoked.

In one case, the IRS stripped a Baltimore church of its tax exemption when it placed full-page advertisements in *USA Today* and *The Washington Times* warning readers that presidential candidate Bill Clinton's positions on abortion, homosexuality, and condom use for teenagers violated the Bible. Losing tax-exempt status is a death sentence for most nonprofits because all the nonprofit's income becomes taxable and donors can't deduct their contributions.

While the consequences are severe and something you want to avoid at all costs, these actions by the IRS are rare. In one recent year, a total of 76 nonprofits were found to have engaged in prohibited political campaign activities and only five had their tax exemptions revoked. The others received advisory opinions stating that prohibited political activity had occurred, but, because they were onetime violations, no further action would be taken. However, the IRS is attempting to step up its enforcement efforts. It established a Political Activities Compliance Initiative to help educate nonprofits about the restrictions on political activity and has assigned more staff to investigate complaints.

Getting Around the Restrictions

The restrictions on lobbying and, in particular, political campaign activity by public charities (Section 501(c)(3) organizations) can be very burdensome for nonprofits that are eager to engage in the political process to help advance their exempt purposes. However, there are ways to get around these restrictions.

Forming a Social Welfare Organization

One alternative is for a public charity (or a coalition of several charities with a common advocacy agenda) to form a separate social welfare organization to engage in lobbying and/or political activity on its behalf. Social welfare organizations are created under Section 501(c)(4) of the Internal Revenue Code and are often referred to as 501(c)(4) organizations. Their primary purpose is to in some way promote the common good and general welfare of the community—for example, "by bringing about civic betterments and social improvements."

Lobbying. Contributions to a social welfare organization are not tax deductible. As a result, unlike a public charity, a social welfare organization may engage in unlimited lobbying as long as it advances its tax-exempt social welfare purpose. For example, a social welfare organization created to help improve public health could spend all of its money lobbying Congress to provide more funding for public health. But it could not lobby Congress to increase the budget for space exploration because that isn't related to its exempt purpose.

Political campaign activity. Unlike 501(c)(3) nonprofits, 501(c)(4) social welfare organizations can engage in extensive political campaign activity. Moreover, as a result of the Supreme Court's controversial decision in *Citizens United v. FEC*, 501(c)(4) nonprofits can spend their money (both voluntary contributions and general treasury funds) to support or oppose candidates for the U.S. House, U.S. Senate, and president. Previously, such advocacy had to be made through Political Action Committees ("PACs") using voluntary donations rather than general treasury funds.

However, there are still some important limitations on 501(c)(4) political activities:

- they can't give money directly to candidates
- the political campaign activity must be undertaken to advance the organization's social welfare purpose—for example, an organization formed to advance public health could support political candidates who agree with its positions, and
- political activity may not be a social welfare organization's primary activity—no more than half of its activities should involve such political work.

In addition, social welfare organizations that spend money on political activity can become subject to a special tax on the lesser of the organization's net investment income or the total amount spent on political activity. The applicable amount is taxed at the highest corporate tax rate—35%. Organizations that don't have investment income need not worry about this tax. (See IRC Sec. 527.)

Legal relationship with charity. Legally, the social welfare organization is a separate entity even though it can be controlled by your 501(c)(3) nonprofit. For example, your 501(c)(3) could appoint the board of directors for the social welfare organization. However, the social welfare organization may not be financially supported by the public charity. This means that the social welfare organization must support itself by raising money through nondeductible contributions.

The public charity and social welfare organization must take care to keep their finances separate. Thus, for example, sharing of facilities and personnel is allowed only if the social welfare organization reimburses the charity for its share of the costs. Good records should be kept showing that tax deductible contributions to the public charity are not being used to pay for lobbying or political activity by the social welfare organization.

Forming a PAC

One thing a social welfare organization can't do is contribute money directly to candidates for federal elective office. This is barred by federal election laws. However, it may form a political action committee ("PAC") to do so. The amount of money a PAC can contribute to a political campaign or party is limited (at most $5,000 per candidate per election), but there are no limits on the amount they spend independently of a candidate's campaign.

The social welfare organization that created the PAC may solicit nondeductible contributions to it (limited to $5,000 per election per donor), but it can't take donations from corporations or other nonprofits. Your 501(c)(3) nonprofit cannot donate money to such a PAC, but it could be involved in its governance.

For more information on PACs, refer to the Federal Election Commission's Campaign Guide for Corporations and Labor Organizations, available at www.fec.gov.

Help Beyond This Book

f you have questions or problems not answered by this book, there are many other resources you can turn to, including websites, books, and tax professionals.

Help From the IRS

The IRS has made an impressive effort to inform the nonprofit community about the tax law, creating many informative publications, an excellent website, and a telephone answering service. However, keep in mind that, unlike the regulations and rulings issued by the IRS, these secondary sources of information are for informational purposes only. They are not official IRS pronouncements, and the IRS is not legally bound by them.

IRS Charities and Nonprofits Website

The first place to go for IRS information is the IRS's own website at www.irs.gov. The IRS website has a special section for nonprofits at www.irs.gov/Charities-&-Non-Profits. The IRS's Charities & Non-Profits website contains a vast amount of information including:

- virtually every IRS form and informational publication dealing with nonprofits
- helpful FAQs (frequently asked questions)
- specialized information for charities, churches and religious organizations, contributors, political organizations, and other nonprofit organizations
- training materials for IRS employees who deal with nonprofits
- articles published as part of the IRS continuing professional education program, and
- the IRS's EO Newsletter, which is issued periodically to keep the public up to date about tax law changes, new forms, and published IRS guidance.

There is also a detailed topic index.

IRS Publications

The IRS publishes over 350 free booklets explaining the tax code, called IRS Publications ("Pubs," for short). Several of these deal specifically with nonprofit issues. Many of these publications are referenced in this book. These include:

- Publication 526, *Charitable Contributions*
- Publication 557, *Tax-Exempt Status for Your Organization*
- Publication 598, *Tax on Unrelated Business Income of Exempt Organizations*
- Publication 892, *How to Appeal an IRS Decision on Tax-Exempt Status*
- Publication 1771, *Charitable Organizations—Substantiation and Disclosure Requirements*
- Publication 1828, *Tax Guide for Churches and Religious Organizations*
- Publication 3079, *Gaming Publication for Tax-Exempt Organizations*
- Publication 3833, *Disaster Relief—Providing Assistance through Charitable Organizations*
- Publication 4220, *Applying for 501(c)(3) Tax-Exempt Status*
- Publication 4221-PC, *Compliance Guide for 501(c)(3) Public Charities*
- Publication 4221-PF, *Compliance Guide for 501(c)(3) Private Foundations*
- Publication 4302, *A Charity's Guide to Vehicle Donations*
- Publication 4303, *A Donor's Guide to Vehicle Donations*
- Publication 4573, *Group Exemptions*
- Publication 4630, *The Exempt Organizations Products & Services Catalog*
- Publication 4779, *Facts about Terminating or Merging Your Exempt Organization*, and
- Publication 4991, *Automatic Revocation of Exempt Status*.

Other useful IRS Publications not written specifically for nonprofits include:

- Publication 15, *Circular E, Employer's Tax Guide*
- Publication 15-A, *Employer's Supplemental Tax Guide*.

Some are relatively easy to understand, others are incomprehensible or misleading. As with all IRS publications, they only present the IRS's interpretation of the tax laws—which may or may not be upheld by the federal courts.

You can download all of the publications from the IRS website at www.irs.gov. You can also obtain free copies by calling 800-TAX-FORM (800-829-3676) or by contacting your local IRS office or sending an order form to the IRS.

IRS Training Programs

The IRS also offers various types of training programs on nonprofit tax issues.

Live workshops. The IRS offers one-day workshops for small and midsized 501(c)(3) organizations in selected cities throughout the United States each year. The workshop, presented by experienced IRS Exempt Organizations Specialists, explains what 501(c)(3) organizations must do to maintain their exempt status and meet their tax obligations. The workshop is designed for administrators or volunteers who are responsible for the organization's tax compliance. For dates, locations, and registration consult the EO Calendar of Events on the EO website.

Web training. The IRS also offers a Web-based version of its live workshop. This free online workshop, *Stay Exempt—Tax Basics for 501(c)(3)s,* consists of five interactive modules on tax compliance topics for exempt organizations. Users can access this training program at www.stayexempt.org.

Phone forums. The IRS offers free periodic phone forums (conference calls) that provide information on topics of special interest to nonprofits. Check the Calendar of Events on the EO website to learn about upcoming phone forums.

Contacting the IRS

You may direct your technical and procedural questions concerning charities and other nonprofit organizations to IRS Tax Exempt and

IRS Nonprofit Tax Forms

Here is a list of the most commonly used IRS tax forms concerning nonprofits, most of which come with instructions that can be very helpful.

- Form 1023, *Application for Recognition of Exemption under Section 501(c)(3) of the Internal Revenue Code*
- Form 1024, *Application for Recognition of Exemption under Section 501(a)*
- Form 1098-C, *Contributions of Motor Vehicles, Boats, and Airplanes*
- Form 4720, *Return of Certain Excise Taxes Under Chapters 41 and 42 of the Internal Revenue Code*
- Form 5768, *Election/Revocation of Election by an Eligible Section 501(c)(3) Organization to Make Expenditures to Influence Legislation*
- Form 8274, *Certification by Churches and Qualified Church-Controlled Organizations Electing Exemption from Employer Social Security and Medicare Taxes*
- Form 8282, *Donee Information Return*
- Form 8283, *Noncash Charitable Contributions*
- Form 8868, *Application for Extension of Time to File an Exempt Organization Return*
- Form 990, *Return of Organization Exempt from Income Tax*
- Form 990-EZ, *Short Form Return of Organization Exempt from Income Tax*
- Form 990-N, *Electronic Notice (e-Postcard) for Tax-Exempt Organizations Not Required to File Form 990 or 990-EZ*
- Form 990-PF, *Return of Private Foundation or Section 4947(a)(1) Nonexempt Charitable Trust Treated as a Private Foundation*
- Form 990-T, *Exempt Organization Business Income Tax Return*, and
- Form 990-W, *Estimated Tax on Unrelated Business Taxable Income for Tax-Exempt Organizations.*

All these forms can all be downloaded from the IRS website at www.irs.gov.

Government Entities Customer Account Services at 877-829-5500 (toll-free number). Direct your questions about employment taxes to the Business and Specialty Tax Line at 800-829-4933 (toll-free).

If you prefer to write, you may write to the IRS at:

Internal Revenue Service

Exempt Organizations Determinations

P.O. Box 2508

Cincinnati, OH 45201

Other Helpful Publications and Websites

There is a vast amount of literature on nonprofits as well as many websites dealing with nonprofit legal issues, including taxes. A comprehensive list of books, articles, and websites on all types of nonprofit legal issues can be found in *Nonprofit Resources* (2nd edition), edited by Victor Futter and Lisa A. Runquist (American Bar Association). In addition, the New York University Law School's National Center on Philanthropy and the Law has an exhaustive online bibliography of books and articles on nonprofit law and taxes that is frequently updated. It can be found at http://ncpl.law.nyu.edu/ncplsearch.

Here are some particularly useful resources.

Nolo Publications and Website

Nolo has several books on nonprofit issues not covered in this book. These include:

- *How to Form a Nonprofit Corporation*, by Anthony Mancuso
- *Nonprofit Meetings, Minutes & Records*, by Anthony Manucso
- *Starting and Building a Nonprofit*, by Peri Pakroo
- *Effective Fundraising for Nonprofits*, by Ilona Bray, and
- *Every Nonprofit's Guide to Publishing*, by Cheryl Woodard and Lucia Hwang.

Nolo's website at www.nolo.com also contains a number of articles dealing with nonprofit matters and new legal developments.

Other Publications

Useful in-depth guides to nonprofit tax issues include:

- *Tax Planning and Compliance for Tax-Exempt Organizations*, by Jody Blazek (Wiley)
- *IRS Audits of Tax-Exempt Organizations*, by Bruce R. Hopkins (Wiley)
- *The Tax Law of Charitable Giving*, by Bruce R. Hopkins (Wiley)
- *The Law of Tax-Exempt Organizations*, by Bruce R. Hopkins (Wiley)
- *Tax Compliance for Tax-Exempt Organizations*, by Steven D. Simpson (CCH), and
- *Understanding Nonprofit and Tax-Exempt Organizations*, by Nicholas P. Cafardi and Jaclyn Fabean Cherry (LexisNexis).

Websites

There are a number of websites that have good information on nonprofit tax issues, including:

- Nonprofit Law Prof Blog at http://lawprofessors.typepad.com/nonprofit
- Don Kramer's Nonprofit Issues at www.nonprofitissues.com
- The Chronicle of Philanthropy at www.philanthropy.com
- BoardSource at www.boardsource.org
- Idealist.org at www.idealist.org
- National Association of State Charity Officials at www.nasconet.org
- The National Center for Charitable Statistics, at http://nccs.urban.org
- The Foundation Center at www.foundationcenter.org
- The NonProfit Times at www.thenonprofittimes.com, and
- Nonprofit Resource Center at www.nonprofitresource.com.

Researching the Tax Law

If you can't find an answer to your question in a secondary source, you might be able to find help in the tax law itself. Or, you may want to consult the tax law to verify (or clarify) what you've learned from the IRS or secondary sources.

The "tax law" of the United States comes from several sources:

- the Internal Revenue Code
- IRS regulations
- court cases, and
- IRS rulings, interpretations, and tax advice.

Every branch of the federal government is involved in creating the tax law. The Internal Revenue Code is enacted by Congress (the legislative branch), IRS regulations and rulings are issued by the IRS (a department of the executive branch), and taxpayers may appeal the IRS's actions to the federal courts (the judicial branch).

Internal Revenue Code

The Internal Revenue Code (IRC) is the supreme tax law of the land. The IRC (also called "the code" or "the tax code") is written, and frequently rewritten, by Congress. The first tax code, adopted in 1913, contained 14 pages. Today, the tax code is more than 3,600 pages long.

The IRC is found in Title 26 of the United States Code (USC for short). The USC encompasses all of our federal laws. "Title" simply refers to the place within the massive USC where the IRC is found.

The entire tax code covers income taxes, Social Security taxes, excise taxes, estate and gift taxes, and tax procedure. It is organized by category and broken down into subtitles, chapters, subchapters, parts, subparts, sections, subsections, paragraphs, subparagraphs, and clauses. The income tax laws are in Chapter 1 of Subtitle A of the Tax Code. Most of the laws dealing with tax deductions are found in of Subchapter F of Chapter 1.

For our purposes, the most important thing to remember about the organization of the tax code is that each specific tax law is contained in a separate numbered section. For example, Section 501 covers the federal tax exemption for nonprofit organizations. For the sake of convenience, tax professionals will often refer to these numbered sections of the tax code.

> **EXAMPLE:** "IRC § 501(c)(3)" means that this particular tax law is found in Title 26 of the USC (the Internal Revenue Code), Section 501, subsection c, paragraph 3.

The tax code is published each year in a two-volume set (usually in paperback). The IRC is available for free on the Internet. You can get to the entire IRC from Nolo's Legal Research Center—go to www.nolo. com. The IRC is also available on the IRS website (www.irs.gov) and several other websites, including www.legalbitstream.com.

IRS Regulations

Even though the Internal Revenue Code contains over 3,600 pages, it does not provide adequate guidance for every situation that arises in real life. To supplement the IRC, the IRS issues regulations, called "Treasury Regulations," "Regulations," or "Regs." Although written by the IRS, not Congress, these regulations have almost the same authoritative weight as the tax code itself.

While the tax code is usually written in broad and general terms, the regulations get down and dirty, providing details about how tax code provisions are intended to operate in the real world. Regulations are slightly easier to read than the tax code on which they are based and often include examples that can be helpful. The regulations cover many (but not all) of the tax code provisions dealing with nonprofits.

To *See* if a particular IRC section is supplemented by a regulation, start with the number of the IRC section. If there is a corresponding regulation, it will bear the same number, usually preceded by the number "1."

> **EXAMPLE:** "Reg. 1.501(c)(3)-1" refers to a Treasury regulation interpreting IRC Section 501(c)(3).

Regulations can be downloaded through the website www. legalbitstream.com.

Court Cases

When a dispute arises between a taxpayer and the IRS, the taxpayer may take the matter to federal court. The courts are the final arbiters of tax disputes. A court may overrule the IRS if the court concludes that the IRS applied the tax code in a manner contrary to the United States Constitution or differently from what Congress intended.

Tax disputes are tried in three different courts: a special tax court that handles only tax disputes, the regular federal trial courts (called U.S. District Courts), and the Court of Federal Claims. If either the taxpayer or the IRS doesn't like the result reached at trial, it may appeal to the federal appellate courts (called the U.S. Courts of Appeals), and even to the United States Supreme Court.

Decisions of these courts are published, along with explanations and discussions of the tax law. These court decisions provide valuable interpretations of the tax laws. Many, but not all, of these court interpretations are binding on the IRS. Thousands of court decisions dealing with tax law have been published, so chances are good that there is at least one decision on the issue that interests you.

To locate a published court decision, you must understand how to read a case citation. A citation provides the names of the people or companies involved on each side of the case, the volume of the legal publication (called a reporter) in which the case can be found, the page number on which it begins, and the year in which the case was decided. Here is an example of what a legal citation looks like: *Smith v. Acme Nonprofit, Inc.*, 123 F.3d 456 (2009). Smith and Acme Nonprofit, Inc., are the names of the parties to the legal dispute. The case is reported in volume 123 of the Federal Reporter, Third Series, beginning on page 456; the court issued the decision in 2009.

Opinions by the federal district courts are in a series of reporters called the Federal Supplement, or F.Supp. Any case decided by a federal court of appeals is found in a series of books called the Federal Reporter. Older cases are contained in the first series of the Federal Reporter, or F. More recent cases are contained in the second or third series of the Federal Reporter, F.2d or F.3d. Cases decided by the U.S. Supreme

Court are found in three publications: United States Reports (identified as U.S.), the Supreme Court Reporter (identified as S.Ct.), and the Supreme Court Reports, Lawyer's Edition (identified as L.Ed.). Supreme Court case citations often refer to all three publications.

Many, but not all, of these legal decisions are available free on the Internet. Tax court decisions and tax decisions from other courts from 1990 to date can be accessed for free at www.legalbitstream.com. Tax court decisions from 1999 to date can also be accessed at www.ustaxcourt.gov, which contains links to all types of law-related websites. Virtually all legal decisions are available on the subscriber websites www.lexisnexis.com and www.westlaw.com. You may be able to access these websites through a library or tax professional's office.

Hard copies of published decisions by the United States Tax Court can be found in the Tax Court Reports, or TC, published by the U.S. Government Printing Office. Tax court decisions can also be found in a reporter called Tax Court Memorandum Decisions, or TCM, published by Commerce Clearing House, Inc. Decisions from all federal courts involving taxation can be found in a reporter called U.S. Tax Cases, or USTC, published by Commerce Clearing House, Inc. These are available in law libraries.

For a detailed discussion of how to research court cases, *See Legal Research: How to Find & Understand the Law*, by Stephen Elias and the Editors of Nolo (Nolo), or go to Nolo's Legal Research Center at www. nolo.com.

IRS Rulings, Interpretations, and Tax Advice

It might *See*m like the tax code, regulations, and court decisions would provide everything anyone ever wanted to know about tax law. But even more IRS guidance is available. The IRS publishes several types of statements (besides Regs) of its position on various tax matters. These pronouncements guide IRS personnel and taxpayers as to how the IRS will apply specific tax laws.

Unlike the tax code and regulations, these statements do not have the force of law. Rather, they are the IRS's own interpretation of the tax law, which is not necessarily binding on the courts (or you, should you choose to challenge the IRS's interpretation in court). However, they give you a good idea of how the IRS would handle the situation involved.

Revenue rulings. IRS Revenue Rulings (Rev. Rul.) are IRS announcements of how the tax law applies to a hypothetical set of facts. The IRS publishes over 100 of these rulings every year. These rulings represent the IRS's view of the tax law, and the IRS presumes that they are correct. If an auditor discovers that you have violated a revenue ruling, you will probably have to pay additional tax. On the other hand, if you can show an auditor that a revenue ruling supports your position, you probably won't have to pay more tax. If you have violated a revenue ruling, all is not necessarily lost. Revenue rulings are not binding on the courts, which can (and do) disregard them from time to time. Thus, it's possible you could win your case on appeal.

You can download free copies of all IRS Revenue Rulings from 1954 to date from: www.legalbitstream.com. Revenue rulings also appear in the weekly *Internal Revenue Cumulative Bulletin*, which is published by the U.S. Government Printing Office. Tax book publishers Prentice Hall, Commerce Clearing House, and Research Institute of America also reprint IRS Revenue Rulings. They are indexed by IRC section and subject matter.

> **EXAMPLE:** "Rev. Rul. 03-41" refers to IRS Revenue Ruling number 41, issued in 2003.

Revenue procedures. Revenue Procedures ("Rev. Procs.") are IRS announcements dealing with procedural aspects of tax practice. Rev. Procs. are used primarily by tax return preparers. They often explain when and how to report tax items, such as how to claim a net operating loss on a tax form or return. Revenue procedures are contained in the weekly *Internal Revenue Cumulative Bulletin*, which you can find in larger public and law libraries, and also are reprinted by tax book publishers and on the IRS website. You can obtain free copies of many revenue procedures at www.legalbitstream.com.

> **EXAMPLE:** "Rev. Proc. 09-15" refers to published Revenue Procedure number 15, issued in 2009.

Letter rulings. IRS letter rulings are IRS answers to specific written questions from taxpayers about complex tax situations. The only person who is entitled to rely on the ruling as legal authority is the taxpayer to whom the ruling is addressed; even if you find yourself in a similar position, the IRS is not legally required to follow the guidance it gave in the letter. However, letter rulings offer valuable insight into the IRS's position on tax treatment of complex transactions. Since 1976, letter rulings have been made available to the general public. You can access free copies of many letter rulings at www.legalbitstream.com. They are also published by tax publishers.

> **EXAMPLE:** "Ltr. Ruling 0913043 (April 3, 2009)" refers to a letter ruling issued on April 3, 2009. The first two numbers of the seven-digit identifier show the year it was issued, the next two indicate the week of the year, and the last three show the ruling for that week. Thus, this letter ruling was the 43rd issued during the 13th week of 2009.

IRS general guidance. From time to time, the IRS gives general guidance and statements of policy in official "announcements" and "notices" similar to press releases. They appear in the weekly *Internal Revenue Cumulative Bulletin*. It doesn't usually pay to search IRS announcements or notices because they are too broad to answer specific questions. You can access many of these for free at www.legalbitstream.com and at the IRS website (www.irs.gov).

Internal Revenue Manual. The *Internal Revenue Manual* (IRM) is a series of handbooks that serve as guides to IRS employees on tax law and procedure. The IRM tells IRS employees (usually auditors or collectors) how specific tax code provisions should be enforced. The manual is available on the IRS website. Part 4.75-76 deals with examinations of nonprofits. Part 7.27 contains the IRS Exempt Organizations Tax Manual.

Consulting a Tax Professional

You don't have to do your own tax research. There are hundreds of thousands of tax professionals (tax pros) in the United States ready and eager to help you—for a price. A tax pro can answer your questions, prepare your nonprofit's returns, and help you deal with the IRS if your nonprofit gets into tax trouble.

Types of Tax Pros

There are several different types of tax pros. They differ widely in training, experience, and cost:

Enrolled agents. Enrolled agents (EAs) are tax advisers and preparers who are licensed by the IRS. They must have at least five years of experience or pass a difficult IRS test. They can represent taxpayers before the IRS, and in administrative proceedings, circuit court, and, possibly tax court, if they pass the appropriate tests. Enrolled agents are the least expensive of tax pros but are reliable for tax return preparation and more routine tax matters. They can be quite adequate for many small nonprofits, provided they have experience handling nonprofit returns.

Certified public accountants. Certified public accountants (CPAs) are licensed and regulated by each state. They undergo lengthy training and must pass a comprehensive exam. CPAs represent the high end of the tax pro spectrum. In addition to preparing tax returns, they perform sophisticated accounting and tax work. CPAs are found in large national firms or in small local outfits. The large national firms are used primarily by large businesses. Some states also license public accountants. These are competent, but are not as highly regarded as CPAs.

Tax attorneys. Tax attorneys are lawyers who specialize in tax matters. The only time you'll ever need a tax attorney is if your nonprofit gets into serious trouble with the IRS or another tax agency and needs legal representation before the IRS or in court. Some tax attorneys also give tax advice, but they are usually too expensive for most nonprofits. You're probably better off hiring a CPA if you need specialized tax help.

Finding a Tax Pro

The best way to find a tax pro is to obtain referrals from other nonprofits. You can also try contacting the National Association of Enrolled Agents or one of its state affiliates. You can find a listing of affiliates at the NAEA website at www.naea.org. Local CPA societies can give you referrals to local CPAs. You can also find tax pros in the telephone book under "Accountants, Tax Return." Local bar associations can refer you to a tax attorney. Be aware that CPA societies and local bar associations refer from a list on a rotating basis, so you shouldn't construe a referral as a recommendation or certification of competence.

Your relationship with your tax pro will be one of your nonprofit's most important business relationships. Be picky about the person you choose. Talk with at least three tax pros before hiring one. You want a tax pro who takes the time to listen to you, answers your questions fully and in plain English, *See*ms knowledgeable, and makes you feel comfortable. Make sure the tax pro works frequently with nonprofits.

Sample Forms

Form **990-EZ**

Department of the Treasury
Internal Revenue Service

Short Form
Return of Organization Exempt From Income Tax

Under section 501(c), 527, or 4947(a)(1) of the Internal Revenue Code
(except black lung benefit trust or private foundation)

▶ Sponsoring organizations of donor advised funds, organizations that operate one or more hospital facilities, and certain controlling organizations as defined in section 512(b)(13) must file Form 990 (see instructions). All other organizations with gross receipts less than $200,000 and total assets less than $500,000 at the end of the year may use this form.

▶ *The organization may have to use a copy of this return to satisfy state reporting requirements.*

OMB No. 1545-1150

20**12**

Open to Public Inspection

A For the 2012 calendar year, or tax year beginning _____ , 2012, and ending _____ , 20 ____

B Check if applicable:	**C** Name of organization		**D** Employer identification number
☐ Address change			
☐ Name change	Number and street (or P.O. box, if mail is not delivered to street address)	Room/suite	**E** Telephone number
☐ Initial return			
☐ Terminated	City or town, state or country, and ZIP + 4		**F** Group Exemption
☐ Amended return			Number ▶
☐ Application pending			

G Accounting Method: ☐ Cash ☐ Accrual Other (specify) ▶ _____

I Website: ▶

J Tax-exempt status (check only one) — ☐ 501(c)(3) ☐ 501(c) ( ) ◀ (insert no.) ☐ 4947(a)(1) or ☐ 527

H Check ▶ ☐ if the organization is **not** required to attach Schedule B (Form 990, 990-EZ, or 990-PF).

K Check ▶ ☐ if the organization is not a section 509(a)(3) supporting organization or a section 527 organization **and** its gross receipts are normally **not** more than $50,000. A Form 990-EZ or Form 990 return is not required though Form 990-N (e-postcard) may be required (see instructions). But if the organization chooses to file a return, be sure to file a complete return.

L Add lines 5b, 6c, and 7b, to line 9 to determine gross receipts. If gross receipts are $200,000 or more, or if total assets (Part II, line 25, column (B) below) are $500,000 or more, file Form 990 instead of Form 990-EZ . . . . ▶ $

Part I	**Revenue, Expenses, and Changes in Net Assets or Fund Balances** (see the instructions for Part I)

Check if the organization used Schedule O to respond to any question in this Part I . . . . ☐

Revenue	**1**	Contributions, gifts, grants, and similar amounts received	**1**	
	2	Program service revenue including government fees and contracts	**2**	
	3	Membership dues and assessments	**3**	
	4	Investment income	**4**	
	5a	Gross amount from sale of assets other than inventory	**5a**	
	b	Less: cost or other basis and sales expenses	**5b**	
	c	Gain or (loss) from sale of assets other than inventory (Subtract line 5b from line 5a)	**5c**	
	6	Gaming and fundraising events		
	a	Gross income from gaming (attach Schedule G if greater than $15,000)	**6a**	
	b	Gross income from fundraising events (not including $ _____ of contributions from fundraising events reported on line 1) (attach Schedule G if the sum of such gross income and contributions exceeds $15,000) . .	**6b**	
	c	Less: direct expenses from gaming and fundraising events . . .	**6c**	
	d	Net income or (loss) from gaming and fundraising events (add lines 6a and 6b and subtract line 6c)	**6d**	
	7a	Gross sales of inventory, less returns and allowances	**7a**	
	b	Less: cost of goods sold	**7b**	
	c	Gross profit or (loss) from sales of inventory (Subtract line 7b from line 7a)	**7c**	
	8	Other revenue (describe in Schedule O)	**8**	
	9	**Total revenue.** Add lines 1, 2, 3, 4, 5c, 6d, 7c, and 8 . . . . . ▶	**9**	
Expenses	**10**	Grants and similar amounts paid (list in Schedule O)	**10**	
	11	Benefits paid to or for members	**11**	
	12	Salaries, other compensation, and employee benefits	**12**	
	13	Professional fees and other payments to independent contractors	**13**	
	14	Occupancy, rent, utilities, and maintenance	**14**	
	15	Printing, publications, postage, and shipping	**15**	
	16	Other expenses (describe in Schedule O)	**16**	
	17	**Total expenses.** Add lines 10 through 16 . . . . ▶	**17**	
Net Assets	**18**	Excess or (deficit) for the year (Subtract line 17 from line 9)	**18**	
	19	Net assets or fund balances at beginning of year (from line 27, column (A)) (must agree with end-of-year figure reported on prior year's return)	**19**	
	20	Other changes in net assets or fund balances (explain in Schedule O)	**20**	
	21	Net assets or fund balances at end of year. Combine lines 18 through 20 . . . . . . ▶	**21**	

For Paperwork Reduction Act Notice, see the separate instructions.   Cat. No. 10642I   Form **990-EZ** (2012)

Form 990-EZ (2012)   Page **2**

Part II   **Balance Sheets** (see the instructions for Part II)

Check if the organization used Schedule O to respond to any question in this Part II . . . . ☐

	(A) Beginning of year		**(B)** End of year
22 Cash, savings, and investments		**22**	
23 Land and buildings		**23**	
24 Other assets (describe in Schedule O)		**24**	
25 **Total assets**		**25**	
26 **Total liabilities** (describe in Schedule O)		**26**	
27 **Net assets or fund balances** (line 27 of column (B) **must** agree with line 21) . .		**27**	

Part III   **Statement of Program Service Accomplishments** (see the instructions for Part III)

Check if the organization used Schedule O to respond to any question in this Part III . . ☐

What is the organization's primary exempt purpose? _____

Describe the organization's program service accomplishments for each of its three largest program services, as measured by expenses. In a clear and concise manner, describe the services provided, the number of persons benefited, and other relevant information for each program title.

Expenses
(Required for section 501(c)(3) and 501(c)(4) organizations and section 4947(a)(1) trusts; optional for others.)

28 _____

_____

_____

(Grants $ _____) If this amount includes foreign grants, check here . . . . ▶ ☐ | **28a** |

29 _____

_____

_____

(Grants $ _____) If this amount includes foreign grants, check here . . . . ▶ ☐ | **29a** |

30 _____

_____

_____

(Grants $ _____) If this amount includes foreign grants, check here . . . . ▶ ☐ | **30a** |

31 Other program services (describe in Schedule O) . . . .

(Grants $ _____) If this amount includes foreign grants, check here . . . . ▶ ☐ | **31a** |

32 **Total program service expenses** (add lines 28a through 31a) . . . . ▶ | **32** |

Part IV   **List of Officers, Directors, Trustees, and Key Employees** List each one even if not compensated (see the instructions for Part IV)

Check if the organization used Schedule O to respond to any question in this Part IV . . . . ☐

(a) Name and title	**(b)** Average hours per week devoted to position	**(c)** Reportable compensation (Forms W-2/1099-MISC) **(if not paid, enter -0-)**	**(d)** Health benefits, contributions to employee benefit plans, and deferred compensation	**(e)** Estimated amount of other compensation

Form **990-EZ** (2012)

Form 990-EZ (2012)   Page **3**

Part V   **Other Information** (Note the Schedule A and personal benefit contract statement requirements in the instructions for Part V) Check if the organization used Schedule O to respond to any question in this Part V   .   ☐

			Yes	No
33	Did the organization engage in any significant activity not previously reported to the IRS? If "Yes," provide a detailed description of each activity in Schedule O	**33**		
34	Were any significant changes made to the organizing or governing documents? If "Yes," attach a conformed copy of the amended documents if they reflect a change to the organization's name. Otherwise, explain the change on Schedule O (see instructions)	**34**		
35a	Did the organization have unrelated business gross income of $1,000 or more during the year from business activities (such as those reported on lines 2, 6a, and 7a, among others)?	**35a**		
b	If "Yes," to line 35a, has the organization filed a Form 990-T for the year? If "No," provide an explanation in Schedule O	**35b**		
c	Was the organization a section 501(c)(4), 501(c)(5), or 501(c)(6) organization subject to section 6033(e) notice, reporting, and proxy tax requirements during the year? If "Yes," complete Schedule C, Part III	**35c**		
36	Did the organization undergo a liquidation, dissolution, termination, or significant disposition of net assets during the year? If "Yes," complete applicable parts of Schedule N	**36**		

37a	Enter amount of political expenditures, direct or indirect, as described in the instructions ▶	**37a**

			Yes	No
b	Did the organization file **Form 1120-POL** for this year?	**37b**		
38a	Did the organization borrow from, or make any loans to, any officer, director, trustee, or key employee **or** were any such loans made in a prior year and still outstanding at the end of the tax year covered by this return? .	**38a**		

b	If "Yes," complete Schedule L, Part II and enter the total amount involved	**38b**
39	Section 501(c)(7) organizations. Enter:	
a	Initiation fees and capital contributions included on line 9	**39a**
b	Gross receipts, included on line 9, for public use of club facilities	**39b**

40a	Section 501(c)(3) organizations. Enter amount of tax imposed on the organization during the year under: section 4911 ▶ _____ ; section 4912 ▶ _____ ; section 4955 ▶ _____

			Yes	No
b	Section 501(c)(3) and 501(c)(4) organizations. Did the organization engage in any section 4958 excess benefit transaction during the year, or did it engage in an excess benefit transaction in a prior year that has not been reported on any of its prior Forms 990 or 990-EZ? If "Yes," complete Schedule L, Part I	**40b**		

c	Section 501(c)(3) and 501(c)(4) organizations. Enter amount of tax imposed on organization managers or disqualified persons during the year under sections 4912, 4955, and 4958 . . . . ▶ _____
d	Section 501(c)(3) and 501(c)(4) organizations. Enter amount of tax on line 40c reimbursed by the organization . . . . ▶ _____

			Yes	No
e	All organizations. At any time during the tax year, was the organization a party to a prohibited tax shelter transaction? If "Yes," complete Form 8886-T	**40e**		

41   List the states with which a copy of this return is filed ▶ _____

42a   The organization's books are in care of ▶ _____   Telephone no. ▶ _____
     Located at ▶ _____   ZIP + 4 ▶ _____

			Yes	No
b	At any time during the calendar year, did the organization have an interest in or a signature or other authority over a financial account in a foreign country (such as a bank account, securities account, or other financial account)?	**42b**		
	If "Yes," enter the name of the foreign country: ▶ _____ See the instructions for exceptions and filing requirements for **Form TD F 90-22.1, Report of Foreign Bank and Financial Accounts.**			
c	At any time during the calendar year, did the organization maintain an office outside the U.S.?	**42c**		
	If "Yes," enter the name of the foreign country: ▶ _____			

43   Section 4947(a)(1) nonexempt charitable trusts filing Form 990-EZ in lieu of **Form 1041**—Check here . . . . ▶ ☐
     and enter the amount of tax-exempt interest received or accrued during the tax year . . . . . ▶ | **43** |

			Yes	No
44a	Did the organization maintain any donor advised funds during the year? If "Yes," Form 990 must be completed instead of Form 990-EZ	**44a**		
b	Did the organization operate one or more hospital facilities during the year? If "Yes," Form 990 must be completed instead of Form 990-EZ	**44b**		
c	Did the organization receive any payments for indoor tanning services during the year?	**44c**		
d	If "Yes" to line 44c, has the organization filed a Form 720 to report these payments? If "No," provide an explanation in Schedule O	**44d**		
45a	Did the organization have a controlled entity within the meaning of section 512(b)(13)?	**45a**		
45b	Did the organization receive any payment from or engage in any transaction with a controlled entity within the meaning of section 512(b)(13)? If "Yes," Form 990 and Schedule R may need to be completed instead of Form 990-EZ (see instructions)	**45b**		

Form **990-EZ** (2012)

Form 990-EZ (2012)   Page **4**

		Yes	No
46	Did the organization engage, directly or indirectly, in political campaign activities on behalf of or in opposition to candidates for public office? If "Yes," complete Schedule C, Part I **46**		

Part VI **Section 501(c)(3) organizations only**

All section 501(c)(3) organizations must answer questions 47–49b and 52, and complete the tables for lines 50 and 51

Check if the organization used Schedule O to respond to any question in this Part VI . . . . ☐

		Yes	No
47	Did the organization engage in lobbying activities or have a section 501(h) election in effect during the tax year? If "Yes," complete Schedule C, Part II **47**		
48	Is the organization a school as described in section 170(b)(1)(A)(ii)? If "Yes," complete Schedule E **48**		
49a	Did the organization make any transfers to an exempt non-charitable related organization? **49a**		
b	If "Yes," was the related organization a section 527 organization? **49b**		

50 Complete this table for the organization's five highest compensated employees (other than officers, directors, trustees and key employees) who each received more than $100,000 of compensation from the organization. If there is none, enter "None."

(a) Name and title of each employee paid more than $100,000	(b) Average hours per week devoted to position	(c) Reportable compensation (Forms W-2/1099-MISC)	(d) Health benefits, contributions to employee benefit plans, and deferred compensation	(e) Estimated amount of other compensation

f Total number of other employees paid over $100,000 . . . . . ▶ _____

51 Complete this table for the organization's five highest compensated independent contractors who each received more than $100,000 of compensation from the organization. If there is none, enter "None."

(a) Name and address of each independent contractor paid more than $100,000	(b) Type of service	(c) Compensation

d Total number of other independent contractors each receiving over $100,000 . . ▶ _____

52 Did the organization complete Schedule A? **Note:** All section 501(c)(3) organizations and 4947(a)(1) nonexempt charitable trusts must attach a completed Schedule A . . . . ▶ ☐ **Yes** ☐ **No**

Under penalties of perjury, I declare that I have examined this return, including accompanying schedules and statements, and to the best of my knowledge and belief, it is true, correct, and complete. Declaration of preparer (other than officer) is based on all information of which preparer has any knowledge.

Sign Here	▶ Signature of officer		Date	
	▶ Type or print name and title			

Paid Preparer Use Only	Print/Type preparer's name	Preparer's signature	Date	Check ☐ if self-employed	PTIN
	Firm's name ▶			Firm's EIN ▶	
	Firm's address ▶			Phone no.	

May the IRS discuss this return with the preparer shown above? See instructions . . . . ▶ ☐ Yes ☐ No

Form **990-EZ** (2012)

Sample Conflict of Interest Policy

Article I

Purpose

The purpose of the conflict of interest policy is to protect this tax-exempt organization's (Organization) interest when it is contemplating entering into a transaction or arrangement that might benefit the private interest of an officer or director of the Organization or might result in a possible excess benefit transaction. This policy is intended to supplement but not replace any applicable state and federal laws governing conflict of interest applicable to nonprofit and charitable organizations.

Article II

Definitions

1. Interested Person

Any director, principal officer, or member of a committee with governing board delegated powers, who has a direct or indirect financial interest, as defined below, is an interested person.

2. Financial Interest

A person has a financial interest if the person has, directly or indirectly, through business, investment, or family:

a. An ownership or investment interest in any entity with which the Organization has a transaction or arrangement

b. A compensation arrangement with the Organization or with any entity or individual with which the Organization has a transaction or arrangement, or

c. A potential ownership or investment interest in, or compensation arrangement with, any entity or individual with which the Organization is negotiating a transaction or arrangement.

Compensation includes direct and indirect remuneration as well as gifts or favors that are not insubstantial.

A financial interest is not necessarily a conflict of interest. Under Article III, Section 2, a person who has a financial interest may have a conflict of interest only if the appropriate governing board or committee decides that a conflict of interest exists.

Article III

Procedures

1. Duty to Disclose

In connection with any actual or possible conflict of interest, an interested person must disclose the existence of the financial interest and be given the opportunity to disclose all material facts to the directors and members of committees with governing board delegated powers considering the proposed transaction or arrangement.

2. Determining Whether a Conflict of Interest Exists

After disclosure of the financial interest and all material facts, and after any discussion with the interested person, he/she shall leave the governing board or committee meeting while the determination of a conflict of interest is discussed and voted upon. The remaining board or committee members shall decide if a conflict of interest exists.

3. Procedures for Addressing the Conflict of Interest

a. An interested person may make a presentation at the governing board or committee meeting, but after the presentation, he/she shall leave the meeting during the discussion of, and the vote on, the transaction or arrangement involving the possible conflict of interest.

b. The chairperson of the governing board or committee shall, if appropriate, appoint a disinterested person or committee to investigate alternatives to the proposed transaction or arrangement.

c. After exercising due diligence, the governing board or committee shall determine whether the Organization can obtain with reasonable efforts a more advantageous transaction or arrangement from a person or entity that would not give rise to a conflict of interest.

d. If a more advantageous transaction or arrangement is not reasonably possible under circumstances not producing a conflict of interest, the governing board or committee shall determine by a majority vote of the disinterested directors whether the transaction or arrangement is in the Organization's best interest, for its own benefit, and whether it is fair and reasonable. In conformity with the above determination it shall make its decision as to whether to enter into the transaction or arrangement.

4. **Violations of the Conflicts of Interest Policy**

a. If the governing board or committee has reasonable cause to believe a member has failed to disclose actual or possible conflicts of interest, it shall inform the member of the basis for such belief and afford the member an opportunity to explain the alleged failure to disclose.

b. If, after hearing the member's response and after making further investigation as warranted by the circumstances, the governing board or committee determines the member has failed to disclose an actual or possible conflict of interest, it shall take appropriate disciplinary and corrective action.

Article IV

Records of Proceedings

The minutes of the governing board and all committees with board delegated powers shall contain:

a. The names of the persons who disclosed or otherwise were found to have a financial interest in connection with an actual or possible conflict of interest, the nature of the financial interest, any action taken to determine whether a conflict of interest was present, and the governing board's or committee's decision as to whether a conflict of interest in fact existed.

b. The names of the persons who were present for discussions and votes relating to the transaction or arrangement, the content of the discussion, including any alternatives to the proposed transaction or arrangement, and a record of any votes taken in connection with the proceedings.

Article V

Compensation

a. A voting member of the governing board who receives compensation, directly or indirectly, from the Organization for services is precluded from voting on matters pertaining to that member's compensation.

b. A voting member of any committee whose jurisdiction includes compensation matters and who receives compensation, directly or indirectly, from the Organization for services is precluded from voting on matters pertaining to that member's compensation.

c. No voting member of the governing board or any committee whose jurisdiction includes compensation matters and who receives compensation, directly or indirectly, from the Organization, either individually or collectively, is prohibited from providing information to any committee regarding compensation.

Article VI

Annual Statements

Each director, principal officer, and member of a committee with governing board delegated powers shall annually sign a statement which affirms such person:

a. Has received a copy of the conflicts of interest policy

b. Has read and understands the policy

c. Has agreed to comply with the policy, and

d. Understands the Organization is charitable and in order to maintain its federal tax exemption it must engage primarily in activities which accomplish one or more of its tax-exempt purposes.

Article VII

Periodic Reviews

To ensure the Organization operates in a manner consistent with charitable purposes and does not engage in activities that could jeopardize its tax-exempt status, periodic reviews shall be conducted. The periodic reviews shall, at a minimum, include the following subjects:

a. Whether compensation arrangements and benefits are reasonable, based on competent survey information, and the result of arm's length bargaining.

b. Whether partnerships, joint ventures, and arrangements with management organizations conform to the Organization's written policies, are properly recorded, reflect reasonable investment or payments for goods and services, further charitable purposes, and do not result in inurement, impermissible private benefit, or in an excess benefit transaction.

Article VIII

Use of Outside Experts

When conducting the periodic reviews as provided for in Article VII, the Organization may, but need not, use outside advisers. If outside experts are used, their use shall not relieve the governing board of its responsibility for ensuring periodic reviews are conducted.

Annual Conflict of Interest Acknowledgment Statement

In compliance with Article VI of the Conflict of Interest Policy of [*name of nonprofit*] (the "Policy"), I affirm that I:

- have received a copy of the Policy
- have read and understand the Policy
- agree to comply with the Policy, and
- understand that [*name of nonprofit*] is a charitable organization, and that to maintain its federal tax exemption it must engage primarily in activities that accomplish one or more of its exempt purposes.

Signature: _____   Date: _____

Rebuttable Presumption Checklist

1. Name of disqualified person: _____

2. Position under consideration: _____

3. Duration of contract (1 yr., 3 yr., etc.):_____

4. Proposed Compensation:

   Salary: _____

   Bonus: _____

   Deferred compensation: _____

   Fringe benefits: _____

   _____

   _____

   Liability insurance premiums: _____

   Forgone interest on loans: _____

   Other: _____

5. Description of types of comparability data relied upon (for example, association survey, phone inquiries, etc.):

   a. _____

   b. _____

   c. _____

   d. _____

6. Sources and amounts of comparability data:

   Salary: _____

   Bonus: _____

   Deferred compensation: _____

   Fringe benefits: _____

   _____

   _____

   Liability insurance premiums: _____

   Forgone interest on loans: _____

   Others: _____

7. Office or file where comparability data kept: _____

8. Total proposed compensation: _____

9. Maximum total compensation per comparability data: _____

10. Compensation package approved by authorized body:

    Salary: _____

    Bonus: _____

    Deferred compensation: _____

    Fringe benefits: _____

    _____

    _____

    Liability insurance premiums: _____

    Forgone interest on loans: _____

    Other: _____

Family and Business Relationship Questionnaire

Attached is a list of all [*name of nonprofit*] officers, directors, trustees, and key employees during [*list year*]. IRS Form 990 requires that the organization report if any of these individuals are related to each other through family or business relationships. Please check the appropriate boxes, provide the necessary information, and sign and date your response to each question as indicated on the questionnaire.

1. Family Relationships

Family relationships include an individual's spouse, ancestors, children, grandchildren, great-grandchildren, siblings (whether by whole or half blood), and the spouses of children, grandchildren, great-grandchildren, and siblings.

☐ I have no family relationship with anyone on the attached list.

Signed: _____

Date: _____

☐ I have a family relationship with someone on the attached list.

Name of related person: _____
Nature of family relationship: _____
(*Use reverse of this form if more than one related person.*)

Signed: _____

Date: _____

2. Business Relationships

Business relationships between two people include any of the following occurring during the tax year:

- One person is employed by the other in a sole proprietorship, or by an organization in which the other person is a trustee, director, officer, key employee, or greater than 35% owner.
- One person (1) directly transacts business with the other in one or more transactions involving transfers of cash or property with

a total value over $10,000, and (2) such transactions are *not* in the ordinary course of either party's business and *not* on the same terms as are generally offered to the public.

- One person transacts business with the other in the same manner as described in the previous paragraph but does so indirectly through an organization with which the person is a trustee, director, officer, key employee, or greater than 35% owner.
- The two people are each a director, trustee, officer, or greater than 10% owner in the same business or investment entity.

☐ I have no business relationship with anyone on the attached list.

Signed: _____

Date: _____

☐ I have a business relationship with someone on the attached list.

Name of related person: _____

Nature of business relationship: _____

(Use reverse of this form if more than one person.)

Signed: _____

Date: _____

Expense Report

Attach all receipts to this Expense Report

Name _____

Address _____

City/Zip _____

Telephone _____ Email _____

Expenditure was for: _____

List Expenditures:

_____ $ _____

_____   _____

_____   _____

_____   _____

_____   _____

Total Expense $ _____

Total Amount Claimed From Above $ _____

Minus Advance Received   _____

Reimbursement Claimed $ _____

Signature _____

Date _____

Index

A

accident insurance for volunteer-employees, 174

accountable plan for reimbursements
  for employees, 204–6
  local transportation costs of volunteers, 159–60, 172–73
  for ODTKEs, 334–37
  overview, 136, 153–57
  return of excess payments, 157–59
  unaccountable plans vs., 158–59, 205–6
  of volunteers, 136, 153–59, 161–62, 172–73

accountants, 63, 84–85, 219, 420–21

accounting, 113–46
  accounting method, 67, 119–21
  balance sheet numbers, 67
  budget, 116
  computerization of, 146
  documentation, 133–37
  independent audits, 94, 139–42
  journals for, 123–27, 130–32, 146
  overview, 114–17
  record retention periods, 138–39
  restricted funds, 144
  and sale of inventory, 63
  See also accountable plan for reimbursements; financial information; GAAP; record keeping; tax year

accounting system, 122–32
  chart of accounts, 124–27
  documentation, 133–37
  example of, 130–32
  expense allocation, 127–28
  financial statements, 116, 129–30, 143–44
  overview, 122–24, 146

accrual method of accounting, 67, 119–21

acknowledgment of contributions, 229–30, 231–32, 286, 288, 289, 293–98

activities
  compliance and limitations on, 14–15
  game activities, 227–28, 310–11, 364
  program accomplishments, 53, 67–70
  program expenses, 127, 144
  program service revenue, 52, 59, 61
  program services, 68, 69, 70
  reporting changes to IRS, 54, 75
  statement of activities, 143
  See also lobbying; lobbying restriction; political campaign activity; UBIT-exempt activities

actual expense method for reimbursement of volunteers, 160

adjusted gross income (AGI) of donors, 218, 219, 251–53

administrative bodies and advocacy, 378–79

administrative expenses, 127, 144

advertising income, periodical, 364–66

advocacy vs. lobbying, 378–82

advocacy vs. political campaign activity, 396–98

affiliated nonprofits and lobbying expenditures, 386

affiliate policies, 92

affinity cards, 362

AGI (adjusted gross income) of donors, 218, 219, 251–53

aircraft as property donation, 259–63, 293–98

antiques as property donation, 269–74

apparently wholesome food, 275–76

⚖ NOLO *Online Legal Forms*

Nolo offers a large library of legal solutions and forms, created by Nolo's in-house legal staff. These reliable documents can be prepared in minutes.

Create a Document

- **Incorporation.** Incorporate your business in any state.
- **LLC Formations.** Gain asset protection and pass-through tax status in any state.
- **Wills.** Nolo has helped people make over 2 million wills. Is it time to make or revise yours?
- **Living Trust (avoid probate).** Plan now to save your family the cost, delays, and hassle of probate.
- **Trademark.** Protect the name of your business or product.
- **Provisional Patent.** Preserve your rights under patent law and claim "patent pending" status.

Download a Legal Form

Nolo.com has hundreds of top quality legal forms available for download—bills of sale, promissory notes, nondisclosure agreements, LLC operating agreements, corporate minutes, commercial lease and sublease, motor vehicle bill of sale, consignment agreements and many more.

Review Your Documents

Many lawyers in Nolo's consumer-friendly lawyer directory will review Nolo documents for a very reasonable fee. Check their detailed profiles at **Nolo.com/lawyers**.

On Nolo.com you'll also find:

Books & Software

Nolo publishes hundreds of great books and software programs for consumers and business owners. Order a copy, or download an ebook version instantly, at Nolo.com.

Online Legal Documents

You can quickly and easily make a will or living trust, form an LLC or corporation, apply for a trademark or provisional patent, or make hundreds of other forms—online.

Free Legal Information

Thousands of articles answer common questions about everyday legal issues including wills, bankruptcy, small business formation, divorce, patents, employment, and much more.

Plain-English Legal Dictionary

Stumped by jargon? Look it up in America's most up-to-date source for definitions of legal terms, free at nolo.com.

Lawyer Directory

Nolo's consumer-friendly lawyer directory provides in-depth profiles of lawyers all over America. You'll find all the information you need to choose the right lawyer.

NIRS3